ETHICS AND HUMAN ACTION
IN EARLY STOICISM

Ethics and Human Action
in Early Stoicism

BRAD INWOOD

CLARENDON PRESS · OXFORD

Oxford University Press, Walton Street, Oxford OX2 6DP

Oxford New York Toronto
Delhi Bombay Calcutta Madras Karachi
Petaling Jaya Singapore Hong Kong Tokyo
Nairobi Dar es Salaam Cape Town
Melbourne Auckland

and associated companies in
Beirut Berlin Ibadan Nicosia

Oxford is a trade mark of Oxford University Press

Published in the United States
by Oxford University Press, New York

© Brad Inwood 1985
First published 1985
Reprinted (new as paperback) 1987

British Library Cataloguing in Publication Data

Inwood, Brad
Ethics and human action in early stoicism.
1. Stoics
I. Title
188   B528
ISBN 0-19-824739-7
ISBN 0-19-824462-2 (pbk.)

Library of Congress Cataloging in Publication Data

Inwood, Brad.
Ethics and human action in early Stoicism.
Bibliography: p.
Includes index.
1. Stoics.   2. Philosophical anthropology—History.
3. Ethics, Ancient.   I. Title.
B528.I59   1985   128'.4   84-20673
ISBN 0-19-824739-7 (Oxford University Press)
ISBN 0-19-824462-2 (pbk.)

Printed in Great Britain
at the University Printing House, Oxford
by David Stanford
Printer to the University

For Nora

Acknowledgements

Work on this book was begun with support from the Social Sciences and Humanities Research Council of Canada and from a Queen Elizabeth II Ontario Scholarship. I owe the opportunity to continue work on the topic to the Andrew W. Mellon Foundation and Stanford University, where I spent a year as a post-doctoral fellow in 1981–2. Many people have helped me with advice and encouragement; Professor J. M. Rist is first among them. Jonathan Barnes, Michael Bratman, Blake Landor, A. A. Long, M. J. O'Brien, Fr. J. Owens, T. M. Robinson, Bruce Rosenstock, and Michael Wigodsky have all been more helpful perhaps than they are aware of. Less tangible are the debts outstanding to all my friends at Stanford and the University of California at Berkeley (where I had the privilege of attending Professor Long's seminar on Stoic ethics). Their warm hospitality helped to make my regrettably short stay among them happy and productive, and reminded me again that the republic of scholars has no national boundaries.

Contents

Abbreviations

Acad.	Cicero *Academica*
Adv. Col.	Plutarch *Adversus Colotem (Against Colotes)*
Aet. Mun.	Pseudo-Philo *De Aeternitate Mundi (On the Eternity of the World)*
Ben.	Seneca *De Beneficiis (On Benefits)*
Comm. Not.	Plutarch *De Communibus Notitiis (On Common Notions)*
Cons. Marc.	Seneca *Consolatio ad Marciam (Consolation for Marcia)*
Const. Sap.	Seneca *De Constantia Sapientis (On the Constancy of the Sage)*
DA	Alexander or Aristotle *De Anima (On the Soul)*
Diss.	Epictetus *Dissertationes (Discourses)*
D.L.	Diogenes Laertius
DM	Aristotle *De Motu Animalium (On the Motion of Animals)*
Dox. Gr.	*Doxographi Graeci*
DRN	Lucretius *De Rerum Natura (On the Nature of Things)*
Ecl.	Stobaeus *Eclogae*
EE	Aristotle *Eudemian Ethics*
EN	Aristotle *Nicomachean Ethics*
Ench.	Epictetus *Encheiridion*
Ep.	Seneca *Epistulae Morales (Ethical Letters)*
Fin.	Cicero *De Finibus (On Goals)*
Leg. Alleg.	Philo *Legum Allegoriae (Allegories of the Laws)*
M	Sextus Empiricus *Adversus Mathematicos (Against Learned Men)*
MM	Pseudo-Aristotle *Magna Moralia*
Met.	Aristotle *Metaphysics*
NA	Aulus Gellius *Noctes Atticae (Nights in Athens)*
Nat. Hom.	Nemesius *De Natura Hominis (On the Nature of Man)*
ND	Cicero *De Natura Deorum (On the Nature of the Gods)*
Off.	Cicero *De Officiis (On Appropriate Behaviour)*
PH	Sextus Empiricus *Outlines of Pyrrhonism*
PHP	Galen *De Placitis Hippocratis et Platonis (On the Doctrines of Hippocrates and Plato)*
Post. An.	Aristotle *Posterior Analytics*
Prep. Ev.	Eusebius *Preparatio Evangelica*
Quod Deus	Philo *Quod Deus Immutabilis Sit (The Immutability of God)*
RE	*Real-Encyclopädie der klassischen Altertmus-wissenschaft* (Pauly, Wissowa, Kroll)
Rep.	Plato *Republic*
Soll. An.	Plutarch *De Sollertia Animalium (On the Intelligence of Animals)*
St. Rep.	Plutarch *De Stoicorum Repugnantiis (Stoic Self-Contradictions)*
Strom.	Clement *Stromates*
SVF	Stoicorum Veterum Fragmenta
Tranq.	Seneca *De Tranquillitate Animi (On Tranquillity)*
TD	Cicero *Tusculan Disputations*
Virt. Mor.	Plutarch *De Virtute Morali (On Ethical Virtue)*

Introduction

This book is about the Stoic concept of human nature, and in particular about those characteristics which, according to the Stoics, make humans different from other mortal animals. There are many such characteristics; but the scope will be limited by concentrating on the definition of man as a rational animal, and by starting from what Zeno of Citium, the school's founder, selected as his own starting-point for a consideration of human nature. This is the question of the difference between human and animal action.

Unfortunately we no longer possess Zeno's discussion of the question in his own words, nor even in an extensive summary by someone who read it. But we do know that his essay *On Human Nature*[1] was given the alternate title *On Impulse*,[2] either by Zeno himself or by someone who read the book. *Hormê*—the Greek term which I translate as 'impulse'—is the central concept in the old Stoic analysis of human and animal action. By giving his treatise on human nature this title, Zeno or some later Stoic indicated that one of the central differences between human and animal nature lies precisely in the difference between human and animal action.

The two factors I shall concentrate on converge. One aim of this book is to demonstrate how rational actions, actions performed by rational agents, differ from irrational actions, which are performed by animals and are not really actions in the same full-blooded sense of the word. It might in fact be preferable to reserve the term 'action' for what is done by humans and to use the term 'behaviour' for what animals do. But that terminological restriction would be awkward, so I shall not bind myself by it. When, however, I use 'action' of animals it should be understood that the term is being applied in a weakened sense.

Thus the consideration of human nature in the doctrine of the older Stoics will be conducted through a study of *hormê* in the relevant fragments and testimony. Such a study is inevitably an exercise in reconstruction and depends on conjecture and hypothesis as well as on hard evidence. The reconstruction of the Stoic psychology of action which I offer cannot pretend to certainty; it must commend itself by its ability to account for the evidence, by its coherence with what we know about other parts of the Stoic system and by the plausibility of its relation to other ancient discussions of the nature of action.

Part I presents a reconstruction of this analysis of action. In Part II, I leave behind the question of how the theory of rational action distinguishes men from animals and examine how this theory of human action was used as a basis for several important themes in Stoic ethics. In a sense, however, Part II is also part of the reconstruction; for in it I discuss topics which employ the concept of *hormê* and if it could not be shown that these topics used *hormê* in a way compatible with the reconstructed theory, its claim on our credence would be weakened.

But I think that these ethical doctrines are compatible with the theory reconstructed and that one may, in addition, make a claim of substantial historical and philosophical significance about the old Stoa. The older Stoics not only elaborated an analysis of human action in greater detail than their rivals did, but they used it, I would claim, deliberately as a basis for their ethics. They seem to have seen clearly that making claims about what sorts of action are good or right should only be done on the basis of a theory about what action is. It is a commonplace that Stoic ethics is based on an understanding of human nature, that it is naturalistic. This they shared with most Greek ethical systems. But it is a significant philosophical advance to have seen that the understanding of human nature which grounds ethics should include a detailed theory of the nature of human action.

An objection to this approach comes readily to mind. 'Surely the most important facet of rationality for any Greek would be its role in the acquisition and contemplation of theoretical knowledge.' This is certainly true of Plato and arguably true of Aristotle (at least some of the time). Antiochus of Ascalon, an Academic philosopher of Cicero's day who argued for the essential unity of Platonic, Aristotelian, and Stoic philosophy, claimed Aristotle as his inspiration for a view of human nature which gave equal weight to the practical and theoretical side of our nature.[3] Later Peripatetics gave more or less weight to the active and contemplative sides of human nature,[4] but these were arguments about which should predominate within a framework which gave an important role to both. Is it reasonable to look exclusively at the practical side of rationality in the Stoic discussion of human nature?

It is impossible to deny that contemplation was a part of the good life according to the Stoics and that, correspondingly, an important part of rationality is the ability to seek out and achieve a grasp of theoretical truths. In Diogenes Laertius (7.130) we are told that the Stoics believed that the best life was neither the theoretical nor the practical, but a life which they called rational (*logikos*). 'For the rational animal is made on purpose by Nature for contemplation and action.' A similar statement is made in Cicero's *On the Nature of the Gods* (2.37): 'man himself was born to contemplate and imitate the world.'[5]

But we must put this in its proper Stoic context. Even a Stoic like Epictetus, notorious for his disinterest in theory and his zeal for practical ethics, can appear to regard man's practical instincts as being parallel to and equipollent with his natural affinity with what is true (*Discourses* 3.3.2–4). We should ask why contemplation of truth is so important for the Stoics. It is not because the life of the theoretical philosopher is in itself a particularly valuable sort of life;[6] for Chrysippus attacked the proponents of the scholastic life in no vague terms, claiming that it was sheer hedonism to drag out one's days in pursuit of the pleasures of intellectual contemplation (*Stoic Self-Contradictions* 1033c–d).[7] Although they no doubt left room for instincts towards the disinterested pursuit of truth,[8] the most important reason for contemplating the world was to facilitate the living of life according to nature. In order to live according to nature in a providentially determined world we must understand it; nature must be perfectly understood before man can live in accordance with it (Cicero *Fin.* 3.73; 2.34). We contemplate the world in large part in order to be able to imitate it, i.e. follow nature, more effectively.[9] It may well be that the most important difference between Posidonius and earlier Stoics was his abnormally high (for a Stoic) valuation of knowledge for its own sake.

It should at least be uncontroversial to claim that the Stoics were frequently inclined to de-emphasize the value of purely theoretical knowledge in a way that Plato and Aristotle were not. In pursuing the question of the Stoic analysis of rational action by means of an investigation into *hormê* we are on the trail of something central to their notion of what it means to be human.

What sort of theory of action did the Stoics have? A detailed answer will emerge in due course. But one or two general characterizations may help at this point. Like Aristotle and like Epicurus, the Stoics analysed actions done by an agent (whether human or animal), in contrast to motions undergone by them as a result of purely external forces, in terms of two basic factors. There is a desiderative state in the animal, which programmes it to pursue or avoid certain things (or, more generally, to act) in various circumstances; and there is an informational component, some sort of awareness of factors or aspects of the situation which indicate that the achievement of a goal is in the animal's power. For the simplest case, these are the only factors one has to mention in explaining an action, for one's desires and one's awareness that they can be achieved suffice on this theory to explain a piece of behaviour. That is because these two factors actually cause the behaviour in question.

In this very simple form, such a psychology of action is similar to a stimulus–response model of behaviour. In such a model, behaviour is elicited by providing stimuli which correspond with desiderative states in the animal. Dogs like to eat meat, so if you make a dog notice that meat is available he will take action to get it. The two causes one must mention in explaining Fido's leap across the room are his desiderative state (fondness for meat) and his awareness that a raw steak is within reach on the other side of the kitchen.

This sort of behavioural model for explaining action lies behind the Aristotelian, Epicurean, and Stoic psychologies of action. Human action was not, of course, explained in terms of such a crude theory; but a theory like this is the basis on which these theorists built, adding elements and modifying others in order to take account of more sophisticated cases of behaviour and action. Something roughly like this theory is the primary model for these psychologies of action, as it is for many even today.[10]

As we shall see, one move which Aristotle made in adapting this primary model to the case of human beings was to posit a separate power in the souls of men, reason. This power can function alone as both the desiderative element and as the informational element in the actions of highly rational and virtuous agents. But in most cases, reason is, as it were, in competition with the functioning of the simple primary model of action. As animals, men are programmed to do certain things in response to certain stimuli. But our reason can intervene in those actions or attempted actions and try to control or quash them. There is, thus, a kind of dualism between man's animal self and his rational self; moral improvement can be seen as turning in part on the battle between these two forces. A proper account of weak will (*akrasia*) can only be given, Aristotle seems to believe, on the hypothesis that there are such opposed powers operating in the determination of human actions.

The Stoics, I shall argue, faced many of the same questions when they came to consider the similarities between human and animal action. And they too added reason to the psychic capacities which operate in animal actions of the simple primary sort. But in adding reason they did not allow it to oppose and struggle with the lower animal soul. They found a way to introduce reason into the functioning of the animal soul without introducing the kind of psychological dualism Aristotle seems to need and want in his theory. There is no trace of a 'divided self' in Stoic psychology. When the rational soul functioned in producing an action, it functioned as a unity. How they did this and what significance it has in their psychology and ethics are stories to be told in the pages which follow.

PART I

Chapter 1

The Aristotelian Background

In 1967 David Furley published his influential book, *Two Studies in the Greek Atomists*. The second study, 'Aristotle and Epicurus on Voluntary Action', describes with exemplary clarity and force the main outlines of Aristotle's analysis of human and animal action. Moreover, Furley argued that Aristotle's approach to the explanation of action had considerable influence on Epicurus' treatment of the same theme. This is now generally accepted, although it is only natural that opinions differ on the details of the two theories and the exact nature of the influence.[1]

The early Stoic theory of human and animal action was influenced by Aristotle as much as was Epicurus'. Like Aristotle and Epicurus, the Stoics too began with a 'two-parameter' analysis,[2] in which a pro-attitude or desiderative state of the agent and some kind of informational component or cognitive state are the two principal elements in the explanation of action. The distinctive features of the Stoic theory are the topic of the following chapters. Here I give a brief outline of Aristotle's theory; such an outline will inevitably pass over many difficulties of detail and appear to be dogmatic on points where general agreement will, no doubt, never be achieved. But the broad outline of Aristotle's theory is sufficient for my purposes, since I do not want to claim that the early Stoics were replying in detail to this or that Aristotelian text. Perhaps, as Furley argued (see pp. 218–19), Epicurus *was* simply adapting Aristotle's theory to an atomistic psychology and a hedonistic ethics; but the Stoics carried out a more thorough rethinking of the theory of action and developed it with complete independence.

Aristotle's general account of animal action is given in the treatise *De Motu Animalium* (*On the Movement of Animals*). He claims that action occurs when some desiderative state of an animal is activated by a realization that the conditions for the fulfilment of its desire are present. In chapter 6 Aristotle groups the various factors which should be mentioned in a causal account of action under two headings (700b18–23). One of these is what I have called the informational component (*nous*) and includes *phantasia*, *aisthêsis*, *dianoia*, and, one supposes, any relevant discriminatory capability.[3] The other heading is desire (*orexis*), and this includes the three varieties which Plato (mistakenly in Aristotle's view) thought should be attributed to distinct parts of the soul:[4] wish (*boulêsis*), spirit (*thumos*), and appetite (*epithumia*). Choice (*prohairesis*), which plays an important role in Aristotle's ethics, is said to be reducible to a combination of the two basic elements (700b23).

Nussbaum has given an excellent account (in essay 4 of her edition of the *De Motu*) of how Aristotle uses these two basic features to explain animal action in general, and how he employs the so-called practical syllogism to illustrate the interaction of the factors. The practical syllogism cannot be examined thoroughly in the present context, but let us look at its use in the exposition of the psychology of action.

In Aristotle's syllogistic model of goal-directed behaviour, the agent is thought of as saying to himself (though he need not do so consciously and certainly not out loud), first: I should taste everything sweet (this is the 'major premiss' expressing his desire); second: this thing is sweet (the 'minor premiss' or informational component, embodying a perception or judgement about one's relation to the environment with respect to the desire). The conclusion, which follows of necessity, Aristotle says, provided that there are no external hindrances, is the immediate performance of the action. The necessity of the conclusion is borrowed from the necessity which characterizes genuine syllogisms in logic and this 'necessity' is supposed to explain (causally) why the action occurs. Let us focus first on one essential feature of the theory.

It is the role of the informational component, when it is itself activated, to activate the desiderative state and so to cause an instance of goal-directed desiderative behaviour. In chapter 7 Aristotle points out that a conscious awareness of the minor premiss is not essential.[5] All that is needed, he says, to cause the action is an activation of one of the informational faculties (*aisthêsis*, *phantasia* or *nous*) with respect to the goal, i.e. what the desiderative state has in view.[6] Then action follows automatically. 'For', he continues (701a31–2), 'the activation of desire stands in place of asking or thinking.'

Aristotle's central idea here is that the information provided by any of the relevant capacities activates or triggers the desire which is ready and waiting among the animal's dispositions. The proximate cause of the action, then, is neither the desiderative state nor the information, but the activated desire which results from the combination of these two explanatory factors. The activated desire is what is meant at 701a33–6: animals are impelled to move and act by this desire, which is activated by one of the informational capacities.

This portion of the *De Motu* is interesting because it contains a peculiar turn of phrase. The Greek corresponding to 'animals are impelled to move and act'[7] employs the idiom which is characteristic of the Stoic description of an animal action.[8] *Hormê* and *horman* are frequently used by Aristotle in the sense of 'desire' or 'activated desire',[9] so this wording should not surprise us. But the usage underlines how close the general framework of the psychology of action is for Aristotle and the Stoics.

The important place of *phantasia* in activating the desiderative state is also a feature of both Aristotle's and the Stoic theory. In chapters 6 and 7 we are given the impression that *phantasia* is one informational capacity among the others. But its role is more central than that, as Aristotle himself makes clear later, in chapter 8 (702a19): *phantasia* 'comes about either through perception or thought'. In the *De Anima*[10] these two kinds are labelled 'perceptual' and 'deliberative' or 'calculative' *phantasia* respectively.[11]

Nussbaum has drawn attention, in her fifth essay, to the importance of *phantasia* in Aristotle's psychology of action. She has emphasized that it provides the interpretive force which brings the object of perception of thought into connection with the animal's desires and presents it as being relevant to those desires. Although the role of *phantasia* in Stoic psychology (and especially in their epistemology) is different from its role in Aristotle's, this feature is common to both. *Phantasia* is the perceptual or noetic stimulus for the activation of desire and, therefore, for action. Nussbaum's discussion brings out this feature of Aristotle's concept of *phantasia*. But on one significant point I must register disagreement with her treatment, although a full discussion of the point would be out of place here.[12]

Nussbaum argues that *phantasia* as an interpretive faculty (the most important role it plays in the psychology of action) is to be contrasted with *phantasia* as a faculty which preserves and presents representations of the content of perception. *Phantasia* as a faculty of 'images' of this sort is in her view a part of a regrettably lame empiricist psychology built around the theoretical device of mental images. By contrast, she finds the interpretive kind of *phantasia* philosophically interesting. She therefore attempts to pry apart the promising texts where the interpretive function of *phantasia* is prominent from those passages where the context demands that images be a part of the concept, treating these two aspects of *phantasia* as alternative types.

As an exegetical approach this is dubious. In the psychological treatises Aristotle speaks of the faculty of *phantasia* as though it were one capacity of the soul. It would be an unfortunate muddle on his part if he used one technical term to refer to two distinct and mutually exclusive psychological powers or processes. It is preferable, if at all possible, to suppose that he had a single faculty in mind throughout the psychological works, a faculty which combined both the interpretive and representational features which are required of *phantasia* at various places in those works. This approach would also enable us to avoid the need to suppose (as Nussbaum sometimes does) that the interpretive *phantasia* is a faculty which goes to work on uninterpreted data provided by *aisthêsis*.[13] If, like perception, *phantasia* supplies images which resemble their objects and also interprets them, we will find it easier to understand why Aristotle emphasizes the similarity of perception and *phantasia* (as he does at *De Anima* 431a15, 432a9–10 and in *De Anima* 3.3 where *phantasia* is a change in the soul (*kinêsis*) derived from *aisthêsis*).

Such a reading of *phantasia* and *phantasmata* would require us to suppose that Aristotle believed that some interpretive images are needed for thought. For he clearly says that *phantasmata* are required in thought: 'and when it thinks (*theôrêi*) it must at the same time think some *phantasma*.'[14] This statement immediately precedes a statement that *phantasmata* are similar to *aisthêmata*. Aristotle is treating thought (as he often does) as a combination of basic concepts all of which are ultimately derived from perceptual experience.[15] Since he conceives of thought in this way, we would not expect him to draw a sharp contrast between the representational images of perception and the discursive or propositional interpretations of them. While the details of Aristotle's theory of *phantasia* are problematic, it will not be helpful to begin, as Nussbaum does, with a sharp dichotomy between perceptual images and thought. Rather, we should try to understand how Aristotle combined the two in a single, although somewhat inchoate, concept of *phantasia*.[16]

Why then did Aristotle single out *phantasia* in his account of action, rather than saying simply that either perception or thought could serve to activate desire? He did so probably because he was looking for a single factor to be the informational component, just as *orexis* (desire) was a single common factor for the desiderative component. In chapter 6 (700b19-20) he proposed *nous* as the common informational factor; but in a general account of animal action as well as human action, this term has drawbacks. It suggests the critical faculties of a rational animal. Aristotle was trying, as Nussbaum rightly emphasizes, to give a general account of the causes of action in all animals; this (and not the desire to isolate the interpretive from the representational aspects of perception and thought) led him to posit *phantasia* as the informational component in his explanation of action.

In *Two Studies* Furley drew attention to the striking similarity between the Epicurean psychology of action, in which action is stimulated by an image (*eidôlon, simulacrum*) of the action, and Aristotle's, where this role is played by the representational *phantasia*.[17] He argued that Epicurus followed Aristotle's account very closely. The Stoics did not adhere rigidly to Aristotle's formulation of the problem and to his presentation of the solution. But there are respects in which they followed up on parts of Aristotle's theory which Epicurus did not pursue, developing them in their own way. For the *phantasia* which informs the animal and so activates its desiderative disposition is, on the Stoic view, representational and also interpretive.[18] Moreover, the Stoics employed logical and grammatical concepts in the elaboration of their psychology of action; and so did Aristotle, when he adopted the syllogism as a model for the interaction of the desiderative and informational elements in his causal explanation of action.

The claim that the practical syllogism is used principally to explain occurrences of goal-directed animal behaviour is somewhat controversial. John Cooper[19] puts the case most strongly, arguing that it is only used to give an account of what happens in the soul at the moment of action and not to represent the process of deliberation which may have preceded it and shaped the agent's rational desires. This may be something of an overstatement, since there are passages where deliberations are cast into quasi-syllogistic form.[20] But Cooper's argument is convincing for the most part. The few deliberative syllogisms are easily explained. Nussbaum claims[21] (and I agree) that the practical syllogism is a framework which displays the relationship of the factors (desires and beliefs) which must be mentioned if an action is to be explained. It would not be surprising, then, if in the case of agents who deliberate rationally some of the factors in the deliberation could also be displayed in syllogistic form. For these deliberative factors will partially explain a rational agent's action. Despite the few readily explained exceptions, Cooper is right to emphasize that the principal use of the practical syllogism is not in giving an account of practical reasoning but in explaining the occurrence of an action.

The two premisses of the practical syllogism (one described as 'through the good', the other as 'through the possible')[22] represent, respectively, the desiderative state of the animal and the information it gets from thought or perception about the possibility of fulfilling that desire. This presupposes that the animal is already in a certain desiderative state, that its disposition has been prepared by previous experience in such a way that it will respond to an appropriate *phantasia*.[23] The so-called major premiss ('through the good') represents the desiderative state; it explains what the animal regards as good in the situation at hand. In a human, such a desiderative state might be a mere appetite, such as any irrational animal might also possess; or it might be a spirited desire, which could be shared by other animals; or it might be a wish (*boulēsis*), if it is a reasoned desire for what is good, formed by previous deliberation about how he ought to live.

Aristotle uses his general model of human action to explain 'weak will' or *akrasia*. The ability of a human to form desiderative states of his soul in conflict with the more rudimentary appetites; his ability to take account of the future consequences of his actions;[24] and his ability to generalize about his experience and use these generalizations in calculating proper principles of action;[25] these capabilities of human beings produce the possibility of acratic action. For if a man has two or more conflicting desiderative states, represented by major premisses 'through the good', then it is possible that he will complete the wrong syllogism and fail to act according to his 'wish', his rational desire for the genuine good.

Aristotle's use of the practical syllogism to account for 'weak will', in the *Nicomachean Ethics* 7.3 and *De Anima* 3.11, is a difficult topic. An important feature of his explanation is a human's ability to form conflicting major premisses representing his desires. These conflicting desires, then, are the 'principles' of action (*archai*) mentioned in the *Eudemian Ethics* (2.8, 1224a23–5). When activated, these desires are the impulses (*hormai*) referred to in the description of acratic motivation in the *Nicomachean Ethics* (1.13, 1102b21).

Aristotle's decision to use the syllogism as a model for the operation of the discriminatory capacities and desires does not commit him to the claim that a person is conscious of such a 'reasoning' process when he acts. Rather, it is an explanatory model which shows how these factors are related in causing an action, quite apart from the question of whether one is aware of them. Nevertheless, it is probable that Aristotle did believe that a human is often consciously aware of at least the 'minor premiss', the informational component of the cause of action. It is more likely that the cognitive component will be conscious than the underlying desiderative state. At *De Motu* 7, 701a25 ff. Aristotle makes a point of saying that sometimes we do not stop to note consciously the minor premiss. This suggests that he believes that a man often will be conscious of this factor.

At this point I want to draw attention to features of Aristotle's various discussions of action which anticipate some of the more striking characteristics of the Stoic analysis. The practical syllogism does not use the ideas of 'assent'[26] and 'commands to oneself' in a systematic way; but these concepts, central to the Stoic analysis of human action, are in several places used by Aristotle to represent the function of the two elements in the explanation of action.

The clearest case of this is in the *De Motu*.[27] Appetite says (*legei*) that the agent is to drink (*poteon moi*); but this has no effect until perception, *phantasia*, or thought also says (*eipen*) that some available object is drinkable. When this report is made—a single event rather than a continuing condition like the desiderative state—the action follows immediately. The decisive report of the information about the environment is a forerunner of assent in the Stoic theory. A similar situation is envisaged in the *De Anima*.[28] Both the desiderative state and the information 'say' their piece. But it is the information which is decisive; it 'says' that the conditions for the fulfilment of desire are available and it is the motive element. The general opinion which represents desire is 'more at rest' (*ēremousa mallon*).

Earlier in the *De Anima*[29] Aristotle considered the case where the information is provided to desire by perception. Its activity is like assertion or denial, depending on whether it perceives something pleasant or painful. The result of such a report is pursuit or avoidance behaviour, and the step between the report and the behaviour is the activation by perception of the faculty of desire (the animal feels pleasure or pain, which are manifestations of desire). But the decisive moment is the statement (*hoion kataphasa ê apophasa*) by the perceptual faculty.

The comparison to a verbal report is worked out somewhat differently in the *Nicomachean Ethics*.[30] Here the soul, not the informational capacity, pronounces the conclusion of the syllogism in theoretical cases, and we are told that the analogue to this in practical syllogisms is action. As the analogy of theoretical and practical syllogisms is used here, the pronouncement of the conclusion corresponds to the action.[31] In the other passages we have looked at it was the activation of the informational component which was described as a kind of report or discourse.

Aristotle's somewhat unsystematic use of verbs of saying to indicate the activating influence of the informational component and the conclusion (which is the action) is picked up and regularized by the Stoics. For as we shall see, they made assent a key part of the informational aspect of human action and the necessary and sufficient condition for the impulse which causes action.

Aristotle also uses imperatival language in describing how action issues from a combination of desire and belief. Again, his remarks are unsystematic, but in several places he associates imperatival force and language with desire. At *De Motu* 701a32 what desire says is 'I am to drink' (*poteon moi*). In the *Nicomachean* text just considered, the motive force of desire is expressed with similar language: at 1147a29, 'one must (*dei*) taste every sweet thing'; the general opinion resisting this 'hinders' tasting (*hê men katholou enêi kôluousa geuesthai*, 1147a31–2).[32] The imperatival aspect of desire, in its rational form, is even clearer in the *De Anima*.[33] Reason orders (*keleuei, epitattei*).[34] Here Aristotle is concentrating on cases where action fails to correspond to the commands of rational desire, but his use of the language of commanding is no less significant.

There are other cases too where Aristotle uses imperatival language to express the force of rational desire.[35] In these cases the analysis of action by means of the practical syllogism is not in view.

An examination of the various cases where Aristotle uses such language shows that he has a strong preference for attributing imperatival forces to rational desire alone. It is as though he were reluctant to dignify irrational desire with the position of 'commander' in the soul. But the passages from the *De Motu* and the *De Anima* indicate that he was ready on occasion to construe the power of lower desires as imperatival too.

The simple observation I want to make about Aristotle's analysis of action is this: he employs logical and linguistic concepts (syllogisms, verbs of saying or deciding, commands) in working it out. This is also a feature of the Stoic analysis of action, although the application of such concepts is different in important ways. Like the Stoics, Aristotle is not very informative on one question which naturally arises: how do such linguistic concepts fit into the analysis of action in non-rational animals? Aristotle and the Stoics are unclear on this, and I suggest that it is for the same reason. They are more interested in human action and extend their analysis to animals without considering this question in sufficient detail.

Aristotle's analysis of human and animal action had a significant influence on the Epicurean and Stoic theories. But the aspect of Aristotle's theory which strikes us as particularly interesting, his use of logical and linguistic concepts, was not picked up by Epicurus,[36] who seems to have left no room for this feature.[37] The Stoics, as we shall see, did follow Aristotle on this point. Indeed, they developed the use of linguistic elements in the analysis of human action even further. One result of this development was that they were in a better position to explain how the intentions and goals of actions can be formulated by the agent. The practical syllogism is a step in this direction, but was not designed expressly to capture this facet of human action. It was left for the Stoics to realize fully that the goal and point of one's actions could be verbally formulated and become a conscious intention. This development, made possible by other Stoic advances in logic and epistemology,[38] had a significant impact on their psychology of action and ultimately on the shape of Stoic ethics.

Chapter 2

Human Nature and the Rational Soul[1]

(a) The Place of Man in Nature

Man is a very special sort of animal. And yet man is an animal for all that. Animals are a distinctive sort of living things, different in important ways from plants. In their turn, plants are a particular and distinctive kind of natural object. If one is to make systematic sense of these vague facts, a good way to do it is to arrange the various forms of natural objects on a hierarchical scale according to a set of criteria which display the various entities being compared in different places on the scale. And if one's criteria are chosen correctly the *scala naturae* which results will account for the similarities and differences observed and will make an important statement about the order of nature.

Both Aristotle and the Stoics approached the question of man's place in nature in this way. But man is not the highest animal for either. Gods have to be accounted for too, or perhaps only one god is needed. God, then, though he is not what *we* would call a part of nature, is placed atop this scale as its highest entity. The effect of this is to delimit human nature from above and below.[2]

Gods and men are both rational. The traditional Greek view of the difference between them focused on human mortality and weakness in contrast with the deathless and ageless quality of divine beings.[3] Philosophers, of course, insisted on rather more points of difference. Gods were eventually expected to display in perfect form the sort of rational characteristics, intelligence and morality, which men display in their imperfect way. Plato certainly expected this of his gods, and if Aristotle's god, the prime mover, displays only intellectual perfection in his self-contemplation that should not count against the general pattern. The Stoics followed this general pattern and insisted that gods are different from men most significantly because of the natural perfection of the gods' rational nature. But men and gods do share a rational nature, and this is basis for the friendship and community which can exist between gods and men.[4]

Aristotle too thought that man was akin to god in the sense that god has in perfect degree some characteristic which men also have. For it is an aspect of our theoretical reason which Aristotle seems to identify with that divine part of soul which is 'separate' and which is not the entelechy of any part of the body.[5] But on the Stoic view, reason as a whole is common to gods and men, and they put special emphasis on the applications of reason in the correct living of life; therefore a Stoic is inclined to say that the gods are naturally virtuous; they are perfect and virtuous by nature, while man must labour long and hard to achieve whatever degree of excellence he may.[6]

When we turn to the *scala naturae* below the level of man, the mortal and rational animal, there are still similarities between the Stoics and Aristotle. In *De Anima* 2.2–3 Aristotle outlines a scheme for organizing the various phenomena of nature. To distinguish living from lifeless nature he introduces soul. The various levels of nature are defined by their possession or lack of certain powers of the soul. For life to be present there must be the power of growth and nutrition. Thus plants are distinguished from things like stones and other inanimate natural objects. The *sine qua non* of animal soul is perception or sensation (*aisthêsis*), the lowest and simplest form of which is touch. Some very simple animals have this alone, but by virtue of that fact they are animals, not plants. The number of senses an animal possesses and the presence and degree of the other powers which characterize soul (the power of appetition or desire, of local motion, the power of thought) can be used to rank all animals on the *scala*. Man, the mortal and rational animal, is at the top of the ladder, except for god. An important fact about this hierarchical scale is that the possession of any characteristic entails the possession of the characteristics below it on the scale.[7] This does not mean that a man's soul contains a bundle of distinct lower souls. Aristotle is careful to tell us that the lower psychic powers are in the soul potentially (*dunamei*),[8] which means that they cannot be separated out in actual fact. Nevertheless, it is clear that in a rational animal the lower powers of nutrition and perception and local motion are distinguishable in the functioning of the animal.

The details of this theory are not as important for the purposes of comparison with the Stoa as is its general outline. For we shall see in the Stoa too a hierarchical *scala naturae* which marks off each level by the presence or absence of certain powers or characteristics; and like Aristotle, the Stoics thought that nature was organized in such a way that the presence of higher powers in a natural object entailed the presence of the qualities below it on the scale.[9]

But before we turn to the Stoic evidence, one more piece of Aristotelian background is needed. Aristotle thought it important to discuss the differences between the way animals moved themselves or were set in motion by something external and the way inanimate natural objects moved themselves or were set in motion. Much of his discussion is to be found in *Physics* 8.[10] It would be out of place to consider the matter in any detail here, but it is clear that the various kinds of movement can be correlated with various levels of the hierarchy of nature. The ability to set oneself in motion in pursuit of something, for example, is only present when the animal in question has the powers of perception and local motion. In contrast, mere motion to the natural place of an object is found in inanimate objects too, at the very bottom of the *scala*. And the power of deliberate action which man has by virtue of reason makes possible a different sort of movement again. For as the fact of acratic behaviour shows, men unlike animals, are able to move in accordance with either of two competing internal powers or principles. In his discussion of voluntariness in *Eudemian Ethics* 2.8 Aristotle contrasts men to animals because human action can occur as a result of either of the two principles in us, reason or unreflective desire, whereas animals, like inanimate objects, have only one principle of motion. An irrational animal's power to act is an irrational *dunamis* (*Met.*Θ. 3 and 5), while man's is rational. He can act or refrain from acting on a stimulus. But an animal must act on an environmental stimulus, just as surely as the dropped stone must fall.[11]

Aristotle's discussion of the kinds of motion forms a supplement to his hierarchy of natural objects. The details of it are not as clear as we might wish, but the broad outline of his position is all that we need for the sake of comparison with the Stoa. For among our sources for the Stoic version of the *scala naturae* are texts which deal with the question of which motions are found at each level of the hierarchy. The details of this doctrine of the hierarchical organization of nature are Stoic; but the problem they are dealing with was set by Aristotle.

It is time to turn to the evidence for the Stoic *scala naturae*. For at this point the introduction of evidence for the doctrine of *hormê* is overdue, and *hormê* is one of the key criteria used to define the Stoic hierarchy.

The Stoic hierarchy of natural objects, like Aristotle's, was organized on the principle that the higher levels on the scale include the characteristics of the lower levels.[12] In the mature Chrysippean form of the doctrine, the continuity and unity of nature through all these levels is assured by the claim that the forces which give each kind of entity its characteristic powers are all modifications of the same material principle, *pneuma*. *Pneuma* is manifested as mere *hexis*, the power of coherence, in things like stones; in plants a more complex form of *pneuma* constitutes the *phusis* which makes them what they are; in animals *pneuma* manifests itself as soul; and in rational animals *pneuma* achieves its highest form and is reason.[13] This doctrine of an all-pervasive *pneuma* is a complex one, and this is not the place to investigate either its origin or the finer points of the physical theory which underlies it.[14] In the evidence we have to consider now, the main importance of this doctrine is in the fact that each level of the hierarchy is characterized by the powers of *pneuma* appropriate to that level of organization and that the unity of nature is maintained through the continuity of *pneuma* at all levels.

The kinds of motion of the various natural objects were set out by the Stoics (and one may guess that Chrysippus was primarily responsible) in systematic fashion; they were almost certainly following up Aristotle's discussion and giving their version of it a more precise and inflexible statement. Several texts from later antiquity report or criticize this doctrine. The clearest report comes from Origen's *De Principiis* 3.1.2–3 (=SVF 2.988).

Of things that move, some have the cause of movement in themselves, while others are moved only from the outside. Thus things moved by being carried (*ta phorêta*), such as sticks and stones and every form of matter held together by *hexis* alone, are moved from the outside . . . Plants and animals and, in a word, everything held together by *phusis* and soul have within themselves the cause of movement. They say that this category includes veins of metal and, in addition, that fire and perhaps springs of water are also self-moved. Of things which contain the cause of movement in themselves, they say that some move from themselves (*ex heautôn*) and others by themselves (*aph' heautôn*). 'From themselves' applies to soulless objects, 'by themselves' to things with soul. For ensouled things move by themselves when a *presentation* occurs which stimulates the *impulse* . . . But the rational animal has reason too in addition to the power of presentation. Reason judges [or distinguishes] the presentations and rejects some and admits others . . .

Plants and animals can be moved by external forces, just as sticks and stones are. But plants and animals have an additional power, self-movement. The lower entities are 'moved *only* from the outside'. Animals retain the power of growth found in plants, but add to it the power to move in response to their environment through presentation (*phantasia*) and impulse (*hormê*), the powers characteristic of animal soul.[15] Rational animals possess in addition the controlling power of reason which makes it possible for this kind of movement to be made not automatically but selectively.

Like Aristotle, the Stoic author of this doctrine refused to allow that any absolutely self-caused movement is possible. Even movements 'by themselves' are the result in part of environmental stimulation. We shall see as more evidence is presented that even rational action is not utterly self-caused; it too depends on stimulation from outside the animal.

In this first text, Origen is discussing the lower four of the five levels of the full Stoic *scala naturae*: inert objects, plants, animals, and men. Gods are not brought into the scheme in the second text from Origen either; their place at the top of the scale must be presented on the strength of other evidence.

In his book *On Prayer* Origen presents similar material (6.1 = SVF 2.989):[16]

Of things that move, some have the mover external to them, as do soulless things and those held together by *hexis* alone. And those things that move by *phusis* or by soul sometimes also move not as beings of this sort, but in a manner similar to those held together by *hexis* alone. For stones and sticks which are cut off from a vein of metal or have lost the power to grow[17] are held together only by *hexis* and have their motive power external to them. And the bodies of animals and the moveable parts of plants which are shifted by someone are not shifted *qua* animal or plant, but in a manner similar to sticks and stones which have lost the power to grow . . . After those, second are those objects moved by the *phusis* or the soul within them, which are also said to move 'from themselves' by those who use words in their stricter senses [i.e. the Stoics]. Third is the movement in animals which is termed movement 'by oneself' (*aph' heautou*). And I think that the movement of rational animals is termed movement 'through themselves' (*di' hautôn*). And if we deprive an animal of movement 'by itself' it is impossible to go on thinking of it as an animal. Rather, it will be similar either to a plant moved only by *phusis* or a stone being carried along by an external agent. And if the animal is aware of its own movement, this animal must be rational, since we have called this movement 'through itself'.[18]

These reports of Stoic doctrine are used in discussions of fate and free will. Similar but much more problematic material is found in Alexander of Aphrodisias and in Nemesius and confirms that this is the context in which Chrysippus set out this elaboration of the doctrines of the kinds of motion found at each level of the hierarchy. The evidence of Alexander and Nemesius will be considered later but it is appropriate to introduce here the testimony of Simplicius. In his *Commentary* on Aristotle's *Categories* (p. 306 = SVF 2.499) Simplicius criticizes the Stoic classification of motions. Although this report is different in several points from that reported by Origen, it is valuable for its inclusion of a reference to the highest level of the hierarchy and for its introduction of some Stoic terminology which Origen does not give us. The Stoics

say that the differences between kinds [sc. of movement] are: 1) moving 'from themselves', as a knife has the ability to cut because of its own proper constitution (for the doing [*poiêsis*] is carried out by its shape and form); 2) and the activation of movement 'through oneself', as natural organisms [*phuseis*] and curative[19] powers carry out their action [*poiêsis*]: for the seed is sown and unfolds[20] its proper potential [*oikeious logous*] and attracts the matter nearby and alters the potential in it; 3) and also doing [*poiein*] 'by oneself', which in general terms is doing from a thing's own impulse [*hormê*]. But another sense 4) is doing from rational impulse,[21] which is called action.[22] And 5) even more specific than this is activity according to virtue.

A comparison of the schemes by Origen and by Simplicius is in order:

Origen	Simplicius
1. *hexis, exôthen* sticks, stones, etc.	1. *eidos*, 'from themselves' a knife
2. *phusis* 'from themselves' plants etc.	2. *phuseis* 'through oneself' seeds
3. soul, 'by themselves' animals	3. from a things own impulse, 'by itself'
4. reason, 'through oneself' rational animals	4. from rational impulse, action
5. ----------------------	5. virtuous action

Although Rieth treats Simplicius' report as a straightforward and reliable report of Stoic doctrine, I think we must give greater credence to Origen. For his discussion of free will shows throughout a

first-hand familiarity with a variety of Stoic doctrine which is confirmed by other sources. Simplicius, however, has omitted the first
level of the hierarchy, that characterized by *hexis*. In its place he
inserts an example of a tool with a power derived from its proper
form. This is probably an addition from the Aristotelian tradition. The terminology of *schêma* and *eidos* is Peripatetic and so is the
notion of a power to act (in this case to cut) being the result of such a
form. One might compare Aristotle's discussion of the form of an
axe in *De Anima* 2.1. The choice of the term 'from themselves' to
describe the motion of the first level suggests that the sort of cases
Simplicius has in mind would be better placed on the second level.
This second level in Simplicius' account is also confused or corrupt;
moreover 'through oneself' is oddly displaced to the second level by
Simplicius.

At least the lower two levels are muddled in Simplicius' account.
On the other hand, he gets the terminology of the third level correct
and he includes a reference, however vague, to the fifth level.[23]
Moreover, Simplicius refers to rational impulse and to 'action'
(*prattein*) as characteristic of the level of rational soul. Origen is less
informative on these points. One may guess that the report in
Simplicius is the result of his attempt to interpret not an original
Stoic text, but a text containing Stoic material as adapted by someone who was sympathetic to elements of Aristotle's doctrine and
who performed a slight conflation of his sources. And we can be
fairly sure who this might have been. For Simplicius introduces his
report of this theory with a reference to 'Plotinus and the others who
follow the Stoic usage' (p. 306. 13–14).[24] The points where
Simplicius' report diverges from Origen's are to be explained by
reference to earlier Neoplatonic adaptation of a Stoic source such as
Origen used.

According to Origen, each level is demarcated by certain characteristics while retaining in its nature the characteristic features of the
lower levels.[25] (1) Mere sticks and stones are held together by *hexis*
and are moved by external forces. (2) Plants are held together by
phusis and as a consequence possess the power of growth. (3)
Animals have soul, and thus the powers of presentation and
impulse which enable them to respond automatically to the
environment. They also grow and can be moved by external force.
(4) Rational animals grow, of course, and can be moved by external
force, as when I grab your arm and swing it; but their power to react

to the environment through presentation and impulse is complicated by reason, which frees it from the automatic response characteristic of animal action.

It would be tiresome to quote and discuss all the texts which use or
allude to the Stoic *scala naturae*. Seneca (*Ep.* 58.14) uses the material
of the *scala* to illustrate the proper method of division and classification and the same procedure underlies Cicero's systematic presentation of things which are useful to men in various ways (*Off.* 2.11).
Seneca brings out the way each level contains the powers of the levels
below it while being characterized by the highest powers it possesses
in *Ep.* 76.8–11.[26]

There are striking similarities between Origen's version of the
doctrine and the one given by his fellow Alexandrian, Clement,[27]
who says in part: 'Of moving things, some move by presentation
and impulse, as do animals'.[28] His account of the hierarchy is condensed, but he mentions the essential points given by Origen. *Hexis,
phusis*, soul, and the power of reason are all mentioned, and we note
that the third level is said to contain or include the first two. The
familiar examples, stones and plants, are also found in Clement.

In Cicero's version of the hierarchy[29] *sensus* and *appetitus* (*appetitio*)
or *impetus* (his translations of *hormê*)[30] are attributed to animals. The
substitution of *sensus* for presentation does not alter the scheme significantly. And indeed Philo's reports of the hierarchy,[31] which are
quite clear and detailed and give every sign of being based on
reliable Stoic sources, include *aisthêsis* along with presentation at
the level of animal soul. These passages of Philo use the familiar
examples for the *hexis* level and so too does the probably spurious
work attributed to Philo, *De Aeternitate Mundi* (75).

The text from Philo's *Allegory of the Laws* offers an explanation of
how the lower levels of the hierarchy are included in the higher. In
higher animals the bones are like stones in being governed by *hexis*
while our hair and nails are compared to plants governed by *phusis*,
because of their obvious ability to grow. Unfortunately, we must
doubt whether this is the Stoic way of explaining the doctrine of the
inclusion of lower levels, since it is not paralleled in any other source
and has a slightly fanciful air to it which may well be the product of
Philo's active imagination.[32] I think it is more likely that the inclusion of *hexis* in a plant is reflected in the fact that all the parts of its
body are held together by *phusis* which performs the function of *hexis*
as well as its own characteristic functions by virtue of being a more

highly organized form of the same *pneuma* which subsumes its powers. Something similar would apply to the inclusion of the power of *phusis* in an animal. One *pneuma*, soul, also possesses the powers embodied in the *hexis* and *phusis* of lower entities.[33]

Eusebius too[34] reflects the Stoic hierarchy in his account of 'things that move', although his terminology is not as consistently Stoic as it is in our other sources. Still, the four levels are clearly indicated and animal movement is characterized by presentation and impulse while human nature is characterized by the additional power of reason.[35]

It is reason which makes man superior to the animals. Reason alters the functioning of the soul's powers of presentation and impulse in the production of actions. Reason makes men superior in other ways too, but the main contrast will be between human and animal action.

And what of the gods? Apart from being immortal and naturally virtuous, how else is the divine superior to man? The full answer to this question will become apparent only when we consider the old Stoic view of man's place in a providentially determined universe ruled by the will of Zeus. But one important point should be made here. We are not told as much about the divine level as we should like. But we may infer that the highest level contained the powers characteristic of lower levels as well. This is strikingly confirmed by an important text from Cicero's work *On the Nature of the Gods* (2.58). We may not have been inclined to doubt that the Stoics credited their only genuine god, Zeus, with the power of perception as well as that of reason. But what of *hormē*? Does god have the power of impulse which accounts for goal-directed actions in other animals? What would god's actions be?

Cicero gives us part of the answer:

And as all the other natural entities are born, grow and are controlled each by its own seeds [i.e. natural potentials], so too the nature of the world has all those voluntary motions, conations and impulses which the Greeks call *hormai*, and he follows these with corresponding actions, just as we ourselves do, who are moved by our minds and sensations. Since this is the nature of the mind of the world [i.e. Zeus] it may therefore be properly called prudence or providence (for in Greek the term is *pronoia*).

Cicero then goes on to characterize the providential actions of Zeus. We do not have to go into this question now; what is important in this passage is the statement that god has impulses and performs actions just as men do. Since god is the mind of the world, who rules it and causes its providentially determined sequence of events, his impulses and actions will be of immensely greater significance than those of mere men.

These impulses of the divine mind are surely to be identified with the 'will' or *boulêma* of Nature to which Epictetus refers in the *Enchiridion* (26), and with what Chrysippus calls the '*boulêsis* of the organizer (*dioikêtês*) of the universe'.[36] If the 'will of god' is a kind of impulse (*boulêsis* is in fact one kind of impulse)[37] is it not reasonable to identify the actions god performs with the events of the providentially determined world? It seems to me that it is. Epictetus associates the governance (*dioikêsis*) of the world by god with his *hormai*.[38] So too does Marcus Aurelius.[39] From these texts it is clear that the results of *hormê* of Providence or Zeus are just the occurrences of the natural order of the world. Since god can be considered the mind of the world as well as its ruler, it would be natural for the Stoics to consider the events of the world as the result of the will of god, as his actions. And just as human actions are the result of *hormai*, so too are the 'actions' of all-powerful and providential Zeus.

In part II we will have to consider the ethical significance of this similarity of god's mind, will, and actions to those of men. In so doing we will shed a little light on man's relations with the occupant of the highest level of the *scala naturae*. The rest of the first Part must be dedicated to the question of man's relation to the next lower level, occupied by irrational animals. And the chief point of contrast will be the psychology of action. How does rational human action differ from that of brute beasts?

(b) The Nature of the Rational Soul

We have learned that animal soul is characterized by the powers of presentation (or perception) and impulse (the power to set oneself in motion in pursuit of goals). And we have seen that human soul has the additional power of reason. We must now examine the nature of soul more precisely, in order to make possible an exact understanding of the way these powers function.

It is sometimes thought that an extreme version of nominalism must have prevented the orthodox old Stoics, Zeno and Chrysippus especially, from believing that there could be enduring 'powers', or if you will, 'faculties' in the soul.[40] In fact, a very battle royal raged earlier in this century between two outstanding German historians

of Stoic thought, Robert Philippson and Max Pohlenz,[41] on precisely this question: did any old Stoics believe in faculties of the soul
or did they all think it was radically monistic, having no powers
beyond the ones being exercised at any given time? And if they did
think so, did they all? Or was there an important difference between
Zeno and Chrysippus on this question?

The reader's time would be wasted by a re-examination of this
scholarly quarrel. But something must be said here, since A.-J.
Voelke has recently announced his support for a modified Pohlenzian position which attributes a radical nominalism to both Zeno
and Chrysippus,[42] in a book dealing with the historical antecedents
of a modern concept of 'will' in Stoicism.

With the wisdom of hindsight it seems clear that at least two infeli-
cities, which we need not repeat, led to the quarrel. First, Philippson
overemphasized the Aristotelian appearance of Stoic psychology in
arguing that it was a faculty psychology. Second, both scholars
failed to distinguish with sufficient clarity these two questions: does
the soul in its entirety or just the *hêgemonikon* have a multiplicity of
powers? and the more important question, does the mind (as I shall
translate *hêgemonikon*) have in it a power which can oppose reason
and impair its functioning in the control of a man's actions and life?

The latter is the key psychological question which bears on Stoic
ethics. I doubt that it can even be framed in an exact form until we
have examined the functioning of the psychology of action in some
detail. When we have done this, it will be possible to see what is
meant by psychological monism in a non-radical but still very
important sense. In this section a general outline of the old Stoic
analysis of the soul's structure will be given. Then an accurate
picture of the functioning of the soul in causing actions will be
possible.[43]

One more point about past confusions. It should be clear that
nominalism, as Voelke invokes it, is a bugbear which we can
ignore. It is doubtful whether any old Stoic was so extreme or
strict a nominalist as Voelke thinks. Indeed, if one wishes to reconcile nominalism, in a materialist psychology, with 'faculties' or
general powers, all one need do is to locate each faculty in some
material entity. The power to have impulses (i.e. to act), for
example, can be located by a nominalist in a state or material
modification of the soul. A general power can in this way exist
quite happily within a nominalist system. This is exactly what the

Stoics did, as will become clear when we have cast our net more widely and brought ashore rather more evidence than Voelke and Pohlenz did.

But now let us turn to this evidence of the old Stoic views on the structure and powers of the soul. We shall see that, contrary to what Pohlenz thought, there is no reason to believe that Zeno's views on the structure of the soul were in any important respect different from those of Chrysippus. We are in general dependent on doxographic reports of general Stoic doctrine which, most scholars agree, reflect what is basically the mature formulation of the old Stoic theories by Chrysippus. The formulations which the doxographers found in their immediate sources may owe something to the handbooks and summaries drawn up by Stoics as late as the second century BC, but there is no reason to doubt their basic orthodoxy. Similarly, there is no reason to believe that on the questions now under consideration Zeno held significantly different views from those of Chrysippus. Where we do have direct evidence of Zeno's views, it coheres fairly well with the general doctrine which we agree to regard as Chrysippean.[44]

We must begin by setting out the evidence for the structure of the human soul and its powers. Then some of the erroneous interpretations of Pohlenz and Voelke must be dealt with. Finally, we shall be able to show how the ascription of 'powers' or 'faculties' to the soul is consistent with Stoic nominalism by finding a location for them in certain states of the material soul.

The main division of the human soul into parts was this: it has eight parts (*merê*), namely the five senses, the part controlling voice, the part controlling reproductive powers, and the mind itself, which controls or regulates all of these.[45] This is a theory also reported by Neoplatonic sources;[46] if the bishop Nemesius is to be believed, this division goes back to Zeno himself.[47]

In addition to these specifically listed parts of the soul, we must remember that the soul also has the functions performed at lower levels of the hierarchy by *hexis* and *phusis*. It holds the animal together, as *hexis* does for things like sticks and stones.[48] By implication too, the soul performs the functions of *phusis*, growth, and nutrition, although they are not listed as 'parts' in these texts.[49] If confusion is to be avoided at certain key points it will also help to keep in mind what we are told in the text of Sextus Empiricus cited in n. 48: since the mind or *hêgemonikon* is the leading and dominant part of the soul it was sometimes designated by the term 'soul' itself.Some information we are given about the powers of the soul obviously deals only with the powers of the mind.[50]

But this eight-part division of the soul sheds no light on the question of the status of *hormê* or the other powers of the mind itself. For this we must turn again to a selection from Iamblichus' book *On the Soul* found in Stobaeus.[51] Here we read: 'The followers of Zeno teach that the soul has eight parts, and that in the soul (*peri hên*) there are several powers. For example, there exist in the mind presentation, assent, impulse, and reason.'

Iamblichus has already attributed to the Stoics and to all proponents of a material soul the view that the powers of the soul are analogous to qualities.[52] He divides powers into two groups: those operating in conjunction with a specific part of the corporeal *pneuma* (e.g. the senses) and those *dunameis* which, as a group, operate through only one *pneuma*. These, Iamblichus says, are distinguished 'by the peculiarity of their quality (*idiotêti poiotêtos*). Just as the apple has in the same body its sweetness and its aroma, so too the mind contains in the same [sc. physical part] presentation, assent, impulse and reason.'

It must be emphasized how important it is to distinguish parts from powers in this text.[53] Parts are spatially distinct bits of *pneuma*, and the *hêgemonikon* is one of these; it is the *pneuma* in or around the heart. It has four powers, i.e. it can do four different sorts of things; by contrast each of the *pneumata* extending to the sense organs is endowed with only one power. The ears can only hear, the eyes can only see, and so forth, while the mind can do several different things, because it has more than one power in the same bit of matter., How this is possible, according to the Stoics, we shall see presently.

Two brief observations are in order at this point. First, it is noteworthy that the powers of the mind which Iamblichus singles out for mention are just the powers which are found in the Stoic analysis of action. This is no accident. Even if the mind does have other powers, these are the ones worth singling out just because of the great importance the Stoics attached to their analysis of action in their account of human nature. Second, this talk of powers of the soul suggests that Aristotelian influence lies behind the Stoic theory. Like Aristotle, the Stoics distinguished different kinds of soul by reference to the different kinds of behaviour or action, the different ways of living,[54] which various animals exhibit. And like

Aristotle, the Stoics supposed that some capability or power to perform that sort of behaviour was a real facet of the animal soul.

Iamblichus' information in this passage is thus very valuable indeed. But it must be used with caution. It proves only that, in addition to the eight parts of the soul, Stoic psychology also recognized in the mind, the part of the soul with more than one power, real enduring distinctions. It does not by itself establish that they were called powers or *dunameis*; but this is in fact the case, as we shall see. Nor does it tell us about their physical status on Stoic principles; we shall, however, be able to make a good guess about this soon enough.

Iamblichus organized the portion of his treatise *On the Soul* which interests us here around the Aristotelian concepts of *dunamis*, *energeia*, and *ergon*, as the titles of chapters 33 to 37 of Stobaeus' *Eclogae* Bk. 1 show. Thus his use of the word *dunamis* is not itself evidence for Stoic doctrine. These powers are compared to qualities inhering in a substance. Iamblichus seems to be thrusting on to the Stoa a substance—quality metaphysical framework which is foreign to their own system.[55]

On the other hand, the fact that Iamblichus' use of *dunamis* is not direct evidence for old Stoic usage does not prove that the Stoa did not refer to *dunameis* in the mind, any more than the oddness of the phrase *idiotēti poiotētos* would mean that the Stoa did not have a place in their physics for *idiōs poia*. And indeed there is a Stoic sense of *dunamis* which is relevant to the present question. Simplicius, in his *Commentary* on Aristotle's *Categories*,[56] attributes to the Stoics a definition of *dunamis* meant to account for the relationship of a mental disposition to the activities which stem from it.[57] A power, he says, is 'that which brings on [i.e. causes] many events (*sumptōmata*)[58] and controls [or dominates] the activities subordinate to it'. A power is some sort of disposition, of the soul in the cases at hand, which can produce and regulate a set of activities or discrete events.

There is confirmation for this testimony from Simplicius about powers. Philo Judaeus[59] confirms that impulse, and so too (one supposes) the other powers of the mind, is a *dunamis* in a Stoic sense. Impulse, he says, is 'according to the *tonikē dunamis* of the mind'. And Arius Didymus gives this as one definition of knowledge (*epistēmē*):[60] 'a disposition (*hexis*) to receive presentations, which can not be changed by argument, which they say consists in *tonos* and *dunamis*'.[61] *Dunamis*, or a power to produce and regulate certain mental events, seems to consist in some tensional state of the *pneuma* of the soul. Thus the *tonos* of one's mind is of critical importance for the nature of one's impulses and in general for determining how an animal will interact with its environment.[62] So it seems also in the case of a *hexis* governing one's cognitive powers. Individual acts of one's cognitive powers[63] are determined by the *tonos* of the disposition which governs them. We shall return again to the question of the relation of *dunamis, tonos,* and *hexis.* For the *hexis,* which we have been translating 'disposition', will turn out to have a material character, just as the *dunamis* has.

There is good independent reason to accept the evidence of Iamblichus in the text we are considering: the mind does have four powers and these exist even when the powers are not being exercised. Thus impulse, like the other powers which are needed in the Stoic psychology of action, has both an active form (a *kinêsis* or *energeia*) and a quiescent or potential form (a *dunamis*).

In most of our sources impulse is explicitly defined as a kind of change, movement or activity of the soul. It is a motion (*phora*)[64] or movement (*kinêsis*)[65] or change (*heteroiôsis*).[66] Similarly, in one of the few texts which seems to be direct evidence for Zeno's views, Plutarch[67] tells us that in the production of an action three *kinêmata* are involved: the action of presentation, that of assent, and that of impulse. That means that three of the four powers mentioned by Iamblichus and needed for the analysis of human action were represented as activities as early as Zeno. It is hard to prove that the theory of powers or dispositions also goes back to Zeno, but it seems to me to be overwhelmingly likely.[68]

So far we have been talking about the human soul, since that is the kind of soul for which we are given the best evidence; and I have been assuming that *hêgemonikon* referred only to the leading part of the human soul, i.e. what is also called reason or thought, and so have translated it as 'mind'. But we should remember that there is a sort of *hêgemonikon* in all animal souls, as we are told by Arius Didymus:[69] 'every soul has some leading part, which is its life and sensation and impulse.' The application of this to animal soul is guaranteed by the reference to *every* soul, by the mention of sensation and impulse, which are the characteristic powers of animal soul, and by the absence of any reference to reason. Clearly animals have souls which are similar in make-up to those of men, except for the absence of reason and, of course, of all the powers made possible only by reason. Cicero confirms this general picture, when he refers to a part of the soul which is analogous to the mind in men and which he calls 'something similar to mind from which impulses for things arise'.[70] I shall continue to use *hêgemonikon* for the human mind alone, since the word is used to refer to a part of the human soul by virtually all our sources. When occasion arises to refer to its analogue in irrational animals I shall call it 'quasi-*hêgemonikon*' or 'quasi-mind'.[71] When we come to consider the differences between human and animal action, the close similarity between the parts and powers of their souls will be important.

If the human soul has these eight parts and the mind has four powers, then in what sense is the psychology of the old Stoa 'monistic'? Not, surely, in the strictest possible sense, that there are no parts in the soul. For there are eight parts. And not even in the sense that the mind has no enduring distinctions within it, as the supernominalist interpretation of Pohlenz and Voelke[72] claims. If the soul is monistic at all, it is going to be in the sense that the various powers of the soul all function together harmoniously, with no internal conflict or opposition. The way the Stoics attempted to guarantee the harmonious functioning of these powers in their psychology of action will become clear in the next chapter. Here we should turn our attention to some critics of the Stoa, ancient and modern, who have supposed that the unity they had in mind was of a different nature.

There is no direct and unpolemical evidence which indicates that the old Stoics, or Chrysippus more particularly, maintained that the soul had only one *dunamis*; certainly there is none which outweighs the evidence of Iamblichus, Simplicius, Arius Didymus, and Philo which has been cited. The idea that there is only one power in the soul according to the old Stoa has its origins in several attacks on the Stoic psychology of action. The Stoic psychology of action was monistic in that it placed the power of reason in charge of the process of generating actions, and did not leave room for a power in the soul which might oppose reason and interfere with its control over the actions of the agent. This control of a polydynamic soul[73] and its activities by reason was caricatured by philosophers who held on to a psychological dualism of the sort which Plato in his mature years and Aristotle seem to have accepted and which did not rule out the possibility of genuine *akrasia*, as the Stoic theory did.[74] When the Stoic psychology of action is compared with such a dualistic analysis, then it does indeed seem to have only 'one power'. But here 'power' is meant in a sense which does not correspond with 'power' in the technical Stoic theory.

In the sense in which the Stoic psychology of action is in fact monistic Zeno and Chrysippus appear to have held views which are indistinguishable from each other. Cicero[75] makes it quite clear that, like Chrysippus, Zeno held that there was only one 'power' in the mind of the kind to which critics of the Stoics referred when attacking them for monism. Plutarch too makes it quite clear[76] that all the orthodox Stoics, Zeno included, were subject to the same criticism, viz. not positing an irrational part or power in the soul.

Yet Pohlenz maintained that Chrysippus' psychology was monistic in a way that Zeno's was not. It is no longer necessary to refute such a view in detail. Even Voelke, who accepts the radical monistic interpretation of Pohlenz, has admitted that there seems to be no difference between Zeno and Chrysippus on this point.[77]

But the interpretation of the old Stoic psychology which Pohlenz defended does deserve examination. He held that the mind has no enduring differentiations within it; there are no powers except that of reason; all of the mind's activities are nothing but fleeting alterations or motions in the mind, mere passing states—*pôs echonta*—of the soul or mind, rather than activations of determinate powers which endure between occurrences of the corresponding activity. Thus impulse would not be a power, contrary to what Iamblichus tells us, since it would have no existence whenever it is not active as a manifestation of the single power of reason.

There are several texts which can be and have been used to support a view like that of Pohlenz.

Themistius[78] contrasts philosophers who believe that the soul has no parts and many powers with those who believe that it has many spatially distinct parts. The latter group includes the Stoics. This text is too vague to be useful, reveals its Aristotelian bias in its willingness to group the Stoics with Plato, and contains no clear statement either that all eight parts had one power or that each part had its own power. Both would seem possible, since the eight parts of the soul are, according to the Stoics, made of one material substance, the *pneuma.*

By contrast we must take seriously what we are told by Alexander of Aphrodisias.[79] His presumably Stoic opponents are not mentioned by name, although Stoic terminology is used frequently in his discussion. Alexander's own views on the soul's parts and powers are quite precise. There is a large variety of different activities (such as reproduction, growth, sensation, desire, practical and theoretical reason), and this variety proves to his satisfaction that the soul has many powers, not just one. But it is clear that Alexander's target is not orthodox Stoicism. First, he attempts to prove that the reproductive power is part of the soul, rather than of *phusis*. But this is already old Stoic doctrine. Panaetius (fr. 86) and other, perhaps eclectic, philosophers attributed it to *phusis*. Next, Alexander does not mention a distinction between the question of many powers in one part (i.e. the mind) and the question of many powers among the eight parts of the soul. Iamblichus is quite clear on this vital distinction. Alexander shifts between saying that actions of the different parts of the soul are not the mind in a certain state and saying the same about the different *energeiai* of the mind itself. Moreover, he refers to activities of the soul which a Stoic would hesitate to recognize.[80]

Either Alexander is attacking a Stoicism highly contaminated with Aristotelian psychology or he is attacking a vaguely grasped Stoic psychology into which he mixes a great deal of his own doctrine. In either case the fragment from this passage which von Arnim prints as SVF 2.823 is untrustworthy. And yet this text is cited as one of the main pieces of evidence for the radically monistic interpretation of Chrysippean psychology, according to which there is only one power in the soul.[81]

Aëtius too[82] has been used in this way. He recorded the Stoic view that the mind was 'what produced presentations and assents and sensations and impulses'. This has been used to argue that there are no enduring powers in the soul, as though it followed from this statement that the mind did not produce these activities on the basis of any *dunamis*.[83] And of course it does not follow. Similar use might be made of Chrysippus' statement that 'our impulses occur according to this part [i.e. the mind] and we assent with this and all the sense organs extend to this'[84] or of the statement that *logos* is a product or outflow of the mind[85] rather than one of its powers, or that impulse, like *katalēpsis*, is an alteration of the mind.[86]

Impulses and other movements are often spoken of as 'transformations' of the mind. And Pohlenz takes one passage where this is done as evidence for his view that there is no other status for impulse in Stoic psychology:[87] 'it transforms itself completely and changes both in passions and in the changes which occur in accordance with a disposition (*hexis*) or a condition (*diathesis*).' Similar language is used elsewhere[88] and we may be confident that the old Stoics did refer to *hormê* as a 'transformation' of the mind. Yet Pohlenz, in his zeal for proving that the mind does not have two powers in the sense which would make *akrasia* possible, goes so far as to argue as though this talk of changes and transformations of the mind excluded the possibility that impulse or anything else in the soul might have been given any other status by the Stoa[89] (despite *hexis* and *diathesis* in the text of Plutarch just cited).

But this cannot be right, since several activities which are described as motions or changes in the mind are also described as enduring dispositions, the very status which the four powers of our text from Iamblichus have. Pohlenz cannot, therefore, argue from the fact that impulse or assent, for example, is called a movement or transformation to the conclusion that it is not also a *hexis* or *dunamis*.[90]

Pohlenz's views rest almost completely on his interpretation of the Stoic category *pôs echon*. He acknowledges that the category is used in a wide variety of applications.[91] But he nevertheless maintains that a *pôs echon* of the soul is a mere passing event, not a settled state which might coexist with another modification of the pneumatic tension or which could continue to exist between active manifestations. 'All mental characteristics and activities are nothing but circumstantial[92] determinations of the one mind', he says.[93] All characteristics, qualities, and modifications of the mind, Pohlenz says, are changes in the disposition of the mind, and the previous disposition is completely erased at each 'transformation'. This is an implausible theory of the soul and Pohlenz has not proved that Chrysippus held it. He does not consider *hexeis* in this connection and he does not discuss the principal text from Iamblichus in his 'Zenon und Chrysipp'.[94] He does not deal with the implications for his theory of the wide use to which the category *pôs echon* is put.[95] It seems to have been used to cover stable states of matter as well as transient modifications of it, and indeed seems to designate any disposition or modification of an object beyond the qualities (*poia*) which individuate otherwise undifferentiated matter (with the exception of purely relational dispositions, called *pros ti pôs echonta*). There was certainly no limit on the range of the term *pôs echon* which confined it to what Voelke calls 'des dispositions momentanées'.[96]

For even the human soul is defined as a *pneuma pôs echon*.[97] In a rather strange text of Plotinus (SVF 2.400) even *poia* are referred to as being *pôs echonta* of matter[98] (*peri tên hulên pôs echonta*).

There is obviously a great deal we do not know about *pôs echon* in Stoic theory.[99] But it is obvious that Pohlenz is not right to use the evidence about 'transformations' of the mind to prove that all *pôs echonta* last only until the next transformation occurs. Nor is it right to say[100] that '*heteroiôseis* are nothing but the transition to another *pôs echein*'. Chrysippus held quite explicitly that several *heteroiôseis* or alterations could coexist in the mind, and moreover that they would endure through a period of time when they were not being exercised. For Chrysippus interpreted presentations as *heteroiôseis* in order to make it possible for them to persist as memory, which is defined as a 'storehouse of presentations'.[101] Obviously, some *pôs echonta* are enduring dispositions and others are fleeting events.

Pohlenz's interpretation of Chrysippus' psychology as a radical monism fails. And Voelke does not add any arguments of weight to what Pohlenz advanced. Indeed, Voelke is in a somewhat worse situation, since Pohlenz at least was in a position to dismiss texts which conflicted with his radical monism as being Zenonian. Voelke cannot do so. Hence when he acknowledges[102] the force of Simplicius' account of *dunamis* and of the evidence for a *hexis hormêtikê*, the disposition to have impulses which we will discuss presently, he is forced to reject this evidence out of hand. And when he does so he can offer nothing but the explanation that there are two irreconcilable tendencies in our sources. According to the one, assent, *hormê*, etc. are powers in the mind; according to the other, they are just activities and nothing more. And only one of these is consistent with Stoic nominalism, according to Voelke. No explanation can be offered for the existence of this alleged contradiction in otherwise trustworthy evidence.

But nominalism is a bugbear we need not fear, and the two tendencies in our evidence are not in conflict. They are complementary. The 'powers' of the mind are modifications, stable dispositions of the mind's *pneuma*, which govern the corresponding activities or movements. We do not need to posit radical monism, after the manner of Pohlenz, nor need we reject evidence as Voelke does, nor is it necessary to suppose that Zeno and Chrysippus disagreed significantly on the structure and operation of the soul. This chapter concludes with a brief look at the physical status of these powers and the way they exist in the mind.

If we are to dismiss nominalism and still hold that the powers which correspond to, generate, and govern activities of the mind are real powers with a definite form of existence between their episodes of activation, then some location must be found for them in the material soul. For even if the Stoics were not the extreme nominalists they are sometimes thought to be, they were rigorous materialists.[103] Even qualities and dispositions are taken to be matter in a certain state. So powers and dispositions in the mind will need to have a material status in just the same way.

The powers of the mind are referred to as being 'in' the mind or heart.[104] This is not a metaphor, but a sober description of what the Stoics believed about the location of the mind's characteristic powers. The mind is located in the heart and it is material. It follows from this, as Plutarch says, that all the states and activities of the mind are also in the heart, including 'impulses and assents'.[105] Plutarch ridicules this doctrine, and in doing so he makes it clear that many, at least, of these things said to be in the heart are enduring and stable entities.[106] If the mind had been the radically monistic thing which Pohlenz said it was, then the criticisms of Plutarch would be totally without point. As it is, his criticisms are exaggerated and unsympathetic; but at least they begin from a comprehensible starting-point. It makes sense to criticize the Stoa for many aspects of its materialistic psychology and one of the weaknesses to which it is genuinely prey is precisely the one Plutarch seizes on here. If one is going to make all the states and activities and powers of the mind material, then one must have a physiological theory sufficiently complex to account for them all. And the Stoics had not. Whatever the philosophical merits of psychological materialism, the use of it to explain the operation of the mind in a scientific way demands more sophistication than the Stoics could possibly have had.

We may gain useful information about the four powers of the mind mentioned by Iamblichus by turning to Arius Didymus. At one point in his brief discussion of *hormê*[107] he reports that one sense of the term *hormê* in Stoic usage is to designate 'the *hexis hormêtikê*, which they indeed call *hormê* in a special sense (*idiôs*); from this the action of impulse comes about.'[108] This last clause is without doubt a reference to the fact that the active impulse, the *kinêsis*, is generated by a disposition, a *hexis*. Here we have direct confirmation for the report of Simplicius mentioned earlier, that a *dunamis* 'brings on many events and controls the activities governed by it'.

Thus we may say that the *dunamis* 'impulse' mentioned by Iamblichus is a *hexis*.[109] And it follows that the other powers in the mind are also *hexis* and govern the activities corresponding to them. What, then, is the physical nature of these powers or dispositions in the mind? One possibility may be ruled out quickly. These dispositions are not distinct bits of *pneuma* in the mind; for that is the way the other seven parts of the soul are distinguished from the mind and Iamblichus contrasts the ways in which parts and powers are distinct.

To answer this question, we must recall the connection found earlier between *tonos* or tension and 'powers', and we must also think of Chrysippus' description of memory. In describing memory as a storehouse of presentations and in understanding by presentation an alteration (*heteroiôsis*) of the *pneuma* of the mind, he displays his willingness to claim that the mind's *pneuma* can retain many distinct modifications of its structure, that is many distinct *tonoi* or tensions, for long periods of time. As memories can lie inactive for long periods of time until they are reactivated, so the powers of the mind should be able to remain quietly in the mind until they are activated. This ability of the mind to retain several distinct physical alterations in it is of course reminiscent of the sort of theory of powers and parts which Iamblichus attributes to the Stoa. And now we can see that even a materialistic psychology can accommodate genuine and enduring powers in one and the same body.[110]

Simplicius' *Commentary* on Aristotle's *Categories*[111] provides useful information again on the topic of *hexis*. He is interested in the topic only because the Stoic use of the terms *hexis, schesis*, and *diathesis* is so different from Aristotle's use of the same terms. The Stoics differentiated *diathesis* and *hexis* only in that the former does not admit of variations of degree while the latter does.[112] The duration or fixity of the characteristics are not relevant, nor are they relevant for the distinction between *schesis* and *hexis*.

Schesis and *hexis* differ in that the former is only a relation to other things and is not any intrinsic characteristic of an object itself. Being a brother is a *schesis*, while being six feet tall is a *hexis*. Since a *schesis* is a *pros ti pôs echon* in the Stoic scheme of categories[113] we may identify *hexis* as a kind of *pôs echon*. What is special about this sort of disposition, above and beyond its ability to endure for some time in an object and to coexist with other *hexeis*? Again Simplicius tells us (p. 238). '*Hexeis* are characterized by activities from the thing itself.' A modification of a substance is a *hexis* if it 'provides from itself the activity of being so-and-so . . . like mud turning into "pottery". For it became so-and-so by itself.'

The kind of *hexis* Simplicius is describing here is not the only sort. But it is the right sort for our present needs, since it seems to be related to some characteristic activity just as the powers we considered above are, just as the *dunamis* 'impulse' or the *hexis hormêtikê* is related to the active impulse, the *kinêsis* or *kinêma hormêtikon*. These *hexeis* or powers in the soul are modifications of its *pneuma*, and they are well suited for the task of causing activities intermittently while themselves enduring between occurrences. For, as Simplicius says (p. 238), the Stoics 'say that the *hexeis* are so constituted that they can remain on their own when inactive (*aphetheisas*), since they provide stability from within themselves and their own nature'.[114]

Hexeis of this type are appropriate for another reason too. Unlike *diathesis, hexis* admits of variations in degree and quality. Since some *hormai* are correct and some incorrect (and similarly for assent), the way an animal or man responds to stimulation must vary with the *dunamis* which governs these activities. The *tonoi* of the *pneuma* which constitute *dunameis* and *hexeis* (*Leg. Alleg.* 1.30) have the sort of variability which makes possible a theory in which actions are determined by the variable dispositions of the agent. There is a correlate in Stoic psychology for the ethical belief that actions are determined by character.

It is almost certain that a power was posited in the soul by Zeno to correspond to and govern at least each of the three motions which he seems to have mentioned in his psychology of action: those of presentation, assent, and impulse.[115] It is impossible to tell what sort of technical terminology he used to describe their status. *Heteroiôsis* is probably Chrysippus' contribution to the vocabulary of psychological description, and *hexis* too seems to be associated particularly with his greater emphasis on the role of *pneuma* in physics. But it is at least possible[116] that some form of the doctrine of the categories was used by Zeno and not impossible that he located the powers in question in some sort of disposition or modification of the *pneuma*.[117]

When we come to discuss the psychology of action of the old Stoa we will have these basic facts about the soul at our disposal: the relevant part of it, the mind, has four powers, reason, presentation, impulse, and assent; each of these is a disposition of the *pneuma* of the mind[118] and each is a power which endures between the occasions on which it is activated. What we shall have to discover, then, is how these powers and their activations interact in the production of an action and in particular how this analysis of action produced that harmony among the various parts and powers which instigated their critics to accuse them of reducing the powers of the soul to just one, an accusation which has done much to foster the supernominalist interpretation of Pohlenz and his followers. When the true sense of the Stoics' psychological monism has been explained, I would hope that any lingering temptation to attribute radical monism to Chrysippus or to any other of the early Stoics will be dissipated.

Chapter 3

The Psychology of Action

(a) The Nature of Impulse

We have seen that the Stoics held that animal soul is characterized by the powers of presentation and impulse and that man has, in addition to these, the powers of reason and assent. These four powers are used in the analysis of animal behaviour and human action. Most of the information we have about the Stoic analysis of action concerns the more complex case of human action which employs all four of the powers of the *hêgemonikon* mentioned by Iamblichus. As a result, human action must be considered first. The Stoic account of animal behaviour and of the behaviour of children, who have not yet reached the age of reason, must be reconstructed in contrast to their account of fully rational action.

The annoying fact that the simpler case of non-rational action is less well documented is probably not accidental. The action of rational, morally responsible agents is not only more complex and philosophically interesting; it is also the sort of action which matters most in ethics. There are other indications that the old Stoics allowed their ethical interests to guide their psychological investigations. If our sources devote more attention to rational action, this may well be a fair reflection of the Stoics' own priorities.

The psychology of action, whether it be rational or irrational action, centres on the concept of impulse. In reconstructing it I shall proceed on the hypothesis that the psychology of action plays a theoretical role like that which I have assigned to Aristotle's analysis of desire and action, schematized in a practical syllogism. That is, I suppose that the Stoic psychology of action is an explanatory analysis of action, meant to account for action and behaviour by presenting it as the result of a complex of mental events. This means that the various elements of this explanatory construct can only be described in terms of the role they play in the analysis of action as a whole. An impulse, on this approach, is not an independently specifiable mental event,[1] but is a theoretical entity posited to do a theoretical job. We cannot describe what it is without describing its function in the explanatory framework of which it is a key element.

Assent and reason are the two powers which mark men off from animals. Assent is in a sense dependent on reason, and we shall see how this is so in the course of this chapter. It is reason which Greek philosophers traditionally used to mark off men from lower animals; even in the psychology of action, the Stoics gave to reason the dominant place in the mind, the leading part of the rational soul.

The power of reason can involve many different things. For the Stoics, reason involves first and foremost the use of language;[2] not the mere utterance of articulate sounds, of which even irrational animals are capable,[3] but the utterance of words backed up by and representing meanings or *lekta*.[4] This is the genuine use of language and the one which distinguishes rational animals from parrots, for instance. The use of reason which backs up articulate utterances is called 'internal logos'.[5] It is this which makes possible inference and thought, and it does this because it links articulate sounds with *lekta*, which are incorporeal entities represented by intelligently uttered words.[6]

Indeed on one plausible interpretation, that of A. A. Long (see n. 6), *lekta* are more than just the entities which give meaning to uttered words; *lekta* are themselves the substance of the internal discourse which the Stoics, following Plato,[7] identified with the process of thought. On this interpretation human thought is parallel to uttered speech in its structure and consists in the occurrence in the mind, through their association with rational presentations, of the *lekta* which also give meaning to rational utterances.

The term *lekton* is virtually untranslatable, but its sense is close to 'what is said' or 'what is meant' in an utterance. Since *lekta* are immaterial, they are technically 'non-existent' in the Stoic system. Nevertheless, the Stoics gave them an important role in their account of the working of the rational mind, arguing that their immateriality did not bar them from being able to affect rational agents[8] and giving them a firm relation not just to the words which express them but to the psychological images or presentations (*phantasiai*) which embody them in the rational mind.[9] Many details of the doctrine of *lekta* are obscure,[10] but it is clear that the ability to form and manipulate *lekta* plays an important role in differentiating rational animals, who reason, infer, think, and speak (in the proper sense of the word) from non-rational animals who do none of these things.

Rationality and *lekta* also distinguish human action from animal

behaviour, and the way they do this will be one of the main themes of
this chapter. I shall argue that reason makes human action distinct
from animal action not just because access to *lekta* allows men to
spell out in thought and language the import of their actions and so
to act self-consciously and reflectively, but also because the power to
give or withhold assent, which properly speaking is given to *lekta* and
so is only possible in rational animals, makes men morally responsible for their actions.

The question of moral responsibility is central to the Stoic treatment of action. They devised a psychology of action which enabled
them to hold men responsible for all their actions. The question of
responsibility was of importance to Plato and Aristotle too—and
that is a sweeping understatement. But it was not until the generation after Aristotle's death that the problem took centre stage in
Greek philosophy,[11] and became a matter of pressing concern to
both Epicurus[12] and the Stoics. The reason in each case was the
same: the challenge to a belief in moral responsibility which stimulated interest in the problem came from a form of determinism.
Epicurus most probably had in mind Democritus' determinism,
which he called 'the fate of the physical philosophers'; the Stoics
faced the problem closer to home, for their own acceptance of a
philosophical determinism made it imperative to find a way to justify ascriptions of praise and blame.[13]

For Aristotle, and for his commentator Alexander of Aphrodisias
(a formidable philosopher in his own right), rationality in human
action manifested itself first and foremost in deliberation. Here is a
major difference between the Stoics and the Aristotelian tradition.
For as Alexander himself says,[14] the Stoics did not make deliberation a part of their notion of rational action. They made assent, not
deliberation, the locus of rationality and responsibility.

We shall have to deal with Alexander's criticisms of the Stoic analysis of responsible action in the course of reconstructing the old
Stoic theory. In those criticisms Alexander tries to interpret the
Stoics as though they shared Aristotle's and his own beliefs about
the connection between rationality and deliberation. It is possible
to be led by this[15] to the belief that the Stoic idea of rational and
responsible action involves deliberation too. But there are no secure
references to deliberation in our sources for the Stoic doctrine. The
conscious evaluation which sometimes precedes assent is not called
deliberation and bears little resemblance to what Aristotle called

deliberation.[16] Indeed, on philosophical grounds we would expect a serious change in the approach to 'deliberation' in a deterministic system, and I shall follow most recent scholars in acknowledging that the Stoics do not disappoint that expectation.[17] The Stoics faced a serious challenge in their attempt to reconcile moral responsibility with determinism, and their solution, which will emerge as our reconstruction proceeds, is of no small philosophical interest.

But we must turn now to the detailed reconstruction of the Stoic analysis of rational action.[18]

A *hormê*, which I am translating by the term of art 'impulse', is not just an instinct or an underlying drive in an animal. This is worth insisting on at the outset, since the recognition of this is hard won[19] and still not universally accepted.[20] There is no clear scholarly consensus as to what a *hormê* is, and it is a measure of the confusion on this point that one distinguished scholar could suggest as recently as 1970 that impulses are bodily movements in Chrysippean Stoicism.[21] Even Voelke, who translates *hormê* as 'tendance' or 'tendance naturelle', fails to provide a clear statement of what an impulse is.[22] Many writers on Stoicism seem to assume a vague conception of *hormai* as drives or desires, instinctual urges which provide the basic raw material of human or animal nature. This uncertain notion is no doubt encouraged by the now entrenched translations 'impulse' or 'tendance'.[23] But it is fundamentally wrong. This is not because the Stoics did not think that animals have innate tendencies to develop and act in certain ways. Such tendencies are very important and are called *aphormai*,[24] inclinations.

But simply to identify *hormai* with instinctual behaviour patterns or primal drives would contradict much of the evidence we do possess about *hormê* in the old Stoic analysis of action. Even the use of the term *hormê* to designate a disposition to have certain kinds of impulses[25] does not justify such an interpretation of *hormê*. For the dispositional sense of *hormê* is dependent on the primary sense, in which *hormê* is a theoretical term in the analysis of action. This analysis gives *hormê* a much wider role. Moreover, these 'hormetic dispositions' are part of one's character and subject to considerable variation and modification, which would not be the case with instincts.

The main elements of the old Stoic psychology of action, which we find recurring with impressive consistency in our evidence, are presentation, assent, and impulse; these precede and generate the action to be explained. This sequence is given by the Stoicizing Academic Antiochus of Ascalon;[26] the validity of this testimony[27] for a reconstruction of Chrysippus' theory is proved by the attribution of the same ideas to Chrysippus himself in a discussion of fate and voluntary action. It is worth while to quote this at some length.[28]

Chrysippus, however, since he both rejected necessity and wanted that nothing should occur without prior causes, distinguished among the kinds of causes in order both to escape from necessity and to retain fate. 'For', he said, 'some causes are perfect and principal, while others are auxiliary and proximate. Therefore, when we say that all things occur by fate by antecedent causes, we do not want the following to be understood, viz. that they occur by perfect and principal causes; but we mean this, that they occur by auxiliary and proximate causes'. And so his response to the argument which I just made is this: if everything occurs by fate it does indeed follow that everything occurs by antecedent causes, but not by principal and perfect causes. And if these are not themselves in our power it does not follow that not even impulse is in our power. But this would follow if we were saying that everything occurred by perfect and principal causes with the result that, since these causes are not in our power, not even impulse would be in our power. (42) Therefore, those who introduce fate in such a way that they connect necessity to it are subject to the force of that argument; but those who will not say that antecedent causes are perfect and principal will not be subject to the argument at all.

As to the claim that assents occur by antecedent causes, he says that he can easily explain the meaning of this. For although assent cannot occur unless it is stimulated by a presentation, nevertheless since it has that presentation as its proximate cause and not as its principal cause, it can be explained in the way which we have been discussing for some time now, just as Chrysippus wishes. It is not the case that the assent could occur if it were not stimulated by a force from outside (for it is necessary that an assent should be stimulated by a presentation); but Chrysippus falls back on his cylinder and cone. These cannot begin to move unless they are struck; but when that happens, he thinks that it is by their own natures that the cylinder rolls and the cone turns.

These are the elements of the old Stoic theory,[29] a view supported by the fact that these three elements correspond to three of the four powers of the rational soul in Iamblichus' report.[30] But what are we to make of the identification of assent and impulse which we find in several sources?[31] And if impulse is an act of assent, several questions arise. How are we to understand the report that Chrysippus described impulse as 'the reason of man commanding him to act'?[32] Such a statement, which immediately brings to mind recent imperatival theories of the will,[33] suggests that an imperative rather than the indicative mood suggested by 'assent' is the grammatical correlate of impulse. Is impulse a cognitive event or an imperatival, practical event in the soul? And what sort of analysis of action and the human mind would use grammatical or logical concepts to explain how a person acts?

The last question at least can be answered readily. An analysis of action which uses grammatical or logical concepts to explain how action occurs is one which looks back to Aristotle for part of its inspiration. He had used the syllogism as an analogue for the functioning of the desiderative and cognitive elements in the generation of an action, suggesting that the action follows neces-sarily from these elements just as the conclusion of a syllogism follows from its premisses. And he occasionally likened the decisive moment in the generation of an action to an imperative given to one-self or to an act of assertion or assent. In a general way, then, the Stoic analysis of action follows this aspect of Aristotle's theory. I believe, in fact, that the Stoics sharpened up this side of Aristotle's sometimes rather vague account of action and gave the grammatical and lin-guistic aspect of it a more vigorous work-out than Aristotle did.

The other questions, about the relation between impulse as assent and impulse as a command, about the roles of cognitive and imperatival elements in generating action,[34] are more challenging. The grammatical tangle becomes worse when the special relation-ship of impulse to predicates is added.[35] The reconstruction I give will, I hope, do justice to the close connections of impulse to assent and to commands to oneself, which lead to their occasional identifi-cation in our sources, and to the distinctions among them.[36] A proper reconstruction will also have to touch on the physical and psycho-physical problems and questions raised by the use of what is basically a stimulus–response model of action within a materialist and empiricist psychology which also gives an important role to immaterial linguistic entities.

An impulse is that psychological event which determines or causes an action. It is a movement or change in the material soul, more particularly in the mind (or in its analogue in the case of irrational animals). The idea that a psychic event should cause an action is not new; we have seen forms of this belief in Aristotle and Epicurus.[37] As we would expect, an impulse is a cause within a theory which makes it possible to ascribe intentionality to human behaviour. For associated with this psychic cause there are invariably statements of the goal or upshot of the action in question.[38] The incorporeal propositions and imperatives which accompany each action are connected to the material soul (and so acquire causal efficacy) by way of their connection to presentations. This connection is presupposed by the Stoics, but never analysed in detail.

Aristotle's theory has a place for such statements too, although it is not quite clear whether this is a distinguishing mark of human action, as it is according to the Stoics, or whether the same analysis is applied to animals.[39] Here the Stoics and Aristotle stand together in contrast to Epicurus, whose analysis of actions seems not to have left room for the causal efficacy of linguistic elements.[40]

A theory like this has philosophical merits and philosophical relatives. Stuart Hampshire at one point[41] argues that the principal difference between the purposiveness of animal behaviour and the intentionality of human action is that men have the ability to state to themselves or for the benefit of others what the point of their action is. It is senseless, he says, to attribute 'intentions to an animal which has not the means to reflect upon, and to announce to itself or to others, its own future behaviour'. The Stoics would agree about this distinction between human and animal action, and they make the ability of a man to state to himself the point of his action the reason that he is responsible for his actions.[42]

What is the evidence that *hormê* is the proximate cause of actions in the Stoic analysis of action? Because Chrysippus held a form of determinism, as did the other old Stoic scholarchs, which extended even to the claim that in some respect each human action is caused, he had to deal with criticisms to the effect that such causation of actions made the ascription of responsibility to agents impossible, or at least unreasonable. This is seen most clearly in a passage from Aulus Gellius which it is worth while to cite at length:[43]

Chrysippus, who is the leading member of the Stoic philosophical school, defines fate, which the Greeks call *heimarmenê*, more or less in accordance with this statement. 'Fate', he says, 'is an eternal and inevitable series and chain of things, rolling and intertwining itself throughout eternal and regular sequences out of which it is assembled and joined together.' I have cited the very words of Chrysippus, as far as memory allowed, so that if anyone should think that my translation itself is obscure, he might compare his own words . . .: 'a natural arrangement of all things from eternity, following on each other and moving among each other, such an entwinement being inevitable'.

But authorities from other philosophical schools make this objection to the definition given: 'If', they say, 'Chrysippus thinks that everything is moved and ruled by fate and that the columns and coils of fate can neither be deflected nor escaped, then the errors and wrong-doings of men should not provoke anger nor be attributed to the men themselves and their wills but rather to a kind of necessity and compulsion which comes from fate and is the mistress and arbiter of all things and through which it is necessary that whatever is going to occur should happen. And for that reason, penalties for the guilty have been unfairly established by the laws, if men do not perform their misdeeds voluntarily but are dragged by fate'.

Chrysippus makes many subtle and clever arguments against this position; but the upshot of almost everything which he has written on this subject is as follows: 'Although', he says, 'it is the case that all things are compelled and connected by fate through a certain necessary and principal set of reasons, nevertheless the temperaments of our minds are subject to fate exactly according to their own characters and qualities. For if they have been fashioned by nature from the beginning in a healthy and useful way, they pass on all that force which presses on us by fate from the outside in a more acceptable and manageable manner. But if, on the other hand, our temperaments are harsh and uneducated and uncultivated and not supported by any help from the virtues, then if they are assailed by a minor or non-existent blow of a fated misfortune nevertheless they rush into constant crimes and into errors by their own weakness and by a voluntary impulse. And that things should happen in this way is a result of that natural and necessary sequence in things which is called fate. For it is in its very nature fated and in natural sequence, as it were, that bad temperaments should not be free of sins and errors.'

Then he uses this apposite and charming example for this state of affairs. 'Just as', he says, 'if you were to throw a cylindrical stone down a steep incline, you would indeed be a cause and initiator for it of its going down, nevertheless soon afterwards it is rolling down not because you are still doing it, but because this is the nature and "rollability"' of its form. In this way the order and reason and necessity of fate moves the kinds themselves and starting points of the causes, but the impulses of our thoughts and minds and the actions themselves are controlled by each person's own will and the temperament of his mind.' Then he cites these words which agree with what I just said: 'And therefore it is said by the Pythagoreans, "He will know that men suffer woes they have chosen for themselves", since the injuries to each man are in his own power and they err through their own impulse and are injured by their own plan and execution.'

Therefore he says that we ought not to put up with or listen to men who

are wicked or lazy and guilty and daring and who take refuge in the necessity of fate as though in the asylum of some temple, when they are con-
victed of crime and misdeeds, and who say that their worst actions should
not be attributed to their own ruthlessness but rather to fate.

Moreover, that wisest and most ancient of poets was the first to make
this point, in the following verses:

> Alas, the way mortals blame the gods for things!
> For they say that their evils come from us; but
> they themselves have pains beyond due allotment
> because of their own outrageous behaviour.

The charge is that a line of causation originating in the external
stimuli to action extended all the way through to the performance
in question. The passage from Gellius just cited and the analogous
text from Cicero[44]make it clear that Chrysippus did not back off
from the claim that a chain of causes extended from the externally
generated presentation to the mental reaction to this (assent if the
stimulus is accepted), which is determined by character and
habit,[45]to the impulse and finally to the action. Rather, he made
certain important qualifications about the character and source of
the causation of assent, the mental reaction to the stimulus of
presentation. The natural conclusion from these passages is that
assent if given does cause impulse and impulse does cause action.

This line of reasoning is confirmed by other evidence. We know
from Seneca,[46]for example, that the early Stoics disagreed among
themselves over the way to describe the relation of events in the
mind to actions. Cleanthes and Chrysippus agree that the pneumatic *hêgemonikon* does something which causes a man to walk, but
disagree over the exact nature of this relation. Cleanthes thought
that the movement in the mind's *pneuma* (and this must be the
impulse) sent out a separate jet of *pneuma* to the limbs as a motor
stimulus. This, he said, should be called 'walking'. The action,
properly speaking, is not the movement of the limbs but the *pneuma*
which made them move. Chrysippus thought that the relation of
mind to body was more intimate, and that the *pneuma* of the mind
could act directly on the limbs and that this should properly be
called 'action'.

One may suspect that Chrysippus was overstating himself for the
sake of emphasis when he said that this movement was itself the
action, as he seems also to have done when insisting that an impulse
was an assent. But the overstatement was not without its justifica-

tion. J. M. Rist has drawn attention to the philosophical significance of Chrysippus' position: in Chrysippus' view a man's actions
are immediate expressions of the personality and its decisions.[47] But
from the point of view of the psychological, causal account of action,
the differences between Cleanthes and Chrysippus are slight, as
Seneca himself realized. Both held that the mind was *pneuma* in the
heart and that actions were causations of bodily movements by
movements in that *pneuma*. They disagreed about the detailed
pneumatic mechanics of setting the limbs in motion and about
which portion of this psycho-physical chain of events should be
designated as the action itself. But these points are less significant
than their shared belief in a cause of action, a motion of the material
mind called impulse.[48]

It is worth recalling at this point that Aristotle distinguished the
analysis of action embodied in the 'practical syllogism', which is a
question of philosophical psychology, from the problem how the
mind then set the body in motion. He found the connecting link, as
we learn from the *De Motu Animalium*, in the *sumphuton pneuma*. He
gave some account at least of the psycho-physical link involved in
bodily action. The Stoic view of the problem is similar; in fact, the
prominence of *pneuma* in Stoic psychology[49] may be partially
accounted for by Aristotle's influence.[50] But the question of the
psycho-physical link was much easier to handle for the Stoics, and
for Epicurus,[51] since they did not have to deal with the problems
posed by the lingering conception of an immaterial soul and its relation to the material body. Accordingly, since they regarded the soul
and its functions as material it is likely that both the Stoics and
Epicurus did not draw a firm line between philosophical psychology and physiology as Aristotle may have done. They could treat
the questions of what happened in the soul to cause an action and of
how the body was subsequently set in motion as distinct questions,
but need not have regarded them as being different in kind.

The language used in our sources also supports the view that an
impulse is the cause of an action. Most often we are told that an
impulse is 'directed at' something,[52] usually an action or its verbal
representation, a predicate.[53] The meaning of this phrase depends
on the theory it represents, and this is still to be reconstructed. But
the relative uniformity of our evidence that impulses are directed at
actions is some confirmation of the causal role so far attributed to
them.

If an impulse is the cause of an action, it should be the necessary and sufficient condition for a specified action. That it is a necessary condition is shown by Alexander of Aphrodisias:[54] 'since the things animals do would not occur unless the animal had an impulse'. Similarly Seneca:[55] 'no action can be done without an impulse.'

We may conclude that an impulse is the sufficient condition for action from this brief argument in Cicero. He is criticizing Antiochus' use of the Stoic argument against scepticism[56] and says, 'For the Stoics say that the senses themselves are acts of assent and *since* impulse follows these [sc. acts of assent][57] action follows.'[58]

This text isolates the point at issue, that impulse is a sufficient condition for action. If it were not, the argument would be invalid. But in broader terms, there are several things which would be puzzling if it were not the case that impulse were the necessary and sufficient condition for an action. Thus the definition of *prattein* as 'doing [sc. something] from a rational impulse'[59] would be strange, as would Plutarch's description of impulses as the '*archê* of actions'.[60] It would be odd that Diogenes Laertius (7.108) reports the use of 'activities according to impulse' to designate what seem to be all morally relevant, responsible actions, if impulse were not the sufficient as well as the necessary condition for action.[61] Equally odd would be the yoking of action and impulse by Plutarch:[62] 'one can neither act nor have an impulse without assent.'

If it is the case that an impulse is the necessary and sufficient condition of an action,[63] then several things are more easily explained. Chrysippus' identification of the action 'walking' with the mind itself, meaning the motion of the mind called impulse, makes sense. If under normal conditions (with no external constraint) the mental impulse to walk did not produce the phenomena recognized by others as walking, then it would be bizarre to identify the two. Further, it is a good deal easier to account for the fact that *praxis*, 'action'[64] is used so seldom in ancient discussions of Stoic ethics and psychology and why *hormê* is so frequent. 'Impulse' refers to what an agent *does* in an important sense, by isolating the act of setting oneself to do something, in contrast to the physical accomplishment of the corresponding bodily movements. And this moment of an action is worth singling out for attention. For one thing, external physical constraints can prevent the physical execution of an action, but one still wants to be able to refer to what one was trying to do and would certainly have done except for the unexpected obstacle. Aristotle was careful to specify that action followed on the conclusion of the practical syllogism automatically unless there were an external hindrance. When the conclusion of the practical syllogism has been drawn the agent is committed to action so far as in him lies. This is the act of setting oneself to do something and it is, one might argue, the locus of moral evaluation. I suspect that Chrysippus' somewhat hyperbolic claim that the movement in the mind simply is the action 'walking' was made at least in part because of this sort of consideration.

We may suppose that the Stoics inserted a similar saving clause in their statement that action followed automatically on the occurrence of an impulse. Only Nemesius[65] attributes such a clause to the Stoics, but his evidence is suspect. Still, some such clause is needed in the Stoic theory, and in fact its presence may be inferred with some confidence from Epictetus' constant assertion that human impulses are unhinderable while our bodily actions are not.[66] The clause I wish to postulate in the old Stoic psychology of action would provide pertinent theoretical basis for his claim.

If this is correct, then an impulse is the cause of an action, as being its necessary and sufficient condition; an impulse invariably produces an action, provided that no external obstacles bar the physical execution of the act[67] (and so is sometimes even identified with the act). An impulse is a little more than an 'intention', 'act of will', 'decision' or *Entschluss*,[68] because of its role as the cause of an action. But like these other terms of art, *hormê* isolates the ethically significant aspect of an action. *Hormê* performs much of the work of 'intention' as well as being an essential element in a causal analysis of action and behaviour.

How well impulse is suited to do the work of 'intention' or 'will' will become apparent when other aspects of its role in the psychology of action have been examined. In particular, the relation of impulse to assent and to imperatives, to propositions, and to predicates, will show how the 'intentionality' of action is expressed in the Stoic theory. This will be the topic of the rest of the present section. Another issue of substantial importance will be deferred to section (c) vi: the claim that impulses are the causes of actions should make us ask about the scope of the psychology of action. What counts as an action in this theory? This question is even more important if the impulse is the principal locus of moral evaluation.

In the texts which set out presentation, assent, and impulse as the steps of a sequence[69] leading to an action, Chrysippus picks out assent as the pivotal term. Presentations are externally caused; impulses generate actions; assent is apparently an unfailing cause of impulses. Man is responsible because of assent. This point will engage our attention again; the relation of assent to presentation and the special role of the latter are our present concern.

A presentation is the initiator of the sequence and is a necessary but not sufficient condition for the entire process. Cicero, reporting Antiochus, claims this.[70] No action is produced spontaneously by the mind; a presentation is needed in every case to 'call forth' the impulse,[71] or to 'stimulate' it.[72] Having such a presentation is not something which we can control. But assent is different; it is 'in our power'.[73] This suggests that men have no control at all over their presentations, and that they are at the mercy of fate for the stimuli to action. This probably is the Stoic view about those stimuli which are derived immediately from the world outside. We may have reason, however, to doubt whether even those presentations which we draw up from our memory, which is a 'storehouse of presentations',[74] are so unalterably beyond our control. But even if the Stoics did believe that some presentations can be summoned up or manipulated (and this is not as clear as we might wish it to be),[75] it is still the case that there must be some presentation to begin any action-generating sequence of mental events.

The question whether the environmental stimuli to action are subject to our control or not and the related question whether our reaction to it is in our power had been raised long before the Stoics addressed them.[76] Gorgias had argued in his *Defence of Helen* that she should be held blameless for her actions because she was compelled to act as she did by the force of the stimuli which she could neither control nor resist. Aristotle seems to have this or a very similar argument in mind when he considers the plea[77] that men might not be responsible for their actions because their actions are dependent on their *phantasiai* and the agent cannot control his *phantasia*. Aristotle's reply to this plea is a denial of the claim that men are not responsible for the way they see things.[78]

It is possible that the Stoics looked back beyond Aristotle to Gorgias' own work when considering this question. For the environmental stimulus is treated by Gorgias as a representational image or *eikôn* which has emotive power,[79] and his use of the word *tupoô*, imprint, is reminiscent of Zeno's definition of a presentation as a *tupôsis* in the soul.[80] The notion that stimuli to emotion and action are pictures in the soul was also used by Plato;[81] and even though Aristotle probably is not thinking explicitly of *phantasia* as an image in *EN* 3.5, it is likely that in most of his uses of *phantasia* in the analysis of action he does think of the stimuli to action as representational images having emotive or interpretive force.[82]

Aristotle's response to this challenge to our ordinary opinions about responsiblity for our actions, in this passage at least, involves insisting that men are responsible for their characters. Accordingly, he maintains that our reaction to stimuli is determined by our characters as well as by the stimuli themselves. It is clear that the Stoics also held that human reaction to stimuli is determined by our characters[83] and that the moral character of the agent determined the character of the action.[84] But they did not follow Aristotle in using this as their reply to the Gorgianic challenge. The Stoic view of a man's responsibility for the formation and development of his character is complex and ambivalent;[85] instead of relying on this, they emphasized the fact that some causal contribution is made by an agent in any reaction to environmental stimuli. Perhaps following a line of reasoning begun by Aristotle in the *Eudemian Ethics* (2.8), they ascribed to an agent responsibility for any action of which something in his soul was even a partial cause. For the Stoics, this internal cause which is the locus of responsibility is assent.[86] This approach enabled them to sidestep the question whether a man could legitimately be held responsible for the shape his character had taken, which was bound to be immeasurably more difficult for a determinist to address than it was for Aristotle.

To return to the presentations which initiate any sequence of mental events leading to action. A certain amount of guesswork and hypothesis is needed to account for the relationships among presentation, assent, the imperatival aspect of impulse, and the predicates which we are told are the principal object of impulse.

The account of Stoic ethics in Stobaeus, thought to have been compiled by Arius Didymus in the time of Augustus, gives a great deal of useful information about the workings of the psychology of action; most of this information is compressed into the severely abridged chapter *On Impulse* (ch. 9, pp. 86–8). This is the only surviving report on this standard topic of Stoic ethics,[87] but it is a reliable report as far as it goes. It is confirmed at many points by less detailed sources, and it fairly bristles with the technical terminology so genial to the old Stoics and so rare in the writings of later Stoics. On the other hand, the text has been abbreviated and contains lacunae, only some of which have been detected by editors.[88]

This report opens with the abrupt announcement that the sort of presentation which stimulates impulse has a special name. It is a 'hormetic' presentation (*phantasia hormêtikê*). It is hormetic because it indicates to the animal the presence of something of interest to it, something which will contribute to its health, well-being, pleasure, the fulfilment of its individual nature, etc. These characteristics are here grouped under the general term *kathêkon*. In other, usually ethical, contexts this term is translated as 'appropriate'; here it might better be rendered 'of interest' or 'relevant'.

This means that the Stoics, like Aristotle and Epicurus, accepted the principle laid down by Plato[89] that all action is goal-directed and purposive, and is undertaken in order to get something worth having for the agent or to avoid something it would be better not to have. The commonest way to express this principle is in the claim that all action is aimed at the good or the apparent good. Aristotle explicitly accepted this.[90] So too did Epicurus, as far as we can tell. Identifying pleasure with the good, Epicurus held that an awareness of pleasure or pain would always be found as the stimulus of action.[91] The Stoic version of this principle is also coloured by their views about the nature of 'the good'; the present claim, that a hormetic presentation of something 'relevant' is the stimulus to action, is expressed in such a way as to capture the general principles of goal-directed behaviour without compromising the special claims the Stoics wanted to make about the nature of good.

Although the standard sequence of the psychology of action lists assent as following on presentation, according to the technical distinctions made in the report of Arius Didymus, assent is not given to presentations. For on p. 88, after asserting that all impulses are acts of assent, Arius qualifies this by stating that assent is given to some propositions (*axiômata*) while impulse is directed at predicates (*katêgorêmata*) which are in a sense contained in the propositions assented to. Assent is given to propositions, and this is reasonable. For an incorporeal proposition is just the sort of thing one would expect to see connected to a notion like 'assent' with its strong cognitive overtones.

Presentations, however, are the stimuli to action which assent follows. A presentation is a representational image in the mind, a physical alteration of the mind's *pneuma* which resembles as an *eikôn*[92] its correlate in the world and refers to it.[93] This is what one would expect from definitions of presentation as an imprint or alteration of the soul.[94]

An entity of this nature is not a likely candidate for receiving assent, and Sextus (reporting Arcesilaus) confirms that this was the Stoic view. 'And if it is the case that comprehension (*katalêpsis*) is assent to [literally 'of'] a cataleptic presentation, then it does not exist; first, since assent does not occur with reference to presentation but with reference to *logos* (for assents are to propositions) . . .'.[95] Nevertheless, some sources do refer to apparently propositional presentations[96] and mention assent as though it were given directly to such presentations.

Fortunately there is a solution for this apparent muddle.[97] The problem of the relationship of presentation, propositions, and assent only arises for what are called 'rational presentations'. All the presentations which rational animals have are rational presentations.[98] It follows that the hormetic presentations which humans have are one kind of rational presentation. The solution to the problem posed by reference to apparently propositional presentations which receive assent is to be found in one description of *lekta* which is exceptionally well attested.[99] We are told that 'a *lekton* is that which subsists in accordance with a rational presentation.'

Propositions are, of course, one type of *lekton*. It seems, then, that those sources which refer to a propositional presentation which receives assent are using a forgivable shorthand expression for the more precise Stoic doctrine, which is that the assent is given to the immaterial entity which corresponds to and accompanies the material presentation.[100]

The *lekton* accompanying the presentation serves to spell out in linguistic form the content of the object presented.[101] The occasional interchange of presentation and proposition suggests that their relationship must be a very close one; but there is more direct evidence in Diogenes Laertius. He reports (7.49): 'for the presentation is basic [or first] and then *dianoia* [= reason ?], which is expressive, utters in language the experience it receives from the presentation.' If this is the function of the *lekta* which accompany presentations, then it would follow that the presentation could reasonably be said to be true if and only if the corresponding proposition were true.[102] Cicero's report of Antiochus (*Academica* 2.21) also confirms that the Stoic analysis of perception involved postulating propositional entities, parallel to the representational image received by the senses and expressing their content in linguistic form.

> And still, those things which are not said to be perceived by the senses themselves but 'as it were' by the senses follow according to the nature of those things which we say are perceived by the senses; e.g. these things, 'that is white', 'this is sweet', 'that is melodious', 'this smells nice', 'this is rough'. Now we grasp and comprehend these things with the mind, not with the senses.

It is understandable that such a metaphysical subtlety should be over-simplified by some sources and even by Stoics themselves when concentrating on other facets of their doctrine. But we should not regard the distinction between the material and prepropositional presentation and the *lekton* (which corresponds to it and spells out in linguistic form its content and meaning) as a pointless piece of logical quibbling. Such distinctions between material entities and *lekta* are frequently used in Stoicism and are important in many areas. We should remember that the distinction between *skopos*, a material object, and *telos*, a *lekton* closely related to it,[103] is significant in ethics, and that a similar distinction is used in the explication of the notion of a 'cause'.[104] Further, the idea that human psychology might involve both representational images and propositional entities in the mind, the latter spelling out the content of the former, had important philosophical support from Plato.[105] Where Plato had spoken in vivid terms of a writer and a painter in the soul, the Stoics apparently chose to advance a definite theory, both metaphysical and psychological, concerning the relationship between perceptual images and discursive thought. And it is understandable that they did so. For their adoption of a firmly empiricist and materialistic psychology made this a problem too obvious and too important to be ignored.

It is only when a presentation occurs to the mind of a rational animal that *lekta* are formed to spell out the content of the representational image in a form appropriate for assent. The fact that the forming of *lekta* is distinct from the giving of assent explains why it is that the list of elements involved in the analysis of human action contains two items not needed for the analysis of animal action: *logos* and assent. *Logos* is not itself an element in the causal sequence of events in the mind; but it is the power of the rational soul which makes possible assent, by bringing it about that the presentation which starts the whole process will be accompanied by *lekta*.

This account makes sense of the relationships among assent, presentation, and propositions. Before going on to deal with imperatives and predicates, it may help to make a few comments on the theory at this stage of the reconstruction. First, it should be emphasized that hormetic and non-hormetic presentations have been considered together so far. I have assumed that in the most basic points they are similar. But clearly they are not similar in all respects, and further consideration will bring out some of the important differences.[106] This initial emphasis on some of the similarities between the two kinds of presentation is encouraged by the Stoics themselves. For some assimilation of the two is essential to the strategy of the anti-sceptical argument from *apraxia*.

The relationship between presentations and propositions just outlined explains why it is that 'assent cannot occur unless stimulated by a presentation.'[107] In fact, unless there is some other way for *lekta* to be brought into contact, as it were, with the human mind[108] it must also be the case that thought itself requires the presence of a presentation in the mind. To entertain a proposition, even without assenting to it, would be possible only with the help of such images. This, at any rate, is the view of Long,[109] and I find no reason to doubt it. It may receive a peculiar kind of confirmation from the fact that Aristotle, at least in one part of the *De Anima*, seems to hold a similar belief.[110]

We have seen that it takes a particular kind of presentation to stimulate action. It would make sense that the propositions which spell out the content of rational hormetic presentations should be distinguished from others. A. C. Lloyd distinguishes in the Stoic theory as well as in the Aristotelian theory two kinds of terms which correspond to the two kinds of presentations and of propositions we are considering. He describes these as 'practical predicates' such as pleasant, painful, good, and bad, which cause action in an animal and 'others which just for abbreviation we might call purely descriptive'.[111] This is roughly the difference we want between the propositions which correspond to hormetic presentations and those which correspond to purely theoretical ones.

If one sort of proposition leads to an impulse and action when it is assented to, it is reasonable to dub it 'hormetic', even though none of our sources does so. But the distinction in the kinds of proposition was clearly in the Stoics' minds, even if we do not have a report of their technical terminology for it. The proof of this is in their recognition of two kinds of assent, the one practical and the other merely informational or theoretical. The doxographical account of dialectic in Diogenes Laertius (7.48) mentions a kind of hasty assent (*propeteia*) to statements which has consequences for behaviour: those with untrained presentations will act in a disorderly and random fashion. Galen preserves a similar distinction.[112] Some hasty and weak assents lead to merely intellectual error, while others are concerned with 'life' and involve knowledge of what is good and bad, what one should have and avoid, etc.

As far as I know there is no evidence that the old Stoics spoke of impulse in connection with merely theoretical matters. Although Long wants to leave room for non-practical impulses,[113] this reservation is unnecessary. For no source for the old Stoa goes further than to treat theoretical presentation, propositions, and assent as analogous to their hormetic counterparts. One text, which has been taken to imply the existence of non-practical impulses need not be taken that way and is arguably corrupt. Discussion of this point may be left until later.[114]

At this point we may leave Stoic epistemology behind us and turn to the next stage in our argument. For we still have to indicate the relation of imperatives and predicates to these hormetic propositions and to impulse itself. But first I should give an example of what I suppose a hormetic proposition to be. Imagine that a man sees a piece of cake. We assume that he has in his character that hormetic disposition which we refer to as a 'sweet tooth'. He is a little like the Aristotelian man who tells himself to taste everything sweet. When he sees the cake and has a presentation of it in his mind, several propositions form themselves to spell out the content of the image he sees. One of these, 'there is a piece of cake', is purely theoretical and whether assented to or not is not likely on its own to stir him to action. But another proposition will surely occur to this fellow too, which spells out the importance for any man with a sweet tooth of such a sight: 'it is fitting for me to eat this cake.' Now, under the broad ethical and prudential considerations which a sage would have in mind such a proposition might well merit rejection. But in the case at hand our sweet-toothed fellow assents and reaches for the cake.

An impulse is not strictly speaking an act of assent; this we are told by Arius Didymus. The reason it cannot be is that an impulse is directed at a predicate and not at a proposition. Moreover, Chrysippus seems to have defined an impulse as man's reason commanding him to act. I propose the following hypothesis to connect these facts with what we already know about the psychology of action.

In addition to propositions there are several other kinds of *lekta*. Predicates, wishes, questions, imperatives, and so on are also *lekta*.[115] Apparently all of these various *lekta* 'subsist dependent on presentations', as Diogenes Laertius puts it (7.43). It seems reasonable to suppose that any of these *lekta* may be available to help spell out the content of a presentation.

Nothing stands in the way of the hypothesis that more than one *lekton* or even that *lekta* of different kinds accompany a single presentation. The statement which explains the relationship between a *lekton* and a rational presentation certainly allows for this possibility: 'a *lekton* is that which subsists with a rational presentation'. Other formulations might not have allowed for it,[116] so the point is not trivial.

Let us suppose, then, that one important distinguishing mark of a hormetic presentation is that it is accompanied by an imperative as well as by a proposition. When our sweet-toothed man sees that piece of cake he not only forms the propositions 'there is a piece of cake' and 'it is fitting for me to eat this piece of cake', but also the imperatival *lekton* 'You, eat that piece of cake.'

Now, the identification of assent and impulse seems to be a short, somewhat exaggerated but effective way to say that an impulse can not occur without assent to a hormetic proposition. The impulse itself is not the assent, but may, I propose, be identified with a parallel process. Impulse is to be defined as a mental event which, it seems, is controlled and determined by, but not strictly speaking identical with, the assent to a hormetic proposition.

Let us consider more closely the relation between this assent, which despite the hormetic character of the proposition involved, is a cognitive event, and action. The result of such an assent is not in itself an action. Rather, it is a judgement about a hormetic or pragmatic matter. Suppose that a presentation consists of an image of a child trapped in a burning house. The associated proposition is, we would hope, 'it befits me to save the child.' The agent in question assents to this proposition; now he knows that he should save the child. Does he move? That is to say, is there an impulse?

No, he does not move yet. For although the proposition is a true statement about what he should do, it does not follow that he will act. Knowing what to do provides no guarantee by itself that one will act. Aristotle had recognized this, both in his discussion of *akrasia* and also in another passage from the *Nicomachean Ethics*[117] which is of more immediate interest here:

Understanding (*sunesis*) is not concerned with eternal things which never change, nor with just any of the things which come to be, but it is concerned with the things one might be puzzled about and deliberate over. Therefore it deals with the same things as does practical wisdom (*phronêsis*); but understanding and practical wisdom are not the same thing. For practical wisdom is imperatival . . . and understanding is only judgemental.

Note the distinction between judging what one ought to do and some imperatival function in addition to it. There is no reason why the Stoics should not have seen the same distinction and realized its importance.

This contrast and the description of impulse as the reason of man commanding him to act suggest how the Stoics bridged the gap between practical knowledge and action. They did so, I suggest, by construing impulse, which is the immediate cause of action, in grammatical terms on the model of a command to oneself which one obeys.[118]

The last clause 'which one obeys' may be startling. But it or something very like it is needed for several reasons. (1) Since forming in one's mind the imperatival *lekton* is parallel to forming the hormetic proposition, we need something more which will be analogous to assent. Obeying the command is a good candidate to be this analogue. (2) If impulse does not have an automatic result in action, then it will not be able to play the role as cause of action which we have seen. If the impulse is obedience to a self-given command it will have this kind of result. (3) We know that the old Stoics believed in a monistic soul, that there was no additional power in it which would resist the decisions of reason and stop them from issuing in action. If some impulses were commands we obeyed and some were commands we did not obey, we would have to explain why some were blocked from having effect. We should need a new power in the soul to hinder some activations of the powers of presentation, reason, assent, and impulse. All the orthodox Stoics are agreed that there is no such additional and obstructive power in the mind of man.[119] Their opponents complained that the Stoics did not leave room for this kind of power in the mind. Galen, Plutarch, and others search high and low for internal contradictions and gaps in the orthodox Stoic theory. Never, to my knowledge, did they charge that they admitted that some impulses failed to issue in action.[120] The closest thing they could find was Chrysippus' puzzlement over a passion (which is a form of impulse) which stopped without a change in the judgement which generated it.[121] But this deals only with the causal relation between assent and impulse. If a similar gap had been left between impulse and action we would certainly have heard about it.

If, therefore, we accept the hypothesis that assent to a hormetic proposition is extensionally equivalent to obedience to a self-given imperative we shall be able to retain the belief that the psychology of action of the old Stoics is a causal analysis, as it seems to be. If we suppose that some impulses do not issue in action, we shall have either to give up the belief that it is an adequate causal theory or to posit some additional power in the soul which blocks the efficacy of the impulse. But we have no evidence of such a power in any of our sources, and the version proposed here enables us to account for the Stoa's Socratic belief that our knowledge fully determines our actions.

The fact that impulses are directed at predicates has still to be dealt with. We have seen that predicates are the *lekta* which represent actions; thus it makes sense that an impulse which causes action should be directed at the *lekton* which stands for the action, rather than at the hormetic proposition or the imperative. If the discussion so far is at all close to the truth we have in hand both a fairly precise notion of what the Stoics thought impulse to be and of their whole psychology of action. It is the sense of the relationship denoted by the term 'directed at' which is still puzzling. With a little more consideration of the grammatical and logical side of the Stoic theory we should be able to make a good guess about the sense of this terminology. This will complete the reconstruction of the analysis of rational action and will shed light on the parallelism which I have postulated between the hormetic proposition and the imperative.

We have seen that the predicates at which impulse is said to be directed are 'contained, in a sense', in the propositions to which assent is given. Although the verbal form of a predicate, when considered on its own,[122] is usually the infinitive as a verbal noun, it seems clear from the discussion of complete and incomplete *lekta* at Diogenes Laertius 7.63–4 that the form of a predicate within a complete *lekton* varies. The predicate itself is 'that which is said of something'.[123] I take this to mean that in the sentence 'Socrates walks' we say 'walking' about Socrates. But the fact that the verbal noun which is the basic form of the predicate in language must change when the predicate is joined with the subject to form a sentence does not seem to affect the fact that the same predicate is involved in both instances.

This is the way in which predicates are contained in propositions. In the hormetic proposition 'It befits me to eat this cake' we may distinguish the logical subject 'me' to which the predicate is applied, the operator 'it befits' which makes the sentence hormetic, and the predicate which is applied 'eating this cake'. Since the predicate designates the action it is reasonable to say that the impulse is directed at the predicate.

But what of the imperative? I suggest that the imperative shares the predicate which is 'contained' in the hormetic proposition. In the same sense that the predicate is said of the subject in the proposition, it is also applied to the subject of the imperative. A logical analysis of the corresponding imperative would, perhaps, contain these elements: the subject 'you' which refers to the same person as the 'me' in the proposition; the predicate 'eating this cake', as in the proposition; and some sort of imperative operator which would apply the predicate to the subject in the appropriately imperatival way. The grammatical correlate of the hormetic assertion operator would be something like the phrase 'it befits . . . to . . .'. The imperatival operator would, in Greek, be certain inflectional forms of the verb of the predicate; in English, we would sometimes have to use the exclamation mark to avoid ambiguity.

In this way the hormetic proposition to which assent is given would be closely parallel to the imperative, and they would share the same predicate. Because of the need for both the proposition and the imperative in the generation of action, on this reconstruction, it makes sense to tie the impulse directly to what they share, the predicate, which is also the description of the action performed as a result of assent to the proposition.

What evidence is there that predicates are related to imperatives in this way? Needless to say there is not as much evidence as we would wish, but there is some support for the hypothesis.

Among the charred and partly legible papyrus rolls found at Herculaneum are extensive fragments of Chrysippus' *Logical Investigations* (SVF 2.298a). The text as printed by von Arnim is difficult to read and in need of some correction.[124] But the portion which interests us here (p. 109) is in fairly good condition and makes reasonable sense.

Chrysippus is discussing the relationship between predicates, statements, and commands in the case of certain ambiguous commands. One of these forms is this: Do x or if not do y. His comment is interesting and I shall translate it as best I can.

Should we then say this or should we say that what is commanded[125] here too is like this proposition: 'Dion walks and if not he sits'[126] and that this sort of thing is a persuasive predicate: 'to walk, and if not to sit' and that if this is so that it is persuasive to command[127] this sort of thing.[128] And next there is another objection of this sort, that perhaps those who command in this way, 'take either of these at random' and 'take whichever of these' are not giving commands. For it is not possible to find that what is commanded is a predicate or anything else of the sort.

The questions about ambiguous utterances which concern Chrysippus here are not important to us, but only his incidental statements about the relation between predicates and other grammatical forms. From this text one fact emerges: a predicate is what is commanded in a properly formed imperative. The presence of a predicate is a necessary condition for the speech act commanding, and it would seem that the other necessary conditions include a subject and the sort of imperative operator mentioned above, which takes the form in Greek of an inflectional change in the verb.

The predicate is contained in the imperative in much the same way that it is contained in the proposition. This is confirmed further by a passage of Plutarch where Stoic views, again almost certainly those of Chrysippus, on forbidding and commanding are reported.[129] If we accept the filling out of a lacuna in the text, as Cherniss does in his edition, the relevant portion runs as follows:

Yet they themselves say indeed that those who forbid *say* one thing, *forbid* another, and *command* yet another. For he who says 'Do not steal' says exactly this, 'Do not steal', forbids stealing, and commands not stealing.

Stealing and not stealing are predicates and are indicated in the Greek by the infinitive form of the verb, which is often used to stand for predicates.

This distinction between what someone says, i.e. his actual utterance, and the content of the speech act which he makes in so uttering indicates a fairly high degree of logical sophistication in Chrysippus. This no longer surprises students of Stoicism. But the hypothesis about the old Stoic psychology of action put forward here entails more than a simple attribution of logical sophistication to Chrysippus; it entails the strong claim that this logical apparatus was put to work in the psychology of action. This would mean that the Stoics made the same move that Aristotle made when he applied his favourite logical tool, the syllogism, in some of his discussions of the psychology of action. If the Stoic theory was as well thought out and neatly structured as the present reconstruction has made it appear to be, then it would be fair to claim a considerable advance over Aristotle on the part of Chrysippus at least, if not also of Zeno.

(b) Human and Animal Action

But our understanding of the Stoic analysis of human action must be deepened. The best way to do this is to contrast it with their analysis of animal action. This topic is best introduced by a brief look at the Stoic application of the psychology of action to the problem of moral responsibility and determinism. It is no exaggeration to say that the reconciliation of fate and moral responsibility was the dominant and characteristic problem of Stoic moral philosophy. One result of their concentration on this problem was, I would argue, the isolation of assent in the analysis of action. The Stoics' concern with the reconciliation of fate and responsibility gave them particular reason to emphasize assent as the characteristic feature of responsible, human action.

In view of the importance of reconciling the power and scope of fate with man's moral 'freedom', i.e. his responsibility for his actions, it is not surprising that a large number of arguments for an accommodation are reported.[130] But the most interesting of these, which is widely reported, is based on the psychology of action.

The main lines of this argument are now well known, and perhaps the best recent account is that of Charlotte Stough.[131]

Other scholars differ in their treatments, of course.[132] But the argument for compatibilism from the psychology of action which Chrysippus made is known as well as any comparably interesting part of the old Stoic philosophy. Roughly, the argument runs like this. If the power of fate is to be preserved, it must be the case that all events and states are caused. The operation of causes is the operation of fate and fate therefore operates differently in different situations. Not all causes are the same, or even the same in kind. Human actions must be caused by something and it is clear that the Stoic division of causes into 'perfect' and 'auxiliary' was partly designed to describe the two distinct factors determining human behaviour, the external cause consisting of information about one's environment and the internal cause (also called the 'perfect' cause) consisting of the relevant disposition of the agent's soul which determines the reaction to the stimulus of the external cause.

In man the relevant disposition is a state of his rational mind. Man is a rational animal, by fate. Thus fate acts in man through his reason. The way reason controls or causes action is through assent. Human action is always controlled by the mechanism of rational assent to the hormetic propositions occasioned by our presentations; thus our behaviour is in our power without being cut loose from the causal nexus of fate. We are 'free', at least in the sense that we are responsible for our actions.

One or two observations need to be made at this point. It is clear that on the Stoic model of action man is not an ultimate and autonomous self-mover. But in this they do not differ from Aristotle to any great degree. Stough argues that Aristotle's talk of man as an *archê* of action points to a serious difference between the Stoics and Aristotle,[133] but if the account of Aristotle given above is on the right track some other sense than Stough's must be found for this phrase: man is an *archê* of action because he can respond through *orexis* to stimuli from the environment.

The reaction of a rational agent to a stimulus is determined by other factors too. The characteristics of an agent's reason are also the result of causes. Fate acts through the agent because he is rational, but also because the experiences of the agent shape his dispositions and so incline him to respond as he does. Chrysippus said (SVF 2.1000) that the way men react to events is determined by the quality of their minds and that this is one reason why they may be held responsible for their acts. He also seems to have held that our characters are caused by external factors, at least to some degree, and that this too represents the power of fate in determining human action.[134]

Critics did not miss the significance of this. If man's response to the environment is determined by his character, and his character is a product of factors largely beyond his control, then how can we hold the man responsible for his acts? Shall we blame those poor souls who have had no opportunity to become good?[135] The Stoic answer appears to be yes. Many have found this an unsatisfactory answer and I must count myself among them. But the harshness and implausibility of the Stoic position are mitigated by several factors.

First, uneasiness about holding a man responsible for the actions he has performed as a result of his character, which is itself caused by external factors, is generated in part by our rather woolly notion that a man is something distinct from his character, that when he acts in a certain way because of his character there is some true inner man being tyrannized by the 'character'.[136] If one accepts the identification of the moral personality with the character, as the Stoics seem to have done, it may ease much of the discomfort one feels at the Stoic position.

Second, the Stoics also spared no pains in their efforts to shape the characters of their fellow men into the best condition possible. They held that character is formed in part by one's actions and did their best to overcome by education the corrupting factors which threaten the life of every man. Each man is born with uncorrupted inclinations and a natural drive to achieve the 'good' appropriate to a man.[137] These inclinations may, as Cleanthes perhaps thought, be to some degree hampered by inherited character flaws;[138] a man's habitat may tend to warp his character, as Chrysippus recognized.[139] But it is certain that all Stoics agreed with the Epicureans in the belief that such factors are never sufficient to block the road to moral improvement.[140]

The third factor explains this curious blind spot rather than mitigating it. Sorabji describes one interpretation (his third) of the argument we are considering,[141] according to which, 'what matters most about this perfect cause [sc. assent] is that it is *internal*; and for the purpose of assessing whether something is in our power, Chrysippus simply does not consider whether it is necessitated, but only whether it is necessitated by *external* causes.'[142] If the Stoics are concerned not about the ultimate freedom of action but about showing that the control of the action is lodged in the agent and not in the external world, then the causes of our assent do not interest them. How a man's character came to be as it is hardly matters if one is prepared to hold him responsible for all actions which he performs regardless of why he performs them. We may find it repugnant to hold a man responsible for actions which he does because of a flawed character which he could not help having. But it is by no means absurd to do so; many societies have done so and no doubt still do. It seems quite possible that a Stoic would admit that Dion, for example, should be held accountable for his misdeeds even though he did them because of his bad upbringing, and at the same time continue efforts to improve Dion's character by education and training. On this interpretation, however, the only factor germane to the question of responsibility is whether Dion assented and so 'acted' in the full sense of the word. Improving his character is a different matter.

This interpretation seems to make the best sense of the peculiar Stoic unconcern with what we take to be an important point, i.e. that whether one is cause of one's own character might affect the moral status of actions done according to that character. But Sorabji's version needs some slight modifications. According to this interpretation of Chrysippus' compatibilist argument, characters are caused and actions are caused. But they are caused in significantly different ways. The cause of an action is internal, an assent. The cause of our characters is largely external. External factors directly determine our characters, but not our actions. Sorabji argues that one would have to regard an internal cause such as assent as being free of the chain of causes called fate, which in his view would be constituted by external causes only. But I see no need to do so. There are indeed two sources of causation, one internal and one external. But both can be fated. If this is so, we can save Chrysippus from the charge of contradicting his frequent claim that *all* events are fated by denying that internal causes are fated. But we save him from this contradiction at a price. For although all things are caused and so fated, they are only describable as fated because of an ambiguity in the word 'caused'. For there are two significantly different senses in which things are caused.

On this interpretation, although our actions are determined by assent, and our assent is determined by our character, and our character is determined by external factors, we are asked to believe that moral responsibility is affected by the causal role of assent but not by the causal role of the factors which shape the character which determines assent. Although there is a single chain of causes, which justifies Chrysippus' claim that all things happen by fate, moral responsibility is only retained by treating these causes as though they were not on all fours with each other. In this sense at least there is an ambiguity in Chrysippus' use of the idea of cause.[143]

If the third interpretation Sorabji offers is correct, and I think it is, then we face an unpleasant choice. Either we suppose that Chrysippus backed off from his claim that *all* things are caused by fate, as Sorabji does, or we allow him to retain this dramatic claim at the cost of confusion generated by his ambiguous use of the idea of cause. It is easier to imagine him saving his position at the price of an ambiguity which conceals the disunity of his picture of the power of fate than to suppose that he did so by acknowledging in so many words that fate does not govern all things.

This compatibilist version of the reconciliation of fate and moral responsibility makes use of the notion of a 'mental act' as an internal cause. But if an external action, walking for example, is attributable to the agent because he has first performed a mental act, assent, are the Stoics not exposed to the charge that their analysis involves an infinite regress? For how did the mental act get performed? By a prior assent to assent? And if so, what is to stop this regress from continuing indefinitely? The Stoics' answer to this suggested regress would have to be that a mental act like assent is not an action in anything like the same sense that walking is.[144] It is the response to stimuli determined by the character and dispositions of the agent, an internal cause but not an action. This is reasonable if assent is part of a causal analysis of the overt action, a theoretical event posited to explain observed actions and not a datum to be explained by any further analysis.

A puzzling passage of Cleanthes' *Hymn to Zeus* raises another question. In addressing Zeus, he says:[145] 'nor is any deed done without you, God, not on earth nor in the divine fiery heaven nor on the sea, except the deeds done by bad men in [or because of] their folly.' It might appear from this that the power of fate, which is identified with the working out of god's will, is restricted in some way. This would be a remarkable thing and calls for comment.

We should notice first that this passage from the *Hymn* brings to mind the compatibilism argument of Chrysippus. Chrysippus was trying to reconcile responsibility for individual actions with the fact that those actions are part of the chain of causes which constitute fate. He did so, at least to his own satisfaction, by saying in effect that assent was a special kind of internal cause which permits us to hold the agent responsible for its effects, which are actions.

It is desirable, if at all possible, to interpret Cleanthes' enigmatic lines in a way which is compatible with the general Stoic position on fate and responsibility.[146] If all human action is responsible because it is the result of assent, that will mean that human action is rational by virtue of being the action of an adult human being.[147] Good and bad men are equally responsible for their actions. What then is the point of Cleanthes' distinction?

These lines have been interpreted as a reference to an autonomous 'free will'.[148] But this must be wrong. For it would be strange indeed if bad men were thought to be free of the chain of cause and effect in a way that good men are not. This would have to mean that bad men are ultimate sources of self-motion while good men are not. This is highly unlikely; but still the lines of Cleanthes must be interpreted in such a way that we can make sense of the distinction between good and bad men.

The first point to notice is that 'without you' is a highly ambiguous phrase. There is no need to make it refer to the issue of 'freedom'. It may make more sense to interpret it as reference to normative values: bad men act contrary to the Right Reason which is identified with Zeus.[149] Bad men are not acting any more freely or responsibly than good men; all men act 'rationally' in this sense. Rather, bad men are acting apart from Zeus, without following normative Right Reason. They have, as Chrysippus said,[150] 'turned their back on Reason'.

There are numerous questions about this part of the *Hymn* which this interpretation does nothing to solve. The existence of evil men will be a problem on any interpretation of the Stoics' providential determinism.[151] Similarly, since there is only one Right Reason, and only one way to follow god's will, the sage or good man who succeeds in doing so must have a peculiarly restricted kind of freedom. But the only point at issue here is the compatibility of

Cleanthes' *Hymn* with the general Stoic position on responsible action; there is no reason to deny this compability.

Assent, then, is vital to the Stoic analysis of action because it is the locus of moral responsibility. From here we must turn to a more detailed consideration of responsible, human action by way of a contrast with the action of non-rational animals.

Assent is given to propositions, which accompany but are distinct from rational presentations. We have seen that the formation of such propositions is a result of the presence in the human soul of the power of reason. While every animal has a leading part of the soul, which is the seat of impulses, in non-rational animals this *hêgemonikon* does not contain the power of reason.[152]

A consequence of their lack of reason is that assent cannot be given by non-rational animals.[153] In the same way that the non-rational soul is analogous to rational soul, non-rational action is analogous to rational action. One consequence of the non-rational character of animal action is that they are not capable of 'passions', *pathê*, which are perversions of rational behaviour.[154] As Seneca says, anger (which is a passion) 'never occurs except where there is a place for reason'. An animal may have something analogous to a passion, since it has impulses. But these cannot be evaluated from a moral point of view; being without reason and assent, animals are free from the burden of morality.

And this is also true of children below the age of reason. Origen[155] says that 'children, who have not yet completely acquired reason,[156] are not able to fall into' passions, and weaknesses and illnesses of the soul. A bit later Origen adds that the children who are not subject to real passions are subject to something analogous to them. The similarity of this remark to Cicero's comment on animals at *Tusculans* 4.31 confirms that animals and children are denied passions on the same basis. The association of animals with children which we deduce from the comparison of these two texts is stated in so many words by Galen (*PHP* 5.7.19, p. 340): 'It is admitted by Chrysippus and his followers that beasts and children do not use reason.'

We know from independent testimony that the Stoics did not attribute reason to human beings from the moment of birth. If we compare the texts assembled as SVF 1.149 and SVF 2.83[157] we see that reason, which Chrysippus defined as 'an assemblage of notions and concepts',[158] begins to be acquired at or about the age of seven and is 'completely acquired' at or about the age of fourteen.

The term for 'complete acquisition' of reason is the same in this context as it is in Origen's discussion of the freedom of children from passions.

Although children are significantly different from animals in that they have the potential for reason, they do not have reason in the sense which matters for the psychology of action any more than animals do.[159] This reduction of the behaviour of children to that of animals from the ethical point of view may seem strange at first sight; but Aristotle took the same position, for reasons of his own.[160] The Stoics had different criteria for responsible action, but on these too children and animals fell into one group and intelligent, responsible adults into the other.

Since animals lack reason, their presentations are not rational. This ought to mean that there are no *lekta* accompanying them to spell out in rational form the significance of the presentation; hence there is no assent. It is rare to find a detailed description of animal action, but the description Seneca gives of the 'quasi-passions' of animals in his *De Ira* (1.3.4–8) suggests that the presentations which mute animals have are different from those of humans because they lack *lekta* to clarify their content and spell out in words their significance for the animal.[161] He compares the deficiencies of the animals' ability to react to presentations to the deficiencies in animal utterance.

This comparison is not casual. From the age of fourteen children have the full command of concepts and notions which constitutes reason; according to Diogenes of Babylon this is the same age at which humans acquire the ability to utter sounds in the characteristically human way, articulately and 'from the mind'.[162]

When an animal lacks reason it cannot be held responsible. One reason for this is that non-rational animals, such as animals and children, lack certain vital moral concepts: Seneca tells us that children and animals lack the notion of 'good', which would seem to be a necessary condition for moral behaviour.[163] Later in the same letter,[164] he connects this to the full awareness of time in rational animals: *mute* animals, he says, have no notion of the future and a very weak grasp of the past. The significance of the ability to use language recurs here.[165]

But as Diogenes of Babylon says, children under the age of reason are also unable to speak in the characteristically human way. Chrysippus seems to have said the same thing, if we may credit a fascinating text from Varro.[166] Here Chrysippus is presented as saying that young children do not really speak (Varro's word is *loqui*) because they have not mastered syntax, i.e. the proper ordering of words. Until they do, their utterances are just quasi-speech (*ut loqui*). The result of this inability to get syntax right is that even the words in isolation are not really words. This condition is attributed to children who are beginning to learn how to speak[167] and, interestingly, to talking birds whom we have met already as possessors of 'external *logos*' only, which is speech not backed up by *lekta*.

Syntax was, for the Stoics, a matter of *lekta* or *sêmainomena* and not of mere words (*sêmainonta*).[168] This is consistent with Varro's view that it is the absence of proper syntax which makes apparent words not really words at all. And it is also consistent with the claim I wish to make about the significance of reason in the theory of action. The power of reason gives man the ability to form *lekta* which spell out the significance of his presentations in clear linguistic form;[169] thus unlike children and animals, whose presentations are confused and inarticulate,[170] an adult has the ability to spell out the meaning of his presentations and so the ability to assent to them.

The power to form *lekta* is important in the Stoic theory of language and in the psychology of action. It seems that this ability comes to man when his complement of concepts is filled out, around the age of fourteen. It is not clear why the presence of *logos*, in this sense an 'assemblage of notions and concepts', should give a man the ability to form *lekta*, to control syntax, to speak articulately, and to form clear presentations accompanied by propositions which can be assented to. The claim that reason in this sense comes all at once upon the completion of one's set of concepts makes little sense in the case of language. But it makes much better sense in the case of action. There is obviously no single point at which a child acquires the ability to speak articulately and rationally; and it is hard to imagine why the Stoics would wish to say that there is. But it is easy to imagine why they would say that the control of *lekta* came at one definite point when we look to their application of this doctrine to action. It is natural for a moralist or even a moral philosopher to wish to say that there is a fixed point after which one is held responsible for one's actions. Our legislators select a variety of more or less arbitrary age limits by which to determine whether an offender should be tried as an adult or as a juvenile, or released as being too young to be held responsible. Such limits are necessary and necessarily arbitrary in the law. The Stoics needed a similar fixed point to distinguish between children, who are not responsible, like animals the mere tools of fate, and adult humans who are to be held responsible for all that they are and do. Without some such demarcation line, any attempt to ascribe responsibility would easily become enmeshed in special pleading or in a sorites-type argument about who can be held responsible and who cannot.[171] As moralists they embraced the same practical necessity which confronts legislators.

Children and animals have a quasi-*hêgemonikon* analogous to an adult's; their impulses and presentations are analogous; they have something analogous to passions; even the sounds they utter are 'quasi-words'.[172] We expect, then, an analogue to assent in non-rational animals. It is not unreasonable to suppose that after selecting assent as the factor in their analysis of action which makes an agent responsible, they posited an analogous factor or aspect of animal action which does not, however, make the animal responsible for its action. There does seem to have been a recognition of such an aspect in the analysis of animal action. But it will take a bit of digging to find it, for we are much less well informed about animal action than about human.

In considering the reaction of animals to presentations in the analysis of perception and knowledge and in the analysis of action we have noted the use of the term 'assent'. But a second term is also found in the ancient sources, and it suggests a possible answer to the problem at hand. Diogenes Laertius says that perceptual (i.e. *aisthêtikai*) presentations occur 'with yielding (*eixis*) and assent' when they come from existing objects.[173] Diogenes' summary here is not well enough organized to permit us to decide whether these two terms refer to exactly the same sort of reaction to presentations, nor even to infer whether they are reactions to the same kind of presentations. For the distinction of rational and non-rational presentations, which we have already considered, is made only in the following section. It is possible, however, that the terms 'yielding' and 'assent' are used to distinguish between two different kinds of reactions to presentations.

In theory of knowledge the Stoics distinguished between presentations called 'cataleptic', which form the criterion of truth because of their irrefutable and unchallengeable reliability, and 'non-cataleptic' presentations which are not adequate criteria of

truth. The nature of these cataleptic presentations is still controversial; it is not clear whether the Stoic view on them changed in any
substantial way. More to the point here, it is not clear whether a
cataleptic presentation was such as to compel the assent of the
rational agent or whether it merely encouraged it.[174] In either case
the Stoics would have said that such an assent was still 'in our
power', i.e. voluntary in the minimal sense which sufficed for the
ascription of responsiblity.[175] On this problem Sandbach's cautious
estimation is best:[176] 'the question remains open whether a cognitive presentation is one such that it is inevitably followed by assent.
. . . I do not think there is any evidence to show what was the
opinion of the older Stoics'.

This limitation does not hinder the present inquiry as much as
one might at first think. For it seems certain that no hormetic presentation, whether rational or non-rational, is cataleptic. As we
shall see, the Stoics distinguished human from animal reactions to
hormetic presentations by man's ability to react or not according to
his character and 'choice', in contrast to the animal's automatic
response to stimuli. It seems possible, at least, that this automatic
animal reaction to presentations was termed 'yielding' by the
Stoics, and that the occurrence of the two terms in Diogenes
Laertius is a reflection of this distinction.

The argument in support of this suggestion is as follows. The
term 'yielding' suggests an automatic acceptance of the presentation, a passive reaction which calls into question the claim of the
yielder to be an agent in any significant sense of the word. This, we
shall see, is an apt description of the way animals react to stimuli,
according to the Stoics. That 'yielding' has this sense is shown by
several applications of the term in Hellenistic philosophy. Sextus
Empiricus uses the term to emphasize the passivity of the true
sceptic's attitude to the impressions and stimuli he is exposed to: he
may 'yield', and this yielding may even be described as 'assent', but
he does not take responsibility for the propositional attitudes and
beliefs to which his behaviour might seem to commit him.[177] Some
critics of the Stoic doctrine of assent and action also used the term
'yielding' to press home the point that they regarded the occurrence of assent in the Stoic sense as insufficient to distinguish
human from animal action.[178] This polemical confusion of assent
and yielding could then be extended to reports of other Stoic doctrines.[179] If it is the case that yielding was originally a term for an

automatic reaction to presentations and was subsequently confused with assent in the strict sense of the word,[180] part of the blame
for this may also be laid at the door of the *apraxia* argument. In
Antiochus' version of it,[181] which Sandbach rightly suggests is not
necessarily in agreement with the Stoic version,[182] *cedere*(the equivalent of the Greek term for 'yield') is used of the mind's automatic
acceptance of cataleptic presentations and this yielding is likened
to the automatic pursuit by animals of what seems to be appropriate for them. This suggests that some Stoics, or at least Antiochus, were willing to support their argument that assent to a
cataleptic presentation is automatic with a claim that animals react
likewise to a perception of their apparent advantage. This is a
dangerous move, since Antiochus does not distinguish humans
from other animals here, and other evidence makes it certain that it
is on just this point that the Stoics did make a distinction.[183]

But it is far from certain that 'yielding' was ever a strictly applied
technical term for the automatic reaction to presentations which
some scholars argue was involved in assenting to a cataleptic presentation and which the Stoics did say was the reaction of animals to
hormetic presentations. But whether the Stoics bothered to coin a
special term to distinguish animal 'assent' from rational assent or
not, the distinction in their doctrine is clear. The distinction's
significance may be best summed up by quoting the apt illustration
of Sandbach:[184]

All animals are impelled to action by a movement in their *psychê* called a
hormê. In a brute beast this follows directly upon the stimulus of a presentation (to invent an instance, a dog that scents a hare immediately wants to
chase it). But in a human being the impulse does not exist without a
mental act of assent. (A man who sees a hare does not immediately desire
to chase it: he must first entertain and assent to the presentation 'that hare
is something to be chased'.)

Non-rational animals, which do not have access to *lekta*, cannot
assent.[185] This is the reason why they not only do not pause to reflect
before they act, but could not do so. This seems to be a sensible
reason for declining to hold animals accountable for their actions
as we do men.

But some polemical texts do attribute assent to all animals, without distinction. The most important are in Nemesius and
Alexander of Aphrodisias. A closer consideration of their evidence
will be needed presently, but for now suffice it to say that all these

polemical accounts which attribute assent to animals contradict the information we are given in discussions of the *scala naturae*: nonrational animals have impulse and presentation while humans have in addition reason and assent. It may be that there is something analogous to assent in brute beasts, but it could not have been 'assent' in anything but a misleading and metaphorical sense. These polemical accounts also contradict the picture of human action and animal behaviour which we are given by Origen in his *De Principiis*.[186] Here we meet the firm distinction between men who assent and animals who do not. The text continues from the passage quoted on p. 21 above.

2   In some animals presentations which summon impulse occur when the power [lit. nature] of presentation automatically [or regularly, *tetagmenôs*] stimulates the impulse, as in the spider the presentation of weaving occurs and an impulse to weave follows, since its power of presentation automatically summons it to this. And one need credit the animal with no further power beyond that of presentation. And the same holds in the case of a bee and the production of honeycomb.

3   The rational animal, however, has reason too in addition to the power of presentation. Reason judges [or distinguishes] the presentations and rejects some and admits others so that it might lead the animal according to the presentations. Therefore, since there are in the power of reason inclinations to contemplate the moral and the shameful following which . . . we choose the moral but reject the shameful, we are to be praised when we give ourselves to the doing of the moral and to be blamed in the opposite case. (One must not be unaware, though, that the greater part of universal Nature is present in some measure in animals, to a greater or lesser degree. The result is that the work of hunting dogs and war horses is pretty close, I might say, to that of the rational animal.) We all agree, then, that it is not in our power whether some particular external thing should occur to us, which stimulates this or that sort of presentation. But the decision to use what occurs in this way or that is the work of nothing else but the reason in us, which activates us with reference to the inclinations which summon us to the moral and our impulses to the appropriate, or turns aside to the opposite course.

4   But if someone should say that the external event is such that it is impossible for him, being of such a character, to resist it, let him consider his own passions and motions [sc. of the soul], to see if perhaps there is not an agreement and assent and inclination of the mind to this act because of these particular persuasive factors [in the situation]. For, let us say, a woman who appears to a man who has decided on sexual restraint and celibacy and summons him to do something against his resolution is not

the perfect cause of him putting aside his resolution. For in each instance he consents to the titillation and smoothness of the pleasure and being unwilling to resist it or to stand by his decision he performs the unrestrained act. Another fellow will behave in the opposite way, when the same circumstances occur, if he has learned and practised more lessons. For the titillations and allures occur, but reason rejects the allures and dissolves the desire, since it has been strengthened and nourished by training and has been strengthened (or close to it) with respect to what is moral through his opinions.

Origen goes on in section 5 to claim that anyone who blames the external stimuli for his actions is in effect distorting or counterfeiting the notion of autonomy.[187] Despite this bold front, there are still problems in Origen's position, which in all essentials is that of the Stoa. Like the Stoics, Origen does not here consider the implications for our ascriptions of praise and blame of the fact that the character which determines our actions is itself caused by factors beyond our control. But that problem has already been dealt with, and what interests us now is Origen's contrast between man and animal. He takes it as undeniable that every human action is the result of an assent, whether the agent is immediately aware of this or not; and he contrasts this situation to that of animals who react automatically (*tetagmenôs*) and who have no power in their souls beyond that of presentation. That is, they have no reason and no assent and they are not, therefore, subject to moral evaluation.

They do, of course, yield or give in to the hormetic presentations which affect them. But this programmed response is not a 'power' in the soul. It is merely what happens when presentation occurs in the animal. The conclusion drawn above that children are in the same case as non-rational animals had perhaps one especially disturbing feature. Children are obviously capable of complex, apparently rational, and goal-directed behaviour. Does it make any sense to deny that such actions are 'rational'? Surely the Stoics did not do so. Or did they?

If children, like animals, yield rather than assent, it does not follow that they do not exhibit complex, goal-directed behaviour which is adaptable to changing circumstances. As Origen's text shows, animals also display all these characteristics, which *we* take to be the hallmarks of rationality. That these are not the criteria of rationality for the Stoics confirms the judgement that moral accountability was their principal concern in demarcating man and beast.

That non-rational animals display complex, adaptable, and goal-directed behaviour was well known to the Stoics; indeed, they seem to have gone out of their way to draw attention to such cases as proofs of the providential character of Nature. Thus the presence of quasi-arts[188] in animals as lowly as the bee and the spider and swallow did not prove that reason was present.[189] The Stoic doctrine on the status of prima-facie rational behaviour generated lengthy debate and inevitably tended to crystallize around certain standard examples.[190] It would be unnecessary and tedious to deal with the question in any detail here; the most interesting example used to show that even the most convincingly rational behaviour of an irrational animal was not rational in Stoic eyes is the 'dialectical dog' first mentioned by Chrysippus.[191] According to Chrysippus, who may or may not have observed what he reported, a tracking dog will apparently reason out the path of his quarry by means of the fifth complex indemonstrable syllogism. For when it comes to a three-way division of a trail, it will sniff the first and second for the spoor, and if it does not pick up the scent it will head down the third path without stopping to confirm that the scent is there. Implicitly (*dunamei*) the dog has inferred: either A or B or C; but neither A nor B; therefore C.

If this degree of prima-facie rational behaviour did not induce the Stoics to grant that animals shared in reason, it can only be because they were most concerned with the question of moral responsibility when they assessed which animals were rational and which not. And as Origen says, this turns on the ability to give assent to presentations or to withhold it; this ability cannot be present in any animal which lacks that ability to use language in the proper sense of the word. For with language use come *lekta*, and it is to *lekta* of a certain sort that assent is given.

On this model of action the act of reason which makes an agent responsible is merely reactive. Reason is restricted to judging the presentations which come along, and it is emphasized that the agent does not have control over which presentations shall occur to him. This is an unnecessarily strong claim to make about the origin of stimulative presentations in any animal, and the suspicion might arise that this doctrine, which the Stoics apparently held, was a result of their narrow concentration on the problem of freedom and determinism, which would tend to concentrate on the question of a man's reaction to external presentations. One might also suspect that the Stoics' concerns with the analysis of action were not so narrow, and that the apparent concentration on this extreme case is a result of the selective interests of our sources. Since we know that the problem of determinism was only one of the issues to which the psychology of action was applied, one may follow the latter suspicion. If one does, it is possible to allow that the Stoics also recognized that stimulative presentations could be drawn from the memory, perhaps even that these presentations could be manipulated by the reason. One often gets the feeling that the Stoics made the dubious move of supposing that since all our presentations and concepts *ultimately* come from our experience of the external world it is acceptable to treat those which are processed and mediated by the mind as though they came directly from the world outside.[192]

But assent is still reactive, even if we suppose that the origin of presentations can be more complex than the sources concerned with determinism and 'free will' suggest. Behaviour, no matter how complex or apparently rational, is a result of accepting the stimulus of the presentation. In animals this acceptance is automatic and may have been called 'yielding'. In man, reason is in a position to control this automatic process, since a man can in principle deny his assent to any presentation which comes along. Since he is able to block this process, he is held responsible for its occurrence whenever he chooses not to interfere with it.[193] This omission may be culpable, as Seneca notes:[194] fools (*insani*) are stimulated by the presentation of some desirable thing, and their deluded minds 'do not refute its falsity'. This failure to see through a false or improper presentation leads to the doing of the action which it stimulates.

The control over actions which assent exercises is, therefore, a negative thing. If an agent is capable of refusing his assent and does not do so, he is still deemed to have given his assent. Origen recognizes that not all assents are conscious when he asks the man who thinks that his response to a stimulus is not in his own power to reflect on his experience more carefully (3.1.4). He is supposing that there is an act of assent in each case but that we are not always conscious of it. This unconscious assent, an implicit assent as it might better be called, is clearly meant to help justify the claim that every action of a rational agent is a responsible action.[195]

When a philosopher takes the position that every rational action is a responsible action, he must come to terms with the apparent fact that rational agents do not display their rationality in every action. This is true if the mark of rationality is deliberation, as it was for Aristotle, and also if it is something like the Stoic assent. This poses a problem for a philosopher who is not ready to make all rational humans responsible for all their actions solely by virtue of their belonging to that class. There are two sorts of moves one might make to bridge the gap between the apparent fact that reason was not involved in an action and the conviction that the action was nevertheless rational. One may suppose, as Aristotle seems to have done, that an agent does not deliberate before each action but that if asked the agent could produce a deliberation to support his action which he might have gone through. In this way an action is backed up by reason even though no actual rational procedure precedes the action.[196]

Alternatively, one might posit the occurrence of the characteristic rational activity in each and every action, whether the agent is conscious of it or not. This is the Stoic response to the problem at hand, and while it is undoubtedly high-handed for a philosopher to claim that there are events going on in an agent's mind of which he is unaware, this high-handedness is something the Stoics share with other philosophical psychologists. One of these is Plato, who seems disturbingly ready to attribute to people desires and thoughts they would not admit to having. No one really desires what is bad for him, we are repeatedly told, no matter what he may actually think about his own state of mind. David Glidden has recently drawn attention to this facet of Plato, and offers an account of it which sheds light on one respect in which his own psychological presumption influenced the Stoics.[197]

The *Lysis* postulates psychological elements in the personality which might remain unknown to the agent himself. It is then possible to claim that an individual would desire something, even though that individual might not make that claim himself. Conflicting explanations would result when the agent's conscious desire presented a different description of his state of mind from that given by the theory. In such a case Plato clearly prefers the theoretical explanation over the conscious avowal. . . . The paradox that an individual may not know what he really desires or may not really desire what he thinks he does can be explained by a psychological theory which provides an independent description of the state of the agent's soul.

In claiming that no action is made without an act of assent, the Stoics are making a similar move. They have postulated certain events in the soul of an agent to explain his action, and if the agent is not aware of them, that is not for them a sign that the theory is wrong. The psychology of action is an explanatory analysis of the behaviour of an agent, and it is not falsifiable by the agent's claims about what he did or did not do or feel. The nature of the theory makes it automatically true that if someone acted he also assented. And implicit assent is all that the Stoics thought they needed to hold a man responsible for his actions.[198] The Stoics seem not to have been reluctant to allow important questions in moral philosophy to depend on postulates and theories which were not in fact independently verifiable.[199]

There is, however, some justification for holding people responsible for such implicit assents and the consequent actions. Since the Stoics postulated in each action the formation of the relevant hormetic proposition and the assent to it, it is possible, they thought, for any agent to make explicit the proposition and his assent. We often read of the importance of clarifying or working out one's presentations as a part of the process of moral improvement. Part of this exercise of one's presentations involves making explicit in one's awareness the propositions which are operative in all of one's actions. A rational agent may act without an awareness of what he is doing, in the sense that his assent is implicit; and when so acting he may seem to resemble mere animals who do not evaluate the stimuli which move them to act. But there is a difference between unreflective animal behaviour and unreflective human behaviour, which consists in the fact that a man is always able to bring the significance of his actions to consciousness and to evaluate it. Having that ability, he is held responsible for not exercising it.

This is different from an Aristotelian characterization of a rational action as one which could be explained and justified by reference to a deliberation which the agent might have gone through. The Stoic theory was expected to justify holding men accountable for individual actions in the face of a chain of cause and effect which includes human actions. The Stoics were nominalists and not inclined to accept the reality of unactualized possibilities or potentialities; an Aristotelian account of responsibility in such dispositional terms would not suffice. They needed and postulated for each action a real event in the material soul which would cause the action and justify the ascription of responsibility. Assent is such an event; in order to hold men responsible for all their actions, implicit assents had to be postulated.

Reason is thus a kind of gatekeeper of the presentations. Origen goes on to say:[200] 'Therefore the argument shows that externals [i.e. the presentations which stimulate us to action] are not in our power,[201] but it is our own job to take reason as a judge (*kritēn*) and examiner of how we should react to these externals and so *use them* in this way or the opposite way.' The idea that man's rationality is expressed in his 'use' of presentations is also found in Epictetus.[202] This way of describing rational behaviour is quite natural in Epictetus, who made the dichotomy between what is in our power and what is not the corner-stone of his ethics; it seems to have been central to the psychology and ethics of the older Stoics as well.[203]

The 'use' of presentations by rational animals means more than merely giving assent or not doing so. It also involves processing our presentations, clarifying the concepts built on them, comparing them, and so on. But time and again Epictetus, like other Stoics, returns to the central question, freedom to give assent or to with-hold it. Epictetus captures this in a vivid passage which illustrates how reason operates in the control of action. Deliberation is not involved. Reason seems to consist in halting the otherwise auto-matic process of response to a presentation, and evaluating it before assent is given. 'Wait for me a little bit, presentation; . . . let me examine you.'[204] The need to pause and reflect before assenting is also a frequent theme in Seneca's *De Ira* book 2.

Throughout all these texts the presupposition is that a presenta-tion will produce the impulse it is naturally designed to elicit unless reason steps in to stop it. Clement[205] illustrates the same point: 'But the power of reason is peculiar to the human soul, and so it should not have impulse as the irrational animals do, but should distin-guish (*diakrinein*) between presentations and not be swept along with them.' Being swept along seems to be the fate of those who do not exercise the power of assent. Clement's language here is echoed frequently by Epictetus.[206]

The presentations which an irrational animal receives are not accompanied and clarified by *lekta*; nevertheless they are stimula-tive. Hormetic presentations are presentations of 'the appropriate' or what is relevant to the animal. And as Arius Didymus tells us,[207] this concept extends to mere animals too, 'for even they act in accordance with their own nature.' Even without *lekta* irrational animals see the world in terms of their interests and needs and behave accordingly. 'Appropriate' (*kathêkon*) is not the only term used to signal this adaptive relationship between an animal and its world. Elsewhere the terms *oikeion* and *allotrion* are used for this sort of suitability and its opposite.[208]

The tendency of any hormetic presentation to elicit action if it is not stopped by the withholding of assent, when combined with the Stoic dogma that many if not most acts of assent are implicit, provided abundant grounds for polemical criticism. Plutarch clearly enjoys the irony that some false presentations are tempting to men in this way, and seems to think that the occurrence of such temptation is an argument against the providential nature of the world.[209]

Plutarch exploits the claim made by Chrysippus that even though hormetic presentations lead a man on to action, it is still the case that he must assent before impulse or action can occur. The contradiction which Plutarch wants to foist on the Stoics is this: despite their conviction that all action requires an assent, they also say that 'god and the sage produce false presentations in us, not wanting us to assent or yield, but only to act and to have an impulse toward the object of presentation, and that we, being fools, assent to such presentations because of our weakness' (1057 ab). This is not, I suggest, a correct report of anything Chrysippus or any Stoic actually said. What Plutarch must have done is to take the stimulative nature of the presentation and the sage's awareness of it and to conclude from these that in Chrysippus' view the sage wants the natural result of the presentation to occur. In fact this need not be the case, since Chrysippus knew that any action would be the result of assent and that whether or not it was done was not in the hands of the source of the presentation but in those of the recipient.

One must allow for the possibility that Chrysippus at some point was forced by persistent criticism to the absurd position which Plutarch puts him in, that he at some time conceded that the knowing production of a stimulative presentation does imply a desire for the action to occur; one could suppose further that having done so he was reluctant to say that either a sage or a god wanted any one man to be the doer of an evil deed. Under this kind of pressure (or in a dialectical argument for a non-Stoic position) it is conceivable, but unlikely, that Chrysippus would have said that what the sage or god wanted was something which according to his own theory was impossible, an action without an assent, i.e. without a genuine agent. But it is far more likely, in my opinion, that Plutarch foisted this on him.[210] Be that as it may, this short polemical passage seems to provide evidence of a doctrine of implicit assent and proof that hormetic presentations will lead, if not stopped by a refusal of assent, to action.

There are theoretical presentations which also tend to lead one to assent, and these are called 'persuasive'.[211] Here too we may see a parallel with hormetic presentations. Just as any ordinary presentation may be met with assent, rejection, or a suspension of judgement (*epochê*), so too any hormetic presentation may be met with assent followed by action, by a rejection of the presentation (that is, a judgement that the proposition accompanying it is false and the action incorrect), or by a pause to evaluate the presentation of the sort which Epictetus recommends. In the case of action the latter two cases may seem to converge. For since while one's mind is pausing to evaluate the stimulus one is not acting, the third case temporarily resembles rejection of the stimulus. But such a stage is only temporary, and the distinction of this pause from rejection would be guaranteed in Stoic eyes by the fact that these two mental acts are constituted by distinct alterations of the material substance of the mind.

We must conclude with a brief look at some arguments and evidence which deny or blur the sharp distinction between animal and human action.

The sceptics of the New Academy, Arcesilaus and Carneades, looked for arguments against the doctrines of Zeno and Chrysippus about the reliability of our knowledge of the world. In particular, they wished to deny that assent was needed for action to occur, in response to the Stoic argument against the possibility and desirability of suspension of judgement. The Stoic argument turned on the claim that assent was needed for action to occur; thus the elimination of assent would mean total inaction or *apraxia*. But, the Stoics pointed out, men do act. Therefore we assent.

In some ways this is a curious argument, since it crosses over from the role of assent in the theory of knowledge to the role of assent in the theory of action.[212] But the confusion of the two roles of assent does no serious damage to the force of the argument, since everyone would have agreed that assent to a hormetic proposition, such as 'It is fitting for me to eat that cake' entailed assent to a non-hormetic proposition, in this case 'There is a piece of cake.'[213]

This set of arguments and counter-arguments is of considerable interest; we have had to deal with it before and much more could be said about it. Only one point concerns us now and that is an aspect of the sceptical attack which seems to have been unnoticed so far.

Zeno claimed that assent was needed for action.[214] He clearly meant to use human action and that alone to press his point against the sceptic Arcesilaus.[215] His response, as reported by Plutarch, is to argue that action is in fact possible without assent and to support this claim by setting out the Stoics' own account of unassented animal action as though it were an acceptable analysis of human action as well. Here is Plutarch's report:[216]

The movement of impulse, aroused by that of presentation, moves man in a *praxis* (*praktikôs kinei*) towards what is appropriate to him (*ta oikeia*); it is as though an inclination and the sinking (*rhopê*) of a balance pan occurred in his mind. Well, those who argue for suspension of judgement about everything do not eliminate this movement either, but they experience [lit. use] the impulse which naturally[217] leads to what is presented as appropriate.

This last phrase is explained a little later:

For action requires two things, a presentation of what is appropriate and an impulse to the appropriate which is presented. Neither of these clashes with suspension of judgement. . . . There is no need of a judgement (*doxa*) in order to generate this movement (*kinêsis kai phora*) to what is appropriate; rather, the impulse occurs automatically (*êlthen euthus*).

The attractiveness of Arcesilaus' response, which amounted to the claim that human and animal behaviour could be analysed in the same way, is no doubt increased by the consideration that the Stoics too would admit that sheer complexity and apparent purposiveness were not enough to make action rational. Only the concern to argue for the uniqueness of moral responsibility in the rational animal made the Stoa distinguish human action and animal action so sharply by means of the concept of assent. Any philosopher who did not share their belief in fate would not feel the need to retain the special characteristics of rational action.

Carneades, if he is the source for ch. 47 of Plutarch's *De Stoicorum Repugnantiis*, seems to have gone even further; for in the text which we have already considered he said that a response to a persuasive, hormetic presentation could occur with neither 'yielding' nor assent. If 'yielding' is the original Stoic term for this sort of automatic reaction, he is taking an even stronger position than Arcesilaus did on the immediacy of our reactions to presentation.

Antiochus of Ascalon faced the same problem as did Zeno and Chrysippus, according to the report in Cicero's *Academica*. As might be expected, his response follows Stoic doctrine in broad outline, but I suspect that it is not wholly orthodox.[218] It is Stoic in so far as it insists that assent is needed for action. But Antiochus gives up the principal point of Zeno's sharp distinction between the human and the animal. Thus Antiochus blurs the distinction between assented and unassented action in a different way.[219] This is a clumsy response, much less sophisticated than Chrysippus' must have been. For it would not really handle the sceptical attack. The sceptics were ready to maintain, with a good deal of plausibility, that assent was not needed for animal action. By granting them the assimilation of human to animal action, Antiochus could only fall back on feeble counter-assertion. Moreover, once he gave up the distinctness of human action, Antiochus was open to criticism for failure to preserve 'free will'.

Two later attacks on the Stoic argument for the compatibility of fate and free will display a disregard for the difference between human and animal action similar to that shown in the arguments against *apraxia*. That is, the success of the polemic depends on denying the difference. The attacks are found in Alexander of Aphrodisias' *De Fato* and in the lengthy treatise *On the Nature of Man* by the bishop of Emesa, Nemesius.[220]

Nemesius pretends to synopsize the familiar Stoic argument, pointing out that each level of the hierarchy has its own proper form of motion by fate. But Nemesius does not distinguish between human and animal life. The top rung on his *scala naturae* is 'animal', without qualification. The powers attributed to all animals are impulse and assent, and although Nemesius elsewhere (pp. 304–5) recognizes in his own way that human behaviour is distinct in an important respect, he shows no inclination to admit that the Stoics made the distinction too. That is to say, he takes the kind of automatic 'yielding' to presentations which characterizes irrational animals as being the pattern for human action too, and disguises this distortion of the Stoic analysis by referring to it as assent. A human action, like 'walking',[221] is presented as being solely dependent on the impulse which follows from environmental stimulus and external conditions imposed by fate. He refers to assent, but does not mention reason, nor does he suggest that man himself determines whether or not assent will be given.

Nemesius is clearly distorting the Stoics' attempt to reconcile fate and moral responsibility by blurring the distinction between rational man and irrational beast, and he does so by a misinterpretation of assent similar to that used by Academic sceptics.[222] He might have argued against it by saying that assent is inadequate to make our actions responsible because it is the result of a determined character; but instead he takes the low road of polemical misrepresentation.

Alexander's debate with the Stoics on this point is much more sophisticated and clear than that of Nemesius. But he too employs for his own ends the amalgamation of human assent and animal 'yielding', in order to contrast the Stoic concept of rational action to his own notion of what rational assent should be, which is a free choice to do either of two opposite actions after due deliberation.[223]

Alexander's discussion is characterized by a deep familiarity with Stoic doctrine (such as the stimulative nature of presentations and their tendency to evoke a definite response: *agei, hepomenoi, endidontes*, p. 180.5–7). At the same time he employs basic premisses which are radically opposed to those of the Stoics. Thus he bases his argument on the presumption that 'what is in our power' (*to eph' hêmin*) is that which enables a man to do either of two opposite actions in a given circumstance and on the firm belief that such a rational control of action is only possible by means of deliberation.[224] He knows that this is not what the Stoics mean by *to eph' hêmin*[225] and that neither of his presumptions is part of the Stoic analysis of responsible action. Yet they form the standard against which the Stoics are criticized.[226]

In his presentation of the Stoic reconciliation of fate and *to eph' hêmin* Alexander gives a version of the hierarchy of entities in which the activity of fate is to be seen.[227] Comparison with other accounts shows again that he knows good Stoic versions of the doctrine, based on the activity characteristic of each level of the hierarchy.

Fate manifests itself in animals, just as it does in stones; there are motions 'through animals by fate' just as there are motions 'by fate through the stone'.[228] He says that the Stoics claim that the power of free action is the activity of fate manifested in animals in their impulses.[229] A little later[230] he says that the Stoics mean by this that animals move by fate because of their powers of assent and impulse. The claim that animals give assent is repeated.[231]

It is not difficult for Alexander to ridicule this notion of free action. As he reports it, there is no more reason to say that an animal is free than that a plant or a stone is free. He represents the reactions of all animals to a stimulus in the Stoic doctrine as one of automatic assent to the presentation which determines the impulse to action.[232] He even equates this assent with the 'yielding' which may be the Stoic term for the automatic animal acceptance of stimuli.

This is not a reliable report, for there is no distinction between man and beast in the 'Stoic' doctrine according to Alexander. According to Alexander, the Stoics treated all animals in the same way, making them fully determined by an automatic acceptance of environmental stimuli to action. This enables him to portray the Stoic reconciliation of fate and free will as a failure, according to which man is no more 'free' than the other animals. The key move in this argument is the assimilation of human to animal action. Nemesius did this too, and to a degree it is a revival of the earlier Academic tactic. In Alexander's case at least, the distortion seems to have been deliberate. Not only does he know that the Stoics reject his conception of *to eph' hêmin*, but he later quotes a Stoic source which stresses the distinction between human and animal action:[233] 'Therefore according to fate animals will perceive and have impulses, and some will merely act (*energêsei*) while the rational ones will act responsibly (*praxei*), and [sc. of these] some will do wrong and some will do right.'

Alexander goes on after distorting and criticizing the Stoic position to present his own theory about rational and responsible action. This kind of action, he says, is the result not of mere impulse, but of rational impulse,[234] which is the product not of mere animal 'assent', but of rational assent.[235] This phrase, which would be a redundancy for the Stoa, is designed by Alexander to distinguish the assent of a rational, deliberating agent from the automatic assent which he claims the Stoics attributed to man.

In Alexander's own view, then, 'the other animals which yield to presentations alone[236] have the causes of their assents and practical impulses determined by these [sc. presentations]; but man has reason as judge (*kritês*) of the presentations pertaining to action which it receives from outside.'[237] The similarity with Origen could not be more clear. He too pointed out that in non-rational animals external presentations are the perfect cause of action, and that man is not like that. He too made reason a judge (*kritēs*) of presentations. But Alexander claims that the Stoics do not share his position.

The reason for this is that Alexander insists that an assent is only rational if it is the result of deliberation. The omission of this element is the flaw in the Stoic theory, he says.[238] He may well have believed that to all intents and purposes the Stoic theory of human action reduced man to the level of an animal. But he did not want his readers to know that in fact the Stoics had analysed human and animal action differently, so he presented a distorted picture of their doctrine which assumes what he should be trying to prove, that the Stoic analysis of responsible action is a failure because it reduces man to the level of the irrational animals.

For Alexander, then, 'free' action is distinguished from what is merely 'voluntary' (*hekousion*) in Aristotle's sense.[239] Even animals act 'voluntarily' in the sense that they act with an awareness of the relevant facts and not under external compulsion. But man is different; he uses his reason to judge his presentations, and for Alexander that is only possible through deliberation. Thus the assent of a rational animal is a 'deliberated assent'.[240] This view of human reason is repeated elsewhere.[241] He claims that this is a universally accepted view of responsible action. In fact, however useful and stimulating Alexander's blend of Aristotelianism and Stoicism might be, it is not the same as the Stoics' own analysis. And the fact that the basic presumptions on which Alexander's own syncretistic view is based are so useful for the attack he makes on Stoicism suggests strongly that it was by reflection on the Stoic approach that much of Alexander's originality in expounding Aristotle on this issue came about. Like other critics of the Stoa, Alexander simply refused to admit the Stoic distinction between human and animal response to presentations.

(c) Some Observations

Before turning to a consideration of the use of the analysis of human action in ethics, which constitutes part II, it is worth while to make a few brief observations about the theory as reconstructed in its own right.

i   The treatment which the Stoics gave to propositions and presentations, and the postulate of assent in both the theory of knowledge and the theory of action provide a means for distinguishing between having a proposition in the mind and assenting to it. When the agent receives a presentation accompanied by a proposition 'it is fitting that I eat that cake', he can pause to evaluate it. Similarly, when someone receives a presentation of a pomegranate along with the proposition 'there are some pomegranates', he can suspend his judgement about that too. In both these cases the person is entertaining a proposition without assenting to it.

This is a considerable accomplishment. The notion that thinking people do entertain propositions has, no doubt, been around since we began to reflect on our own mental processes. But for the first time in the old Stoa there appears a logical and psychological theory which can adequately account for the phenomenon. Ideas and concepts can, in Aristotle's analysis of mind, be held and contemplated; but propositions are still considered to be combinations of such terms, however complex.[242] Once they are combined to make a sentence in the mind, assertion has occurred. It is only with the Stoic 'discovery' of the *lekton*, an immaterial entity which is itself in discursive form, that it becomes possible to capture in a theory the phenomenon of considering, without assenting to, entire propositions.

ii   Consider for a moment the relationships among the hormetic presentation and the two *lekta*, propositional and imperatival, which accompany it and spell out its significance and import for the agent. The first thing which strikes the observer is that the relationship between the corporeal, representational entity, the presentation, and the incorporeal entities is unanalysed. By this I mean that we are nowhere told how a presentation and a *lekton* are structured so as to define how the one corresponds to the other.[243] Similarly, the Stoics seem not to have said anything very helpful about the 'subsistence' relationship between the two sorts of entities. We are told little more than that when these presentations occur in the minds of rational animals *lekta* 'subsist according to them'. This silence on an important ontological and logical puzzle may well be a result of the limited information we have about Stoic logic and philosophy of mind. But it is possible that the gap was left by the Stoics them-

selves; it is not counter-intuitive to say that thoughts corresponding
to perceptual experiences just come into our heads. Faced with the
ancient analogue of the problem of the relation of brain processes to
thoughts, even Chrysippus may have left the question right there.

iii One of the most interesting features of the theory as reconstructed is its ability to capture certain important insights drawn
from the theory of speech acts as well as from imperatival analyses
of 'will'. The parallelism between propositions and imperatives
called for by the theory requires the isolation of the common element in sentences such as 'You, eat that cake!' and 'It is fitting that
you eat that cake' (both addressed to oneself). This common element is very like the unasserted sentence content used in the speech
act analysis of Searle[244] or Hare.[245] If this content is common, one
also needs the analytical machinery to describe what is different
about two such sentences; and this is the *way* such sentences are
asserted, their mode of assertion ('assertion' here being a logical
term, distinct from the action of assenting discussed in (*c*) i above).
An imperative sentence is such and such a content asserted im-
peratively, the corresponding factual proposition is the same content asserted as a fact, as 'You are eating that cake'; and the
hormetic proposition asserted with its own characteristic modal
force.[246]

   This distinction between content and mode of assertion is at least
as old as Frege; at least, it is to Frege that most twentieth-century
philosophers refer in tracing the ancestry of their theories. And by
now there are many varieties of the analysis available. Some of these
are more like the Stoic theory than others. For instance, the form in
which Bennett introduces imperatives into his imaginary language
Tribal[247] does not preserve the grammatical parallelism of the sentence governed by the imperative operator and the assertion operator as closely as Searle's and Hare's analyses do. Bennett makes the
imperative operator govern a sentence already cast in propositional
form: 'the supper is prepared' is the basic propositional form; this
is turned into an imperative by adding an imperatival operator
and a designator indicating the agent who is to bring it about that
the supper is prepared. Thus in his formulation 'd-Imps-s' is the
imperative formed on the basic statement 's', where 'd' is the
person-designator and 'Imp' is the imperative operator. By
contrast, Searle does not make the statement of fact primary. He

isolates an absolutely unasserted sentence content and makes the proposition and the imperative co-ordinate to each other as ways of asserting that content. Thus:[248]

Diagram A

Hare's version would have roughly the structure of Searle's.[249]

It would be implausible to claim that the Stoic version of this fundamental idea was worked out with anything like the logical sophistication used in the twentieth century. We do not find the terminology which might correspond to the idea of assertoric mode operators,[250] although the discussion of predicates and imperatives in the *Logical Investigations* of Chrysippus encourages me to suspect that elsewhere in his now lost logical works he may have employed such terminology. The strongest claim which can be supported by the evidence we have is that the parallelism of propositions and imperatives and the fact that both predicates and presentations were considered in their different ways to be common to propositions and imperatives both suggest that the fundamental idea must have been in the minds of the logicians of the Stoa. The weakest claim we should make is that the Stoic theory of the relationships among presentations, predicates, propositions, and imperatives is a valuable and interesting anticipation of more sophisticated theories.

Within the framework of this general similarity to speech act theories like those of Hare and Searle, several differences may be pointed out. Most important, what corresponds to the unasserted sentence content in the Stoic theory is not of the same order as the various complete *lekta*. For what is common to the imperative and the proposition are a certain presentation, which is a material and representational modification of the mind, and the predicate, which is not a grammatically complete entity as Searle's unasserted 'R-P' is. (By grammatically complete I mean having a subject and predicate designator.) It does not seem to be the case that the Stoics had the idea of a grammatically complete but unasserted (in this sense) *lekton*.[251] Presentations are the occasion of two parallel complete *lekta*; and a predicate is asserted differently in the two parallel complete *lekta*. But for the analogy to a speech act theory like Hare's or Searle's to be complete, it would have to be the case that the Stoics isolated a subject-predicate complex from its mode of assertion. And they appear not to have done this.[252]

iv   Since the action is caused by the assent which the agent gives to a definite hormetic proposition, the Stoics had the logical machinery in hand to reason about actions. One of the persistent questions of action theory is how things we do, actions, can be related to thoughts, sentences, and the other more or less mental entities used to describe and talk about the things we do. Deliberation presupposes some means of getting proper linguistic designations of actions into our calculations. Indeed, this is the way Hare and Kenny use the propositions which the imperatival theory of the will entitled them to postulate in considering how deliberation can influence actions.[253]

The Stoics, on this theory, had the same right to deal with actions in words and argument; for they had a means of tying action unambiguously to proper linguistic descriptions of them. In the Stoics' case, of course, they did not need this logical machinery to deal with the problem of deliberation in its relationship to action. They wanted to be able to say that an agent is responsible because he realized and accepted what he was doing. And to say this about an animal which is essentially a language-using animal, they had to have some way of representing to the mind of the agent a clear and correct statement of what he was doing. When we turn in the consideration of ethical applications of the theory of action to the question of how actions are to be consistent with each other and with the will of god, this logical machinery of the Stoic analysis of action will be put to use once more.

v   It is not uncommon to suppose that intentional actions differ from non-intentional but purposive actions because in intentional actions the agent can or does state to himself what it is that he is going to do. The hormetic proposition clearly fulfils this function; if one wants to know what someone's intentions are, one simply checks to see what hormetic propositions receive assent. If there is a quarrel about what an agent was intending to do, the dispute is in principle soluble. Did Dion *intend* to wound Theon when he threw the javelin across the playing field? We need only ask what proposition he assented to in performing that action.[254] (If he did not intend to wound him, it does not follow that he will go unpunished. Non-intentional, negligent actions can still be punished, but perhaps they will be evaluated differently from intentional actions.) Since these acts of assent to hormetic propositions are private mental acts, this method of stating in principle what someone's intentions are is not necessarily of any practical use. But it is a merit of the Stoic theory that, like Aristotle's and unlike Epicurus', it could find a theoretical place for the stateability of intentions.

On this theory, only a rational animal, that is an adult human or a god, has intentions. Action will be purposive in other cases, of course. It is possible for us language users to put the purpose and upshot of an animal's action into words; but this is different from the case of rational agents who can in principle state their actions to themselves explicitly and, according to the Stoics, do so implicitly every time they act.

On this theory, intentions are always followed by actions unless external obstacles intervene. It is never possible for a man to be sure that his intentions will succeed. Since, however, we would not hold a man responsible for such hindrances to his actions, it follows that intentions are the correct locus of moral evaluation. This would not be a reasonable procedure if assent to a hormetic proposition were to fail to produce an action because of anything but an external cause. If there were some other psychic force which could check and oppose our assent, then we would not want to evaluate a man's moral character solely with reference to his assent; if there is something anti-rational in man, it is surely relevant to the moral evaluation of the whole man. Plato and Aristotle, who believed that there is such a force in the human soul, certainly thought that it was relevant. That the Stoics speak so frequently of evaluating a man's moral status by reference to his assents is explicable on the current reconstruction of the relationship between assent, which is in some sense an intention, and action.[255]

Perhaps a clarification is in order. It does not follow that 'assent' or 'impulse' should be identified with intention or will in general or with those items in any other system. My claim is that the Stoic analysis can do a great deal of the work which systems which use these terms do, and that this partial adequacy is a merit from the perspective of current theories of the will. As Long says,[256] there is in Stoicism no traditional Kantian or existentialist 'will' as a distinct power and faculty in the human soul; and we ought to feel uncomfortable with attempts to identify anticipations of such notions in the Stoic theory.[257] Still, in the same sense in which Kenny[258] claims that it is correct to say that Aristotle has a 'theory of the will', the Stoics may be said to have a theory of will or intention. They have their own analysis of the phenomena to which the terms will and intention are usually applied. But the Stoic system is an independent analysis of those phenomena and must be dealt with in its own terms and not as an adumbration of other systems.

It is likely that in the Stoic theory the cause of an action is not logically independent of the action itself. For the action is properly described in terms of the proposition to which assent is given. This is an unpopular way to regard the relation of cause to effect,[259] and it leaves the Stoics open to some criticisms about the meaningfulness of these causes. But whether these criticisms are valid or not, it is tolerably clear that the Stoa did leave itself open to them. This is not the place for a general discussion of causes in Stoicism, but one of the principal texts on the topic informs us that Zeno (and by implication Chrysippus too) recognized some causes which are connected to their effects very closely indeed from a logical point of view.[260] 'A cause is something because of which (di' ho) something happens [or comes into being], for example "being prudent" happens because of prudence and "living" happens because of soul and "being temperate" happens because of temperance.'[261] But I do not think that the Stoics would have thought these statements of causality to be empty, any more than they would have thought that it is meaningless to say that assent to the proposition 'It is fitting for me to run' causes the running. The state of the soul, prudence, and the assent are both states or movements of a material soul. As such they are in principle describable independently of their effects. The material description of the state of the soul or of the movement in it is independent of 'being prudent' or of 'running'. The fact that they were not able to produce these material accounts of psychological states is, of course, an embarrassment; but it is an embarrassment to which many psychological materialists are liable.

One can clearly perform the same bodily actions as a result of assent to different propositions. 'Climbing the ladder', 'fetching the trunk from the attic', and 'helping mother with the spring cleaning' are all possible and sometimes appropriate descriptions of the same act. In describing an action a variety of factors and purposes must be taken into account,[262] and we are familiar with the idea that the same action can be intended under several different descriptions. Can the Stoic theory handle this insight? If it cannot be supposed that the Stoics themselves at least thought that it could, then there will be serious problems in the application of the analysis of action to ethics; for their ethics, like almost any other, will require the notion of doing an act under a certain description.

It is easy to see in principle how the Stoic theory could handle this requirement. The propositions to which assent is given may be varied to produce different descriptions of the same act. I can assent to the propositions that I should climb the ladder, that I should fetch the trunk, or that I should help mother. But the difficulty with this application is just as easy to see. Propositions are tied to presentations. It is possible to believe, as so many empiricists have, that there is a representatonal image to correspond with even the most abstract and complex facts or states of affairs and the Stoics are committed to some such belief on other grounds. So this is not an objection to attributing the theory to the Stoa; it it just a weakness of the Stoic theory. More worrisome is their tendency to claim that we as agents cannot control our presentations, that they are simply given to us by the environment.

This too is, I believe, a serious problem in the Stoic theory, but not a reason to deny that the Stoics believed that they could account for human behaviour and the moral evaluaton of it within the framework of their theory. They were, after all, determinists and psychological materialists (who also recognized the need for immaterial entities in the description of mental life). It would perhaps be unrealistic to expect a detailed and convincing account of how we can choose to see an action under one description or another, even if their general theory requires them to be able to produce such an account. One may suppose them thinking that one's character, which is a material state of the material soul, determines which presentations will come to mind in which circumstances. A good man will, on hearing the command to fetch the trunk, form the mental presentation which corresponds to helping his mother by getting the trunk; a bad man will no doubt form the presentation of laboriously climbing the ladder and dragging the trunk down.

But it remains true that if the Stoics want to apply the psychology of action in any detail to mental life as most people experience it, they will have to solve the problem of explaining thought in materialist and empiricist terms, within the framework of a deterministic system.[263] That such a task was beyond their powers is certain. That they supposed they could carry it out is almost equally sure. When discussing Stoic ethics and dealing with the application of the theory of presentations, propositions, and assent to rational action, we shall, I suggest, have to do as the Stoics did: suppose that these problems are soluble and get on with the business in hand. For the Stoics this is describing and prescribing human action; for us, reconstructing what they had to say. Impulse and assent are so frequently used in ethics that we must suppose that the Stoics proceeded as I suggest or attribute to them a fundamental and conscious incoherence in their system. It is more faithful to the picture of the early Stoics which emerges from our fragments and other sources to suppose that they were misled by the boundless optimism with which they approached some of the thorniest philosophical problems of their own or any other day, than that they *consciously* propounded a visibly incoherent doctrine. In part II, I shall suppose that the Stoics felt justified in holding that actions could be performed under different and complex descriptions and that their determinism did not stop them from giving descriptions of mental behaviour which seem to presuppose an ability to select and manipulate presentations at will. That this procedure on the part of the Stoics is not justified should not stop us from believing that they followed it.

vi   What counts as an action on this theory? That is, what is the scope or range of phenomena which the theory is meant to account for? In the case of human action, this will be equivalent to the question, 'What is a man responsible for?' What a human action is will determine what a man is accountable for, since on the Stoic theory rational action, assented action, human action, and responsible action emerge as coextensive terms.[264]

Overt bodily motions of the sort which are potentially under conscious control are the most obvious instances of actions: walking is one of the favourite examples of both the Stoics and their predecessors.[265] As I have already suggested, complex actions falling under various descriptions also count as actions if assent is given under those descriptions. A predicate can in theory be of almost any degree of complexity or generality; and since predicates are common to hormetic propositions and to commands, this should give actions the same flexibility.

In general, anything caused by an impulse will be an action. Thus refraining will sometimes count as an action.[266] The question about what constitutes an action becomes a question about what an impulse can cause. In addition to the relatively obvious sorts of actions so far considered, we shall see that certain internal and 'emotional' responses to external events count as actions.[267] The details and significance of this will be considered in Chapter 5 on 'passions' or *pathê* and on *eupatheiai*. But at this point two observations may be made which support the claim that passions and affective reactions come under the theory of action. First, a passion is defined as a kind of impulse; this is an explicit and clear definition, frequently repeated in our sources. Moreover, the prolonged ancient controversy between orthodox Stoics and their critics about the relation of passions to judgements reveals that the early and orthodox Stoics made the same sweeping claim about the relation of passion and assent as they did about impulse and assent in general. They were so serious about their identification of passion and impulse that they denied, as we have seen, that an animal not endowed with the mature power of reason could have passions in the proper sense of the word.

Second, we expect that if a passion is a kind of impulse there will be an intentional object of it which is the internal and emotional analogue of overt action. We are told by our sources and in one instance in Chrysippus' own words what these internal actions are. They are certain contractions and expansions of the *pneuma* of the soul, the mind in particular. Chrysippus[268] distinguished in technical terms between the contraction of the soul and 'the impulse to the contraction'.

The importance of the reduction of emotional responses to events to the status of internal actions cannot be overemphasized. Nor can the seriousness with which the early Stoics made this move. Consequently we are justified, I would argue, in using the correspondence of a report, which is of dubious status on independent grounds, with the psychology of action as a criterion for its reliability as a report of early and orthodox Stoic doctrine. In some texts whose reliability as reports of Chrysippean Stoicism is doubtful in any case, we read of impulses in adult human beings which take place without assent or before assent. The details of the discussion must be deferred to their appropriate place, but in a consideration of the range of the theory of action we can say as a general principle that any action or response to the environment, whether overt or internal, is a human, rational, responsible action if and only if it follows on assent, at least an implicit assent. Since the mind, according to the early Stoics, functions at all times as a whole and is in all respects dominated by reason, we would have to regard unassented responses to the events and circumstances of the external world as not the soul's doing and so not the man's doing at all. This is a very strong and difficult position; but Chrysippus held it. We shall not be surprised to find indications that some later Stoics declined to maintain this view.

One final point about the scope of the theory should be mentioned. The analytic framework which constitutes the psychology of action is not used in the description or explanation of cognitive states or events.[269] It is true that because of the role of assent in the theory of action, certain judgements of fact are entailed by any action one might make. This is the realization which enabled the early Stoics to concoct and use the argument from *apraxia* against the Academic sceptics. But it is quite a different thing to use the theory of action which centres on the concept of impulse in the analysis or description of an 'act' of perception or cognition. It has sometimes been held, implicitly and explicitly,[270] that the Stoics did so. But the evidence which leads to this conclusion is very weak and easily impugned; and the cumulative weight of virtually everything else we know about the theory of action is so great in the other direction that we may with some confidence believe that the theory of impulse in the early Stoa was a theory of action and of action only.[271]

PART II

Chapter 4

Applications to Ethics

The psychology of action is an integral part of the ethical doctrines of the old Stoa. Their conception of what it is for a human being to act is interwoven with their views about what is right and wrong, how to live as a rational man in a providentially ordered world, and the practical significance of being a part of the universal Reason which permeates and governs the world. Much of their ethics is, of course, not built directly on the theory of action. In considering applications of the theory of action we shall see at least two kinds of relationship between it and ethics: in cases of mere compatibility between the psychology of action and ethics the most we can do is to show that some doctrines can be expressed in terms of the theory, making use of its distinctions and terminology; in other cases, such as the doctrine of passions and the Stoic position on the traditional problem of *akrasia* or weak will, it can be argued that the theory of action guided and controlled the answers which the older Stoics gave to important ethical questions.

(a) Consistency

Let us look first at a case of compatibility with a central ethical doctrine. The goal of life according to the Stoics is described in a variety of ways, but the dominant formulation involves the concept of consistency (*homologia*). 'A smooth flow of life' and 'living consistently' are descriptions of what the ideal life should be, and were current from the time of Zeno on.

If we are to believe the report of Arius Didymus, Zeno himself did not add the specification 'consistently with nature' to the formula for the goal of life, 'living consistently'.[1] That, we are told here, is the work of his followers. But it is a mistake to think that Zeno differed substantially from his orthodox successors on this subject.[2] For one thing, Zeno is also credited with the fuller formulation by Diogenes Laertius[3] who says that he gave this definition of the goal of life in his book *On Human Nature* (which was also entitled *On Impulse*). Moreover, there are abundant indications that later Stoics understood the two formulations as being complementary, if not as meaning the same thing. According to Arius Didymus[4] the disharmony of the fool is a disharmony both with himself and with god. Seneca, who frequently emphasizes the need for consistency with oneself,[5] also says that the way to achieve this is to be correct in one's actions and desires (which means that they should agree with Nature or god's will). 'If you wish to want the same thing always, you must want *vera*,[6] i.e. what is true and right. 'No one can always be pleased by the same thing unless it is by what is right.'[7] Chrysippus is making essentially the same point when he explicates the goal of life as 'living according to our own nature and that of the Universe',[8] which he then identifies with the smooth flow of life.

And a convergence of self-consistency and consistency with the Nature of the Universe is exactly what we would expect. For in a rational and therefore consistent Universe, consistency with one's own life will be a necessary condition for consistency with the whole of which one is a part. This consistency with oneself will also be a corollary of consistency with Nature as a whole. But the Stoics would also have claimed that in their deterministic but providential world, if one failed to achieve harmony with nature, sooner or later one would fall out of harmony with oneself. Only if one's plans and actions are in accord with all-mastering fate will one be safe from defeat, disappointment, and regret. And since man has fundamental and inborn inclinations to live the moral life, any falling away from the moral commands laid down by Zeus will be by the same token a repudiation of one's own true self and deepest nature. Thus to live consistently with oneself is possible if and only if one lives consistently with Nature as a whole.

A life is made up of actions. How can the Stoics talk about the consistency of actions, either with each other or with Nature? Here we can see a useful application of the psychology of action. For each action is accompanied by an imperative sentence and a proposition, connected in such a way that when the imperative is obeyed the corresponding proposition is assented to by the agent. Thus there is a truth-valuable entity associated with each action, which serves to identify the action. (A hormetic proposition of the form 'it is fitting that I . . .' is truth-valuable since the Stoics believed that such ethical judgements were matters of fact, the criterion of truth being accordance with Right Reason, i.e. Zeus.) The imperatives and the actions themselves are not truth-valuable; but since each action is defined by a proposition, it makes excellent logical sense to speak of the consistency of one action with another and with Nature. The consistency of the actions which make up life is the mutual compatibility of the principles and propositions which correspond to the actions and imperatives.

Since there is one fully determined and providentially ordered plan for the world and all the men in it, which is the will of Zeus[9] and never changes,[10] only one set of mutually consistent principles can define for an agent a set of mutually consistent actions. Odd as it may sound, this set of principles must have been what the Stoics meant by the virtue of prudence (*phronêsis*). For it is defined as an 'art concerned with life'[11] and an art is a set of assented propositions or *katalêpseis*.[12] Prudence is also a virtue; and virtue is described in various ways as a kind of knowledge[13] and as something concerned with the governance and consistency of one's entire life.[14] 'Life in accordance with virtue' is another description of the goal of life, and if virtue is a set of firmly held beliefs there must be some way of translating those beliefs into the actions which actually make up the life a man lives. The psychology of action provides the logical mechanism to bring such beliefs to bear on action. In fact, it makes the Stoic identification of virtue with a certain sort of knowledge something more than a stubborn adherence to Socratic slogans in the face of Aristotle's brilliant dispositional analysis of virtue; it makes this identification appear as a reasonable consequence of their analysis of action.

The need to live by one set of principles was incorporated by Zeno into his account of the goal of life, if 'by a single set of principles' is not an over-translation of the phrase *kath' hena logon*.[15] The only set of principles which could guide a man unerringly through life is the set of principles recognized as the Law of Nature, the Common Law, the will of Zeus, or Right Reason.[16] For the Law of Nature is a set of commands, concerned with what to do and what not to do. Thus the commands of the Law of Nature are the same in content as the Right Reason and the prudence which is the virtue by which a man is supposed to steer his life.[17] The imperatival law of Nature may be identified with a set of principles, propositional in form. Just as in a man the ethical propositions correspond exactly to imperatives, so in the Universe.

If the parallelism which holds between propositions and imperatives in men is part of an analysis of impulse, should it surprise us if the same is true on the divine level? The imperatives of the Law of Nature are also linked to impulses; for the Law is also the will of Nature[18] or of Zeus who is the arranger of the Universe.[19] And this will (*boulêsis*) is, as we shall see,[20] a kind of impulse. Cicero too refers to impulses of god which are like those in men.[21] These divine impulses are an imperatival expression of what god wants men to do and what he wants to happen in nature. That his will is among other things a command to men is a strange feature of this system, but is readily explained by the Stoic belief that men are parts of the Universal *logos* which governs and rules the world.

The logical machinery of the psychology of action thus gives a degree of precision to a set of beliefs about the relation of man and god, about the proper role for man in the world, about the foundation of human happiness. I doubt that the Stoics who elaborated this theory in such detail thought that the application of the psychology of action had probative force. They expressed their ethical beliefs in this form but did not ground them on the analysis of action. Still, it is appealing to think of the old Stoic zeal for logical precision and technical analysis being applied in such depth.

This reconstruction also helps our understanding of the old Stoa in another way. It is a good deal easier to understand now why Plutarch cites important fragments of the psychology of action from a work by Chrysippus bearing the title *On Law*.[22] *On Law* must have been a work setting out in detail the relation of man to the will of Zeus, an explication of how a man can best live his life, how he can achieve the goal of life, in the providentially determined world. In doing this he seems to have developed a theory of the similarity of the mind of man and of god, and of the consequent need of a man to assimilate his will to that of god.[23] A man's correct actions (*katorthômata*) are the result of his impulses, obedience to commands to himself which are at the same time the commands of the Law of Nature, the will of Zeus. Man's job in this world is to obey the commands of Nature which tell him what to do and what not to do, according to a text in Arius Didymus.[24] This means *doing* certain things, performing certain *praxeis*, each one adding something to the coherent structure of the happy life, according to the blueprint laid up in the mind of Zeus.

Man, Cicero said,[25] is born for contemplating the world and imitating it. This statement, which is the Stoic pantheistic version of the injunction to assimilate oneself to god, now takes on a richer and more definite meaning. By contemplating Nature, the world, one learns the one set of true principles which man is to live by; life in accordance with this will also be life in consistency with oneself. It is by internalizing the correct set of mutually consistent propositions that man, the rational animal, perfects his reason and makes it the equal of god's—literally, for it will be made up of the same set of statements and commands.

'Only the wise man is free.' What can the sage's freedom be?[26] It cannot be an indeterminacy in his response to stimuli from the environment, such as one may be able to find in the deliberation which is so important to Alexander and to Aristotle.[27] For according to the Stoics, all human actions are the result of assent, and deliberation has no place in the determination of an action. One may at best pause to evaluate the stimulus to action by comparing it to the standard of Right Reason[28] before giving or refusing assent.

If a man knows what Right Reason prescribes in a particular situation, he will not be in doubt about what to do. The wise man never needs to 'deliberate' nor even to make that pause for reflection about whether or not he should assent.[29] He has wholly assimilated Right Reason and when faced with one of the binary choices whether or not to assent which make up his life he responds immediately on the basis of his firm moral disposition. As Long says of the Stoic sage, the good '"completely" determines his choice'.[30]

Further, why is the wise man the *only* free man? It would be tempting to suppose that the unwise man is more free—for he does not know the good. The unwise, at least, could hesitate about what is right or wrong before acting; they could act according to different principles at different times; and since in any particular situation in a deterministic world there is only one right action but (in so far as there is any possibility) many wrong ones, those who act wrongly might be supposed to have a choice among the many possible ways of being out of harmony with nature. Such a 'freedom' to be wrong in one's own way would be unattractive. Even this, however, would not be genuine freedom; for the outcome of any situation is still always determined by the character of the agent at the time and could be predicted by an omniscient observer, even if not by the agent's fellow men.[31] The unwise can only appear to be free.

The wise man does not even have the ability to make a significant change in his moral character. For he cannot vary the kind or degree of his virtue and cannot cease to be virtuous except under the most unusual and morally irrelevant circumstances. According to Chrysippus, the sage can lose his virtue through madness, drunkenness (*methê*) or the effect of disease or strong drugs and poisons.[32] But as Simplicius says (SVF 2.238), he thought that virtue could only be lost when the rational powers of the soul were taken away. Only by losing his entire moral personality could the sage change from his virtuous state.[33] The freedom to cease being wise by becoming non-rational is hardly worthy of the name freedom either.

Seneca speaks for the old Stoa when he says[34] that 'the good man cannot not do what he does; for he would not be good unless he did it' and 'there is a big difference between saying "he cannot not do this" because he is forced and saying "he cannot not want to".' The latter form of necessity binds the sage. As we have seen, it is compatible with moral responsibility and it must be compatible with the 'freedom' of the wise man, such as it is.

But in fact, for the Stoics freedom cannot be based on any contingency or possibility. For these are mere epiphenomena of human ignorance.[35] What will happen will happen and, according to the doctrine of eternal recurrence, will recur again in future world cycles just like the one we live in now. Rather, the freedom of the wise man is a result of his harmony with Nature, his consistency with the will of Zeus.[36] With all contingency banished, this is the only freedom left for a man. The wise man is free because nothing external to himself ever impairs or hinders him. Indeed, it could not, since he has achieved a state in which he is at one with the flow of events in the world.[37]

Seneca also expresses this early Stoic belief in one of his terse epigrams:[38] 'we are born in a kingdom—freedom is to obey god.' The wise man alone is free, because only he knows the commands of god and Right Reason and only his character is such as always to obey them. This is, to be sure, a paradoxical idea of freedom; but it is far from unreasonable from the point of view of a determinist. To avoid fighting against the inevitable and providentially ordered flow of events is the negative freedom of the man whose plans are never frustrated and whose apparent hardships are never unforeseen.[39] Freedom in the indeterministic sense of Alexander or perhaps Aristotle[40] cannot find a place in Stoicism. But the smooth flow of life *is* possible and this is the freedom which the wise man alone enjoys. It is the inevitable result of a complete consistency with himself and with the will of Zeus.

(b) Planning and Purpose

An ethical system which is based on an analysis of action and claims to be comprehensive must be able to take account of and describe various forms of purpose which are more specialized than 'intentional action' without qualification; and it must also be able to deal with questions about long-term planning and the over-all organization and co-ordination of a human life. Some suggestion that the Stoics are under a particular obligation to be clear about this wider application of the idea of intentional action has already emerged from the discussion of consistency with Nature or the will of Zeus. For the will of Zeus is not merely a set of general moral injunctions; it is also identified with fate, the providentially determined sequence of events in each world cycle. It is the job of a rational agent, the collaborator and imitator of the rational and ordered cosmos, to fit himself smoothly into this sequence of events. And to do this requires long-range planning and projection.

Nature's will is, of course, very hard for men to fathom; but since the Stoics were determinists, they believed that this will, which determines the course of events in the world, was in principle knowable. Still, specific skills are needed to acquire as much insight as possible into the plans of this rational world-order.

A. A. Long has argued in two important articles[41] that logical analysis and the study of valid inference were employed by the Stoa in order to help men see what the natural course of events would be and thus to be able to follow it with their own assent. This is a convincing account of the main purpose the Stoics had in view in their study of logic (as well as of physics, the study of how the world works), and one may suspect that Chrysippus would not have immersed himself so deeply in the debate on possibility, necessity, and causation if not for his concern with the problem of responsible action in a deterministic but uncertain world.

It would be pleasant to think that this overarching ethical motivation stimulated the Stoics only to such philosophically interesting and intellectually respectable methods of attempting to read the plan of events in Nature. Unfortunately we must attribute to the same interests the Stoics' commitment to and interest in

astrology,[42] divination, and the other less appealing ancient tech-
niques for determining what the gods have in store for mankind.
But the way in which man gets his understanding of how the world
works is not to the point here. The question which will engage us is,
rather, this. How can this knowledge be put to work in his actions?
How, in terms of the analysis of action and in terms of the ideal of
consistency, can a man undertake the more complex and long-
range actions which are required if a rational agent is to fit himself
smoothly and intelligently into the determined flow of events?

The answer to this sort of question cannot be given in the detail
we should prefer to have, but in this section it will be shown that at
least an outline of the old Stoic answer can be elicited from our
sources and that this answer turned on the concept of impulse.
'Impulse with reservation' was an essential concept in the Stoic discussion of the ethical problem of rational action in a determined
world; and the fact that their solution of the problem centred on
impulse is a confirmation of the vital role which the technical analysis of action played in old Stoic ethics.

'Impulse with reservation' is not the only special type of impulse
which deals with the more complex and elaborate forms of intention and action which are employed in Stoic ethics. These other
'kinds' of impulse, as our sources call them, are set out in an elaborate array; but since our information about virtually all the other
kinds of impulse (and much of that concerning 'reservation') comes
from sources which are more difficult to interpret than most others,
the exposition and interpretation of this material presents unusual
problems. Our principal source for information about the old Stoic
classification of the kinds of impulse is a short discussion in the
doxography of Stoic ethics by Arius Didymus preserved by
Stobaeus.[43] This text contains an incomplete list of kinds of impulse
together with brief descriptive formulae which usually suffice at
least to make clear how these kinds of impulse are related to each
other. The text has been discussed previously, but never with the
aid of a general reconstruction of the Stoic analysis of action and
never with an appreciation of the over-all importance in Stoicism of
a detailed categorization of the types and subtypes of impulse. The
details of my discussion will be found in Appendix 2; here I will give
the general results of that investigation and place the Stoic classification of impulses in its broader context.

Despite the fragmentary character of our information about the

Stoic classification of the kinds of impulse, one fact is apparent. The original version of this classification had a very wide scope. It seems to have been intended as a comprehensive framework into which all forms of human planning and purpose could be placed. That impulse is the item in the analysis of rational action which was chosen for this classificatory role confirms once again its central importance and associates it with the concept of 'intention', in a very broad understanding of that term. Another general characteristic of the Stoic categorization is less certainly known but important for our historical judgement about the Stoics' place in the ancient tradition of discussion of rational action and planning. Many of the technical terms used to designate kinds of impulse are drawn from Aristotelian terminology, but given radically new meanings within the framework of the Stoic analysis of action.[44] This suggests that the Stoics intended to offer a system for talking about rational action and intention which would displace that provided by the Aristotelian tradition. Certainly, their co-option of Aristotelian terminology was not the result of a lack of imagination in coining new technical terms; Zeno and his followers showed sufficient ingenuity in that department to dispel any such suggestion. A similar co-option of traditional terminology may also be seen in the case of *pathos*, which is put to work expressing fundamentally new ideas in the Stoic system, as we shall see.

The first distinction among kinds of impulse made in Stobaeus is between rational and irrational impulses. This is the distinction between the impulses of adult humans and those of non-rational animals which was the subject of much of the discussion of the preceding chapter. A further distinction is between impulses which cause an action in a narrower sense and those which cause either avoidance behaviour or the abstention from action. The latter kind of impulse has a distinctive name, *aphormê*, and it too is distinguished into rational and irrational forms. A special sense of the word *hormê* is also noted; the hormetic disposition (*hexis hormêtikê*) which has been discussed already is also referrred to as an 'impulse' by the Stoics.

The main type of impulse is rational impulse, which is also called 'practical impulse'. This kind of impulse, we have seen, is the one that matters most for ethics. For it is the general designation for all the impulses of rational animals, which are the proper cause of responsible actions. In the text of Stobaeus under consideration we are told about two main branches of practical impulse. These are designated by the technical terms *orexis* and *orousis* which it is perhaps best not to translate.

Orexis and *orousis* are not necessarily opposed kinds of impulse. For they are defined with reference to distinct differentiae which leave open the possibility that some form of *orexis* might also be an *orousis* and vice versa. But this raises the question of how impulses can be distinguished one from another. The predicates at which various impulses are said to be directed admit of logical classifications: predicates may be of greater or lesser degrees of complication, they may contain some sorts of terms and not others and the verb element in the predicate may be in various voices and tenses. The factor which distinguishes various forms of *orexis*, then, from impulse without qualification is the fact that any *orexis* is in some way an impulse to the acquisition of 'the good'. Any action whose object is the good or what the agent takes to be good will be caused and defined by the form of impulse known as an *orexis*. It is somewhat more speculative to claim that all forms of *orousis* are directed at actions in the future, actions which are to be performed at some time subsequent to the giving of assent to the hormetic proposition. But this is the most plausible interpretation of the evidence available. Thus the various forms of *orousis* would be used to describe what we would call plans and long-range intentions. The morally significant act of assent, then, corresponds to the act of committing oneself to a course of action.

If this is the correct account of *orexis* and *orousis*, it follows that they are not mutually exclusive forms of impulse. For one could easily assent to a hormetic proposition designating a long-range plan to do something which counts as pursuit of the apparent good. The resolution 'I will help my friend with his problems when he returns from abroad because it is the right thing to do', when assented to, would be the sort of impulse which is both an *orexis* and an *orousis*.

The various forms of *orousis* may be understood in contrast to impulses which are directed at predicates in the present tense and cause immediate action. The various forms of *orexis*, on the other hand, must be understood in contrast to those impulses which are not aimed directly at the attainment of what the agent takes to be good. This is a point which can best be understood in the context of technical Stoic doctrines about what is good and what is not. It is true, the Stoics would say, that all ordinary men aim at what they think to be good. But most of the things men suppose to be good are not good in the strict sense of the word which the Stoics reserved for 'what is truly beneficial', that is, 'virtue or that which partakes of virtue'. The more mundanely advantageous things, such as health and wealth, which can in fact be used well or badly, are not genuine goods. But they are worth having most of the time, as even the most ascetic Stoic would have agreed. *Orexis* is that kind of impulse which we have when we pursue things or undertake actions because we think they are good. But the educated man, who knows the difference between true goods and the more mundanely advantageous things, though he is not yet a sage, will still pursue these lesser goods. He will pursue them, however, under a different description than the ordinary man, only because he thinks they are worth having in the weaker sense.

This is the kind of impulse which is to be set in contrast to the various forms of *orexis*. It seems clear that the Stoic term for this kind of impulse is 'selection'.[45] When the early Stoics set down their ethical doctrines in the schematic form which most of our sources preserve for us, the contrast between selection and *orexis* is clearly made. That is only reasonable, for they were writing for those who already had an introduction to Stoic ethics. But the later Stoic Epictetus, whose use of some of these same ethical terms is also of importance in the present context, was speaking to a wider audience. Epictetus' use of the terms *hormê* and *orexis* is usually precise too, but the terms are used differently than by the old Stoa. A short discussion of how his use of these terms differed from that of the old Stoa will serve to show how his divergent usage is compatible with his substantial orthodoxy on important points of ethics and will help to introduce the important type of impulse which still remains to be discussed, impulse 'with reservation'.

In old Stoic usage *orexis* is a kind of impulse; the latter is the more general term and *orexis* is logically subordinate to it. But in Epictetus' system the terms *orexis* and impulse are apparently co-ordinate with each other. They are in fact used to distinguish and characterize the first two of the three topics of his systematic scheme of ethical teaching.[46] It has often been noted that Epictetus' use of these terms is significantly different from that of the old Stoa; and Bonhoeffer tries to minimize the significance of the difference in terminology.[47] But his discussion is somewhat unsatisfactory on this point, and the essential accuracy of his intuition is undercut by lapses into special pleading. There is no virtue in an attempt such as Bonhoeffer's to minimize the actual difference in usage. But how much should the terminological variation be expected to matter anyway?

The fact that Epictetus made significant changes in the terminology for the kinds of impulse does not prove that there are any substantial differences in ethical approach or doctrine. It is more worth while to consider what Epictetus does with his reformed terminology, to examine his concept of *orexis* and how he puts it to work, and thus to see whether he has made any fundamental changes in the content of Stoic teaching. To anticipate the results of the discussion to follow: the changes he has made are changes in terminology only, and he has made them in order to give new emphasis to a cardinal aspect of his own ethical doctrines which he shared with the old Stoics.

In old Stoic terminology *orexis* is an impulse to the apparent good. Epictetus shares this view.[48] Epictetus also follows the old Stoa in making *ekklisis* or avoidance the proper contrary of *orexis*; as such it is concerned with what is ethically bad. The first division of Epictetus' ethics is said to 'concern *orexis* and *ekklisis*' and is characterized by learning how not to 'desire something and fail to get it' or to 'try to avoid something and yet encounter it'.[49] Thus it is an essential part of *orexis*, whether it is in fact correctly used by an ethically sound agent or not, that it should succeed in achieving its objective. This is what it 'promises' or 'announces'.[50] And if *orexis* is aimed at the good properly conceived it cannot be frustrated, since the good is virtue, a state of one's own soul and something wholly within one's own power—unlike the externals, such as health and wealth, which the uneducated suppose to be 'good'.

Hormê, for Epictetus, is quite different from *orexis*. The second division of his system is that which 'concerns *hormai* and *aphormai* and, in a word, the appropriate' (i.e. *to kathêkon*) and the goal of the second division is to learn how to act 'in an orderly fashion, reasonably, not carelessly'.[51] Two important contrasts with the first division must be noted. The apparent good is nowhere said to be the concern of this division. And nowhere is it said that *hormê* shares with *orexis* the essential characteristic of achieving its objective.

The difference between Epictetus' and the old Stoa's treatment of *orexis* and *hormê* as technical terms may be seen more clearly if we look at the *kathêkonta* (appropriate actions) which are said to be the object of impulse by both Epictetus and the old Stoics.[52] For Epictetus as well as for the old Stoa these appropriate actions include among other things correct behaviour in various social relationships; Epictetus sometimes seems to restrict the term to such behaviour, but the characterization of the purpose of this division quoted above shows that although they are Epictetus' star examples of the sort of thing the second division deals with, its content is not exhausted by them.

Nevertheless, the scope of appropriate action does seem to be narrower for Epictetus than it was for the older Stoics, and this is the important point now. For the old Stoics, morally correct actions, *katorthômata*, are also a kind of *kathêkon*. They are referred to as perfect *kathêkonta*.[53] In so far as impulses are to appropriate actions, some are also to 'the good'. For the old Stoics, *orexis*, an impulse to the good, is one kind of rational impulse to the appropriate.

But Epictetus at no point sets out this relationship between the appropriate and the good, and clearly considers that they are the objects of two distinct and mutually exclusive kinds of impulse. Impulse is directed at the appropriate and *orexis* at the good, and the two are not thought of as overlapping.[54] In some places, such as *Diss.* 3.3.5, he goes so far as to contrast appropriate actions to the good, a view which could not have appeared in the old Stoa. 'Appropriate' is clearly used by Epictetus deliberately in a significantly narrower sense than by the old Stoa. Instead of being the genus of a *katorthôma* it is a co-ordinate species. This is precisely the same sort of change which he introduced into his use of the terms *hormê* and *orexis*.

Two sketches in Diagram B will clearly show the difference between old Stoic usage and that of Epictetus.

The old Stoics may have used their general terms for the more specific form of impulse and its object, selection and things according to nature, when the contrast with *orexis* was not important. In fact, there are signs that it was not at all uncommon for old Stoics to transfer the label for the genus to one of its species when it would not produce misunderstanding.[55] But Epictetus did not leave *hormê* in place as a genus-term. Because he makes such a sharp contrast between *orexis* and *hormê* (and their respective objects) it is difficult for him to use *hormê* as a genus-term. We have by far the greatest

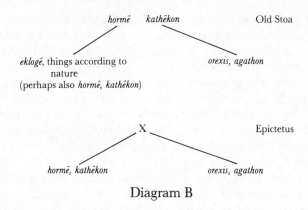

Diagram B

part of his works, in the form set down by his student Arrian, and nowhere do we find a term to stand for the X in this diagram.

The reason for this change in usage by Epictetus can be surmised. We recall the other peculiarity of his discussion of *orexis*, the great emphasis he puts on the determination of *orexis* to succeed in acquiring its object, which stands out in contrast to the absence of this determination in his concept of *hormê*. Like all Stoics, Epictetus analysed ethics in such a way that the good was the exclusive goal of moral endeavour, believing that happiness, the goal of human life, consisted in success in this endeavour.[56] Thus happiness depends on the attainment of the good,[57] and the good is the axis around which the moral life revolves.[58]

Epictetus' rearrangement of technical terms was almost certainly a deliberate change from the old Stoic usage he knew from the orthodox treatises he read and lectured on in his school. For the terms *orexis* and *hormê* are still described as being directed at the same objects as they are in the old Stoa, and the rearrangement of them corresponds with a change in his use of the terms *kathêkon* and good. The effect of this change is to emphasize the special importance of *orexis* and the good in contrast to all other kinds of impulse and all other appropriate actions. This effect must have been his purpose in making the change, and it is easy to guess why he wanted to enhance the emphasis on *orexis* and the good. His was a philosophy of practical moral education. He addressed his lectures to would-be philosophers who came already determined to seek happiness through moral living and philosophy, but were not yet adept in the essentials of Stoic ethics. Therefore he paid particular attention to the distinction between moral actions which his audience would regard as so important that frustration would result in a *pathos*[59] or passion, and moral actions which do not automatically arouse such anxious zeal.

In keeping with this heightened emphasis on the central goal of ethical activity, the pursuit of the good in contrast to merely appropriate actions, Epictetus urged his students to suspend all *orexis*[60] so that eventually their *orexis* might become *eulogos* (reasonable, i.e. correct).[61] Until the would-be philosopher's conception of the good was correct, and he saw that its attainment was wholly in his own power, one dared not unleash his vehement but natural urge to attain the good. The old Stoics also believed that *orexis* was the form of impulse directed at the attainment of the good, but they set out a system for the benefit of those who had already learned what is truly good. Epictetus deemed it safer for his eager but untrained students to suspend all *orexis* until their notion of the good had been corrected. For if their idea of the good were erroneous, it could lead to upset in one's entire life.[62]

For confirmation that this is the reason for Epictetus' change in the technical terms *orexis* and *hormê*, we may turn to a consideration of Epictetus' use of the old Stoic views on impulse 'with reservation'. We know of this special application of the theory of action from the works of Epictetus himself, from Seneca, from a reference in Arius Didymus' summary of Stoic ethics, and most significantly from a fragment of Chrysippus.

'Reservation' (the Greek term is *hupexairesis*) is an important theme in Stoic ethics.[63] It is employed to explain how a rational agent can deal with the situation he is in *vis-à-vis* the providentially ordered and determined cosmos, how he must react to things which are not in his power. It is his duty to adapt himself to this cosmos, to want events to occur as they in fact will. Ideally, a man should never be in the position of wanting something different from the actual course of events, since what happens in the world is the will of Zeus, is the best possible way for things to occur, and since man as a rational agent should assimilate his will to that of the supremely rational agent, who is Zeus. Moreover, if one does try to resist the will of Zeus, one will never succeed. Like the dog tied behind the cart[64] one will be dragged along if one does not follow willingly. But the problem of man is that he is not prescient, he does not know for sure in every case what Zeus has in store for him.[65] It is all well and good that one should try to ascertain the probable course of events, but most of the time even the sage will be acting in uncertainty.

One is to act in a way that is consistent with the will of Zeus and one is also to act amid uncertainty. With the interpretation of consistency already developed, the problem can be formulated more precisely. If one is to act or plan, one does so by assenting to propositions of a certain sort. These propositions must be logically consistent with the propositions which correspond to the will of Zeus, i.e. those which describe the actual course of events in the world. If I act to preserve my own health, I may do so by committing myself to the truth of 'I will be healthy.' But if I am fated nevertheless to fall ill, then the will of Zeus contains the conflicting proposition 'You will not be healthy.' The problem of the rational agent is to act in pursuit of one's reasonable goals in such a way that one does not commit oneself to anything which might be shown by events to be contrary to the plan of Zeus.

Chrysippus faced this dilemma. In a fragment preserved for us by Epictetus[66] he described the attitude which a sensible man will take in just this kind of case. The terminology of impulse 'with reservation' is not used here, but that is clearly what is being talked about and we may use this important fragment to introduce the texts which do talk about reservation in more explicit terms.

For as long as the subsequent events are unclear to me I cling to those things which are better suited for the attainment of natural things [i.e. what is in accordance with nature]. For god himself made me inclined to select them. But if I knew that it is now fated for me to be ill, I would even direct my impulse to that. For the foot too, if it were intelligent, would direct its impulse to being muddied.

If one goes ahead in one's uncertainty about the future, acting in pursuit of one's own health, one may avoid conflict with the will of Zeus if one acts with a tacit reservation: if nothing comes along to interfere, i.e. if it is really fated to turn out so. Thus when Seneca discusses reservation (the Latin term is *exceptio*) he says that the reservation one employs in acting amid uncertainty is the clause, 'if nothing happens to prevent it'.[67] Acting with this reservation, he says, brings it about that the agent is never frustrated, filled with regret, or required to change his mind.

These are the advantages which impulse with reservation is said to confer on the wise man's action in the ethical doxography of Arius Didymus.[68] 'Nothing happens to the sage which is contrary to his *orexis* or his impulse or his purpose [*epibolē*, a kind of *orousis*], since he does all such things with reservation and none of the adversities which befall him comes unexpected.'

An impulse with reservation is one which is directed at a predicate describing an action, like all impulses, but it has an added clause which considerably modifies its nature. Instead of assenting to the proposition 'it is fitting that I should be healthy', one assents instead to 'it is fitting that I should be healthy, unless something comes up to interfere' or 'unless it goes against Zeus' plan'. In this form, the impulse will not contradict the plans of Zeus, nor will it be inconsistent with the set of propositions which describes fate. But in addition to helping us to preserve our consistency with Zeus while acting in the midst of uncertainty, reservation also makes it possible for someone to adapt smoothly to events not in his own power, the unforeseen events of life. Reservation involves keeping in mind that one may be frustrated; thus, like Anaxagoras, who reacted to the news that his son had died by remarking that he always knew that he had fathered a mortal child,[69] one may take the cruellest blows of fate smoothly and without shock.

Seneca also emphasizes this favourable result of acting with reservation. In the treatise *On Tranquillity*[70] he refers to the need to impose a sort of limit on our plans and desires. A man's

safest course is to tempt fortune rarely, always to be mindful of her and never [when action is called for] to put any trust in her promises. Say 'I will set sail unless something intervenes' and 'I will become praetor unless something hinders me' and 'my enterprise will be successful unless something interferes.' This is why we say that nothing happens to a wise man contrary to his expectations. We free him not from the misfortunes but from the blunders of mankind, nor do all these things turn out as he has wished but as he has thought; but his first thought has been that something might obstruct his plans. Then, too, the suffering that comes to the mind from the abandonment of desire must necessarily be much lighter if you have not certainly promised it success. We ought also to make ourselves adaptable, lest we become too fond of the plans we have formed and we should pass readily to the condition to which chance has led us and not dread shifting either purpose or positions, [provided we avoid fickleness]. . . . For obstinacy, from which fortune often wrests some concession, must needs be anxious and unhappy.

Seneca speaks of the fate which a man cannot foresee as chance or fortune; like all Stoics he believed that there is no true contingency in the providentially ordered world. But from the point of view of men, who cannot foresee the future, fate intervenes in our plans in the guise of 'chance', the unknown cause. If one is to live smoothly, that is consistently with oneself and with the will of Zeus, one has to perform all one's actions with an awareness that one may be frustrated and with the appropriate reservation in one's impulse.

These texts do not present the doctrine of reservation in the technical terms of the orthodox psychology of action. But it is easy to see how the notion of acting with a certain mental reservation can be fitted into the framework of the doctrine as we have reconstructed it. Since the action one is committing oneself to do when one assents to a hormetic presentation is already described by a proposition, one may simply add the clause which constitutes the 'reservation' to the proposition. Acting with reservation would be harder to represent in a theory of action which lacked the means at the Stoics' disposal for expressing the relationship between the agent's thoughts and his actions. The analysis of action plays a useful role in the statement of an important ethical doctrine—at least in the early Stoa, for as we have seen Seneca is less interested in the technicalities of the doctrine.

Epictetus is interested in the orthodox analysis of action, at least to the extent of operating within the general framework of the theory. When we consider what he has to say about impulse with reservation (for which he uses terminology essentially the same as that used in the doxography of Arius Didymus and in Marcus Aurelius[71]) we shall see not only that his position on this central doctrine about human action in a deterministic world is consistent with that of the older Stoics, but also that the thesis advanced above about Epictetus' motivation for the change in the terminology of *orexis* and *hormê* is confirmed.

When Epictetus urged his students to suspend all *orexis* he very pointedly did not urge them to suspend all impulse, or even any impulse. Instead, when giving his novices advice in the area of the second division of his ethical system, he draws on the traditional doctrine of impulse with reservation. In section 2 of the *Enchiridion* he says that happiness depends on restricting one's *orexis* and *ekklisis* to those things which are within one's own power, for these things are free of any possible frustration at the hands of external factors (i.e. fate). What is in a man's own power are one's own psychological and intellectual responses and actions, the states and actions of one's *prohairesis* or 'moral personality'. It is in this realm that the Stoics placed the 'good', virtue, the achievement of which was said to be totally in one's own control. But, Epictetus goes on, for the present his students should abolish *orexis* altogether since they are not yet ready to exercise it properly.

For if you should use *orexis* on things which are not in our power, it is inevitable that you will be unfortunate; and you have as yet none of the things which are in our power which it is morally right (*kalon*) for you to use *orexis* on. Rather, use only *hormê* and *aphormê*, but lightly (*kouphôs*)[72] and with reservation and gently.

Later in the *Enchiridion* (48.3) Epictetus says that the man who is making moral progress will 'use a gentle *hormê* with respect to everything'. Similar advice is offered in fragment 27 of Epictetus.

The result of using reservation with one's impulses is an ability to adapt smoothly and without shock or distress to the unforeseen events which fate has in store for us. Thus it is completely appropriate that Epictetus should urge the use of reservation in that area of one's life which inevitably deals with 'externals', things not under the control of the moral agent. To show how this works in practice for Epictetus, let us adapt an example from *Enchiridion* 3.[73] One might try to preserve a piece of pottery intact or to keep one's child or wife alive. But if it turns out to be of no avail and they are lost, one must acknowledge that one's failure is according to nature, part of god's plan for the world and not something at which one should be completely surprised. One must admit that the outcome of such efforts is ultimately beyond one's own power. One must adapt to fate and do it smoothly and without distress. This is made possible by the fact that all along one was acting with the reservation that something might come up to hinder one's plans and efforts.

This reservation ensures that all one's plans are going to 'work out', as Seneca said,[74] because they include a conditional clause allowing for such failures. It is only possible if one has an awareness of how the world works, if one keeps in mind, for example, that children and wives are merely mortal, the sort of things which are subject to illness and death. In the passage we are considering Epictetus says:

With everything which wins your heart, is useful, or of which you are fond, remember to say, beginning with the least important, 'What is its nature?'

If you are fond of a jug, say 'I am fond of a jug', for if it is broken you will not be upset. If you kiss your child or wife, say that you are kissing a human being; for if it dies you will not be upset.

He is not, of course, advocating utter indifference to one's loved ones, any more than Chrysippus (in the fragment considered above) was advocating indifference to one's health. Epictetus is, rather, illustrating the approach to life characterized by reservation and exemplifying how it makes accommodation to fate possible. Similarly, in a passage from the *Discourses* (3.24.84 ff.) Epictetus likens this practice to the Roman habit of having a slave ride in the chariot of a general in the triumphal parade to remind him that he is a mere mortal. We are to remember that fame, like all desirable things, is given by fate and may be taken away by fate at any time. The point is driven home with brutal force (88): 'What harm is there if right while you are kissing your child, you whisper and say "Tomorrow you will die"? ' Anaxagoras, who always kept in mind that he had fathered a mortal child, might as well have been following Epictetus' advice. He certainly illustrates the Stoic's point.

It must be remembered that this readiness for setbacks does not rule out determined efforts and actions to achieve one's proper goals: staying healthy, keeping one's children alive, executing the various plans and actions which make up a life of appropriate actions. But in the uncertainty of a human life, all these actions and plans, which are or depend on forms of impulse, should be carried out with the addition of reservation. In this way one may attain the smooth flow of life which is characterized by consistency with oneself and with the will of Zeus.

But what is truly good is held to be totally within one's own power and free from possible frustration at the hands of fate. Hence one does not expect that 'the good' should be subject to reservation. And indeed it is not. Epictetus tells us[75] that when one does set about the pursuit of what is in one's own power, i.e. the state of one's soul, it should be done *ex hapantos*, with all one's effort, that is without reservation; but what is outside one's power (*to allotrion*) should never be pursued in this way. Achieving virtue is in our power, and it is good in the proper sense of the term. To pursue what is not good as though it were is an error about the nature of the good and can only have disastrous moral consequences.

The old Stoics too urged that the pursuit of the good should be without reservation, when one has a clear conception of what it is. For they described *to haireton* (the truly choiceworthy, a technical designation for 'the good') as that which 'stimulates an unreserved (*autotelês*) impulse'.[76] Epictetus ordinarily tells his students to avoid *orexis*, the pursuit of the good, at least until they have a clear notion of what is in their power and what is not, which is a result of gaining a correct general view of what is truly good. Once they have this proper knowledge of the good, then reservation will not be needed. Until then, he thought it too dangerous for his students to try to pursue the good at all, even with reservation.

At one point[77] we learn that the old Stoics did recommend that *orexis*, the pursuit of the good, should be subject to reservation. This can, however, be easily reconciled with the designation of the 'good' as that which stimulates unreserved impulse and with Epictetus' position. For presumably *orexis* is being used here in the sense of 'pursuit of the apparent good'. As the discussion in Appendix 2 shows, the term is used to cover both the normatively correct form of pursuit of the good and the pursuit of what the pursuer takes to be good without regard to whether his opinion is correct or not. A correct *orexis*, aimed at the good properly conceived, stimulates unreserved impulse. But when there is a possibility that the conception of the good which the agent is working with is incorrect, reservation is called for.

Epictetus would have agreed with this position in its essentials. But once again, his awareness of and sensitivity to the emotional needs of his audience impelled him to recommend for his beginners not a reservation in their pursuit of the good but a temporary suspension of it. Epictetus seems not to have thought it possible for his students to exercise reservation about what they supposed to be good; the older Stoics did. Again, we see Epictetus making changes in the presentation of his practically oriented ethical system in order to mark off the pursuit of the good from the rest of one's ethical activity more sharply than the old Stoics did. But I am confident that he believed correctly that his essential ethical doctrine was compatible with that of the old Stoa. *Orexis*, the pursuit of the good properly understood, should never be subject to reservation. Only the pursuit of those things which are not in one's own power, the 'externals', requires reservation. And it requires reservation in order to make possible the smooth flow of life, the inner tranquillity which comes from consistency with oneself and from a complete avoidance of inconsistency with the will of Zeus.

The good for which *orexis* is the appropriate form of impulse is 'virtue or that which partakes of virtue'. It is a certain way of reacting to the world and acting in it, and as such it is wholly internal and subject to one's own control. Marcus Aurelius makes the distinction between *orexis* and impulse in a broader and more inclusive sense clear in the following passage from his *Meditations*.[78] It shows how long Stoics went on casting their ethical pronouncements in the terminology of the analysis of *hormê* and action developed by the old Stoa. It is a fitting conclusion for this discussion.

But if someone uses force and opposes [sc. your actions], change over to being content and not distressed and use the obstacle for another virtue. And remember that your impulse was with reservation, that you did not have *orexis* for the impossible. For what then? For some impulse of the sort which you had. And this you did achieve.

Chapter 5

The Passions

(a) Passions and the Theory of Action

After looking at some of the less obvious, but nevertheless important, ways in which the old Stoics applied their psychology of action to ethics, we turn now to a discussion of the application of the theory which is particularly prominent in our sources. The orthodox Stoic doctrine of *pathê* is one of those areas where we may see the psychology of action determining important aspects of ethical doctrine.

We must begin with a few clarifications. *Pathos*, the word which I translate as 'passion', is a term of art for the Stoics. In earlier philosophy the word *pathos* is used more widely, even within the area of moral psychology. For Aristotle[1] it covers a set of phenomena at least as large as that designated by 'emotion' in English, although even there it is clear that 'emotion' is not always the way we should choose to translate *pathos*. Among the other changes the Stoics made in their use of the word, they treated *pathê* as wrong by definition. Thus the word 'emotion' will be a very misleading translation for the term in its Stoic uses. 'Passion' is perhaps only slightly better, but at least it has the advantage of suggesting that every *pathos* is wrong. No translation of the term is adequate, for *pathos* is a technical term whose meaning is determined by the theory in which it functions. So 'passion' must be understood in this discussion as a mere substitute, just as 'impulse' is for *hormê*.

Cicero too had difficulties in choosing a term to use in place of the Greek *pathos* in its technical Stoic sense. This was inevitable, but unfortunately Cicero's discussion of the appropriate rendering of the term reveals that he was the victim of a misunderstanding which he need not have fallen into and which we must still be careful to avoid. He discusses the term at length twice,[2] and each time his position is the same. In the *Tusculans* he says of the passions, grief, fear, pleasure, and anger, that

these are the sort of thing which the Greeks call *pathê*. I could call them 'diseases' (*morbi*), and that would be a word for word translation. But that would not not square with our [i.e. Latin] usage. For 'to pity', 'to envy', 'to exult' and 'to rejoice' are all called 'diseases' by the Greeks, motions of the mind not obedient to reason; but I think that we would best term these same motions of the excited mind 'disturbances' (*perturbationes*), but to call them diseases would be somewhat unusual. Or do you disagree?

His respondent of course agrees with Cicero on the question of translation. While we may sympathize with Cicero's difficulty, it is impossible to avoid the judgement that he does not have a firm grasp of the nuances of Greek when he claims that 'disease' would be a literal translation for *pathos*. For that is not a normal sense of the word.[3] The Greek for 'disease' is *nosos*. Where Cicero seems to have gone wrong is in confusing the state of the soul which produces *pathê* with the *pathos* itself. For Chrysippus and other Stoics did compare the weakness of character lying at the root of moral errors with a bodily disease.[4] Of course, the habit of talking about the weaknesses of the soul's moral disposition by means of an analogy with the body's illnesses goes back to least to Plato's *Republic*.[5] But as it is applied to the Stoic analysis of *pathos* the comparison has particular interest.

We have seen that a *hormê* is usually defined as a change or motion (*kinêsis*) in the soul, and that this change is determined by a certain disposition (*hexis*). The *hexis hormêtikê* is part of the psychological make-up of any animal, and it appears from *Ecl.* 2.87 that the Stoics would sometimes also refer to this *hexis* as *hormê* without qualification. It is obviously important to make the same distinction when we consider the special kind of *hormai* which constitute *pathê*.[6] And indeed, most definitions of *pathos* which do not define it as a special kind of impulse define it instead as a particular sort of *kinêsis* in the soul. It is clear from the accounts which we have of *nosos, nosêma*, and the related terms *euemptôsia* and *arrostêma* that these are dispositions to act or react in a certain way. That is to say, the illnesses of the soul are dispositions (*hexeis*) which correspond to the passions; and the passions strictly speaking are changes, motions, or events in the soul.

What Cicero has done, then, in saying that *pathos* would most accurately be rendered as *morbus* in Latin, is to confuse the disposition with the activity or event which it governs. We should be careful not to do the same thing.[7]

The most important guide we have to the interpretation of the doctrine of passions is also the simplest. Passions are defined as impulses of a certain sort, where impulse must be taken in the sense of the motion in the soul rather than the disposition corresponding to such a motion. If we are to take these definitions seriously, we must conclude that the doctrine of passions is a subset of the general psychology of action. Before turning to the detailed discussion of the psychology of passions, it will be useful to consider some of the ways in which the old Stoic decision to treat passions within the framework of the general psychology of action shapes and limits their doctrine.

Passions are impulses of a certain sort, but we may be more specific. Recall the cardinal importance for the old Stoics of the distinction between rational and non-rational impulse. Only rational impulses are the result of assent, strictly speaking, and more important, only rational impulses are subject to moral evaluation. Only the impulses and actions of a rational agent are in the agent's power and 'responsible' and all the actions of a rational agent are responsible. There is nothing such an agent can be said to *do* for which he cannot be held responsible.

Passions, as a morally wrong kind of impulse, are a kind of rational impulse. We have seen how the Stoics concluded from this that neither children under the age of reason nor irrational animals could have passions. Critics of Stoicism, and Galen stands out in this connection,[8] have often been unable to understand this claim and this can only be because they fail to appreciate the central importance and dominant theoretical role of the problem of responsibility. It may well seem ridiculous to deny that children and animals have *pathê* and then to say that after all they do have something similar to *pathê*, quasi-passions which look similar to the observing eye.[9] But unlike Posidonius the older Stoics were not investigating the phenomena of moral psychology with a keen interest in accurate causal explanation;[10] nor, of course, like so many of their ancient critics including Galen, were they piously defending the moral psychology of Plato or Aristotle. The orthodox denial of *pathê* to children and animals only makes sense as a corollary of their decision to analyse the passions within the framework of their general psychology of action.

The decision to treat passions as a part of the theory of rational impulse had other results which were controversial in antiquity. It is clear from what we have said about the role of assent in the analysis of rational action that the much criticized claim that passions are judgements (*doxai*[11] or *kriseis*) or the result of judge ments is nothing more than a natural consequence of the basic decision about how the passions are to be analysed. It is not only that the older Stoics considered the wide range of phenomena which could be grouped under the heading 'emotional' or 'affec-tive' and realized how important cognitive considerations must be in any adequate account of them—although that was no doubt a part of Zeno's motivation.[12] For if that were the only reason for emphasizing the role of judgements in the analysis of *pathê* we would not expect the sweeping claim that all *pathê* are the result of judgements and the even more startling claim that *pathê* can be identified with judgements of a certain kind. But these are among the features of an analysis of *pathê* which we might expect if the key factor were the decision to treat them as a part of the general theory of rational action.

Passions are by definition wrong and vicious, and the need to give an account of wrong actions and reactions as such lies behind the Stoic theory of passions. But as Cicero tells us,[13] they were also concerned when formulating their definitions of passion to make the point not only that all passions are wrong but that all passions are 'in our power' (*in nostra potestate*, i.e. *eph' hêmin*). We recognize here too a natural result of the general theory of rational action. In many ways the features of the doctrine of passions which are so baffling if it is seen as an independent attempt to give a reasoned description of emotional behaviour seem quite unsurprising when we realize that the principal motivation of the old Stoic doctrine of *pathê* was in fact quite different.

There is a traditional puzzle about the old Stoic doctrine of *pathos* which disappears when it is seen in the framework of the analysis of rational impulse. Chrysippus is supposed to have identified the passion, i.e. the incorrect impulse, and the judge-ment, while we are told that Zeno had taken a somewhat different position in holding that the *pathos* was a result or consequence of the judgement. The problem for the interpretation of early Stoi-cism has been to decide whether this is a mere difference of expression in the theory, a slight shift of emphasis by Chrysippus, or whether it is a radical revision of the theory of Zeno.[14] But when this question about the analysis and description of *pathê* is seen within the context of the theory of impulse, it is immediately obvious that those critics who have seen Chrysippus' position as at most a verbal refinement of Zeno's must be right.[15] The judgement which is at issue in the definition of passion is clearly the same thing as the assent in the general theory, and we have already seen in our discussion of the general theory that the relationship between the impulse and the assent is such that it is a matter of relative indifference whether one identifies them or treats the impulse as the result of the assent. They are both mental events; they always occur together, since assent is the cause of the impulse; and their 'objects' partially coincide, since the predicate at which the impulse is directed is a part of the proposition which receives assent. If this distinction and the fact that assent is the cause are stressed, then the Zenonian formulation of the definition of *pathos* seems most natural. If one chooses to concentrate instead on the constant conjunction of assent and impulse and the fact that the former wholly determines the latter, then the Chrysippean identification will seem appropriate. But the substance of the theory of passions is not affected by one's choice of formulation,[16] and this no doubt explains why Zeno was willing on occasion to describe passions as being opinions of a certain sort, and not the results of such opinions.[17]

Closely connected with this are questions about the number of ethically relevant powers of the soul. We have seen already that the orthodox Stoics were criticized for not recognizing that human action could be governed by more than one power. The familiar slogan of such attacks on what may be called psychological monism recurs in Galen's attack on the monistic analysis of the passions.[18]

The fact that the old Stoic analysis of the passions was 'monistic' is now generally accepted, although some doubt may remain about the nature of Zeno's theory in the minds of those who suspect that Chrysippus' changes in the theory of action and passion were substantial. It is clear that later Stoics, especially Posidonius, abandoned this monism for a more complex analysis of human psychology which granted considerable importance to the sort of non-rational powers of the soul which Plato and Aristotle had both recognized.[19] One of the main reasons for Posidonius' abandonment of the monistic model of human psychology was his belief that there are important phenomena which cannot be explained without the postulate of more than one power in the soul. Kidd correctly emphasizes how much weight such a consideration could be expected to carry with the 'aetio-logist' Posidonius. But our question now is about Chrysippus: for we know from Galen[20] that he recognized how difficult it was to explain some psychological phenomena on the monistic hypo-thesis, and yet he persevered with the attempt to do so.[21]

If Chrysippus had been concerned like Posidonius to search for causes in a relatively disinterested spirit, it is doubtful whether he would have strained so hard to retain the monistic hypothesis. The fact that he did so can, I think, best be accounted for again by refer-ring to his determination to stand by the decision to describe the passions in the terms of the general psychology of action, a move which, he thought, justified holding men responsible for all that they do.

The adaptations made in the Stoic analysis of action by later philosophers, innovative Stoics like Posidonius and non-Stoics alike, could be the object of a separate study. It would be of some interest and importance for the present examination of the ortho-dox Stoic psychology, if only because so many of the innovators who looked back beyond Stoic monism to the psychological observa-tions made by Plato and Aristotle continued to use the terminology of the Stoic theory in setting forth their own doctrines.[22] But these developments cannot be considered here except in so far as they are needed to help distinguish reliable from unreliable evidence.

I have been arguing that the orthodox Stoics' adherence to a defi-nite analysis of rational action shaped their treatment of the passions and other aspects of their ethics in several important ways. Ultimately we must justify the claim that the psychology of pas-sions is a part of the psychology of action by a closer look at some of the key evidence. But first there is a related question to be examined. We have been considering ways in which the doctrine of passions is affected by the commitment to a monistic psychology of action. This commitment has a significant impact on the orthodox Stoic position on the traditional problem of weak will, a position which may be compared profitably with some contemporary work on the same problem.

(b) Weak will

Let us begin by distinguishing two different senses of weak will. What I shall call the strict sense is best captured by Davidson:[23] we say that 'an agent's will is weak if he acts, and acts intentionally, counter to his own best judgement.' The broad sense of weak will is not subject to such exact description, but in outline it occurs when an agent fails to stand by a previous decision about what he will do or by some general plan or programme of action. The difference between the two may be clearer if an example is given. When some-one gives in to the desire to smoke a cigarette through weak will, two different things may be going on. On the broad interpretation, the smoker has perhaps committed himself to the plan to stop smok-ing. He decided two days ago that this was what he wanted to do, but he could not live up to his general plan. When he lit the cigarette he had changed his mind: at that very moment he wanted to smoke more than he wanted to stop. On the strict interpretation of weak will, we should have to say that at the very moment of lighting up the weak-willed man still wanted to stop more than he wanted to smoke. He acts intentionally counter to his resolution, to which he is still fully committed at the time of action.

I have deliberately used an illustration in which the principle vio-lated by the weak-willed man is a prudential one rather than a moral one. One of the strengths of Davidson's discussion is his insistence that the problem of weak will is a problem in action theory and not just in ethics. The question whether an agent can act against his own best judgement and if so how, is a general one, and the tendency to look first at the special case in which the judgement which the weak-willed man acts against is a moral judgement has not always been helpful.[24]

Only the strict sense of weak will is of interest in the present dis-cussion. For the centre of my interest here is the difficulties which the Stoics had to face in dealing with cases of weak will because of their psychology of action, and the broad sense of weak will is so loose that virtually any psychology of action could accommodate it. If we take as a paradigm case of weak will the situation of Leontius in book 4 of the *Republic* or of Medea,[25] we seem to be dealing with examples of weak will in the strict and more interesting sense. I shall be arguing that weak will in the broad sense does not present serious problems for the Stoic or any other psychology of action. But weak will in the strict sense does. Why?[26]

Any psychology of action which postulates a close linkage between what may in general terms be called 'practical decisions' and the causes of actions (be they wants, desires, or whatever) will have difficulties in the analysis of strictly construed cases of weak will. If one's conception of action is such that all intentional actions are the results of practical decisions and that practical decisions normally cause intentional actions, then situations where, prima facie, the intentional action of an agent conflicts with the relevant practical decision of that agent will be puzzling. Such situations will be very hard to analyse within the framework of that theory of action. One may even be driven by this difficulty to deny that these situations are in fact cases of weak will in the strict sense. They are explained away rather than being incorporated into one's theory. The old Stoics share with Davidson, Hare, and the Socrates of Plato's *Protagoras* the sort of analysis of action which must face these problems concerning weak will in the strict sense.

According to C. C. W. Taylor[27] there can indeed be cases of weak will in the strict sense. In order to maintain this, he loosens the connection between practical decision and action which in his view the philosophers he criticizes have kept too closely connected. Thus he maintains[28] that 'cases of *akrasia* are cases where an agent judges that it is better to do x than to do y, but does y, and this is possible because the agent's judging it better to do x than to do y does not imply either that he does x in preference to doing y or that he wants to do x more than he wants to do y.' He claims that the common 'error' of Plato (i.e. the Platonic Socrates of the *Protagoras*), Hare,[29] and Davidson is a 'failure to appreciate the complexities of the concept of desire and of its relations with judgement on the one hand and action on the other'.

The Socrates of the *Protagoras* does seem to hold a theory of the sort which Taylor criticizes. Vlastos asks why it is that Socrates is confident of the absurdity of the suggestion that a man might choose the lesser of available goods, knowing it to be lesser. The answer which he gives is, I believe, essentially correct and it shows clearly that Socrates is committed to just the sort of theory of action which Taylor blames for the 'mistake' about weak will. Vlastos claims[30] that Socrates tacitly holds two propositions:

S1 If one knows that X is better than Y, one will want X more than Y.

S2 If one wants X more than Y, one will choose X rather than Y.

This is not the place for a detailed discussion of Hare and Davidson, who have been dealt with by Taylor and others. Philosophers who are committed to such a theory of action may deny that there are cases of weak will in the strong sense which we are considering. If they do so, they must explain away the cases of prima-facie *akrasia* which are frequently referred to and accepted as such on the basis of introspection. But another approach is possible, one taken by Plato in the *Republic*[31] and, I would argue, by Aristotle in his discussions of *akrasia*. If the problem of *akrasia* arises when the practical decisions of the agent do not cause actions as they should, one may explain this by reference to another power in the agent's soul which is able to interfere with, even counteract, the decisions of practical reason. Desires of the irrational sort are said to be able to do this: they oppose and interfere with[32] the practical decisions of the agent after he has decided what he will do, on balance and taking into account all his desires. As Aristotle says, one's over-all judgement may say to avoid eating something sweet, but 'desire leads' and so prevents one's practical decision to abstain from being acted on.[33] In the *Eudemian Ethics*[34] Aristotle is willing to speak of the part of the soul which loses out in such a conflict as being compelled by the other.[35]

In the *De Anima* (3.9) Aristotle employs an imperatival analysis of practical reason. *Nous* is said to command one to act. This imperatival element is also central to the Stoic psychology of action. But the Stoics thought that each self-directed imperative had to be obeyed. The result of that is an inability to account for weak will. Aristotle, who believes in the existence of weak will and has the psychological machinery to account for it, does not postulate that all self-directed imperatives are obeyed (433a1-3): 'And again, when reason commands and thought says to flee something or pursue it, [the agent] does not move but acts according to appetite (*epithumia*), as in the case of the weak-willed man.'

Unlike the theories of action and motivation which maintain the close, almost analytical, link between practical decision and action, this sort of theory can succeed in explaining cases of the strict sort of weak will. But it does so at the cost of sacrificing the close link just mentioned. This is one way of doing what Taylor argues must be done if we are to give an account of weak will: it gives a sufficiently complex account of the relationships among judgement, desire, and action. But the price of this solution is high. In this alternative theoretical framework weak will becomes explicable, but in some sense the soul of the agent is divided. Agency is no longer such a simple matter, and the wedge driven between practical decisions and action jeopardizes the idealistic conception of man as an ultimately rational agent.

This division of human agency contains in it the seeds of another undesirable consequence, one which is particularly important for the Stoics. It is always tempting for philosophers to identify a man's true self with his reason.[36] Certainly all the philosophers of antiquity whom we are considering felt this temptation. If the soul is in the present sense divided, our conviction that the agent is responsible for all of his actions may appear to be threatened. Thus Aristotle is very careful to insist, with less than perfect plausibility, that a man may be held responsible for what he does when moved by either of the *archai* of action in him. But this position is ultimately unstable.[37] There will always be a temptation to say that someone who is overcome by his base, irrational tendencies was in some sense compelled and so is not truly accountable for his actions. Glibert-Thirry has recently suggested[38] that the return of Posidonius to a form of the divided soul doctrine of Plato entailed his admission of an alien power in the soul, a foreign entity which could compel us to act against our will, i.e. involuntarily. There are hints of this in Plato, and the conclusion is drawn explicitly by the Middle Platonist Albinus. In ch. 32 of his *Epitome* he says that actions occur in our soul which are not only opposed by us[39] but are against our will (*akousi*). These actions are called by Albinus 'our own but not voluntary'.

Given the Stoics' sensitivity to questions of moral responsibility it seems reasonable to suggest that Zeno and his followers detected the instability of the Aristotelian position. This, and the Stoic allegiance to what they supposed to be the Socratic legacy, help to account for their refusal to drive a wedge between practical decision—represented in their system by assent—and action. In dealing with action and with the passions the Stoics were firm in their rejection of any suggestion of a divided self. They followed Socrates in declining to treat ethical problems in terms of internal psychological conflict.

Thus it is on theoretical grounds, as Striker says,[40] that the phenomenon of weak will is rejected by the Stoics. Perhaps if they had shared Posidonius' bent for searching first and foremost for a sound causal account of psychological phenomena they would have proceeded differently. In their rejection of weak will, as in other areas, the old Stoics preferred to adhere to their theory of action as the basis for ethics because it guaranteed certain general features, such as the connection between reason and responsibility, to which they felt a prior commitment.

The silence of the old Stoics themselves on the phenomenon of weak will is significant. It is true that the adjective *akratês* is used by Chrysippus to describe a movement in the soul which is out of the control of the reason,[41] but there is no reference to psychic conflict. Chrysippus is using the word to indicate that in some sense during a passion the impulse is beyond reason's control, that it cannot easily be changed or recalled; he does not mean that the impulses which are described as *akrateis* are the products of any power in the soul except the reason. Weak will also occurs once[42] in a list of vices, and of course *enkrateia* (strong will) is often listed as a virtue. But strong will, like temperance (*sôphrosunê*), can be conceived as a virtuous disposition of the unitary soul[43] and need not refer to the control by reason of a separate part of the soul. These are dispositions to stand by one's long-term plans and not to change one's mind. In this sense strong will is the ability to avoid changing one's mind and abandoning one's plans and resolutions.[44]

The Stoic refusal to follow Aristotle and the later Plato in positing the separate powers of the soul needed for weak will in the strict sense was, as we have seen, the reason why their critics accused them of believing in a soul with only one power. It is clear from Plutarch's essay *On Moral Virtue* that the phenomenon of internal conflict was one of the key reasons for adopting the divided soul. It had been so since Plato wrote book 4 of the *Republic* and it was still taken to be the clearest refutation of the monistic soul by a critic as intelligent as Alexander of Aphrodisias. It is probable that he has the Stoics in view in this passage as well as Democritus:[45]

That there are several powers of the soul and that it is not the same one which seems to be several by changes and different activities at different times, both with respect to different objects and through different means, as Democritus and some others think, there is a sufficient proof in the mutual conflict of the powers of the soul in strong-willed and weak-willed men.

Plutarch makes very similar criticisms of the Stoics, in particular Chrysippus, accusing them of being unable to give an account of weak will because they did not postulate an emotional part of the soul distinct from reason. His description of their psychology reveals how the orthodox old Stoics attempted to explain away cases of prima-facie weak will (in the strict sense).[46]

It is obvious, then, that there is in the soul an awareness of a distinction and difference of this type in connection with desires, as though there were something fighting against them and contradicting them. But some say that passion is not different from reason and that there is not a disagreement and strife between the two, but that the one reason changes into both, and we do not notice this because of the suddenness and speed of the change . . .

Where Aristotle or the Plato of the *Republic* and later dialogues, or Plutarch or Alexander or Galen for that matter, saw a conflict of one part, power, or aspect of the soul with another in cases of weak will and of strong will, the Stoics preferred to suppose that there was a rapid shift between different opinions and impulses.[47] At no one time does one part or power oppose another; the same part changes over a very short span of time. If a man fails to act on his practical decision, according to this view, it is only an apparent failure. For the agent has actually changed his mind, or his assent was not sincere in the first place.[48] As we should expect from the nature of their psychology of action, the Stoics maintain that all real assents are acted upon and that apparent counter-examples are to be explained away as instances of a very rapid change of assent and impulse.

The problem with this solution is that it is counter-intuitive. As Plutarch and Alexander pointed out, the feeling of psychological conflict is one which we all have. Anyone, they thought, who is not blinded by theoretical blinkers must recognize that sometimes there are two warring elements in the soul. The Stoics' move to negate this evidence is not in the end fully satisfying except (or perhaps even) to those who share their theoretical commitments. Where a modern philosopher *might* respond to this sort of evidence by denying the validity of introspection in philosophical psychology, the Stoics tacitly accepted their opponents' evidence as an account of what we see when we look into our souls, but explained it away by resolving simultaneous conflict into temporal succession. They then had to make the unconvincing move of postulating that this temporal succession occurred at unobservable speed. Plutarch did not hesitate to point out how implausible this was.[49] This is a sad witness to the strength of the Stoics' theoretical commitment to their psychology of action. But it is also a clear indication of what is meant by saying that the Stoics believed in a unitary soul or had a monistic psychology of action.[50]

(c) Passions and the Unitary Soul

If the old Stoic analysis of passions is in fact a subset or application of the general psychology of action, then it should be the case that the passion itself (i.e. the impulse) is the product of the assent or judgement to a certain kind of presentation. If the monistic character of the psychology of action is carried over to the analysis of passions, then passions and impulses should not be spoken of as resisting or overpowering the assent of the reason which produces them. Impulse should be, as it were, the creature of reason and a conflict between reason as it gives assent and generates an impulse and the impulse itself should not be possible. The most we should find in the way of a conflict between reason and passion or emotion is this: at one time a man may give assent rashly and incorrectly to the wrong sort of presentation and in so doing fall into a *pathos* which is against his long-term better judgement. The Stoics believed that there was always a right and a wrong way to respond to the stimuli which we receive from the environment and that man as a rational animal is designed by nature to respond in the right way. When we fail to do so, as everyone but the sage does, we are falling short of our own proper nature, we are not being all that nature meant us as rational agents to be. When we respond hastily and foolishly to the presentations we receive, we fall into conflict with our own reason in so far as it has achieved its goal of becoming assimilated to Right Reason which, ultimately, is the will of Zeus. But at no time do we experience impulses or passions which are produced independently of our assenting reason or which conflict with and resist it.

This is why the acquisition of virtue is essentially a matter of learning certain things, of converting the inconsistent and hesitant opinion about the good into a firm knowledge which always governs life. This is also the reason why the old Stoics believed that the only way to make men better was to educate their reason, not to produce a properly obedient disposition in some lower and fundamentally non-rational power of the soul, as Aristotle did. Confirmation that this was understood to be the position of the early Stoa is provided by the role that Chrysippus gave to the alteration of opinions in the cure of the emotions and by the vigorous but usually misguided polemic against his views that is preserved in books 4 and 5 of Galen's *De Placitis Hippocratis et Platonis*.[51]

In examining some of the evidence for the monistic analysis of passions we must beware of several pitfalls. The worst of these is Galen himself, who was not above significant distortion (deliberate or as a result of misunderstanding) of the Chrysippean doctrine for which he gives us so much valuable evidence. One general point must be made here: it seems clear that Galen and Posidonius could find no unambiguous statements of dualistic psychology in Chrysippus' treatise on the passions (*Peri Pathôn*). What they did find and what Galen exploited for his polemical purposes were descriptions of the condition of people in the grip of passions which had been cast in popular and non-technical language. He spoke, for example, of a person failing to control himself and giving in to an emotion, or being pushed into irrational actions. These turns of phrase are in fact compatible with a monistic psychology and Chrysippus used them in order to show how his theory could reflect conventional beliefs about the emotions. At one point (SVF 3.462) we find Chrysippus appealing to the way we ordinarily speak about the passions as a support for his own views: 'and in ordinary usage (*en tôi ethei*) we say that some are "pushed" and "irrationally swept along" without reason and judgement.'[52] This is offered as an illustration of part of his own account of how a passion is irrational. Galen makes extensive use of the apparent conflict between the phrase 'without reason and judgement' and the doctrine that all passions are judgements or produced by them. Yet it is clear that Chrysippus is referring to a common manner of speaking which can be argued to agree with his doctrine, and not in these words outlining that doctrine.[53]

Galen is obviously suspect and must be used with great care; in general I shall use the quotations he gives from Chrysippus and shall ignore his unenlightening polemic. The other pitfall which awaits us is more subtle. In the first century BC and later, reinterpretations of the orthodox theory of the passions appear which obviously attempt to adapt it to a dualistic model of the soul's function such as Posidonius argued was needed to account for the phenomena of human psychology. There are various forms of this adaptation, but they all share the conviction which Cicero announces at *Tusculan Disputations* 4.10–11. In expounding the doctrine of the emotions, he says,

I shall follow that ancient division adopted first by Pythagoras and then by Plato, who divide the soul into two parts, the one which shares in reason and the other which does not. In the one which shares in reason they place tranquillity, i.e. a calm and peaceful steadiness; in the other one, turbulent emotions both of anger and of desire which are opposed and hostile to reason. Let this be our starting point. Nevertheless, let us use in our description of the passions the definitions and divisions of the Stoics who seem to me to have engaged in this investigation most subtly.

Cicero then proceeds to give a perfectly good translation of Zeno's definition of passions[54] and indeed in the rest of book 4 there is a great deal of orthodox material on the passions.

Unfortunately, this breathtaking assumption of the compatibility of what is unmistakably a conflation of some Platonic and Aristotelian views on the powers of the soul[55] with Stoic doctrine is not just the product of Cicero's own pragmatic eclecticism. The conflation also turns up in many later authorities. Many of these do not claim to be offering an account of old Stoic views, and their adoption of Stoic jargon can be easily spotted. But Arius Didymus, who is often an excellent source of information on the old Stoa, also conflates this dualistic treatment of the powers of the soul with otherwise reliable information.

The Stoicized treatment of a dualistic psychology is a feature of Arius' treatment of the Peripatetic discussion of *pathos* near the beginning of Stobaeus' selection from Arius' ethical doxographies.[56] The adaptation of orthodox Stoic formulas to a theory fundamentally at odds with Stoic monistic psychology is unmistakable:

A passion, according to Aristotle, is an irrational excessive motion of the soul. By the 'irrational' he means that [sc. part or power] which lacks commanding reason, for it has subservient reason by virtue of which it [sc. the irrational part or power] is naturally inclined to obey reason. By 'excessive' he means that which is naturally inclined to receive excess, not that which is already excessive. For at some times it is excessive and at others it is deficient. And he also defines it thus: a passion is an excessive motion of the irrational part of the soul caused by a presentation of the pleasant or the painful.

The eclecticism of this report is interesting in its own right. The emphasis on pleasure and pain is genuinely Aristotelian,[57] and the re-definition of a *pathos* in terms of a mean between excess and defect is also Aristotelian in spirit. In fact, Antiochus[58] and

Plutarch[59] also discuss passions in terms of excess and deficiency in the motions of the irrational part of the soul. A Platonic precedent might have been read into *Timaeus* 86b–c, but the terminology of excessive and deficient impulse is inspired by the Stoic formula. A sure sign that the underlying psychology is 'dualistic' and discrepant with the Stoic doctrine, however, is the addition of the reference to deficiency in the eclectic versions. For the old Stoics never mention deficiency when they deal with the ways in which an impulse is incorrect and so a passion.

But Arius Didymus allows this eclecticism to affect the testimony which he offers concerning Zeno, which follows directly on the Peripatetic report just quoted. Although there are orthodox elements in the report, notably the concentration on passion as a *kinêsis* rather than a disposition, the treatment Arius gives to the notion of *ptoia*, fluttering, is certainly a distortion of a genuinely Stoic doctrine. Arius explains that *ptoia* is a term derived 'from the movement of birds, likening them to the easily stirred-up character of the passionate part of the soul (*to eukinêton tou pathêtikou*)'. It is a hallmark of eclectic dualism to say that the passions are due to the instability of an irrational power not sufficiently controlled by reason. *to pathêtikon* is not an old Stoic term for a part or power of the soul. It is apparently a synonym for *to orektikon* used by those who conflated the Stoic terminology for the passions with a dualistic psychology.[60]

Grave doubt must also fall over another report which Arius gives of the Stoic doctrine of passions.[61] My remarks on this text (*Ecl.* 2.89.4–90.6) may be brief, since it has been realized already[62] that it is influenced by Posidonius or some other Platonizing philosopher. The comparison offered here of the irrational and rebellious part of the soul to a horse struggling against its driver, reason, is Platonic (cf. *Phaedrus* 246a ff.). In Plato the two horses represent the two distinct irrational elements in the soul. When a dualistic contrast of reason and the irrational part of the soul in its undifferentiated formulation was preferred, an analogy with only one horse was substituted.[63]

Arius' use of the horse comparison is a sign of his eclectic recasting of the old Stoic theory of the passions. This approach is also evident in the rest of the passage under consideration. For although the interpretation of 'contrary to nature' which he gives is correct, and despite the fact that Arius seems to interpret the Chrysippean formula 'turning one's back on reason' correctly as a reference to the rejection of Right Reason (see below), he nevertheless concludes this passage on a dualistic note. Passions are said to 'force' men to act in a certain way, despite their opinions. The excessive impulses which are equivalent to the passions are presented as though they were independent agents with the power to dominate the reason like a tyrant.

Arius, or his source, is commenting here on a central text of Chrysippus (SVF 3.462, p. 113.12–114.17)[64] and his comments are generally much more intelligent than those of Galen who grossly distorts Chrysippus' intention. Arius has grasped the point that the 'irrationality' of the impulse is not the result of an error in deliberative reasoning but is meant in a special sense (*idiazontôs*). Nevertheless, in the course of explicating Chrysippus in terms of the contrast between practical and theoretical knowledge, Arius slips badly. He says that men in the midst of a passion cannot stop even if they change their opinions and are convinced 'that they should not be in grief or afraid'. Yet, as we will see, Chrysippus recommends convincing such men of just this sort of point in order to put a stop to the immediate ill-effects of the emotion. To be sure, Chrysippus granted that it was foolish to try to convince a man in the midst of a strong passion.[65] But Arius says that *even if* you do convince the man, still the passion will continue. He seems, in fact, to be rejecting the doctrine that emotions are (a result of) erroneous moral opinions. This bald opposition of reason and the emotions is not found in the old Stoic theory.[66]

(d) Chrysippus' theory of passions

The Chrysippean theory of the passions is in all essentials[67] the same as the theory of Zeno and the other early Stoics. Galen and Posidonius argued that he made significant innovations in the theory of Zeno and Cleanthes, but this is generally recognized to be a polemical interpretation. It is easy to see why such a revisionist interpretation of the earliest Stoic scholarchs would appeal to Posidonius, with his interest in adapting the doctrines of his school to incorporate what he took to be the valuable insights of Plato.

The Chrysippean theory is complex, and the best way to present it is by explaining in terms of the psychology of action the various qualifications which are applied to impulse in the orthodox definitions and discussions of passion. It is relatively easy to explain what is meant by saying that a passion is an irrational or unnatural impulse. The real difficulties become apparent when we consider the description of passion as an 'excessive impulse' (*pleonazousa hormê*), and when we attempt to account for the role of the 'fresh opinion' (*prosphatos doxa*) which plays such an important role in the theory of passions and their cure. One important aid is to broaden the inquiry, and to consider the doctrine of passions in the context of the doctrines which the Stoics held about the place of human action in a deterministic world governed by providence.[68] This approach to the problem of the nature of passions will not shed light on all its problems and obscurities; but in many respects it will help to see the doctrine in terms of the search for a virtuous and unruffled life.

As we have seen, a passion is a kind of impulse; more particularly, it is a kind of impulse in the sense of a change or movement in the soul. It is important to distinguish the passion from the degenerate disposition of the soul which produces it.[69] Like all impulses, a passion is said to be directed at a predicate[70] and to be the product of an assent to a complete proposition containing that predicate.[71] Thus Chrysippus in his work *On Passions* said that the Stoics including Zeno identified the passion with a judgement.[72] The result of this is that the passion may be said to be totally in the agent's control, since the opinion or judgement is the assent given to a proposition embodied in a presentation.[73] Thus the agent is responsible for his passions just as he is responsible for everything else that he does. But the actions which are caused by passions are in some respects different from other actions.

There are four basic kinds of passion in the old Stoic theory, and their character is sufficiently different from the psychological phenomena picked out by the words conventionally used to translate the Stoic passions that a word of explanation is in order. The four basic passions are desire (*epithumia*), fear (*phobos*), pleasure (*hêdonê*), and pain or distress (*lupê*). Desire and fear are incorrect forms of *orexis* and *ekklisis*; that is, desire is an incorrect form of the impulse to acquire the (apparent) good and fear is an incorrect form of the impulse to avoid the (apparent) bad. These two passions, then, are not basically kinds of 'feelings'; the affective side of the pursuit and avoidance is not emphasized in the Stoic account of these passions and they seem not to have used these words principally to designate what we would call affective reactions.[74] That is the job of the other two passions. 'Pleasure' and 'pain' are also impulses. They are not themselves affective states or reactions[75] and this is the first major difference from the phenomena to which the Greeks generally applied the terms *hêdonê* and *lupê* and to which we apply the terms pleasure and pain. What then are pleasure and pain impulses to? They are directed at certain changes in the *pneuma* of the soul, contraction and expansion.[76] These contractions and expansions are pretty much what we call affective reactions.[77]

It is also important to emphasize that pleasure and pain in the present sense have nothing whatever to do with bodily feelings.[78] 'Pain' or 'grief' (*lupê*) is not for a Stoic the sort of thing a person feels when a hammer drops on his toe; nor is pleasure the sort of feeling he might get from a first-rate back massage. Mere bodily feelings of this sort were inevitably referred to by the same terms; but the technical use of these words as designations for certain reactions in the soul, dependent on judgements, is clearly something quite different. Mere bodily pleasure and pain are classed as 'things indifferent' to the moral status of the agent. But the passions of pleasure and pain are vicious impulses, the product of a defective moral constitution. They are the very stuff of moral evaluation and anything but 'indifferent'.

There is a difference in modern usage between pleasure and pain as sensations and pleasure and pain as emotions.[79] When we are talking about pleasure and pain in the Stoic theory of passions it is important to remember that as passions pleasure and pain are analogous to emotions and not to bodily sensations. It is perhaps regrettable that the Stoics did not clarify this distinction by coining new terms for the affective reactions in the soul which they held to be the result of assent and occur in adults. For once, their penchant for neologism seems to have let them down. No doubt the ambiguity of *hêdonê* and *lupê* in ordinary Greek (referring to both sensations and emotions) led them to feel that the traditional words could be used for their new concepts. The long legacy of misunderstanding which the Stoic doctrine of *pathê* and *apatheia* has left shows just how wrong they were.

We have seen how the four standard kinds of passion in the Stoic theory fall into two dissimilar pairs. Let us look a little more closely at the differences between pleasure and pain and, on the other hand, desire and fear. For by doing this we shall be able to cast some light on the question of the role of the 'fresh opinion' (*prosphatos doxa*).

(e) The 'fresh opinion' and passion[80]

There are, as we have seen, four basic passions in the mature Stoic theory. Only once in our sources do we find a truly comprehensive discussion of their relationships to each other. This is unfortunate, because the four passions are divided into two distinct pairs which are dissimilar in important ways. The text which does give us relatively full information is *Ecl.* 2.88–9. There we are told that

desire and fear are primary [or lead off—*prohêgeisthai*], the one being to the apparent good and the other to the apparent bad. Pleasure and pain are subordinate [or subsequent—*epigignesthai*] to these, pleasure occurring when we get what we desire or escape what we try to avoid and pain when we miss what we desire or run into what we fear.[81]

Fear and desire are oriented to future states of affairs; they are impulses to get or avoid something. Such impulses may fail or succeed. In so far as desire and fear are directed towards things not in a man's power, the achievement of them is in the hands of fate. Yet these impulses are directed at the apparent good and bad; that is, they are forms of *orexis* and *ekklisis*. The success or failure of one's pursuit of the apparent good and attempt to avoid the apparent bad is crucial to the agent's happiness. Therefore it is not surprising that the failure or success of such impulses is a central feature of the moral admonitions of Epictetus.[82] One can see from a consideration of this text of Arius Didymus that a conflict between a man's endeavour and the fated events of Nature's will is important in the doctrine of passions.

The primary passions are different from the subordinate in two important ways. The primary are directed at getting (or avoiding) the apparent good (or bad),[83] while the subordinate are directed at internal psychic reactions to the results of these endeavours. This means that the subordinate passions are concerned with a present state of affairs, while the primary are oriented toward the future. Yet the other accounts of the basic passions desire, fear, pleasure, and pain[84] tend to de-emphasize these distinctions and treat the difference between present and future, good and bad, external and internal as being of equal importance. This is the result of an excessively schematic presentation.

The same text of Arius Didymus indicates the role that the 'fresh opinion' plays in the theory of passions. For at *Ecl.* 2.89.2–3 we are told that 'fresh' is used to mean 'stimulative of an irrational contraction or expansion'. Since only pleasure and pain are productive of contraction or expansion in the soul, this should mean that the *prosphatos doxa* is only relevant to the discussion of the subordinate passions. And this is pretty much what we find in the rest of our evidence about the 'fresh opinion'. With a minor exception,[85] only pleasure and pain are involved with the fresh opinion, since they are the passions involved with affective contraction and expansion in the soul.

The fresh opinion, then, is important for our understanding of the subordinate passions and more must be said about it.[86] The most important fact about this fresh opinion is that, for both Zeno and Chrysippus, it does not refer primarily to a temporal recentness of the object about which the opinion is made, but rather to the fact that a fresh opinion is one which still has a certain kind of force for the agent. Bonhoeffer established this beyond any doubt; he did this by a careful examination of the evidence of Cicero in *Tusculan Disputations* 3 esp. 74–5 and of Arius Didymus' explicit statement of what 'fresh' means (*Ecl.* 2.89.2–3). This evidence is clearly preferable to the tendentious account offered by Posidonius and preserved for us by Galen.[87] Posidonius claimed that Chrysippus intended 'fresh' only in the sense of 'temporally recent', and this emphasis suited his claim that despite himself Chrysippus was in effect supposing that there was an irrational power in the soul.[88] Posidonius' case was built on the fact that Chrysippus did acknowledge some difficulty in explaining why some passions, such as pain, faded away with the passage of time even if the opinion that produced the passion originally did not change. We shall return to this question about the cessation of passions shortly, but for now it suffices to note that Posidonius had a clear polemical motivation for taking Chrysippus' notion of the 'fresh opinion' in a one-sided way as referring only to the temporal recentness of the object of the opinion.

What sort of opinion is this *prosphatos doxa*, if it is not just an opinion formed about a good or bad state of affairs which the agent has suddenly and recently become aware of? If we are to follow Arius Didymus,[89] it is the judgement that some object or state of affairs is the right sort of thing about which to have a contraction or expansion of the soul (*eph' hôi kathêkei sustellesthai* or *epairesthai*).[90] That is, the 'fresh opinion' is a judgement that what has happened is appropriately responded to with the affective reactions which are associated with pleasure or pain. This account fits perfectly with several pieces of information we have about these passions and the 'fresh opinion'. For one thing, it makes good sense of the explanation of 'fresh' as that which is stimulative of irrational contraction or expansion in the soul. The prominence of the judgement that a certain kind of reaction is appropriate (*kathêkei*) is also just what we would expect from the general account of the presentations which stimulate all impulses: at *Ecl.* 2.86 the hormetic presentation is said to be 'of the appropriate'. In terms of the psychology of action, we may explain the fresh opinion as assent to the proposition that such and such a state of affairs is the appropriate sort of thing to have this or that affective reaction to.

But why is this called 'fresh'? Cicero explains this for us with an admirable clarity.[91] In a discussion of pain (grief would be a better translation, but I shall often retain the conventional term) he says that

pain is an opinion about a present evil, and in this opinion there is this element, that it is right (*oporteat*) to feel pain. Zeno properly makes the addition to this definition, to the effect that this opinion about a present evil is 'fresh' (*recens*).[92] This word they interpret thus: by 'fresh' they do not mean only that which occurred a little while before, but as long as there is a certain force in that supposed bad thing (*opinato malo*) so that it is strong and has a certain 'vitality' (*viriditas*), for just so long it is called 'fresh'. Thus the famous Artemisia, the wife of Mausolus the Carian king, who built that splendid tomb in Halicarnassus [i.e. the Mausoleum], as long as she lived, lived in grief and wasted away, consumed by it. For her that opinion was fresh every day. The opinion only ceases to be called 'fresh' when it is exhausted by the passage of time.

Zeno called fresh the opinion that some unpleasant event was the sort of thing to feel pain about, for as long as it continued to be active; and by this he must have meant as long as the agent kept assenting to it, explicitly or implicitly. This might go on for twenty minutes or for twenty years; passage of time is a factor which may influence whether the opinion retains its vitality, but 'freshness' is not determined by the clock or the calendar. The attitude of the agent is far more important.

But Zeno (and Chrysippus too) did admit that the passage of time was not irrelevant to the process. This brings us back to the acknowledgement by Chrysippus of a certain difficulty in explaining how a passion such as pain passed away with time and

Posidonius' use of this in his polemic. Let us begin by quoting the passage in which Chrysippus states the issue:[93] 'One might enquire also about the relaxation of the pain, how it comes about, whether when some opinion changes or when all of them remain the same, and why this will be the case.' Galen here says that Chrysippus continues, but we may suspect a slight abridgement.

It seems to me that an opinion of this sort remains, that the very thing which is present is bad, but that as it [sc. the opinion] lingers the contraction relaxes and, as I think, the impulse to the contraction. Perhaps even if this [sc. the opinion][94] remains the things which follow will not obey, as these things occur by some other supervening disposition which is hard to account for (*dussullogiston*). For it is in this way that people cease weeping and weep even when they do not want to weep, whenever underlying circumstances produce dissimilar[95] presentations and something or nothing interferes. For in the same way that the cessation of laments and weepings occur, it is reasonable that such things should occur in those cases, since things are more stimulative at the beginnings, just as I said occurs in the case of things which stimulate laughter; and also things similar to these.

Note that this entire discussion of the cessation of passions is focused on the passion of pain or grief alone. Posidonius and Galen selected this as the weak point in Chrysippus' account. Posidonius' principal argument here is that the discrepancy between the overt manifestations of grief, such as weeping, and the opinions of the agent is proof that there must be some irrational power in the soul which can be sated by wearing itself out in the course of time, regardless of what the rational power in the soul may be opining. If, as Posidonius thought, Chrysippus is in effect acknowledging that this is the case when he admits that the discrepancy occurs, this need not affect the rest of his discussion of the passions. Glibert-Thirry[96] concludes that in this case Chrysippus is modifying his theory to acknowledge (grudgingly, it might seem) the facts of experience. Some such qualification is perhaps inevitable, if indeed his basic approach to the passions is determined by his decision to interpret them according to the general psychology of action. This would not be the only instance when the rigours of such an approach were modified to bring it more into line with the apparent facts of affective experience.[97]

But let us look more closely at Chrysippus' position and ask whether such a concession is in fact being made. First, let us consider the implications of the variation in the interpretation of what

is said to remain while the overt signs of grief fade away. [98] The fact
that both the impulse to the contraction and the opinion can be
taken to be the persistent factor is puzzling, until we consider the
relation of the assent to the impulse in the psychology of action. For
if an assent is the cause of an impulse and they always occur
together, it should not matter a great deal which is said to remain
the same. By the general psychology of action there can be no
discrepancy between them. This is presumably what Posidonius
was relying on when he made the substitution of the impulse for the
opinion in his criticism of the passage we are considering.

But Posidonius' interpretation must be wrong. For in Chrysippus' text the affective reaction in the soul (the contraction) and the
impulse to it are said to relax at the same time, while a certain sort of
opinion remains the same. This opinion is described thus by Chrysippus: that the very thing which is present is bad. How can it be
that this sort of opinion remains, but the contraction in the soul and
the overt signs of grief such as weeping (which are presumably
caused by the affective reaction in the soul) fade away? Chrysippus
himself says that this phenomenon is hard to account for (*dussullogiston*). The solution to this problem which Chrysippus should
have given, and which neither Posidonius nor Galen had an interest
in preserving for us, has been suggested already by Bonhoeffer.[99]

The key to the solution is to note carefully the opinion which
Chrysippus says remains the same: the very thing which is present
is bad. This should be compared with the opinion which is said by
our better sources to cause pain. At *Ecl.* 2.90 pain is said to be
caused by the opinion that a fresh bad thing is present, about which
(*eph' hôi*) it is appropriate to suffer a contraction (sc. in the soul).
Similarly at SVF 3.391(pseudo-Andronicus): pain is a fresh
opinion of the presence of something bad about which they think
they should suffer a contraction. A similar description is given by
Cicero in his discussion of the opinion which Zeno said was the
cause of pain (quoted above, *TD* 3.74–5).[100] His definition of pain
(*aegritudo*) in book 4 of the *Tusculans*[101] has the same features: pain is
a fresh opinion of a present bad thing in relation to which (*in quo =
eph' hôi*) it seems to be right to be downcast and to suffer a contraction (*demitti contrahique*) in one's soul.

The opinions which cause pain, then, are not simply judgements
about the goodness or badness of what is present. They include the
judgement that it is appropriate to suffer the affective reaction, that

is, the contraction of the soul. We may infer from *Ecl*.2.89.2–3 that it is the addition of this judgement about the appropriateness of this affective reaction which makes an opinion 'fresh'. For Arius tells us there that *prosphaton* is used in place of 'stimulative of an irrational contraction or expansion'.

Chrysippus' answer to the problem at hand is now clear. The opinion which remains the same is the judgement that something bad is present. But by itself this is not enough to produce the passion of pain. For that one needs a contraction in the soul; for this one needs an impulse to contraction; and for this impulse to occur, one must assent to the proposition that such a contraction is appropriate. When the opinion stays the same while the passion fades, it is because the part of the complex opinion that gave it the power to stimulate this affective reaction has ceased. The 'fresh' part of the complex opinion has also stopped when the passion stops. Thus when Chrysippus notes a discrepancy between the continuation of an opinion and the cessation of a passion, he can solve the problem he sets for himself by distinguishing between the two parts of the complex opinion.[102]

This is probably what the text of Chrysippus we are considering was leading up to. Note how careful Chrysippus is in specifying that it is an opinion of a certain sort (*toiautē*) which remains and in stating exactly which opinion he means. It is obvious that Galen does not reproduce Chrysippus' entire discussion of the problem; he cuts it short at the end, probably abridges it by omitting a passage in the middle, and gives us no help in understanding Chrysippus' reference to his previous remarks about the causes of laughter.

For Chrysippus the passion of pain is the product of a complex set of opinions, not just one.[103] This is the point of his mentioning the possibility that *all* the opinions might remain the same, a possibility which we may be sure that he rejected.

But Chrysippus did admit that there was something hard to account for in his analysis of pain and its cessation. The very neatness of this account might make us suspicious of its faithfulness to Chrysippus' own position. But it need not. For one thing, the preliminary recognition of a difficulty is a natural prelude to the solution. Aristotle admits to many an *aporia* on his way to philosophical solutions with which he is himself satisfied. But perhaps there is in this case a puzzle for which Chrysippus still felt unable to find a complete solution. How *does* it come about that the opinion which produces the impulse to contraction (and so the overt signs of grief) stops? This is what Chrysippus is asking about when he says that the things which follow (the overt signs of grief) do not obey or conform to the opinion that something bad is present, and that the cause of this is some other disposition which is hard to account for. The lines which follow are difficult to interpret, not least because of a serious uncertainty about the correct reading of our text (see n. 95). But what he seems to be saying is that whether or not there is an external obstacle or interference, our presentations change. This is obscure, but the best guess as to its meaning may be this. Our presentation changes, which means literally that we take a different view of the situation which we think to be bad. Chrysippus elsewhere[104] said that when something unexpected happens we often suppose it to be more serious than it really is 'because there is no time to consider how serious what has happened is'. Perhaps in the text from Galen Chrysippus means that our initial evaluation of some occurrence is often hasty, so that we think that it is not only bad but also such as to justify feeling a contraction in our soul over it. With the passage of time our presentation of the situation changes, when we get a chance to consider it more carefully, and we then think that it is bad, but no longer such as to justify feeling grief. What will be hard to account for, on this interpretation, is why we should change our evaluation of the misfortune solely because of the passage of time. And this is a genuine puzzle.[105] Nevertheless, however it is resolved (if at all), the solution which has been given for the discrepancy between the opinion and the passion remains valid.

A degree of confirmation for this solution is available in Chrysippus' views about the proper way to 'cure' the passion of grief. In the same context (book 2 of his treatise on the passions) Chrysippus noted that once the 'inflammation of the passion'[106] had died down in this way, then and only then could reason find its way back into the soul, as it were, and go to work on exposing the irrationality of the passion. This point was expanded in book 4 of his treatise on passions, the so-called 'therapeutic' book dealing with their treatment. For in *Tusculan Disputations*, which seems to draw on Chrysippus' book at one remove (at least), we are told (4.59) that the safest initial treatment for a bout of, say, regret over one's poverty (an example of *lupê*) is not to argue that poverty is not bad, but rather to say that one ought not to bear it badly (*aegre ferre*

= *sustellesthai*). 'This is certainly the better course, to avoid having to agree to the *aegritudo* (= *lupê*) if you do not carry your point about poverty.' The direct assault on the error about the badness of poverty is said to be correct, but less useful (4.60). The first task is to relieve the contraction in the soul (4.62).

Here the situation envisaged is one where there is a deliberate effort on the part of another person[107] to quench the 'inflammation of the passion'. This might also occur by the agent's own eventual second thoughts about the seriousness of the misfortune he is suffering over; that is the kind of case which Chrysippus dealt with in book 2. In book 3 of the *Tusculans* Cicero also refers to that kind of case, and calls the sort of reflection which leads to the elimination of the fresh opinion (and so the extinguishing of the pain) a *cogitatio diuturna* (3.74). This, Cicero says, and not the mere passage of time, accounts for the cessation of the passion. But whether the passion is alleviated by the advice and consolation of someone else or by one's own eventual return to a more balanced view of the situation, the proximate cause of the cessation of the passion is the same: the abandonment of the fresh opinion, i.e. the belief that one ought to react to the misfortune with a contraction in the soul.

In one interesting passage (3.76) Cicero contrasts Cleanthes and Chrysippus. The former thought that the only cure for pain was to rectify the error about something bad being present. Chrysippus, on the other hand, thought that the first job was to remove the conviction that it was right to suffer contraction in the soul because of it, or (we may add[108]) at least to wait until this change of opinion came about in due course. The essentials of the doctrine of the fresh opinion were laid down by Zeno, although Chrysippus may be responsible for spelling out the meaning of 'fresh' in the form which appears in Arius and pseudo-Andronicus. It also seems, from Cicero's contrast of Cleanthes and Chrysippus, that the latter was the first to make full use of the doctrine of the fresh opinion in formulating an effective theory of the short-term alleviation of pain.[109] He seems to have seen that it is easier to change someone's mind about the belief that one ought to suffer grief and distress over a misfortune than to convince him that the misfortune is not, in the proper sense of the word, a bad thing at all.[110]

I have been emphasizing the subordinate position of the fresh opinion and the passions of pleasure and pain in the Chrysippean theory of the passions. The root cause of all the passions is a set of mistaken beliefs about what is good and what is bad. For desire and fear are caused by such beliefs; they are the pursuit and avoidance respectively of what is mistakenly thought to be good and bad. For the properly conceived good is the sort of thing which an agent cannot fail to achieve, when he goes after it in the proper way, and the converse holds for bad. Good, which is 'virtue or that which partakes in virtue' is completely in the power of the agent and not subject to hindrance from things which are not in his power.

This is why the cure of pain which consists in removing the fresh opinion alone is not a true cure for the root causes of pain. As long as one continues to hold mistaken views about what is bad, one will be subject to incorrect responses to the misfortunes of life. It is worth emphasizing at this point that the error about good and bad which Chrysippus considers to be the root cause of all the passions is not an error about the degree of goodness or badness which certain things have. For the orthodox Stoic view on the nature of good (and of bad) is that it is an absolute, not admitting of any variation in degree.[111] The error about good which is fundamental to all of the passions, and indeed to all moral error, is simply an error about *which* things are good.

But other views were taken on the nature of good, according to which it could vary in degree. Posidonius in particular, whether he shared this view or not, seems to have used it in an attack on the orthodox theory of the passions which made use of an alleged difficulty which Chrysippus would have in accounting for the passions of a man making moral progress (a *prokoptôn*).[112] We do not need to consider this criticism and the orthodox response to it[113] here. It suffices to point out the difference in the interpretation of the good which Posidonius uses in his polemical attack from the one used in the orthodox ethics which he is criticizing.

It is important to emphasize this point about the nature of the good because Posidonius is also presuming that the impulse one has towards an object of pursuit varies in magnitude according to the degree of goodness one attributes to it. This premiss, if it were Chrysippus' own, would have an important bearing on the meaning of the 'excess' of an impulse which makes it a passion.[114] The question of what the excess of an impulse is (perhaps the most difficult aspect of the theory of passions) will soon have to be addressed. For now, note that Chrysippus did not think that the magnitude of a impulse varied according to the degree to which a thing is good. The relation which he thought did hold between the error about the good and the 'excess' of the impulse is best indicated by the following Chrysippean quotation which Galen gives in connection with the Posidonian criticism we have been looking at:[115] 'for these conditions are not said to be infirmities (*arrostêmata*) because they consist of judging that each of these things is good, but also in that one is attracted to them in excess of what is natural.'[116] The reaction to something which is erroneously judged to be good (not something which is thought to be more good than it really is) is an attraction to it in excess of what is natural. We shall return to the problem of excessiveness shortly; but first we must discuss the other characteristics which a passion is said to have, irrationality and unnaturalness.

(f) The Irrational and Unnatural Movement of the Soul, or Excessive Impulse[117]

Chrysippus discussed the meaning of this standard definition of passion in a long text preserved for us by Galen.[118] This explanation makes it plain that 'irrational', 'unnatural', 'disobedient to reason', and 'excessive' (which are all specifications of the kind of impulse which constitutes a passion) must be elucidated in terms of one another. It also makes it clear that Chrysippus dealt with the doctrine of the passions in the broad context of the proper goal of man's life and the place of a rational animal in a rational universe.

The doctrine of the passions has been discussed abundantly, but puzzles remain. There has yet to be a fully satisfactory account of what it means for an impulse to be excessive;[119] there has not yet been a consideration of this 'excess' in the light of the psychology of action, nor a sufficient awareness of the broader context of Stoic ethics in the detailed examination of the evidence on the passions.

The text containing Chrysippus' discussion of the standard definition of a passion is important enough that it should be quoted at length.

We must first keep in mind that the rational animal is by nature such as to follow reason and to act according to reason as a guide. Nevertheless, he often moves toward some things and away from some things[120] in another way, disobediently to reason, when he is pushed too far [or to excess]. Both definitions, [sc. the one mentioning] the unnatural movement which arises irrationally in this way and [the one mentioning] the excessiveness in the impulses, are in terms of this movement. For this irrationality must be taken to be disobedient to reason and turning its back on reason.[121] And it is in terms of this motion that we also say in ordinary usage that some people are 'pushed' and 'moved irrationally without reason and judgement'. For we do not use these expressions as if someone is moved mistakenly and because he overlooks something that is according to reason, but most especially according to the movement he[122] outlines, as the rational animal does not by nature move this way in his soul, but rather according to reason.

Galen tells us that the second part of the quotation follows directly (*ephexês*) on the first.

The excess of the impulse was also spoken of in terms of this, because they overstep the symmetry of impulses which is proper to themselves [*kath' hautous*] and natural. What I say would be made easier to understand by means of these examples. In walking according to impulse the movement of the legs is not excessive but is in a sense coextensive with the impulse, so that it can come to a standstill when he [sc. the walker] wishes, or change direction.[123] But in the case of those who are running according to impulse, this sort of thing is no longer the case, but the movement of the legs exceeds the impulse so that it is carried away and does not change direction obediently in this way as soon as they start to do so. I think something similar to these movements [sc. of the legs] occurs in the impulses because of the overstepping of the symmetry which is according to reason, so that whenever one has an impulse (*hormâi*) he is not obedient with respect to it, the excess being beyond the impulse in the case of running and beyond reason in the case of impulse. For the symmetry of natural impulse is that according to reason and is as far as reason deems proper. Therefore since the overstepping is according to this [sc. standard] and in this way, the impulse is said to be excessive and an unnatural and irrational movement of the soul.

A passion is an impulse disobedient to reason. Those who had adopted a dualistic psychology very naturally interpreted this as a disobedience of the impulse to one's own reason. But this cannot be right for Chrysippus, since the fundamental hypothesis of the monistic psychology leaves no room for the disobedience of an impulse to the reason of the agent as it gives assent and issues its command to act. Thus when we are faced with texts which refer to the disobedience to reason in terms broad enough to permit either a monistic or dualistic interpretation,[124] we should choose to interpret them in a monistic fashion.[125] For this will also agree with those texts which specify that the reason which is being disobeyed in a passion is Right Reason,[126] the normative standard of all proper conduct, which Chrysippus identified with Zeus.[127]

The unified mind of an agent is both reason and impulse. That is, it contains these two powers and they always work together. Thus the disobedience can only be to the divine Reason of Zeus.[128] Man is naturally made so as to obey this; thus it is unnatural to reject it.[129] It is clear from Chrysippus' own words that he intended the qualifications 'unnatural' and 'irrational' to be explained in terms of each other in just this way. But we must also remember that human reason is essentially the same as divine Reason. When human reason is perfected it will be completely assimilated to that of Zeus; thus man's normatively ideal and perfectly natural reason is also something which he can fall short of in individual actions, just in so far as he is not perfect. By turning his back on the Reason of Zeus, a man is also turning his back on the best that he himself can be and should be.

I have been emphasizing the need to consider the passions in light of the broader sweep of Stoic ethics. This is in part dictated by the information which Arius Didymus gives us about the passions at *Ecl.* 2.88–9. There, as we have seen, an important distinction is drawn between primary passions which are misguided attempts to acquire the good or to avoid the bad and subsequent or secondary passions which are the result of success or failure in those attempts. This should bring to mind the problems associated with the need to act in a determined world, where only what is 'in one's own power' can be relied upon to turn out as one wishes. But there is another indication that this wider perspective is appropriate. An important fragment of Chrysippus which deals with the passions is revealing. In his treatise *On Inconsistency* (*Peri Anomologias*),[130] he deals with the problem of the relation of passions to man's commitment to reason in a way which is strikingly reminiscent of the passage from *On Passions* which we have examined. At one point he said: 'Although the rational animal has a nature such as to use Reason in every situation and to be guided by it, we often turn our back on it, when we are subject to another more violent motion.' The similar phrasing of this text and parts of the fragment *On Passions* underlines the similarity of content. Again we have man's natural commitment to reason's guidance contrasted with the fact that we often reject it and allow ourselves to be carried away by the violent motions in the soul which constitute passions. (Passions are specifically mentioned earlier in the fragment.) Yet note the title of the work from which this text is quoted by Plutarch. In writing a treatise on the failure to achieve the goal of life, which is consistency with one's own nature and with universal Nature, Chrysippus has felt the need to make the same point about reason and the passions which formed the foundation of his explanation of the standard definition of passion. We cannot tell precisely how this material was worked into the treatise on the goal of life, since Plutarch only quotes it to facilitate the same sort of dualistic criticism of Stoic psychology which Galen also revels in. But its occurrence in such a work is sufficient to confirm the propriety of approaching the passions with broader issues in mind.

But let us return to the fragment from *On Passions*. A passion occurs when a man fails to achieve the naturally prescribed ideal, when he fails to follow the lead of Reason, turns his back on it, and goes beyond the limits which Reason prescribes. The ideal behaviour which Reason dictates is called the natural symmetry of impulses; it must not be overstepped if man is to be what he is intended by Nature to be.

Since this text from Chrysippus is explaining what the definitions of passions mean, we expect to find in it a clue to the meaning of the 'excessiveness' which is characteristic of the impulses which constitute the passions. Chrysippus explains excess by referring to the overstepping of something he calls 'the symmetry of impulses which is proper to themselves and natural' and the two qualifications of this symmetry may reasonably be supposed to refer to the fact that the desired symmetry is in accord with the universal Nature as well as with the individual nature of the agent. The symmetry here mentioned is echoed in other discussions of the passions, and this confirms its importance. Clement[131] for example explains 'excessive' impulse as that which 'extends beyond the measures which are according to Reason' (*ta kata ton logon metra*). Epictetus too[132] seems to be following the Chrysippean interpretation of 'excess' in a text which is worth quoting because it neatly unites Epictetus' own favourite ethical themes with an orthodox interpretation of the passions:

What has pain to do with you? For of those things of which there is fear when they are anticipated there is also pain when they are present. What then do you still desire? For you have a symmetrical and stable *orexis* for things which are in the realm of moral purpose (*prohairesis*) since they are morally good (*kala*), and you have no *orexis* for any of the things not in the realm of moral purpose so as to give room for that irrational element which also pushes and thrusts beyond the measures (*metra*).

Freedom from passions of desire, fear, and pain is here connected with not being pushed beyond certain limits, and also with restricting one's *orexis* to those things which are truly in a man's own power, the *prohairetika*. This *orexis* is described as *summetros*, a clear verbal echo of Chrysippus.

Obeying Right Reason is also to obey one's own reason in its natural and proper condition. The convergence of perfected human reason with divine Reason is analogous to the relationship between human and divine Nature in Chrysippus' explanation of the traditional formula for the goal of life.[133]

And again, to live according to virtue is the same as to live according to experience of what occurs by Nature, as Chrysippus says in book 1 of his *On Goals*. For our [sc. human] natures are parts of the Nature of the universe. Hence the goal is to live following nature, that is, according to one's own and that of the universe, doing nothing which is usually forbidden by the common Law (which is Right Reason,[134] passing through all things, the same as Zeus who is the leader of the disposition of things). This [sc. the goal] is the virtue of the happy man and a smooth flow of life, when everything is done according to the harmony of each man's *daimôn* with the will of the Director of the universe.[135]

The discussions referred to in notes 134 and 135 confirm the validity of interpreting the demand for a life according to Reason, which is the natural life for a man, in terms of avoiding passions. Posidonius wished to reinterpret the sense in which living according to reason was the avoidance of living according to passions; this was necessary in view of his adoption of a dualistic psychology. This comes out clearly in this text quoted from Posidonius by Galen:[136]

The cause of the passions, i.e. of the inconsistency (*anomologia*) and the unhappy life, is not following in every respect the *daimôn* in himself which is akin (*sungenês*) and has the same nature as the Disposer of the entire cosmos, but sometimes turning aside with the worse and beastlike [sc. part of themselves] and being swept along. Those who did not see this do not in these matters give a better account of the cause of the passions nor do they hold the right opinion in matters concerning happiness and consistency (*homologia*). For they do not see that in this [i.e. consistency] the primary thing is to be led in no respect by what is both irrational and unhappy and godless in the soul.

Posidonius is correcting what he takes to be mistaken in the connection which Chrysippus made between leading a consistent life and the freedom from passions. Let us concentrate on Chrysippus' version of the connection. Following Zeus, the common Law, and Right Reason is a matter of doing certain acts, that is, having certain impulses. To reject this Reason is to abandon one's own true, rational nature. It means not following or adapting oneself to those things which happen by Nature. The commands of Zeus are the common Law and the sage shares in these,[137] making the commands which rule the universe the commands or impulses which rule his own life. The events of the world, which are what occur by Nature, are the will of Zeus,[138] and they are rational and providentially determined. It is man's proper nature to assimilate himself to these.[139]

Assimilation of one's actions to the commands of Zeus is another way of describing the accommodation of oneself to fate, since Zeus' will determines the events of the providentially ordered world. For Chrysippus[140] defined fate as the Reason and 'Law of the events in the cosmos governed by providence'. The Law governing events is the same as that which guides men. If one obeys this, then like the dog tied behind the wagon[141] one's actions will be in harmony with events as they unfold. The account of reservation which has already been given explains how this accommodation to fate can be reconciled with the need of man to act even in ignorance of what in particular is fated.

I suggest, then, that the natural symmetry of impulses is that coordinated set of impulses which constitutes the complete set of commands issued to man by the common Law which is the will of Zeus.[142] This will is, like all impulses, imperatival and so the identification of it with the Law and a set of commands as well as with Right Reason should not be puzzling. We are told that actions according to this set of commands are right actions (*katorthômata*) and that actions in contravention of it are wrong actions (*hamartêmata*) and some of these latter will also be, as the passage of Epictetus just considered suggests, passions. Since passions are identified with impulses and no action whether right or wrong can be done without an impulse to cause it, the assimilation of our own impulses to those of Zeus (which means that we give to ourselves the commands which constitute the divine Law) is a necessary and sufficient condition for actions which accord with the will of Zeus and so are in accordance with Right Reason.

This account of the relation of human action to Right Reason and the will of Zeus will enable us to explain the sense in which a passion can be contrary to reason and still the result of one's own assent. For normatively man's reason is at one with Right Reason; what is natural is also what is proper to men as rational animals.[143] Thus when in his comment on the example of the runner (used to illustrate what excessiveness in impulses is) Chrysippus says that those who are excessive in their impulses go beyond their proper reason (*para ton idion logon*)[144] he is referring to the fact that in such a situation a man acts against Right Reason which is his own reason, from a normative point of view.[145] The agent who acts against Right Reason is in a significant sense less than his true self when he does so.[146] By turning his back on Reason, a man also turns his back on himself.

In the same passage[147] Chrysippus says that when men act in a passion they do so not 'in accordance with themselves', which must be understood in the sense we have proposed, but 'according to some other force outside them' (*kat' allên tina bian exôthen autôn*). Galen, of course, protests that this other force should be said to be within the man, i.e. that it is the irrational part of the soul. But Chrysippus' reference to an external power is comprehensible in terms of his monistic theory.

There are many references to the force of some other power; a man is said to be 'pushed' or 'thrust' too far by something. The motion in the soul which is identified with a passion is said to be 'more violent' and even to displace our reasoning processes (*ta pathê ekkrouei tous logismous*).[148] Sometimes the language used in such passages seems to suggest a more dualistic account of the passions than Chrysippus actually held. That, after all, is one of the reasons why critics cited them. But there cannot be any serious doubt about what this power is. The presentations we receive from the environment and which we cannot control have within them a certain persuasive force. They tend to lead us on to assent to them, and it is the job of the rational agent to examine them carefully and only to give his assent to the ones which accord with the principles of Right Reason. But they do exert their influence over us, and indeed this very 'persuasiveness of things' is one of the two causes of the corruption of rational animals who start out in life with uncorrupted inclinations.[149] If we give in to these stimuli without examining them (assenting implicitly) or give them conscious but erroneous assent, then we will be swept away by them and we will be allowing ourselves to be pushed too far.

This way of accounting for the reference to an external force which pushes an agent into a passion also points to the way in which the term chosen to describe passions is in fact appropriate. *Pathos* in Greek does connote passivity; it suggests that something is done *to* the agent. Yet since the *pathê* are the results of assent and so intentional actions, it seems odd to call them by such a name. For they are in fact actions, things which the agent *does*. The point of calling them *pathê* is that a *pathos* is a very special kind of action. An agent gives his assent to the persuasive presentation which he receives without proper consideration and so is swept away by it.[150] By assenting to these persuasive presentations without due circumspection he allows himself to be acted on. In doing so, of course, he is still giving his assent and so is responsible for this rather strange sort of action. Truly human action, in a normative sense, is not passive in this or any other sense. When an agent attends to and obeys Right Reason he is *acting* in the true and proper sense of the word.

Let us now consider what it is about the agent which causes him to respond to presentations in this defective way. What is there in the condition of his mind which constitutes his weakness, his disease of the soul. We are asking, more specifically, about the weak *tonos* of the soul of the fool, the non-sage, who is subject to passions in certain circumstances.

An adult human is the only animal which can have a passion. It is no coincidence that adults, i.e. humans who have reached the age of reason, are deemed to have acquired their full complement of moral notions.[151] Chrysippus believed that a man has in him, potentially, the moral principles which enable him to act properly, i.e. according to Reason, if they are applied consistently and correctly. These need not be innate principles; the potentiality to acquire them is inborn, but they come, like all concepts, from experience. By the time a person is at the age of reason this process of acquiring the basic moral notions is expected to be complete. At this stage a person is rational; he has become responsible for living according to Reason and has within himself all that he needs to do so.

One can, of course, fail to act according to one's principles. This will happen in any case where the agent has not yet made explicit these principles and accepted them as a guide for his conduct. But it can also occur in men who have begun the process of moral education. Before a man has adopted these principles strongly enough that he is immune to the persuasiveness of external things, but after he has in general adopted them as guides to conduct, it is possible to act weakly. Fools are said to act *apostatikôs* and *endotikôs*, that is, falling away from Right Reason and giving in to the persuasiveness of external things.[152] Throughout chapter 6 of book 4 of Galen's treatise this weakness (called *astheneia* and *atonia*) is described in terms of a failure to stand by one's decisions or judgements. At one point Galen accurately describes Chrysippus' position[153] in very enlightening terms. The failure to control onself, i.e. *akrasia*, weak will, is a matter of departing from 'these very same decisions' which one has previously made, under the force of external circumstances (*en tois sumpiptousi*). This is what is meant by being overcome by the passions. This sort of weak will, as we have seen, is perfectly consistent with a monistic psychology;[154] Galen, however, is primarily interested in using this discussion of weak will by Chrysippus as a proof that there must be some distinct and irrational power in the soul.

Despite this bias Galen still gives us valuable information about Chrysippus' analysis of how it is that a man can fall away from the rational decisions he has already made. The fundamental cause of all passions is the same as the cause of all incorrect actions. A man's reason is not yet in perfect condition, and this means that the *hexis* or disposition of his mind is not yet completely in accord with nature. The *hexis* which produces any action is a *hexis hormêtikê*; when this is in such a condition as to produce passions, it is called sickness of the soul. This disease in the soul is, however, an opinion or set of opinions.[155] Arius describes it as a 'judgement of [= leading to?] desire which has settled and hardened into a *hexis*, according to which they think that things which are not worth choosing (*haireta*[156]) are worth choosing strongly'. Diogenes Laertius' version is more condensed but essentially the same: 'a *nosêma* is an opinion of what seems to be worth choosing strongly.'[157]

These characterizations of the condition of the fool's soul apply even to the utter fool who despite his possession of the full complement of moral notions has formed explicitly no correct opinions.[158] The cases which Galen is interested in, however, are cases where a man falls away from his own better judgement. This can only occur when the set of opinions relevant to action is internally inconsistent, and Galen tells us this when he returns to criticism of Chrysippus on this point at *PHP* 5.4.10 ff.[159] There he explains that according to him the ultimate cause of the passions under discussion is a conflict between two judgements.[160]

This means that when a man falls away from his own better judgement, through a failure to act with the necessary circumspection and reflection, it is because he has in his soul a set of inconsistent opinions. This would not be the case if the agent had fully assimilated his reason to Right Reason. A sage has done this, and this is why all of his actions are according to Right Reason. When a man has in his soul conflicting opinions, then the over-all condition of his soul is weak. His judgements on practical and ethical matters are liable to be reversed when external circumstances lead him to assent according to one of his incorrect opinions and so to issue to himself incorrect commands.[161]

This account of the weakness of the soul explains why it is that a failure to achieve complete consistency with Right Reason also causes inconsistency with oneself.[162] Virtue is the unfailing correctness of one's judgements and impulses and it can only be achieved by internalizing completely the judgements and commands of Right Reason. Thus only the sage can be said to do everything properly.[163] It is also why excellence of soul is so often said to be a matter of harmony or consistency in one's opinions.[164] This is precisely how Chrysippus explained the weakness in the soul which produces passions: a failure to achieve harmony or consistency (also called symmetry) among the parts of the soul, where by parts he understands (much to Galen's annoyance) the concepts and notions in the ruling part of the soul.[165] This is the harmony among 'parts' of the soul which Chrysippus identified with the soul's health and beauty. It seems obvious that this strange way of talking about the harmony among parts of the soul is Chrysippus' attempt to redefine what Plato meant by psychic harmony.

These concepts and notions are the stable opinions according to which assent (a *kinêsis* in the soul) is given; they are enduring *hexeis* and the collection of them is termed *logos*. At this point it is helpful to recall that *logos* and assent are said to be distinct powers in the soul, just as are assent and impulse, and that these powers are described in terms of tension and *hexis*. Weak *tonos* also has its physical manifestation in the condition of the *pneuma* of the mind; but it is weakness in the dispositional aspect which explains the occurrence of passions. For Chrysippus, psychic disharmony or sickness in the soul was the weakness of the soul's disposition, its tendency to assent inconsistently because of the presence of conflicting opinions and principles.

Assent which is given in accordance with an unharmonious set of principles is bound to be weak and unstable.[166] The sage is free from this vacillation,[167] since his set of principles is in complete harmony with itself and with Right Reason. The ultimate goal of moral improvement is the complete eradication of such inconsistent opinions. But for the rest of mankind, who are on the way to perfection, the road to follow is one of constant effort to give one's assent only according to the proper opinions in one's soul and to examine very carefully all the presentations received from the world around us.[168]

As long as one's soul has this inconsistency of opinions and moral notions, one will be liable to fall prey to the persuasiveness of external things. This is the reason why Chrysippus used the example of Menelaus' surrender to the charms of Helen, despite his resolve to kill her for her misdeeds, in his account of the passions.[169] A passion is intrinsically unstable. Only impulses which are the result of a completely harmonious disposition of the soul are free of this fluctuation.

Now let us return to the problem posed by the identification of passions with excessive impulses.

(g) Excessive Impulse as Unreserved Impulse[170]

A consideration of the relationship between man and Right Reason (which is the same as the will of Zeus) has shed light on the sense in which passions are irrational. I suggest we look to the same area for help with the problem of excessiveness.

The impulse which constitutes a passion is excessive in a trivial sense—trivial for us but not for the Stoics. All impulses are motions in the *pneuma* of the *hêgemonikon*; this psychological materialism was taken very seriously by the Stoics, although we find it relatively unenlightening to be told that such and such a psychological event is identifiable with a certain set of movements in the stuff of the mind. In one sense, then, an impulse will be excessive because of a certain sort of motion in the *pneuma*. This is certainly one meaning of the fluttering (*ptoia*) in the soul which is attributed to passionate movements of the soul in a standard definition[171] and also in a quotation from Chrysippus.[172] Its importance for the Stoics is indicated by the further description of this kind of motion as 'ruffled', as a 'random movement'.[173] This may also be a part of what Chrysippus meant by calling such impulses 'uncontrolled' (*akrateis*).[174] But it is not the main significance of that reference to being out of control, or of other references to this characteristic of passions. Chrysippus himself explained it differently, and we must look at his own explanation for clues to the meaning of the excessiveness of the impulse.

I have argued that the doctrine of impulse with reservation was an important part of the orthodox conception of correct behaviour. It is through checking one's impulses with reservation that one is able to remain consistent both with oneself and with fate, the course of events in the world which is the will of Zeus. The passions too are closely linked to the need for a rational animal to adapt to fate.[175] Among other things, reservation in one's impulses makes possible the smooth flow of life which can never occur if one is subject to the inconsistencies and vacillations of the passions. Let us look at an example[176] of how this connection of reservation to the passions works. A man who is making moral progress (a *prokoptôn*) realizes that holding public office is appropriate, for he knows that service to one's fellow man is in accordance with our nature.[177] Men are, after all, *phusei koinônikoi*. This earnest citizen therefore decides to run for office. In doing so he assents to the proposition that it is appropriate to be a magistrate and to take the actions which are means to that end. So he campaigns and waits eagerly for the results when the votes are counted. Since he is only a *prokoptôn*, we may suppose that he acts as though winning office were a good thing; therefore his impulse to act in this way is a desire (*epithumia*), a mistaken impulse in pursuit of what is thought to be good. His impulse, therefore, is an impulse without reservation.

When the votes are counted it turns out that the poor man has lost. How does he handle this defeat? An ordinary man feels disappointment and frustration, which are forms of pain, since he is not able to follow fate willingly, wanting only what the will of Zeus decrees. He assents, therefore, to the proposition that something bad has occurred and that he should suffer a contraction in his soul. Perhaps later the bitterness of defeat induces him to ease his pain by convincing himself that the office was not really worth winning after all. So now he believes that nothing bad has happened. (Perhaps he thinks of all the labours of high office which he is spared.)

He is relieved of his pain, but at the cost of inconsistency with his previous opinions and actions, which were themselves inconsistent with the will of Zeus.

His original passion, desire, occurred because of a misevaluation of winning the election. The fact that his opinions and actions have shifted inconsistently is closely connected to his mistake about what is good and what is merely 'preferred'. His impulse to win office was unreserved when it should have been reserved, and so it was uncertain of success and potentially the cause of frustration and regret. The passions which he fell into were a result of inadequate knowledge of the good and how one should act amid uncertainty about what fate has in store for one.

On the other hand, consider the action of the sage. He would not have desired to win public office for its own sake, but only to do his best to do so. For that is the good in his action, the moral rightness in his decision, and this is wholly within his power.[178] He wants that good unreservedly and this desire cannot be frustrated by external events. This is correct *orexis*, not desire.

When the sage hears the news of his defeat, he feels no pain. Nothing bad has happened and no contraction of the soul is called for. Did he not want the magistracy? Yes, but only with the reservation 'if it is fated for me to win it; otherwise not'. He never forgets that his desire was only for something truly good, an impulse of the correct sort to win office.[179] Therefore the sage is never disappointed and is utterly free from passions and regret. Nothing he wants, in the special sense in which a sage may be said to want things, is beyond attainment.[180]

I suggest, then, that an impulse which is not protected by reservation when it should be is 'excessive'. This gives a comprehensible and important meaning to the term, which avoids the problems and obscurity of talking about the 'degrees' of impulse in a more ordinary sense. For if an impulse is excessive in the sense that one wants something more than one should because one thinks it better than it really is, then it is hard to see why there should not also be deficient impulses too. Plutarch, as we have seen, does adapt the theory in this direction; but his eclectic blend of Peripatetic and Stoic psychology cannot readily be substituted for the orthodox Stoic doctrine. Moreover, if we think back to the psychology as reconstructed above, we shall find no aspect of the theory which admits of the sort of variation of degree which would be needed for a more familiar quantitative sense of 'excessive'. But reservation is an integral part of that theory.

Epictetus described this way of exercising impulse as using impulse 'lightly and in a relaxed fashion'.[181] That this is consistent with the orthodox psychology of action (and *pathê*) is shown by Epictetus' description of it in fr. 27[182] as an 'art of giving assent'. But more important here is the fact that the kind of language used by Epictetus to describe impulse with reservation recurs in apparently orthodox discussions of the passions. Both Seneca[183] and Cicero[184] are discussing the state of the soul which produces the passions. They are describing the erroneous judgements according to which the mistaken assent which produces a passion is given. Seneca describes this disease of the soul as a stubborn judgement that 'those things which should be chosen lightly are to be chosen strongly (*valde*)' and Cicero echoes this. An illness in the soul is 'a very strong (*vehementem*) opinion concerning a thing which is not to be chosen . . . as though it were to be chosen strongly (*valde*)'.[185]

Cicero's text is virtually a translation of what we read in Arius Didymus.[186] For there a *nosêma* is defined as an 'opinion according to which they suppose that things which are not to be chosen are to be strongly (*sphodra*) chosen'. That this is meant to explain what it is for an impulse to be excessive is suggested by the occasional use of *hormê sphodra* in place of *hormê pleonazousa*[187] and by the rather more frequent references to *sphodrotês* in discussions of the passions.[188] But if I am right to connect this material with the passages which deal with 'using impulse lightly', it follows (with a bit of charity for the state of our sources) that the opposite of excessive impulse is reserved impulse.

This account of overstepping the natural symmetry of impulses applies primarily to the primary passions, desire and fear. To the extent that the subordinate passions occur as the result of these, the general description of passions as excessive impulse also has a certain application to them. But pleasure and pain are also 'excessive' in their own right. For they too overstep the limits set by Right Reason, and this was probably thought of in several ways. Pleasure and pain also lack that easy reversibility which is missing in desire and fear. We have already seen how this works in some detail for the case of pain.

Pleasure is an impulse to expansion in the soul. It will be excessive when it is an unreserved impulse to expansion on account of something which is not genuinely good. For merely preferred things, a reserved impulse to expansion may have been thought to be correct; this would give it the ability of easy reversal which would be needed when the preferred thing turned out not to be an advantage after all. With pain, however, the situation must have been different. For we are told[189] that there is no correct form of impulse corresponding to pain. This means that no impulse to contraction can be correct, not even a reserved impulse to contraction on account of something 'rejected'. This asymmetry between pain and pleasure would tell us a good deal about Stoic views on the values of the various indifferents.[190] But that is not our concern here. The claim that contraction in the soul is never justified is explained in general terms with reference to the strong Stoic commitment to the providential nature of the universe and to their belief that nothing which is really bad (i.e. vice or that which partakes in vice) is incurable. When one realizes that something truly bad is present, the appropriate response is not pain and grief, but redoubled efforts at moral improvement. Any impulse to a contraction in the soul is *eo ipso* an overstepping of the symmetry established by Nature.

It remains only to see whether this is consistent with Chrysippus' own explanation of the excessiveness of impulse. I take it as established that Chrysippus had a doctrine of impulse with reservation, even though we do not have any certain use by him of that term.[191] In his explanation of excessiveness (p. 155–6 above) Chrysippus did not use the language of reservation either, except in so far as he spoke of passions going too far. We must, therefore, allow for the possibility that the term itself was not used by Chrysippus. But it is the idea we wish to trace here.

Chrysippus spoke of the excessive impulse as one which goes beyond the proper symmetry of impulses. I suggest that this symmetry, also called the 'bounds' or 'limits' set by Right Reason,[192] is the result of the fact that impulses should not be unreserved when a reserved impulse is appropriate. That is, one's impulse will be within the bounds set by Right Reason and will be in accord with the natural symmetry of impulses if all one's impulses to things which are not good (or bad) are reserved and only one's impulses for the good properly conceived are unreserved. For if that is the case, then all one's actions will be in accord with the will of Zeus as well as with each other. The natural symmetry of impulses is identifiable with the will of Zeus, which is not surprising if we recall that Zeus' will (*boulêsis*) is a kind of impulse, one that is perfectly rational and correct. If one goes beyond this natural set of limits for one's impulses, then one's impulse is a passion, an irrational desire or fear. And the pleasure and pain which follow upon the success or failure of these primary passions are also passions; they too go beyond the bounds set by Reason. For they incorporate the judgement that what has happened is really good or bad when it is not, as well as the 'fresh' opinion that a certain affective reaction is called for. Thus the excessiveness of impulse is not, as Plutarch thought,[193] a reference to the exceeding of some ideal and moderate degree of motion in the soul; nor is it, as Galen thought,[194] a reference to a lack of rational control of an intrinsically irrational psychic movement. Rather, excessiveness is, as Chrysippus said, a result of overstepping the bounds and symmetry set by Right Reason.[195]

In Chrysippus' explanation of what it means for an impulse to be excessive he uses the analogy of a person running, in which the following parallelisms are said to apply. The motion of the legs of a runner or walker is analogous to the impulses of the agent when he is acting in a passion or correctly, respectively. The analogue of the Reason which one should follow is the impulse which governs walking or running. Then Chrysippus explains what it means for an impulse to exceed the bounds which it should keep to by comparing this with the way in which a runner's legs exceed his impulse. When one walks, the motion of the legs is always in correspondence with the impulse. A walker can stop or change direction[196] at will. What is lost in running is this ability to alter or adapt the motion of the legs in accordance with one's impulses. Similarly, if the agent's impulses exceed the symmetry of Reason, he loses the ability to alter or adapt to the commands of Reason.[197] This symmetry is described in this way: it is 'according to Reason and is as far as Reason deems proper'.[198] We see here the important connection of the symmetry of impulses with a correct estimate of value and with a limit on impulse.

Applying the analogy, we may conclude the following. The Right Reason of Nature issues for agents a set of commands, one after another. If he obeys these, he will adapt to the events of life as they occur with correct actions and so will regulate his life properly, according to the limits and values which Reason sets down. Different orders are given at different times, as the events of the providentially ordered world unfold; that is, in different circumstances of life different impulses and actions are called for in order to maintain harmony with Nature. If our impulses stay within the symmetry laid down by Nature, we will be able to adapt to events. That is, we can stop having an impulse to something (such as being elected to office) when it is clear that it is not what the will of Zeus has in store for us, just as the walker could stop; or we can change the object of our impulse (so that we want what actually occurs[199]), just as the walker can change direction. To exceed this symmetry and to want things unreservedly means losing this ability to adapt to events.

Reason's commands are tied up with value judgements and on that basis they set limits to an agent's impulses. An impulse should be only 'so much'. Some objects (the good and the bad) merit un-reserved impulse and others (the indifferents) merit reserved impulse. If a genuine good is pursued unreservedly no inconsistency or passion will ensue. Passions never occur in men who have a firm grasp of what is truly good; and men who do not are prone to pursue things which are not good as though they were. All such impulses are unreserved and incorrectly so. In this sense all impulses which constitute passions are 'excessive'. The error of the passions[200] is therefore not one of miscalculation, but of refusing to follow Reason, which would have told us how much to value the objects and events which we are concerned with. By turning our back on Reason and refusing to accept its valuation of things, we make it inevitable that we shall use our impulse incorrectly in pursuit of what we mistakenly suppose to be good.

Chrysippus went on[201] to say that such impulses or movements of the soul are *akrateis*, out of control. They do not control themselves, but are 'runaway' (*ekpheromenai*) like the motion of the runner in the text just considered.[202] This makes good sense on the proposed interpretation of 'excessive'. Right Reason ceases to regulate the actions of a man who has turned his back on it, and just as the runner's motion is not readily alterable by his impulses, so the agent's impulses and actions are beyond the limits set by Reason and therefore not alterable in accordance with its dictates. They do not follow Reason 'whatever it might be like', i.e. as it gives a man different commands. A rational agent resolves to follow Reason wherever it may lead, whatever it may command for him. Thus Chrysippus was prepared to say,[203] 'If I knew that it is now fated for me to be ill, I would even direct my impulse to that.' A man's job is to want what Zeus wants, i.e. to want that what actually occurs should occur, no matter what the cost to his own erstwhile desires. For in this accommodation to fate lies a man's true good and ultimate benefit.

Those, however, who do follow Reason, Chrysippus continues,[204] and steer their lives by it are able to control their impulses and be persuaded and adapt to what actually occurs and is revealed as god's will. Thus impulses which are irrational in the sense in which Chrysippus is using the word (*houtôs*),[205] i.e. by rejecting Reason, are called 'passions and unnatural, in that they exceed the rational constitution of man', which is to follow Reason wherever it leads. Chrysippus makes one additional remark of significance somewhat later.[206] He says that were it not for the excess an agent would preserve Reason (*toutou sôstikon*), i.e. remain within the rational constitution which is natural to man. In the phrase 'being swept away in a rush' (*athroôs pheromenê*) we may see a reference to the hasty and weak assent which is a result of giving in without due circumspection to a persuasive presentation.

Everything which Chrysippus says in the texts from *On Passions* which Galen preserves for us is at least consistent with the proposed interpretation of 'excess'. Some passages only make sense on this reading. Others might seem to lend themselves to a dualistic interpretation of the sort which Galen claims is actually implied by them. But that sort of interpretation is precisely what Chrysippus wants to avoid, since it conflicts with his entire psychology. Many of the suspiciously dualistic phrases which Galen quotes were used by Chrysippus, I suggest, at least partly because he wanted to show how the customary language used to talk about the passions could be reinterpreted to accommodate his new psychology of action. At times we may suspect that this simply is not so, that ordinary language is fundamentally linked to a dualistic model of the soul's operation; Posidonius and Galen certainly thought that it was, and moreover, that the facts of psychology could not be accounted for on the monistic hypothesis. I have tried to give a sympathetic reading of those quotations which critics selected for their purposes and, with the help of the general psychology of action and a broader look at the place of the doctrine of passions in Stoic ethics, to make sense of what Chrysippus said about the passions. Other attempts may fare better than my own and be more convincing; but the basic approach I have taken to this material seems to be the only one which has a serious chance of revealing the original force and meaning of the old Stoic psychology of the passions.

Before this chapter is concluded, two subsidiary problems demand a brief consideration.

(h) Good 'Passions' or Eupatheiai

It is not clear when the term *eupatheia* first came to be used in the Stoa. Nor is it known when they were systemized into the canonical trio *boulêsis* (will), *eulabeia* (caution), and *chara* (joy), although there is a strong presumption that this is the work of Chrysippus.[207] But certainty on this point is not essential. For the proper understanding of the Stoic ideal of the freedom from passions, which might be summed up in the slogan '*apatheia* is *eupatheia*', makes it clear that an *eupatheia* is simply the impulse of a fully rational man.[208] Just as the passions are analysed in terms of the Stoic psychology of action, so are the *eupatheiai*. And the doctrine of *apatheia*, which is at the heart of Stoic ethics, is in all essentials the work of Zeno. Freedom from passions is, I have argued, closely linked to consistency in one's assents and actions; therefore Zeno's ideal of the smooth flow of life and consistency are simply other ways of expressing both *apatheia* and *eupatheia* as ideals for living the life of a naturally rational animal.[209]

The identity of *apatheia* and *eupatheia* is also reinforced by the close connection of both to virtuous activity.[210] Note that *chara*, *euphrosunê*, and *tharros*, as well as the typical example of a virtuous action *phronimê peripatêsis*, are classed as *telika agatha*[211] although they are not themselves virtues[212] because they are not constant states of the soul of the sage.[213] Like *euphrosunê*, *chara* is an effect or product (*epigennêma*) of virtue.[214]

I shall not spend time here on the subtypes of the three *eupatheiai*,[215] although it might be worth while to point out that at least two of them are explained in terms of a readiness to accept fate gladly.[216] Bonhoeffer's discussion of this is adequate.[217] Nor shall I deal with the use made of the doctrine of *eupatheiai* by Antiochus and Philo.[218] It seems better to limit my comments to one or two further observations which confirm the analysis of passions presented in this chapter.

Boulêsis, like *hairesis* and *orexis* in its normative sense, is directed to the good,[219], i.e. virtue or virtuous acts. Like *chara*, then, it is not itself a virtue.[220]

Joy (*chara*, the Latin *gaudium*) is more discussed in our sources than the other *eupatheiai*. Sandbach raises a problem about *chara* which is worth considering more closely.[221] He argues that it is not clear whether joy is an expansion of the soul aroused only by what is truly good, or whether a proper, rational, and limited reaction to the attainment of preferred things would also count as a case of joy. Perhaps the explanation of excess in terms of reservation will help clarify the matter.

Plutarch[222] and Lactantius[223] do little more than indicate that joy is a correct (*eulogos*) expansion of the soul, which is the counterpart of the passion pleasure. In the *Tusculans* Cicero adds that what the Stoics call joy is a smooth and consistent expansion (*elatio*). Pleasure, its opposite, is a vain *elatio*, a reaction to what is not truly good (*TD* 4.12–4). Seneca is making the same point in letter 59 when he describes joy as a sage's 'expansion of the soul relying on goods which are its own and genuine' (*Ep.* 59.2).

Sandbach is worried that a proper reaction to something which is merely a preferred thing might occur in someone who is not yet a sage. If it does, he asks, why should this too not be a case of joy? It is clear that it should not, but the vague definitions of joy might suggest that it is. The reason why only a sage can experience an *eupatheia* is that when he has an expansion in his soul for something which is merely preferred, he does so with the proper reservation based on a fully reliable knowledge of the good. Only genuine goods are irreversible and reliable. Thus the sage, who is the only man who can have genuine goods or even know with complete conviction what they are, will have expansions of the soul for those goods and the impulse to this expansion will be unreserved. A merely preferred thing, for which the ordinary man might feel an expansion in his soul, is always liable to turn into something disadvantageous. The sage can *rely*, Seneca says, on the things for which he feels an expansion in his soul. But anyone who has an unreserved impulse to expansion is not in a position to rely on the object of his feeling being good; therefore, since joy must, as Seneca says, not stop nor be turned into its opposite, the reaction of the non-sage to anything cannot be joy. For only with genuine goods, which only the sage can have, is there no chance of regret or need for a change of heart.

Moreover, even when an ordinary man does one thing correctly this cannot be a case of *eupatheia*. For as the discussion of excessive impulse has suggested, full correctness in action is only possible when a man's entire system of beliefs and actions is correct and harmonious. Unless one is a sage, even a proper response to a stimulus will be in conflict with something else in one's life or in one's set of dispositions and opinions. Since consistency of one's whole life is the goal, something is radically wrong with each action or belief until all of one's actions, dispositions, and opinions are brought into harmony with one another and with the will of Nature. Ultimately the Stoics wish to apply moral evaluation to the whole man and his entire life, not to one isolated action.[224] From this perspective one can see the point of the Stoic paradox that all sins are equal: until the whole man is in complete harmony, something is wrong with everything he does.

But let us return to the sage. Nothing in Seneca's discussion rules out the possibility that the joy *of a sage* might include a reserved impulse to expansion for the presence of something which is merely preferred. Such a reserved impulse could easily be stopped if god wills that subsequent events bring unfortunate results. It is tempting to think of this kind of reserved response to something indifferent as a form of joy. But even this should not qualify, unless there is in the preferred thing some genuine good. Joy is a response to genuine goods, and so can only be felt for virtue or that which partakes of virtue.[225] If a sage or a friend of a sage acts virtuously, then joy is in order. One would like to think that joy is especially appropriate on those rare occasions when a man finally attains virtue.[226]

(i) The problem of the 'preliminary passions'[227]

We have already pointed out several important ways in which the Stoic decision to treat passions as part of the psychology of action shaped their theory. One consequence is that the term *pathos* can only be applied to a very narrow range of phenomena. In this section I want to look briefly at the results of this restriction in one area of psychology.

Since every passion is (the result of) an act of assent, any affective reaction which an agent has to something in his environment which cannot be considered, even in principle, to be the result of an assent will lose its claim to be called a *pathos*. Now the chief sign that assent is involved in some action or reaction is that the agent can if he wishes withhold his assent and so prevent this action or reaction. Any affective reaction which is completely beyond the voluntary control of an agent is therefore not a passion in the proper sense of the word.

Before looking at the complications which this theoretical restriction imposes on Stoic psychology, a closely related issue should be raised. It should be clear that no orthodox Stoic could say that an impulse could occur in an adult human either before or independently of an assent. But there are traces of such a view in the texts which we use to reconstruct old Stoic psychology, and they should be considered. In Cicero's *De Fato*, section 40, there is a reference by an unnamed philosopher[228] to an impulse (*impetus*) which precedes and determines human assent. By contrast, Chrysippus' response to this philosopher in sections 41–3 mentions only presentation as an external cause of assent and makes impulse a result of this.[229]

In an important letter of Seneca[230] there is another reference to an impulse preceding assent, which is then either confirmed or quashed by reason as it gives or refuses assent. Unlike the philosopher of *De Fato* 40, however, Seneca does not think that these preliminary impulses determine assent, so that despite the novelty of the analysis of action Seneca can retain the old Stoic conclusion that all actions are responsible, since the confirmation of assent is needed before any action occurs.[231]

Let us turn now to the question of the 'preliminary passions'.[232] It is obvious that a man has affective reactions which are radically involuntary. For example, we turn pale or tremble at a sudden shock; the most we can do is to reject this involuntary response and to refuse to give our assent to the proposition that something frightening has occurred. We can stop ourselves from having an impulse to avoidance or to contraction of the soul. But still, the involuntary response has occurred and it is at the very least peculiar to deny that it is a case of fear. For it *is* very similar to fear in its effects on us and is caused by the same stimulus. Yet the Stoics are committed to denying that it is fear, or even a cause of fear, not least because they conceded that even a sage would have these affective reactions. Whatever the mechanism by which this involuntary pallor or trembling is produced, it cannot on their theory be the result of an impulse. It might be tempting to blame these reactions solely on the body; but that was not the old Stoic manœuvre. It would be appealing to deny that the leading part of the soul was involved at all, but the importance of soul in all perception and sensation makes this impossible.

There are one or two important pieces of evidence which indicate the Stoic way of dealing with these phenomena within the framework of their psychology of action. Aulus Gellius preserves an important fragment of Epictetus which he claims is consistent with the doctrines of Zeno and Chrysippus. It is long, but worth quoting.[233]

Presentations in the mind . . . with which the intellect of man is struck as soon as the apppearance of something which happens reaches the mind are not voluntary or subject to one's control; but by a force of their own they press themselves on men to be acknowledged. But the assents . . . by which the same presentations are acknowledged are voluntary and occur subject to human control. Therefore, when some frightening sound from the sky or a collapsing building or the sudden announcement of some danger, or something else of the sort, occurs it is inevitable that even a sage's soul be moved for a short while and be contracted and grow pale, not because he has formed an opinion of anything evil but because of certain rapid and unreflective movements which forestall the proper function of the intellect and reason. Soon, though, the sage in question does not give assent . . . to such presentations . . . but he rejects and refuses them and judges that there is nothing in them to be feared. And they say that the difference between the mind of the sage and the fool is that the fool thinks that the violent and harsh presentations which first strike his mind (*primo animi sui pulsu*) really are as they seem; and he also confirms with his own assent these initial reactions, just as though they really were to be feared, and he *prosepidoxazei* (for the Stoics use this word when they discuss the matter[234]). Whereas the sage, when he has been affected briefly and in a limited fashion in his colour and expression, does not assent but retains the condition and strength of the opinion which he always had about such presentations, as things not at all worthy of being feared which try to frighten us with a false show and empty dread.

This is confirmed by a passage of Seneca[235] which attributes to Zeno similar views about the sage:

'What then? when the sage faces something like this, will his soul (*animus*) not be touched and will he not be moved more than usual?' 'I admit it', [says Seneca to his imaginary interlocutor], 'he will feel a certain light and feeble motion. For, as Zeno says, there remains even in the sage's soul, even when his wound has healed, a scar. Therefore he will feel certain hints (*suspiciones*) and shadows of passions, but passions themselves he will not have.'

It is clear that these involuntary responses occur in the soul, and even in the *hêgemonikon*, and that even a perfected soul is not free from this sort of reaction.[236] This is also the position attributed to the Stoics by Cicero in book 3 of the *Tusculans* (83): *morsus tamen et contractiuncula quaedam animi relinquetur* ('nevertheless, a "bite" and a certain small contraction of the mind will remain'). He adds that this reaction is natural.[237] Clearly, this acknowledgement of involuntary psychic reactions could be a serious modification to the monistic psychology of action; and the Stoics only avoided the need to concede that such a psychology was untenable by arbitrarily denying that these 'preliminary passions' are passions at all and so excluding them from the range of phenomena covered by the psychology of action.

Further evidence comes from Plutarch,[238] who takes the not unreasonable view that such reactions are really passions, but that the Stoic commitment to a monistic psychology would not allow them to admit it.[239] One may recall here that Aristotle, who was not committed to such a psychology, also referred to such involuntary reactions of fear and desire[240] and was not at all troubled by saying that they were involuntary, and that they were not the result of a command by reason (even though they could be the result of a thought as well as of a perception). But then, Aristotle believed that there was an irrational part of the soul. The Stoics, Plutarch says, took refuge in re-labelling such reactions with terms like *dêgmoi* (bites, cf. Cicero's *morsus*), *prothumiai* (eagerness, in the Loeb translation), and so forth.[241]

But the terminology is not the main problem here. For it is reasonable to apply new terms to phenomena which one *claims* are significantly different from the passions. And the difference between such reactions and true passions, however tenuous it seemed to others who were not committed to psychological monism, is not something which an orthodox Stoic could give up. For these reactions are not the result of assent and impulse.[242] Plutarch has a point. How can it be reasonable to deny that such reactions are essentially similar to the passions which they so closely resemble?

Seneca deals with the phenomena of preliminary passions frequently, but most extensively in book 2 of his *De Ira*.[243] It is likely enough that this account is intended to be orthodox. For he stresses that the preliminary reactions which resemble and may lead to the passion of anger are like involuntary bodily reactions[244] and are themselves involuntary.[245]

But there are features in his discussion which bring out the instability of the Stoic position. It is true that these involuntary responses are not here attributed to impulses. He calls them 'blows': *primus ille ictus animi*.[246] He stresses that such reactions are passive (*patitur magis animus quam facit*), compares them again to bodily reactions,[247] and insists repeatedly that they are not the result of assent.

But Seneca also says that they occur 'after the opinion that one has been injured' (2.2.2; cf. 2.3.4 *putavit se aliquis laesum*). No doubt he means by this simply that they occur after one has received a presentation to that effect (*speciem acceptae iniuriae*), which is the same claim that Epictetus made.[248] But the talk of opinion is striking and, to my mind, natural in reporting such phenomena. (One might also question how the mere acceptance of a presentation without assent could produce such reactions.)

Even more worrisome is the startling resemblance of this passage to the unorthodox psychology of action in *Ep*. 113.18 discussed above.[249] These preliminaries to passion are so similar to it that if they are not quashed by refusal of assent they will result in a passion. This is like the situation described in *Ep*. 113. We have the same sequence: initial response, confirmation of this response (*adprobavit* 2.3.5; *animo adprobante* 2.1.4; *confirmavit Ep*. 113.18), and then impulse. The only detectable differences are the avoidance of the term impulse for the initial response in the *De Ira* and the fact that *Ep*. 113.18 deals with ordinary voluntary actions and not passions.[250] In fact I would suggest that the similarity is best accounted for by supposing that the unusual sequence of *Ep*. 113 (nowhere paralleled for the early Stoics) may stem from a later attempt by a post-Chrysippean but orthodox Stoic (Diogenes? Antipater?) to refine the psychology of action in order to make it capable of accommodating *propatheiai* within the theory, without moving towards psychological dualism. (If this modification was made by someone after Chrysippus and with this purpose it would help to explain both the rarity of the theory as given in *Ep*. 113 and the frequency of the corresponding analysis of *propatheiai*.) The Stoics in general faced a serious problem in their application of the psychology of action to the passions; to exclude 'involuntary preliminaries to passions' from the framework of the theory was an essential but dubious task. The ambivalence in Seneca's position and the modification made after Chrysippus and reflected in *Ep.* 113 are signs of the general problem.

Seneca, though, goes beyond the old Stoic position in his other discussions of or allusions to the preliminary passions.[251] Sometimes, as in *De Ira* 1.7–8, he seems to attempt to reconcile a more dualistic discussion of the passions with the demands of Chrysippean orthodoxy.[252] Elsewhere he clearly thinks of these preliminary passions as involuntary reactions of an irrational part of the soul.[253] In other cases this is his tendency, although his position is less perspicuous.[254] In several places he attempts to describe these involuntary reactions as a product of the body alone.[255]

This tendency to dualism in the interpretation of the preliminary passions is understandable in Seneca. For although it is not the case (as Holler thought) that Posidonius originated the doctrine,[256] it is certain that he greatly elaborated it in terms of his own psychology. And he, of course, with his more complex non-monistic psychology, could do so with little difficulty. Fragment 154 of Posidonius reveals that he used the term *pathos* very broadly; he developed a classification of *pathê* which included 'psychic passions concerned with the body' (*peri to sôma*) and 'bodily passions concerned with the soul' (*peri tên psuchên*) and which would be a very useful framework for the accurate discussion of these involuntary psycho-physical phenomena. He could deal with them all the more easily since he accepted irrational powers in the soul which could respond independently of reason and assent.[257] It is tempting too to connect the 'passionate pull' (*pathêtikê holkê*) to the sort of automatic reactions which Seneca describes. For Kidd[258] describes this 'pull' in a way which suggests nothing so much as the preliminary passions.

The early Stoics acknowledged as genuine passions only those phenomena which could be squeezed into their psychology of action. Here again the theoretical constraints of the psychology of action prevent them from giving a fully satisfying account of psychic phenomena such as the 'preliminary passions'. But they did try. Is there no virtue in their attempt? Despite its precarious position in old Stoic psychology, it seems to me that it has its merits as a description of a special kind of emotional response, the feeling of cool detachment from involuntary emotional reactions. This is a familiar experience and it occurs most often in the case of fear. As evidence, I append three quotations gathered in the course of random unphilosophical reading, all of which describe (more or less seriously) a sort of detached fear which is unpassionate in a sense which Chrysippus would have welcomed.

From Oliver Wendell Holmes:[259]

But I remembered the story of Sir Cloudesley Shovel, who was seen all of a tremor just as he was going into action. 'How is this?' said a brother officer to him. 'Surely you are not afraid?' 'No', he answered, 'but my flesh trembles at the thought of the dangers into which my intrepid spirit will carry me.'

More circumstantial is this account by Tom Wolfe of John Glenn's feelings during space flight:[260]

Occasionally he could feel his heart skip a beat or beat with an odd electrical sensation, and he knew that he was feeling the tension. (And at the biomedical panels the young doctors looked at each other in consternation—and shrugged.) Nevertheless, he was aware that he was feeling no fear. He truly was not. He was more like an actor who is going out to perform in the same play once again—the only difference being that the audience this time is enormous and highly prestigious.

Perhaps best is this from John Gardner:[261]

Nor had he thought about death at night when he returned to his tent—except once. Once in the middle of the night a cannonball had crashed through his tent and knocked his cot out from under him—it seemed the same instant, though it couldn't have been, that he had heard the muffled thud of the cannon's exploding black powder. But even that he had not registered as fear. It had been, he would say, an extreme of startledness, a slam of heart that had nothing to do with his mind, his beliefs, and convictions.

Chapter 6

Moral Evolution

With the passions we leave behind those areas of Stoic ethics where the psychology of action exercises a dominant influence on the content of their ethics. We consider again ways in which the psychology of action is used in the formulation of ethical doctrines which might have received expression in terms of another moral psychology or might even have been set out with no technical psychological doctrines to support them. But even in this area, where the role of the old Stoic psychology of action is less crucial, it plays its part.

The Stoics gave a great deal of attention to the moral evolution of the individual man, giving an account of his development from the time when he is born. At birth a person has a soul which is in many respects a *tabula rasa*, but nevertheless contains within it certain uncorrupted inclinations to develop into a creature which loves morality and reason above all else. They also gave an account of why human development never follows this ideal course.[1] Someone who did develop perfectly would be a natural sage.

The sage was thought to be as rare as the phoenix, but a sage who was not first a fool is impossible. Zeno's remark that even the sage carries with him the scars of his former passions is applicable to all sages, and it is clear that the Stoics did not expect anyone to develop morally without first falling into folly.[2]

Nevertheless, they gave a normative account of a person's development from the time of the first inclinations and actions of the infant to the achievement of perfected reason. At each stage of this development there are characteristic actions and consequently characteristic kinds of impulse. If we follow this development through, we shall see how the doctrine of impulse plays its role at each stage. Two restrictions on the scope of this discussion should be noted. There are many problematic aspects of Stoic ethics which must be dealt with and a thorough examination of them all is impossible here; an outline of my own considered view will have to suffice. The second is a more important restriction. In this discussion I shall be trying to reconstruct what Chrysippus' position was on these topics. The formulation which Stoics after Chrysippus gave for the goal of life (*telos*) changed considerably, although opinions differ over the question whether any of the Stoics down to Antipater intended to change the substance.[3] As always in attempting to reconstruct Chrysippean views, some use must be made of general doxographic material whose formulation must date from the time of Diogenes and Antipater. But enough can, I think, be recovered of Chrysippus' own views to allow us to use this material with cautious confidence.

The question of the evolution of Stoic ethics before Chrysippus is much more difficult, and I shall try to say as little as possible about this question. Our evidence for Zeno and Cleanthes is scanty and, in places, apparently contradictory. Still, the reader deserves to know the approach I take to this question. I am most impressed by the apparent unity of the Stoics on fundamental points from Zeno to Antipater and the burden of proof seems to me to lie on those who would argue for substantial change between the time of Zeno and that of Chrysippus. We seldom have the evidence needed to support that burden.[4]

In looking at the doctrines associated with the moral development of man from the viewpoint of the psychology of action we shall be considering several kinds of impulse. The 'primary impulse' of animals to self-preservation and the other impulses of the pre-rational stage of human life must be carefully considered. The rational selection (*eklogê*) of which men become capable at the age of reason is also a kind of impulse, and its importance will have to be examined. And further, the special sort of impulse which is involved in the virtuous actions of the fully mature rational agent, the sage, also demands some sort of account, although here our evidence is very limited indeed and a certain amount of speculaton will be needed.[5]

First, some general remarks. The Stoics broke with tradition and posited two distinct kinds of value, the 'selective value' (the term is Antipater's)[6] of things which are 'indifferent' for human happiness and the moral value of good and bad things. These two sorts of value, explicitly distinguished by the Stoics, are incommensurable with each other and no amount of the former can outweigh the latter. Moral value's contribution to the consistent and smoothly flowing life of harmony with Nature is of a different kind from the contribution of non-moral values. Yet both kinds are important and are reflected in the actions of a human life.

The difference between these two kinds of value and action must be understood from the point of view of the *archê* of value, which is Nature. The starting-point for all value is the desire of all animals, including humans, for self-preservation. Even the ultimate value in human life, which is virtue, has its roots in this basic animal desire. It is a development of this basic desire and is understood by analogy to it. Since even the 'good' which is unique and proper to man is rooted in this fundamental desire, we must begin as the Stoics did with this primitive orientaton to self-preservation and consider its relationship to and development into the moral commitment of the rational man.

One conclusion of some importance for the old Stoic understanding of human nature may be pointed out in advance. The human animal, we have seen, develops from being irrational to being rational. That is, pre-rational children (like animals) neither form propositions to help guide their actions, nor control their actions by assent. They are, consequently, not responsible as adults are. It follows that at some point human nature undergoes a radical change. Instead of being, from the point of view of action and moral responsibility, similar to brute beasts, the newly rational human becomes responsible, susceptible of good and bad action in a way that animals never are. After this transformation of its nature, the human being is capable of passions and correct actions, neither of which are possible for irrational animals or children. With this transformation there comes a change in the values relevant to the agent. Yet despite this radical change in nature and its values, there is a continuity in both. There is a sense in which the values of the rational and pre-rational human are natural; there is a vitally important analogy which gives unity to human life at all its stages. But to see what this analogy is, we must begin at the beginning, with the desire for self-preservation.

(a) Orientation

'Orientation' is the translation I use for the term of art *oikeiôsis*, adopted by the Stoics to describe their novel theory of the basic state of affairs which grounds all human and animal action. No single translation can capture the various nuances of the Greek word. The verb from which this noun is derived, *oikeioô*, suggests the process of making something one's own, i.e. acquiring it or adopting it;

it also suggests that one feels affection for something, is well disposed to it; and the thing to which one has an *oikeiôsis* is also thought of as being one's own, the proper possession of the agent or something he has a strong natural kinship to. But these are connotations. *Oikeiôsis* and the verb from which it is derived, as well as the adjective *oikeios*, are technical terms for the old Stoa. I choose the term 'orientation' because it brings out the important relational meanings of the word, and because it seems well adapted to expressing the importance of *oikeiôsis* in grounding other ethical ideas which are derived from it. An advantage of this translation is that it makes the verb 'orient' available for the Greek *oikeioô*, in the active and passive voices. A disadvantage is that the adjective *oikeios*, which refers to something to which one has an orientation, cannot be easily translated by a form of the English word I have chosen;[7] it will often be transliterated. Moreover, we lose the sense of endearment and belonging which is also important. But the word is ultimately untranslatable.[8]

That the doctrine of *oikeiôsis* was original in the Stoa and of fundamental importance for their ethics may be taken as established, although both points have been controverted.[9] I shall not be much concerned here with the many historical problems surrounding it, but I should say that I regard the doctrine, if not the term, as a part of Zeno's attempt to ground ethics in a naturalistic way. In doing so he was probably influenced by Epicurus,[10] as Pohlenz argued, but also by Academic and Peripatetic philosophers.[11] It seems unlikely that any one philosopher decisively anticipated Zeno, although strong claims have been put forward for Theophrastus. Rather, we should think of the Stoics as having formed their characteristic views on the foundations of ethics in a milieu where these problems were subject to lively and incisive debate from all sides. But it is hard to say much more about Zeno's theory.[12]

The Stoics said that man's basic orientation was to himself, and that his primary impulse (on which more will be said below) was to self-preservation. In this he was like all other animals. These claims form the starting-point for the story the Stoics told about the development of man's specifically human commitment to the good, i.e. virtue. By contrast, hedonists such as Epicurus said that all animals, including man, had a basic commitment to pleasure and that even in man this did not fundamentally change throughout his life; even the virtues were sought for the sake of pleasure. The most important use of the concept of orientation was in just this sort of debate about the goal of life, the *telos*. But eventually the term *oikeiōsis* came also to be used in discussions of the foundations of one specific virtue, justice, and the Stoics talked of our basic orientation to other human beings as being the root of all justice and the social bonds which hold together human society.[13] This second use of the concept is quite distinct from the orientation to oneself which is the basis of general discussions of moral evolution.[14] The relationship between these two forms of orientation is more problematic than has usually been thought.[15] Fortunately the relationship between them need not concern us here, since the two are distinct and only the orientation to oneself is brought into connection with the problems we are considering; only it is linked to impulse and the psychology of action in our sources for the old Stoa.

Let us look at the most important single piece of evidence that we have for the views of Chrysippus on the moral development of human beings (D.L.7.85–6).[16]

They say that an animal has its first impulse to self-preservation, since Nature oriented it ⟨to itself⟩ from the beginning, as Chrysippus says in book one of *On Goals*, stating that the first thing each animal is oriented to is its own constitution and the awareness of this.[17] For it was not reasonable [sc. for Nature] to alienate an animal ⟨from itself⟩ nor, having created it, neither to alienate it nor to orient it [sc. to itself]. So it remains to state that having constituted it, She oriented it to itself. For it is thus that it repels harmful things and pursues things it is oriented to. They claim that what some people say is false, viz. that an animal's primary impulse is to pleasure. For they say that pleasure—if there really is any [sc. at this stage]—is an aftereffect [sc. occurring] when nature itself by itself seeks out and acquires things that fit its constitution; as animals *thrive in good health*[18] and plants flourish. And Nature, they say, did not operate differently in the cases of plants and of animals, because[19] it controls them too, without impulse and perception. And in our case too some plantlike processes occur. Since in addition impulse is a further feature of animals, using which they pursue things they are oriented to, for them the natural [sc. comes about] by being governed in accordance with impulse. Since reason has been given to rational animals as a more perfect superintendent, the rational correctly turns out to be natural for them. For reason supervenes as a craftsman upon impulse.

Before discussing it in more detail, it is worth emphasizing certain features of this text. Orientation to oneself is the starting-point for the discussion of human nature. All animals start life, as a result of this basic orientation, with an impulse to self-preservation, and this entails the avoidance of harmful things and the pursuit of things which are *oikeia*, i.e. things to which the animal is oriented as a result of this basic orientation. This is changed for men when reason supervenes (on the growth of reason see SVF 2.83). For a rational animal the natural life—which is still the goal, despite the fundamental change brought about by reason—is a life according to reason. But an irrational animal is living naturally if he lives only according to impulse, i.e. impulse as it is before reason comes along to dominate it through assent, which means pursuing those things which naturally elicit impulse, the *oikeia*. According to this text, until a human being develops reason, his action and the life which is natural to him are basically similar to those of irrational animals.

The details of this development must be worked out as the evidence is presented. But one point should be emphasized here. In keeping with the old Stoa's almost exclusive concern with the role of reason in altering animal nature, Chrysippus neglected any serious study of the gradual growth of the human (or animal, for that matter) from birth to maturity. It is only the moral development he is interested in, and so the one basic distinction he has in view is this: rational or irrational animal. We should be accustomed by now to this rather rough and ready approach to the observation of human nature in the older Stoics.[20] It is not in the least surprising that Posidonius took Chrysippus to task for his inadequate observation of young children.[21] Given his strong interest in the evaluative point of view, Chrysippus did not emphasize the fact, which is obvious to us, that children grow and mature in easy stages which blend into one another. He set aside this biological and organic point of view and stressed the demarcation between rational agents capable of assent and the irrational who are not.

Thus we find that Chrysippus (and probably Zeno too) did not have a detailed theory about the gradual evolution of humans. Their interests were narrower that that. When they spoke about 'primary impulse' or the 'primary natural things' (if the early Stoics used this term at all),[22] they did not have in mind a distinct form of impulse and specific behaviour patterns which are characteristic of newborn animals only.[23] This has sometimes been assumed, but the evidence does not support the claim.[24] These terms seem to refer only to the irrational impulse and its objects, which are characteristic of any irrational animals, including pre-rational humans of all ages. 'Primary', for Chrysippus, designates this irrational or pre-rational stage, not just the neo-natal period. This 'primary' element is also more elementary in a logical sense, as we shall see. But let us turn now to a closer consideration of the basic text.

Chapters 85–6 of book 7 of Diogenes Laertius are the basic source of our information about Chrysippus' theory of orientation and primary impulse, and this text is one of the most densely informative and reliable sources on a topic of significance which is available to students of early Stoicism. We do not, of course, know the origin of Diogenes' extract on Stoic ethics; but it must have been a fairly late compendium, if we are to judge by the references to Hecaton and Posidonius in the section on the *telos* which follows immediately (7.87). On the other hand, the first book of Chrysippus' *On Goals* was clearly used in a systematic way by the compiler and we may suppose that the reports of Zeno's and Cleanthes' opinions on the goals which follow in sections 87–9 were taken from Chrysippus' discussion.[25]

It is significant that Chrysippus' views on orientation and the primary impulse came in book one of his treatise *On Goals*. For it clearly set the pattern followed by most later Stoic writers of treatises on ethics. This is true of Diogenes' source, of the source for Cicero's *De Finibus* 3, and of Hierocles. The only important exception to this is Arius Didymus, in the extract on Stoic ethics preserved in Stobaeus.[26] As far as we know, Zeno did not write a treatise *On the Goal*. But since his views on the *telos* are reported as being given in his work *On Human Nature* or *On Impulse*, it is safe to conclude that whatever he had to say on the topic of the primary impulse also came in a work dealing with the goals of life. So Chrysippus himself may well be following a pattern already established by the founder of the school. Whether Cleanthes expressed his views on the topic of the primary impulse and *oikeiôsis*[27] in his *On the Goal* or in his two books *On Impulse*, we cannot know. But it is certain, given the wide influence of Chrysippus' works and their status as authoritative expositions of orthodox Stoicism, that Chrysippus' manner of presenting this material was the model for later discussions.[28]

The reliability and centrality of the basic text for Chrysippus' views on ethics justify using it as the principal evidence for reconstructing early Stoic views on *oikeiôsis* and primary impulse and judging later elaborations of the theme by comparison with it. My procedure will be to use later material to fill out the account only where it is coherent with what we have in the basic text. For the material it presents, it must be authoritative.

Probably the most striking feature of the basic text is the fact that Chrysippus assigns to Nature the role of an agent.[29] We are told that the primary impulse is the result of something which Nature does. The primary impulse is what it is because Nature orients an animal to itself from the beginning of its life.[30] The causal force of the verb 'orients'[31] is confirmed by the references of Alexander, Gellius, Plutarch, and Hierocles.[32] (On the other hand, the author of the pseudo-Philonian *De Aeternitate Mundi* (35) seems to have taken *phusis* as the individual nature of the animal, as the word is also used in D.L. 7.86. Cicero's version in *De Finibus* 3 lacks this emphasis on Nature's agency at this point.[33] But this is a less reliable source for Chrysippus' exact wording; Plutarch and Alexander are likely to have had direct access to Chrysippus' account.[34])

What, then, about the relationship between the orientation[35] and the primary impulse? Are they to be identified or are they distinct dispositions?[36] Clarity on this is worth pursuing since these dispositions are the psychological starting-point in the process of moral evolution.

That the two dispositions are in fact distinct is suggested by the difference between their objects. As we might expect from the general psychology of action, the primary impulse is directed at a predicate representing an action, in this case preserving oneself. The orientation, however, is directed at the animal's constitution and the awareness of this. These objects are not actions, and so it would be surprising if the orientation were ever identified with this impulse by Stoic authors. But it is not. This distinction is important and it is worth while to insist on it at this stage. For Chrysippus also says here that the act of orienting is the cause of the primary impulse which the animal has.[37] And this would not be sensible if the two were to be identified.

This causal relationship is better understood if we think back to the psychology of action. An impulse may be one of two things. As a *kinêsis*, a movement in the soul, it is stimulated by a presentation of something appropriate to the agent (*phantasia tou kathêkontos autothen*). But not every animal finds the same things appropriate to itself, and the reason for this is to be found in the basic constitution or make-up of the animal. This natural aptness to find some things appropriate and so stimulative of impulse is rooted in a disposition, a *hexis*. The disposition of the soul which determines what will be stimulative of impulse for each animal is a hormetic disposition (*Ecl.* 2.87), and this is the source of the *hormê* as a *kinêsis*.

As we shall see, the primary impulse is a form of hormetic disposition. Since this is a disposition to act in a certain way in response to certain stimuli, it is different in an important respect from some modern and particularly Freudian notions of instinct. These dispositions to act in a certain way are not to be thought of as dynamic pressures to act in a certain way which demand expression, and which find expression in some sublimated or distorted form if they are repressed. Rather, the hormetic disposition is an innate plan which regulates selective response to stimuli. The drive to act does not build up and push the animal from within into action. The Stoics thought of the disposition as something which governed responses to stimuli when they occurred and as simply lying dormant, doing nothing, when not stimulated.

The primary impulse is a disposition which directly regulates action and it does so in such a way as to preserve the constitution[38] of the animal (or the animal itself[39]). The constitution itself is also a disposition. For Seneca gives a definition of *constitutio* which is almost certainly derived from Chrysippus: it is the *hêgemonikon* in a certain relation to the body.[40] The orientation seems to function as a bridge between the constitution and the primary impulse, being an inward-turning or reflexive relationship with strong affective overtones. The primary impulse governs actions directed at external benefits and threats, and the orientation explains why this primary impulse is the way it is by relating it to the animal's constitution. The orientation explains why animals act as they do, i.e. in their own self-interest.

Thus in the first part of the basic text three dispositions are mentioned: the constitution, the orientation to it, and the primary impulse, a form of hormetic disposition, as a result of the orientation. The orientation establishes the animal's interest in itself and affection for itself and so produces a *hexis hormêtikê* which determines definite kinds of action in response to environmental stimuli. And the result of this complex state of affairs is that the animal undertakes action to preserve itself, avoiding things which harm it and pursuing things which are appropriate or natural to it—here referred to as *oikeia* because their value to the animal is determined by its *oikeiôsis* and its *prôton oikeion*.[41]

Chrysippus also introduces here a concept which remained important in later treatments of the fundamental principles of Stoic ethics. I refer to self-perception or self-awareness.[42] The relation of this concept to the other basic features of Chrysippus' theory of orientation is somewhat obscure.[43] It seems clear enough that to have an orientation to one's constitution one must in some sense be aware of it; self-perception is the *sine qua non* of orientation to oneself. But the relationship of this self-perception to the primary impulse is not clarified in any of our sources.[44] I venture to say, however, that self-awareness does not play the role of stimulating the impulse to perform self-preserving actions.[45] For such actions would most naturally be stimulated by perceptions of threatening or life-enhancing situations, i.e. external states of affairs. The discussions of Seneca and Hierocles suggest, in fact, that the self-perception is closely bound up with the ability of the animal's constitution to have an effect on the way in which it reacts to such external stimuli. This is suggested by some of Hierocles' arguments for the existence of this phenomenon,[46] in which the ability of animals to know what is beneficial or harmful to themselves or what their powers and natural strengths are, is cited as proof that self-perception is a fact of animal nature.

Hierocles' text is on many points close to Chrysippus' own account, although it does not give us additional information about the primary impulse. Thus he shares Chrysippus' emphasis on the agency of Nature (col. 6.40–3) and echoes his terminology quite closely, as at 6.51–3: it is oriented to itself and its own constitution.[47] But the most striking case of this is the close parallel in Hierocles to the teleological argument which Chrysippus gives in the basic text to show that it is oneself to which an orientation exists, and not to pleasure.[48] Although Hierocles emphasizes[49] the affective connotation of the *oikeiôsis* relationship more explicitly than Chrysippus does (note *dusarestein* and *euarestein*, dissatisfaction or satisfaction at the presentation of oneself), the structure of the argument is the same as that in D.L. 7.85.

In this argument Chrysippus begins in familiar Stoic fashion from a division of the possible situations into two contraries and an intermediate. Either an animal is oriented to itself or against itself or neither way. The latter two possibilities are then ruled out as being inconsistent with the teleological presumptions made about Nature and its rational purposiveness by Chrysippus (and of course by Plato and Aristotle too[50]).

Reflection on this argument can shed some light on the nature of the primary impulse. Chrysippus does not seem to be disputing what it is that animals are doing when he offers this argument that the primary impulse is not to pleasure but to self-preservation. Anyone could see what the overt behaviour of animals was: young mammals are seeking the breast, for example, and young birds are huddling under their mother's wings.[51] This is not what the disagreement with the hedonists is about. The debate, rather, is over how best to describe such actions.[52] Chrysippus is looking for demonstrations that animal behaviour is essentially self-preservatory and not hedonistic.

Hierocles and Seneca[53] use similar anti-hedonistic arguments for somewhat different purposes. But in both cases the general approach is the same as it seems to have been in Chrysippus. Instances of animal behaviour are cited which could only be the result of an impulse to self-preservation (or the preservation of one's constitution), such as fear of the dark (7.5–15), perseverance despite unpleasantness (7.15 ff.), and the need of a tortoise to right itself when turned over on its back. The assumption which makes the argument effective is that only one general impulse is to be posited as underlying a wide range of animal behaviour. Accordingly, if some actions could only be described as being aimed at self-preservation, then all must ultimately be motivated in the same way. The conclusion is that the pleasures involved in any of these acts must be purely incidental.

Given that this is the general character of the Stoic arguments about the primary impulse, some conclusions can be drawn about the nature of this impulse. It will not be the *kinêsis* which causes a particular action; for one would not quarrel about the basic description of an overt action. Nor will it be the hormetic disposition which governs that particular action. For that will be just as specific.[54]

The primary impulse is a more general disposition which determines the many particular impulses which generate actions aimed at self-preservation. Chrysippus refers to both the primary impulse and individual acts of self-preservation; but, I suggest, we should think of the primary impulse as a sort of mediator which comes between the very general orientation to oneself and individual actions aimed at self-preservation. Thus he concludes: 'So it remains to state that having constituted it, Nature oriented it to itself. For it is thus[55] that it repels harmful things and pursues things it is oriented to.'[56]

It follows that the term 'primary impulse' does not refer to some special desires or activities of recently born animals.[57] It is, rather, a general description of animal behaviour which brings out the relationship of such behaviour to the basic orientation which it has throughout its life. The impression that the primary impulse is a specific neo-natal desire is encouraged by a hasty reading of *De Finibus* 3.16. Here the specific actions aimed at self-preservation which Cicero refers to are presented as the actions of young children, at a time before pleasure and pain can influence them.

Cicero gives this as an argument to show that the orientation is directed to the object which Chrysippus said it was directed to.[58] But this is only one argument among many that are designed to show that Chrysippus' description of animal behaviour is the only one that fits all the facts. Thus Cicero quickly moves on to other arguments based on behaviour not restricted to newborn animals.

Hierocles argues in the same way. He describes how young animals act to preserve themselves (col. 6.54–9) and he offers the additional example of the child's fear of the dark. But he then passes (7.15 ff.), without a break or any indication that he has begun to argue a new point, to cases which have no bearing on a newborn animal at all. Seneca (*Ep.* 121.8) shows the same pattern.

There are indeed texts which emphasize that the orientation to oneself exists from birth onwards (see n. 57). Seneca (121.10–13) and Hierocles (5.40–6; 3.54 ff.) are also concerned to show that self-perception is a fact of animal nature from the moment of birth. The reason for this is well known. Uncorrupted infants are a valuable test case; no one can argue that the character or behaviour of the animal has yet been distorted by experience. But the importance for these naturalistic arguments about the foundations of ethics of the crucial test case of the behaviour of infants has muddied the waters surrounding the primary impulse of Chrysippus' theory, by encouraging an exclusively temporal reading of the word 'primary'.

But it must be emphasized again that this was only one

argument among many. Hierocles drew the same conclusion from the behaviour of adults in difficult and trying circumstances (col. 7.16 ff). The primary impulse which Chrysippus refers to in the basic text is best seen as a fact of the most elementary and universal animal nature, one which helps to unify and explain a wide range of behaviour. Animal actions, and this includes a great many human actions, are accounted for by reference to this basic feature of animal nature which is present from birth onwards. This primary impulse itself is made comprehensible and integrated into a wider teleological framework by reference to the animal's basic orientation to itself.

It is clear from the anti-hedonistic thrust of the text of Chrysippus which we are considering that Chrysippus wanted to make good his point about orientation because his entire system of ethics would be founded on it. Man's commitment to virtue could be derived, he thought, from the basic instinct of self-preservation more plausibly than from a basic instinct to pursue pleasure. But the theory has more value than this. It offers a coherent way of understanding the significance of a wide range of animal behaviour by reference to a fairly simple principle with considerable explanatory value. He would, I suspect, have wanted to claim that his theory of orientation was the most economical explanation of animal behaviour, within the framework of certain teleological assumptions about nature as a whole, as well as being the necessary condition of his mature ethical theory.

(b) The pursuit of things in accordance with nature[59]

We have seen how an animal's orientation to its own constitution gives it a primary impulse to self-preservation. This is primary in the sense of being the impulse an animal has from the beginning of its life, but it is not restricted to some particular actions characteristic of very young or newborn animals. For it is also primary in a 'logical' sense; it is the general hormetic disposition with reference to which actions characteristic of irrational animals are performed. Thus in the basic text we are told that as a result of the orientation the animal has to itself, it avoids harmful things and pursues things which are *oikeion* to it. And by *oikeion* here must be meant anything which is appropriate or proper to the animal in view of its primary *oikeion*, which is its constitution and the awareness of it. These derivative *oikeia* are also called 'natural' (see n. 41); these things which are in accordance with nature may, for the sake of brevity, be termed 'natural things'.

In this section we look primarily at merely animal action; in (*c*) and (*d*) the ways in which human action is different will be taken up. This examination of the lower level is important for the study of man, since in his early years he has so much in common with the animals. And his nature in the pre-rational years is still of importance to the mature rational agent.

The natural life for rational animals is to live according to reason; but we are told that the natural life for mere animals is to be governed in accordance with impulse. It is this notion of being governed in accordance with impulse which needs explanation at this point. But note first a fact of importance for the understanding of the relationship of human to animal nature. Each has its way of living according to nature. In mere animals impulse is the highest power in the soul (jointly with presentation) and to live naturally is to live according to that. Similarly for men; since reason is their highest power, it is reason which they must live by if they are to achieve the life according to nature. It is immediately apparent that what is natural for the two main branches of the animal world is the same by analogy, and so there is an important continuity within the animal kingdom. But more important, since humans in their pre-rational years are, for evaluative purposes, similar to mere animals, this provides an important continuity within the life of one human being as he grows to his full rational maturity. The onset of reason may change his life, but the analogical continuity provided by the concept of living according to nature prevents his life from falling into two separate and unrelated periods.

This use of a relational analogy to unify the various stages of a person's life is reminiscent of Letter 121 of Seneca. There the question is raised (*Ep.* 121.14–18) how an infant can have an orientation to the rational constitution which is characteristic of human beings, when his own constitution is not yet rational. The answer to this shows how orientation to oneself or one's constitution can be the same throughout life despite the fact that this constitution changes as life progresses. Each age has its own constitution and one is always oriented to the one which one has at any single time. But the relational disposition, which is what the orientation is, remains the same because the structure of the relationship is constant although one of the terms of the relationship changes in character. The structural features of the relation of orientation to oneself ensure that there is an analogical continuity in one's life, despite the radical changes it undergoes.

But we return to the notion of being governed by impulse. We shall see that there is abundant evidence in the doxographers for the Stoic claim that natural things stimulate impulse, by which it is meant that in animals the presentation of something which is in accordance with its nature automatically produces an impulse to pursuit behaviour.[60] Animals do not have assent, of course; they cannot evaluate their presentations rationally as humans can. But this does not mean that they are completely undiscriminating in their reactions to presentations. The animal's nature and the accuracy of its perceptual mechanisms will have considerable impact on how it reacts to its environment. But without reason to put the upshot of its presentations into words, the kind of complex and morally significant evaluation of which humans are capable is not possible. The best that an animal can do is to live with complete efficiency in accordance with its impulses, never pursuing un-natural things by mistake and always pursuing what accords with and enhances its nature.

The natural things and unnatural things are also important in human life, in so far as they determine the values in accordance with which rational selection is made (see section (c) below). In adult humans they are no longer the only things which are natural or unnatural, nor indeed are they so in the most important sense. But they are still important for the life in accordance with reason, whatever else it may be which reason adds to the life which is merely according to impulse. So it is worth while to take a closer look at the foundations of this sort of value. In effect we are asking why it is that natural things are natural.

We already have the beginnings of an answer to this question in the interpretation of the basic text which has been advanced. On this reading, natural things are natural because of the orientation to one's own constitution. All animals are oriented to this; and while in men this constitution is defined as a relation of the rational *hêgemonikon* to the body, in the animal it will be some analogous relationship of soul to body. The whole animal, then, the parts and powers of its soul and its body, are its constitution and it is to this which one has an orientation.

But this is general and behaviour is particular, and so as we have

seen the primary impulse is posited to link the two and to make all
the particular actions explicable in terms of the basic assumptions
which the Stoics made about the rational teleology of Nature and
all her works. Accordingly, actions or objects which promote self-
preservation and the enhancement of one's nature[61] are also *oikeia*
and stimulate impulse. Since the orientation and the primary
impulse, as well as the constitution of the animal in question, are
the work of Nature, the behaviour pattern produced by the fact that
these things stimulate impulse is reasonably enough called
'natural' itself, and the things one pursues are called 'natural
things'. The role of the primary impulse as that in reference to
which all particular actions of irrational animals are judged to be
natural or unnatural is clear; this is the logical sense of primariness,
and it complements the loosely temporal sense of 'primary' according to which the word designates the pre-rational period of a
human's life when he is deemed by the Stoics to behave similarly to
an animal.

Several texts support my claim that the orientation (and hence
the primary impulse) is the factor by reference to which the Stoics
determined what is natural. Alexander (SVF 3.180) makes the
orientation the criterion for the natural life. Gellius (SVF 3.181) says
that self-love and self-preservation lead to a pursuit of the primary
natural things. Seneca too shows how pleasure and pain, which are
sometimes referred to as natural and unnatural,[62] are derived from
the orientation: 'first the animal is oriented to itself; for there must
be something to which other things are referred.'[63] This is the same
sort of relation mentioned in Arius' account of Stoic ethics: the
indifferents are relational in character.[64]

Natural things are important in Stoic ethics because they underlie a number of central concepts. They are rooted in the orientation,
which men share with animals, and therefore they are prior (temporally but also logically) to the ethical concepts which are of most
importance to human life. Thus the relationships between what is
natural in this sense, impulse, value, preferred things (*proêgmena*),
and appropriate acts are worth some consideration, both to show
how the impulses to what is natural underlie a large and important
part of Stoic ethics and also as background to section (*c*) below.

The relationships in question are illustrated (though often not
very clearly) in the standard accounts of indifferent things (*adiaphora*) and appropriate acts (*kathêkonta*) in the handbooks of Stoic

ethics which have come down to us.[65] The central concepts all go back to the first two scholarchs, however,[66] and we may suppose that the substance of the doctrine is reliably old Stoic. In looking briefly at this material, we will find confirmation for the other evidence that what is natural or the natural life is the basis, i.e. the point of reference, for value (*axia*), preferred things, and selection.[67]

Indifferent things, Arius' version begins,[68] are neither good nor bad. An important distinction is made immediately between two kinds of indifference. One of these, 'absolute indifference', is of no ethical significance.[69] But the other sort, things which are indifferent only in the sense that they do not contribute to happiness and may be used well or badly since *per se* they do not do moral benefit or harm,[70] this kind of indifferent is of moral significance. For unlike the absolutely indifferent things (e.g. whether the number of stars in the sky is odd or even), these indifferents have important relationships to value (*axia*) and to impulse.

The indifferents which matter are defined as those which stimulate *hormê* or *aphormê*;[71] absolute indifferents do not do so. This obviously applies to the other animals as well as to man. But our sources, which are primarily interested in the human side of this theory, go on to look at their application to rational animals too. Thus Arius' account goes on to single out the significant indifferents as that class which is selected or rejected.[72] This selection is a special kind of impulse.[73] At this point too another concept is added. 'Value' has two principal senses in Stoicism. Moral value is not in question here, but only the lower sort of value which determines a more rudimentary notion of the natural life, which could be shared by animals.[74]

According to Diogenes Laertius' account (7.105–6), value in this sense is the criterion for preferred status. He says, 'preferred things, then, are those which also have value.'[75] But value in this sense also has a criterion. For we are told by Arius (*Ecl.* 2.83) that it is the natural things which have value, while Diogenes (7.105) mentions the importance of contributing to a natural life (this must be a life which aims at and achieves a sufficient number of 'natural things'). Arius also tells us that naturalness is important for determining what will be stimulative of impulse. He says:[76] 'the things we said were according to nature are, then, what stimulate impulse.'

We may stand back now and survey the conceptual relations extracted from the doxography. It seems clear that the idea of naturalness is the central concept. Diogenes Laertius includes, in the basic text, the Stoic account of how this is grounded in the orientation and broader principles of rational teleology. Arius does not. But both sources make naturalness, which must be interpreted with heavy emphasis on the animal's own nature, the most important concept for deriving the others. Thus naturalness determines what will be stimulative of impulse and what is valuable, and it seems that being stimulative of impulse and being valuable are not derived one from another. They are parallel to each other and each has a direct relationship to naturalness. Not so with the concept of preferred status. For it seems to be defined by reference to what is stimulative of impulse and so only derivatively by reference to naturalness. Since these concepts are important in Stoic ethics, it is interesting to note their relationship to each other. A comparison of impulse and value here tells us something about the relation of psychology and normative ethics. Being stimulative of impulse and having value are co-ordinate, both determined by their relationship to naturalness. It would seem that the Stoics do not want to say that normative value judgements are grounded in facts about what we are attracted to, nor that we are attracted to things principally on the basis of their normative ethical value. They do not aim to deduce ethical facts from psychological ones, nor vice versa. Both are deduced from their concept of nature. Nature is a complex and extraordinarily rich concept in Stoic psychology and ethics,[77] and its richness permits the Stoics to align claims of fact and claims of value in a way that avoids the now traditional dichotomy between the two. The problem of the 'is' and the 'ought' does not arise in the Stoic version of naturalism.

The parallelism of value and being stimulative of impulse is interesting in another respect too. It recalls the distinction drawn in the reconstruction of the psychology of action between the two *lekta* which accompany a rational hormetic presentation, an imperative and a proposition. Obedience to the imperative is the impulse and assent to the proposition which accompanies it is an ethically significant assertion to which the action commits the agent. Value, then, is what is expressed in the ethical judgement associated with an action; and the stimulative power of the presentation of an object corresponds to the imperative. And the parallelism of proposition and imperative is like that of value and being stimulative of impulse which we see in the doxography.

The correspondence will appear even closer when we consider the contrast between rational and irrational animals. Value is not a factor in animal action; but that some things are stimulative of impulse obviously is. Animals do not make judgements when they act, because they lack reason. But there is—must be[78]—something which takes the role played by the imperative in men and provides the motive power which causes action. Animals lack reason and so value is not a factor for them. But the causal role of impulses in actions is something common to human and animal psychology. Men, unlike animals, make a value judgement (at least implicitly) every time they act. That is the cardinal point of Stoic intellectualism.

The concept of an appropriate action is closely linked to those which we have been considering. While the connections are more complex, naturalness is very important in determining what is *kathêkon* in any one case.[79] It would not be accurate to say that what is appropriate is always *kata phusin*; special circumstances, for example, might make it appropriate to seek illness,[80] and illness is unnatural. But still what is natural for an animal is an important guide in determining what is appropriate and both Diogenes and Arius confirm that the Stoics wanted to emphasize this point.[81] Indeed, the concept of *kathêkon* is in a sense even more closely tied to the concept of naturalness than the others. For just as *to kata phusin* applies even to plants,[82] so too does *to kathêkon*.[83] The other concepts which do not have meaning where action is not a possibility, such as orientation and impulse, do not extend below the animal level.[84]

In animals though, both rational and irrational,[85] the appropriate is tied to the other concepts which we have been considering, since the appropriate in animals is a matter of actions. Thus Diogenes says that appropriate acts are 'activities carried out in accordance with impulse'.[86] Arius tells us that appropriate acts are 'measured' with reference to the indifferents, i.e. the preferred and rejected things,[87] and Chrysippus used to say that nature and the natural are the *archê* (by which I take him to mean primary point of reference) for what is appropriate.[88] What this means for human beings will become clear in the next section. For the problem of selection will be the problem of determining what is appropriate in any one situation. The definition of the appropriate as that of which a reasonable defence can be given[89] clearly fits well with this human application and indeed it was almost certainly devised with that application primarily in view. But it also applies to animal action.

We need not suppose that the defence mentioned in the definition is to be given by the agent. Evaluative judgements can only be made by rational animals; but they may be made about others, provided that we have a set of relevant standards to apply. And in the case of evaluating what is *kathêkon* for an animal we do have those standards. The criterion of rational defensibility in this case is, of course, what is natural for the animal, its orientation to itself and the primary impulse to self-preservation.[90] Food in general is good for an animal's constitution, which is why it is natural to it and why it elicits an impulse. Action in pursuit of food in general is defensible on this basis. But of course the pursuit of food is not always appropriate, for sometimes it may be poisoned. Then it is not appropriate, with reference to the same standards. Whether in wolfing down the poisoned food the animal is acting appropriately or not depends on whether the animal is expected to be able to discern the poison. The notion of an appropriate action is used outside the ethical sphere in a case like this, and a certain amount of debate and even casuistry about our evaluation of its action by the criteria in question is possible. But our principal interest in looking at the notion of the appropriate and the other concepts we have considered is to see how they work in ethics; so let us turn again to human beings.

(c) The first function of reason: selection among natural things[91]

We have not been able to avoid a certain amount of anticipation of human conduct, since the doxographical sources used as a basis for discussing naturalness are themselves primarily interested in human matters. But with the exception of value, a distinctively ethical concept, most of the material in section (b) applies to lower animals and children as well as to adults. The life which is natural to animals may differ according to species, but it is the same by analogy. For the pursuit of what is in accordance with each animal's nature, what will preserve and enhance its non-rational constitution, is common to them all. This life is natural for animals *tout court*, and since man is an animal as well as being rational it is also natural for man to live in this way. But since man *is* also rational, this life is only natural to man *qua* animal, not *qua* rational.

Impulse is the power which all animals use to pursue natural things. But as we are told in the basic text from Chrysippus, in humans reason comes along in addition to impulses and becomes its 'craftsman'. In this section and the next we will look at two ways in which reason alters the functioning of animal nature. In both cases the advent of reason affects how the animal acts, i.e. it changes the impulses from what they had been before it had reason. We shall see in a concrete way how it is that human nature differs from animal nature.

In this section we shall examine a function of reason which does not introduce us to its full possibilities. We shall not be considering virtuous action, but merely the way in which reason makes it possible for a man to select the fully appropriate thing to do. For selection is a kind of impulse which only rational, assenting animals can have. Unlike animals, men can select consciously which hormetic presentations to assent to, and so the issue of what a man can be reasonably expected to do becomes much more complex. The appropriate act for any animal must be one that is susceptible of a reasonable defence. This is true for men, but because they have the power of rational selection the standards of reasonableness are much higher. But it is important to insist that this function of reason does not introduce the profound gulf between man and the rest of nature which comes when virtue and the concept of the good are introduced. One might almost say that at this level of reason's activity men are doing no more than what animals do—pursuing what is in accordance with their nature—but doing so more efficiently and with responsibility. Even when a man selects his actions with complete appropriateness, he is still not virtuous. The two stages or aspects of reason's activity in human nature are not ultimately separable from one another, but the first alone does not represent the final stage of moral development.

Preferred things are what we select 'on the basis of a predominating reason'.[92] I take this is to be a terse expression of what we are told somewhat earlier in Arius' exposition[93] that selective value is that 'according to which *when circumstances permit* we choose these things in preference to those, for example health instead of illness . . .'. The general tendency of a man is to select preferred things and to reject their contraries; but man can make an intelligent evaluation of a large number of other factors and select his particular actions rationally in accordance with the circumstances.

But at the root of all these choices there will still be the nature of the human animal. It is with reference to this that the structure of values and choices exists. Thus when Chrysippus stated the principle of appropriate action and of virtue (which is appropriate action plus another factor to be considered in section (*d*)), he said that it was nature and what is natural.[94] And when he considered the way that humans had to choose the action appropriate in each circumstance, he found that the basis of a man's choices was the fact that god had made him such as to select the things in accordance with nature.[95] This is essentially the same doctrine that we are given in the basic text, that animals pursue certain things and avoid others because of their relationship to their nature and the primary impulse to self-preservation.

Seneca discusses selection in a very interesting passage of Letter 92.[96] He deals with the question of the value of attractive clothing for men. 'A man should pursue the selection of attractive clothing; for by nature man is an attractive and tasteful animal. Therefore attractive dress is not good in itself, but the selection of attractive dress, because the good is not in the thing but in selection of a certain kind.' We shall see below in section (*d*) what this kind of selection is. But note here Seneca's other point, that a man selects attractive clothing because of some natural aptness of that to his nature.[97] It is a preferred thing and, circumstances permitting, a rational agent will select that over its contrary.

This rational selection of the appropriate thing is what distinguishes a human being's pursuit of what is in accord with its nature from that of an irrational animal or a child. Chrysippus, then, may well have added a clause concerning selection to his formulation of the *telos*, as two passages in Cicero suggest.[98] This fuller version is 'to live applying a knowledge of what happens according to nature, selecting what is according to nature and rejecting what is against it'.

The significance of this formula for the *telos* is seen in the fragment quoted by Epictetus at *Diss.* 2.6.9, translated at p. 120 above. It seems clear that the policy of aiming at natural things is only a general policy. Whenever one knows what exactly it is that Nature has in store, then it is necessary to select that. The desire to select what is natural is overridden by the knowledge of what Nature wills in this particular case. Our unavoidable ignorance of god's will forces us to settle for selecting among natural things; direct knowledge of his will would be preferable. We see too the explanation of the reference to experience in Chrysippus' formulation of the *telos*. Experience of the world's functioning is needed if one is to know what is likely to promote a natural life.

But even this experience of what happens according to nature is not certainty. It will still be necessary for a man to make his selection of what is appropriate in the midst of significant uncertainty. Our experience of what happens according to nature will give us no more than a general guide to what will be appropriate in any one case. Thus when the Stoics defined the appropriate act, they did so in terms of reasonableness or probability (*to eulogon*).[99] Here we need a distinction. We want to deal separately with the question of the appropriateness of any one particular action, an act token, and with the question of the appropriateness of an act type. For given the need to rely on probabilities in selecting the appropriate act token for any particular situation, we form general rules about which types of actions are generally appropriate and which are not. And it is these general rules which ethical theorists most often deal with, while individuals select an act token for an individual case.[100]

Thus when the doxographers give us lists of appropriate actions they are working on the level of general rules. None of these can be absolutely reliable, and this may have been part of what impelled Ariston to abolish all ethical distinctions except that between good and bad. For his position seems to have some resemblance to an extreme form of nominalism, and the need to rely on generalizations (which, on this account, he thought were of dubious ontological and epistemological standing) in giving an account of all ethical concepts except the absolute terms 'good' and 'bad' may well have led him to avoid notions which had to be expressed in such suspect terms.[101]

The importance of special circumstances[102] in determining what is appropriate in a particular case is strongly suggested by the following passage from Arius Didymus (*Ecl.* 2.86): 'if we do not take [sc. natural things] or if we reject them when circumstances do not prevent us, we will not be happy.' The reference to the role of special circumstances is clarified by Diogenes Laertius (7.109). Some actions (and he must mean action types) are appropriate without regard to any special circumstances; such would be care for one's health and so forth.[103] These are actions which are generally appropriate, and their appropriateness derives from our orientation to our constitution. But some types of acts will only be appropriate in very special circumstances. Examples of this would be self-mutilation, self-impoverishment or the pursuit of illness. If being sick meant that someone could avoid service to a cruel tyrant which would involve his death, then sickness would be the appropriate thing.[104] It is possible for an action of the type 'being sick' to be appropriate, but only under unusual circumstances. The type then is called 'appropriate in special circumstances'.

Reason's first job is to determine the appropriate act in particular circumstances, and the impulse to action which results from this determination is called a selection. This function of reason is influenced by a large number of factors, which have not been mentioned in the preceding pages.[105] If this function of reason is carried out well, then a man will have a natural life in the weak sense of the word—for he will not yet be living happily nor virtuously nor in complete harmony with his reason and the Right Reason of Zeus. It is a lamentable part of man's lot that he cannot know for sure what the will of Zeus is in every particular case. For if he did, he could then follow him at all times with a willing and informed intent. In the next section we shall look at the problem of how man's reason carries him beyond the limits of rational selection to the achievement of a life completely in accord with nature in the highest sense.

(d) Virtuous action[106]

As we have seen in a text from Arius Didymus, the correct selection of things which accord with nature (due regard being had for special circumstances and other relevant considerations) is a necessary but not sufficient condition for happiness (p. 204 above). This idea is also behind the statements by Seneca and Cicero[107] that it is a certain kind of selection which can be characterized as good. Cicero makes it particularly clear that this is a result of a factor above and beyond selecting with full appropriateness (*cum officio selectio*) and he refers to this selection as being 'consistent and in agreement with Nature'.

Thus the need to select rationally among things which are natural but indifferent with respect to happiness is the foundation of virtuous action. This is the meaning of Chrysippus' statement that nature and the natural are not only the principle of the appropriate, but also the raw material of virtue.[108] But in this section we must make an attempt to describe the additional factor which action must have in addition to fully appropriate selection if it is to be right action (a *katorthôma*). For it is right actions which are done according to virtue and which constitute the very substance of the life of virtue and happiness, which is according to nature in an even higher sense than that which has been considered so far. It is impossible to say something about every important aspect of virtue and virtuous action, and the account which follows will have a narrow focus. But the focus will, I hope, be on the essentials.

One or two central points should be made here. First, we must recall that there is a distinct kind of impulse which is directed at the good, called *hairesis* or choice.[109] Ordinarily impulses are differentiated with reference to the content of the propositions to which assent is given. Second, the good is a concept which enters only with the attainment of reason. Its relationship to the lower natural things is at first sight somewhat problematic, but it becomes clear on further examination what this relationship is. Diogenes Laertius[110] says that the good is 'what is perfect according to nature for [literally, of] something rational *qua* rational'. The definition's meaning is a little obscured by the condensation of the doxographical report, but its significance is brought out by a consideration of Seneca's Letters 121 and 124 and of Cicero's discussion of the concept of good in *De Finibus*.[111] When a human attains his rational nature, he is at the peak of the hierarchy of nature. He is not good, but he is capable of the good. The good is natural to man as a fully rational animal in a way which is analogous to the way in which the merely natural things are natural to non-rational animals. There is an analogy between the nature of any animal and what is natural to it; as merely natural things are to irrational animals, so the good is natural to the rational animal *qua* rational. The adjective 'perfect' applies to the good and to human nature in the full and proper sense of the word, because reason is the top of nature's hierarchy. Other things, Seneca says,[112] can be perfect in their own kind but they cannot be really perfect because they lack reason. As Cicero says, the good is both *sui generis* and is also understood by analogy to the merely natural things. Like them, it is defined as the thing appropriate to an animal's nature, but it is *sui generis* because the rational nature of man is so special.[113]

The addition of '*qua* rational' to the definition of the good is significant and raises a problem. For even when a man is mature and finds his ultimate fulfilment in the pursuit of good which is natural to him, he is still an animal who finds the merely natural things significant in his life. It does not belong to him *qua* rational to pursue them, but they are still the material of virtue. In asking in the pages which follow about the characteristics of a fully virtuous action we will also be investigating the way in which a man's commitment to virtue relates to his weaker commitment to merely natural things. I suggest that the relation between the good and the indifferents, which has long been found mysterious, will become clear in a concrete way only when we consider the difference between selection and choice.

The third point I wish to make here is simple. In asking what a *katorthôma* is and how 'choice' differs from mere selection, we must keep in mind the cosmic perspective. After all, Chrysippus said that the goal of life was to live according to one's own (i.e. rational) nature and also that of the universe. So we expect both to be relevant to the description of the virtuous act. The importance of reason has already been mentioned. We should keep in mind two important texts. Seneca[114] says: 'Other things are perfect only in their own nature, but not truly perfect; they lack reason. For this alone is perfect which is perfect in accordance with universal Nature and the universal Nature is rational.' Cicero[115] makes the point that the awareness of the good which a man acquires when he has reason comes from a reflection on consistency and order in actions. The kind of consistency meant is not completely clear in this condensed passage; but if what was said about consistency in chapter 4 i above is at all close to the truth, it should include consistency with oneself and with Nature (this is suggested by the gerundive *agendarum*). Thus it is the *ordo rerum agendarum* and its consistency, both with Nature and with itself, that strikes a man when he is first able to appreciate its significance. It is important, therefore, when we are looking for the special characteristics of virtuous action, that we keep our eyes on the role of consistency with oneself and with Nature. For in this, Cicero seems to be saying, lies the chief good of man.

The good is defined in several ways, and one of them brings out its role in producing the smooth flow of life, which Zeno said was the goal (see n. 110). The good, therefore, will have a role in determining action which will be consistent with the will of Zeus. Similarly, Chrysippus insisted that the good could not be understood without reference to happiness and the common Nature which guides and disposes the events of the world.[116] This confirms again that the good (i.e. virtue and that which partakes of virtue) will be closely connected with a certain kind of action.

The good is the object of a special kind of impulse, given the technical designation 'choice' (*hairesis*). This is different from the impulse which is concerned only with the indifferents, and the contrast between the two is made explicit by Arius Didymus.[117]

They say that the choiceworthy (*haireton*) and what is to be taken [*lēpton*— clearly a reference to selection] are different. For the choiceworthy is what stimulates an unreserved impulse (*autotelēs hormē*) ⟨and what is to be taken in what we select reasonably⟩. As much as the choiceworthy differs from what is to be taken, by the same degree the *per se* choiceworthy also differs from what is *per se* to be taken and in general the good [sc. differs thus] from what has value.

The *lēpta* are obviously natural things, indifferents; the pursuit of them is a necessary condition for happiness, but such actions are still merely 'intermediate appropriate actions'.[118] But something more is needed for happiness, and in another fragment Chrysippus tells us something about what this additional factor in actions is:[119]

The man who has made the greatest moral progress fulfills all appropriate actions in all respects and omits none; but his life is not yet happy. This supervenes when these intermediate actions (*mesai praxeis*) acquire the additional properties of firmness and consistency (*to hektikon*) and they take on a certain solidity of their own.

As Bonhoeffer points out (see n. 119), this seems to be an attempt by Chrysippus to characterize the difference between a merely appropriate action and a perfectly appropriate action.[120] A perfectly appropriate action is a virtuous action, and it is *always* appropriate as well as being perfectly appropriate. The emphasis on consistency and firmness in this fragment reminds us of Cicero's emphasis on consistency in the idea of the good, but also of the fact that virtues were held by the Stoics to be a special sort of disposition. Virtues were called *diatheseis* and they differed from ordinary dispositions (*hexeis*) in that they were invariable in degree.[121] Arius Didymus tells us (*Ecl.* 2.85–6) that there is a difference between these perfectly appropriate actions and intermediate appropriate actions, and gives examples of each. Going on an embassy is a case of the latter while doing a just action is a case of the former. Yet surely one can be just by going on an embassy. A very large number of actions, if performed in a certain way, will also be virtuous actions. What we are looking for now is some sort of account of what that certain way of acting is.

Let us go back for a moment to the relation of the mature man to the good. The presence of reason does more than make a man capable of rational selection. It also makes possible an awareness of the good, which comes from analogical reflection on things which are advantageous or natural in the lower sense. Once we are aware of the good it changes, or ought to change, the way we act—our human nature. For we see, or ought to see, that the good is truly advantageous; we see that it is natural to us or *oikeion* in a way different from that in which merely natural things are natural to us.[122]

But there is also a continuity between the good and merely natural things. And this continuity is what is needed to explain why the Stoics said that the goal, a virtuous life, is derived from our basic orientation to ourselves which is shared with all animals.[123] A result of this is that the good can also be referred to as *oikeion*,[124] just as merely natural things can also be called *oikeia* because they promote the well-being of what is primarily *oikeion*, our own constitution. Just as natural things promote the natural life (in the lower sense) so the good promotes the consistent life which is perfectly natural for a rational animal.[125] Because man's nature is special, what is natural to him in the strict sense of the word must also be special. As all of our reliable sources tell us, the good is special in the sense that it is different in kind and not merely in degree.[126]

Antiochus adopted the Stoic view that the natural is the basic reference point for ethics; unlike the Stoics, however, he did not think that the advent of reason was a dividing line in a human's moral development after which the values relevant to him were fundamentally different. Since he did not share their interest in this line of demarcation between the pre-rational and the rational, he criticized them for making the highest attribute of man seem to be his only attribute.[127] This seemed to break the continuity of moral development which the Stoics claimed to uphold. Posidonius also criticized Chrysippus for saying that man was oriented only to the good, i.e. that the only thing which is *oikeion* to an adult is moral virtue.[128] Plutarch charges him with similar distortion of the facts about human nature.[129] There is a certain amount of polemic in these criticisms. For the orthodox Stoics would say that throughout life it is the constitution to which a man is primarily oriented, and that the good, like the merely natural things, is derivatively *oikeion*. It is simply not correct to say that according to the Stoics, at any stage of moral development, a man was oriented to the good and the good alone. The importance of selection among indifferents in a virtuous act proves that.

But these critics are driving at a point worth making. Because of the radical transformation of human nature when reason supervenes, there is a serious question to be asked about how the two kinds of value are related to each other. The presupposition behind the polemic is that the commitment to the good obliterated the significance of lower values and left the agent with no affinity whatsoever to the preferred things which promote his self-preservation. This is a crucial question for the old Stoics, and unfortunately we do not have an explicitly formulated answer among the fragments which survive.

An answer can be given, though, which has some plausibility. I suggest that the theory of action will help us to fill in the gap in our sources. For we do know a certain amount about the relation of selection to choice, and by interpreting it with reference to the rest of what we know about the psychology of action a hypothesis may be put forward about the problem at hand. The critical steps will be to recall that for the Stoics the doctrine of consistency with Nature and the need to fit in with the will of Zeus are always in the foreground and to exploit what we know about impulse with reservation.[130]

I suggest that we should think of the relation between preferred things and the good in this way. An adult continues to pursue those things which are preferred, but always in such a way that in case of a conflict with his pursuit of the good the impulse to the good will override his selection of the preferred thing. This means that in every case a man will make the pursuit of the good the ultimate criterion of impulse and action. This seems to be the practical significance of the often repeated statements that virtue alone is to be chosen for its own sake, and that the good has a kind of value different in kind from that of natural things.[131] But in some texts the point about overriding lower values is made more explicitly. Cicero compares man's commitment to wisdom (by which he means the practical wisdom which is identical with

virtue) and his commitment to merely natural things to the situation which occurs when you grow to love a friend more dearly
than some other friend who introduced you to him.[132] They are
both still your friends, but if the two should come into conflict
you would put the second one before the other. A sensible man
would do his best to keep the two from conflicting. Seneca
describes the relation of lower virtues to wisdom in terms which
make it clear that *in cases of conflict* one must let morality be the
overriding determinant in action.[133] The later account given by
Gellius[134] puts the point clearly: 'if there be some external obstacle
. . . which is a thing to be rejected (*incommodum*), it is disdained.'
When the Stoics say that we select the natural things but choose the
good, this seems to be what they mean. In cases of conflict the good
always comes first.

Let us see if we can make sense of this 'overriding' relationship in
terms of the psychology, remembering that the goal of a life according to Nature and Right Reason will be one which is made up of virtuous actions. In so far as Right Reason commands that a man do
virtuous actions, it is obviously a necessary condition of this sort of
life that a man should do a virtuous act in preference to a non-
virtuous act whenever either is possible. But everything the sage
does is virtuous and nothing done by a non-sage is virtuous. It
follows from this that there is no obvious type of overt action which
can only be done virtuously. The difference between virtue and vice
is ultimately not a matter of what one does but of how one does it.
Someone making a moral judgement about a person's actions
needs to know not about his bodily movements, but about his
impulses and assents.

A virtuous action is always appropriate.[135] I take this to mean that
a right action (*katorthôma*) is susceptible of a defence which is more
than probable or reasonable. It has a justification which *always*
holds good, *always* prevails over other considerations of the circumstances. To say that an act is an act of a virtuous disposition is to give
it a defence which is always valid, since the virtuous act cannot, like
the pursuit of lesser natural things, be frustrated. But how, we must
ask, is this dominant value and the consequent stability and un-
varying reliability expressed in ordinary actions? And it must be
expressed in ordinary actions and selections; every *katorthôma*
would be a mere intermediate appropriate action if it were done in
the manner of one who lacked virtue.[136] If there were a set of

characteristically virtuous things to do, and virtue did not consist in a special way of doing the things which can also be done by non-sages, it would be impossible to understand what is meant by saying that the natural is the raw material of virtue, that a right action is a perfectly appropriate action, and that the good consists in a certain kind of selection.

The ultimate standard of goodness and happiness is not the doing of conventionally moral actions. It is harmony with the will of Zeus, wanting to happen just those things which actually do happen and wanting to do just those things which Zeus commands one to do on each individual occasion. If one could achieve that state of complete harmony with Zeus, one's life would be smoothly flowing and fully rational, sharing in the rationality of Zeus himself. How can this harmony be achieved by mere men who must act in ignorance of the details of Zeus' will? They must act with reservation in all cases where the outcome of their action is not totally within their control and without reservation only when they can by themselves ensure the success of their actions. Let us apply this to the specific question of the relation between choice and selection; for this will tell us the difference between a right act and a merely appropriate act.

In pursuing the indifferents a man can be frustrated by events beyond his control, but in the pursuit of good he cannot. For virtue is completely within his power. Reservation is therefore to be used with selection, while choice need never be reserved. In the contrast between the object of selection and the object of choice reported by Arius Didymus (*Ecl.* 2.75, above, p. 208), the object of choice (i.e. the good) is said to stimulate an *autotelês hormê*. This, I suggest, is a reference to the unreserved impulse and it may remind us of the terms used to indicate the corresponding features in its object. For the good is called 'independent' or 'self-sufficient' (*autarkes*) and 'needing nothing' (*aprosdees*), as well as perfect (*teleion*).[137] Similarly the impulse to the pursuit of the good is independent and needs nothing else; since it can never be frustrated by external factors and depends for its success on the agent alone, the reservation which protects selection from disappointment and keeps it in harmony with the will of Zeus is not needed. The good, which is virtue, is certain and reliable and immune to reversal or frustration.[138]

The well-known illustration of the pursuit of the goal used by Cicero in *De Finibus* 3.22 is apposite here. An archer is doing his best to hit a certain target. He must do his best to do so, but even the best marksman cannot guarantee the success of his shot. External factors may intervene and affect the course of the arrow on its path. It would be unreasonable to make our judgement of an archer's skill depend on the effect of an unpredictable puff of wind or the sudden movement of the target. Therefore to strike the target is something which an archer should select (and he should use reservation on this impulse), but not choose. What he should choose is what corresponds to the good and is completely under his own control, i.e. that he should do everything he can to hit the target. That goal can never be frustrated or interfered with. Neither can the pursuit of the good. In this example it is suggested that the pursuit of good consists in nothing beyond excellence in selection of things according to nature, but that is only a result of the limited aims of the author of this analogy.[139]

But if this later adaptation of the old Stoic doctrine omits a feature we are interested in, it does give prominence to something we have already stressed. Any choice, action in pursuit of the good, is also a selection, action in pursuit of natural things. There are no distinct virtuous actions, only actions done in a virtuous way. Every right act is a kind of appropriate act. If choice is to be performed without reservation (because it is an impulse to the good) and selection is to be subject to reservation (because its attainment can be frustrated by external obstacles), how can one and the same act be both?

Only a hypothesis can help us proceed any further. Since an action is virtuous if done from a virtuous disposition, the distinction between the selection and the choice must be in the mind of the agent. Let us suppose that the Stoics made use of the fact that actions can be described in more than one way. The same action may be described as 'going home for Thanksgiving', as 'honouring one's parents', and as 'doing a just act'. The wise and virtuous man is the one who construes his actions as acts of virtue, as things which ought to be done. Simply making the right selection does not constitute virtue, although it is essential for it. The virtuous man thinks of his action as being right and in accordance with Nature's will. He thinks of himself as doing the action because man was made for acting thus. So when the virtuous man goes home for Thanksgiving, he does not just assent to the proposition 'I should go home for Thanksgiving'; he also assents to 'by doing so I honour my parents' and 'by doing so I do a just act'. If his selection of the appropriate action is also to be virtuous, he must also assent to these propositions. In so acting, the virtuous man sees his actions as expressions of virtue.

In this way the sage can ensure that his actions and intentions will never be frustrated. For the impulse to going home is reserved (after all the plane might crash); but the impulse to doing a good act cannot be frustrated and so no reservation is required. By assenting with reservation to one proposition, his action is a selection and merely appropriate; by assenting to the other (which contains reference to the good), it becomes a choice too and an expression of virtue. If a man assents to the proposition which describes his action as virtuous, then his action will never fail of his objective. For although one may not achieve one's goal under the description 'honouring one's parents' or 'going home for Thanksgiving', if the action is construed by the agent as a just act it cannot fail. For to do one's best, consciously to do all that is in one's power, is in itself a just act if it is done with an awareness of the good as one's reason.[140] Since the act cannot possibly fail under the description of 'just act', the action has the solidity and consistent reliability required by Chrysippus' concept of happiness as an addition to the flawless selection of the appropriate thing to do. The addition of an awareness of the good turns one's selections into choices (which are impulses to the good); it also makes one's purpose unhinderable and in perfect accord with the will of Zeus. Only if a man acts virtuously in this way can he assure himself of complete harmony with the will and course of Nature; only thus does he act fully in accordance with his own rational nature.

We might wonder whether it is the virtuous motivation or the consequent certainty of success that commended such actions to the old Stoa as being truly advantageous for the agent. Following Socrates, they put great emphasis on the claim that the good and virtue are the only truly beneficial things. But I doubt that a clear answer can be given to this question. Virtue for the Stoics was both essentially a matter of morality and essentially secure and reliable. It would be pointless to press the question whether deontological or teleological considerations were dominant in their conception of virtuous action. An attempt to separate the two aspects of moral action would founder on the cardinal principle of Stoic naturalism. Moral action is what a man ought to do simply because it is in his nature to be drawn to it and fulfilled by it more than by anything else; it is part of what it means to be a man to find one's greatest fulfilment in the overriding commitment to a virtue which is unshakeable and self-sufficient.

It was not a startling novelty to say that the reason we give to ourselves for doing an action is important for determining its moral character. Aristotle too said that doing the proper action was not really an act of virtue unless it was done 'on account of the noble' (*heneka tou kalou*).[141] Chrysippus' claim that human nature, as rational, could only be perfected and happy if we did all of our actions because of their relationship to the good, recognizing that it overrode the significance of all other values, was based on his views about the dominant position of reason in the human soul. The presence of reason radically changes human nature, rather than simply adding a new and higher but ultimately separate aspect to the functioning of the animal soul. Reason transforms human nature and human values, and this belief is intimately connected with a belief in the unitary nature of the soul.

Conclusion

The Stoics prided themselves on the coherence they had forged among the various parts of their philosophical system. Logic, physics, and ethics were all woven together into a virtually seamless fabric. This unity can still be discerned in many areas of their philosophy, despite the fragmentary state of our information. In the reconstruction I have offered of the early Stoic analysis of human action the same sort of coherence is visible. The description of how the souls of men and animals function falls within the realm of physics; man is part of the natural world, and the Stoics assigned him what they thought was his proper station therein and gave a speculative account of the operation of those powers which justified his privileged position. But to offer this account of the functioning of the human mind the Stoics had to draw on logic, a discipline which they conceived rather more broadly than we do. Zeno and Chrysippus taught ethics last of the three parts of philosophy,[1] and this is consistent with what we find in the analysis of human action. Several of the central doctrines of early Stoic ethics could only be presented after the ground had been cleared by accounts of the functioning of the rational human soul.

But it would be a mistake to think that the influence ran in one direction only, from the psychology of human action to ethical doctrines. That pattern is seen in, for example, the discussion of passions; but elsewhere the lines of influence are reversed. A strong intuition about moral responsibility left its mark on Stoic physics, shaping the doctrine of causes and modifying their determinism, which might otherwise have developed into a form which made ethics in any meaningful sense impossible.

We do well to take the Stoics at their word when they say that no part of their philosophy can be separated from another and that its exposition must at all stages draw on all three branches.[2] As we have seen in the area of the psychology of action, the key to the Stoic system is not the dependence of one part on another, but the integration of all three into one. A rational ethics cannot exist without a well-developed psychology; nor can psychology be complete without ethics. The Stoics believed this and built this conviction into their analysis of human action. It is difficult to decide which discipline, as practised today, is more at risk from the centrifugal tendencies of modern specialization. Whatever the particular merits of their system, the early Stoics offer a valuable example by integrating their inquiries into the functioning of the human animal with their arguments about the good life.

Appendix 1

Primariness in the Old Stoa

In Chapter 6 I have argued that the primary impulse in Chrysippus' theory is a general impulse to self-preservation, not restricted to or characteristic of newborn animals. It is a basic fact of animal nature in terms of which other and more complex behaviour patterns may be explained. This raises questions about other uses of the term 'primary' in Stoic psychology and ethics, and a survey of the issue will support the conclusions arrived at concerning primary impulse. The meaning of terms such as *prôtê hormê*, *prôtê oikeiôsis*, *prôton oikeion*, and *ta prôta kata phusin* has been discussed by various scholars,[1] but it is odd how little attention has been devoted before now to the important problem of identifying the *prôtê hormê*.[2] It is also disappointing to find that previous discussions of the matter have suffered from a lack of attention to the details of the evidence we do have about this terminology and its significance. Rieth, for example, reads *prôtê hormê* into *Fin.* 5.17[3] where it is not to be found, and Kerferd's reference to *prôtai hormai*[4] is a similar figment. The same lack of careful criticism of our sources vitiates much recent discussion of the *prôta kata phusin*.[5] So let us take a closer look.

The term *prôtê oikeiôsis* is not attested for Chrysippus. Despite Kerferd's interest in it (loc. cit.), it is represented only in Cicero. The *prima conciliatio* of *Fin.* 3.21–2 has for its objects the things which are *secundum naturam* and perhaps also the *principia naturae*. This should indicate that his source, certainly post-Chrysippean, used *ta kata phusin* and/or *ta prôta kata phusin*. But if this *prima conciliatio* were the same as the Chrysippean orientation, its object would be the *prôton oikeion*, the self or its constitution and the awareness of it. But Cicero, who also suppresses reference to the primary impulse, is not giving us the details of a doctrine of direct Chrysippean inspiration, and it is unclear whether this is because he had access to such a doctrine in his source but muddled it, or whether his source gave him a heavily adapted Stoic doctrine. One thing is certain; we have no other evidence for the term *prôtê oikeiôsis*.[6] The value of Cicero's testimony as a source for Chrysippus is also called into question by the fact that only the Academic Eudorus (*Ecl.* 2.47) joins Cicero in making primary natural things the object of orientation. And Eudorus' text applies the *Carneadea divisio* (see below) in a manner reminiscent of Antiochus (cf. *Fin.* 5.17–18).

But what of the term *prôton oikeion* in the basic text? Surely it suggests a primary orientation? We do have evidence that other things were called *oikeia* in a secondary sense, with reference to the primary *oikeion*,[7] but none that the early Stoics said that an animal is ever oriented to anything but its constitution (see *Ep.* 121). This evolves, of course. But the orientation clearly stays the same. If Chrysippus ever mentioned a primary orientation (in any sense of the word primary), it has left no trace in our sources. Since the *prôton oikeion* is primary as a point of reference and not as essentially temporally prior,[8] there is no need to suppose that the *oikeiôsis* itself was qualified in a similar way.

In the basic text Chrysippus' use of the phrase *prôton oikeion* is most naturally interpreted in the same way as *prôtê hormê*. It is a point of reference which accounts for other affinities and behaviour patterns.[9] This reading is supported by Alexander (SVF 3.183): in this text *prôton* no more refers to the first period of our life than *eschaton orekton* in the same context refers to the wishes of our dying days. (Alexander's use of *oikeiôsthai* in SVF 3.185 is a different matter. He is being polemical in the manner of Plutarch (*Comm. Not.* 1069f–1070a) and used *oikeiôsthai* much as it is used by Posidonius in his critique in fr. 169.[10])

We have seen that primary impulse is primary in the sense of being a point of reference. It explains why some actions which are not obviously natural for the animal (such as the beaver's self-mutilation, Hierocles 3.9 ff.) are in fact natural with reference to the over-all goal and rational plan of Nature for its creatures.[11] Self-preservation is primary as a point of reference for describing or explaining other actions, just as one's constitution is the primary object of orientation in that it can explain why other things too are *oikeia*.[12] These things are also primary in a temporal sense, for in humans the primary impulse and *oikeion* (while never ceasing to exist) are considerably modified and restricted by the alteration of human nature which occurs with the acquisition of reason.

In Chapter 6 I have argued that natural things (*ta kata phusin*) are natural because of the orientation which all animals have. They are, therefore, *oikeia* in a derivative sense. I wish to argue further here that the old Stoics did not distinguish within this class of natural things any that were primary in the sense of being natural especially for newborn animals. It has been held quite widely that they did so, and that their special term for such things is *prôta kata phusin*. But it is very doubtful whether anyone, let alone a Stoic, used the term before Carneades' day. Moreover, when it was introduced into the debate on the foundations of ethics it did not seem to differ in its application from the *kata phusin* of earlier days. When these points are established it will be clear that there is no reason to suppose that the use of the term *prôton kata phusin* and its meaning have anything to tell us about the structure of Chrysippean ethics or the use of the term 'primary' in the early Stoa.[13]

It is arguable (but not absolutely certain) that the term 'primary natural things' was not used before Carneades. It is prominent in the *Carneadea divisio* and Pembroke (op. cit., pp. 134–5) has rather generously assumed that all aspects of its use there may be attributed with confidence to Carneades' Stoic predecessors and opponents. But he neglects to mention how little independent evidence there is for any use of the term by any pre-Carneadean Stoic, even Chrysippus for whom our evidence is the best. Thus other scholars have thought that the term originated in the debates with Carneades and not before; these scholars either provide or rely on careful examinations of the evidence for the term.[14]

Fin. 5.16 ff. shows that Carneades was the author of a classification of all the possible objects of the impulse of a newborn animal: they were pleasure, freedom from pain, and the 'primary natural things'.[15] It would be incorrect to identify the neo-natal impulse used in the *divisio* of Carneades with the primary impulse of our basic text. For not only is the intent of Carneades' doxographic review different from Chrysippus' purpose, but Carneades was not bound by the old Stoic analysis of *hormê*, and indeed the psychology of action which is central to the Stoic theory of *oikeiôsis* is absent from the generalized Academic account. This is not to say that I think that even Carneades is envisaging an exclusively neo-natal state of affairs with his doctrine of the primary natural things; far from it. But even if such a case could be made, it would not be evidence for the Stoa.

Indeed, the only text which can be argued to be evidence for a use of primary natural things by Chrysippus (*Acad.* 2.138, see below on its evidential value) mentions neither impulse nor the newborn animal. If the fragment is genuine, all Chrysippus is doing is setting out the three possible views about the goal of life, in order to refute two of them, no doubt. He does not connect these goals to neo-natal impulse, which ought to cause hesitation in anyone wishing to insert a doctrine of primary natural things into Chrysippus' theory of *oikeiôsis*. Carneades' use of the *prôta kata phusin* differs from this fragment in that he does link them to new-born animals (*Fin.* 5.17).

Texts which can be traced to the *Carneadea divisio* as their source must not be used as evidence for the old Stoa. Thus we may eliminate from consideration the following: *Acad.* 1.22–3 (cf. *Fin.* 4.15 and *Strom.* 2.22.133); *Acad.* 2.131; *Fin.* 5.16–21, 2.34–5, 5.34 ff.; *Comm. Not.* 26;[16] *Ecl.* 2.47.12–48.5.[17] Not all of these texts derive from Carneades by the same route, of course,[18] but of their dependence on his *divisio* there can be no doubt. Posidonius at one point[19] criticizes the followers of Chrysippus for their views on the *telos* which include reference to the primary natural things. But the target of this criticism is surely Antipater; indeed, he is probably the originator of the Stoic use of the term.[20]

When Cicero attributes use of the term 'primary natural things' (*prima naturae commoda*) to Chrysippus at *Acad.* 2.138 we have good grounds for suspicion. For the similarity of this passage to the Carneadean *divisio* is striking (see especially *Fin.* 2.34). Such a classification is not elsewhere attested for Chrysippus and the context in which it is embedded is wholly Academic and derived from Carneades through Clitomachus.[21] The source of Cicero's information is tainted, and even if it were reliable, we could never be confident that Carneades or Cicero had not recast Chrysippus' classification in terms of the familiar Carneadean division.[22] The attribution of the term to Chrysippus is, then, highly doubtful and our doubts are not in the least allayed by the one other indication that he may have used the term *prôta kata phusin*. Lucian in his *Sale of Lives* (23) employs the familiar later Stoic term in his satirical sketch of Chrysippus as the typical Stoic.[23]

In my opinion the evidence of the passage from the *Academica* must be rejected too. But it is accepted by Glucker[24] as a genuine fragment and it is just possible that he is right. Even on such a generous evaluation of what is very poor evidence, we can see that Pohlenz's claim is too exaggerated to be correct:[25] 'dass für Chrysippus die *prôta kata phusin* wie für die spätere Stoa. . . ein fester

Bestandteil auch der eigenen Lehre gewesen sind, lässt sich nicht bezweifeln'.

But let us suppose for the sake of argument that the term is Chrysippean in origin and that Carneades took it over from him. Would this make any difference to our view of early Stoic ethics? I think not, and the reason for this is simple. As far as we can tell from the lists and descriptions of the primary natural things, they are no different than the natural things with which we are familiar from reliable Stoic sources.[26] This is certainly the case in *Acad.*2.138 and throughout *Fin.* 3. Both terms refer in Stoic texts and in later texts of Carneadean inspiration to what Academics called bodily and external goods (cf. *Acad.* 2.131, 1.22; *Fin.* 4.15, 5.21; *Strom.* 2.22.133; *Ecl.* 2.47; *NA* 12.5.7; Lucian *Sale of Lives* 23; also *Ecl.* 2.82 although the sense of *prôta* is different there—see below).[27] It is difficult to discern any significant difference in meaning or application among the terms *prôton kata phusin*, *kata phusin* and 'external' or 'bodily' goods. None of the lists of primary natural things is restricted to items which a newborn or very young animal would be especially drawn to.

It is doubtful, therefore, whether even post-Chrysippean philosophers regarded primary natural things as specific to newborn animals. When Antiochus (following Carneades) draws attention to the impulses of the newborn (*Fin.* 5.17–18) he, like the Stoics, is merely appealing to infant behaviour as valuable and particularly clear evidence for a nature common to all non-rational animals (similarly at *Fin.* 5.55). At *Fin.* 5.61–2 it is said explicitly that the same sort of instincts are seen in older ages as in children (here called the 'mirrors of nature'), but that the behaviour patterns have become stable with age; it is not said that they have changed.

In SVF 3.181 from Aulus Gellius primary natural things appear as objects of neo-natal perception and affection. The Stoic source for this text is probably as late as Panaetius,[28] and the immediate source is an Academic philosopher. Even this text does not suggest that there are any subsequent natural things in contrast to these primary ones, except the higher values appropriate to rational adults. Again, the *prôta kata phusin* seem to be the external and bodily goods, not a set of infantile desires which evolve into temporally posterior inclinations.

At *Fin.* 3.60–1 and throughout 17–23 Cicero uses various

apparent translations for *ta prôta kata phusin* (such as *prima naturae*) as though they were equivalent to *ta kata phusin*. He clearly regards them as synonymous. But the clinching proof that Cicero does not regard the primary natural things as just temporally primary is this. The first orientation, Cicero says at 3.21, is to things which are *kata phusin* (*secundum naturam*). If the primary natural things were the objects of animal striving only at or near their birth, surely they would be made the objects of this primary orientation. (I am supposing for the sake of argument that Cicero intends the primary orientation to be temporally primary.) Cicero, it seems, did not think that there was a significant difference between primary natural things and natural things without qualification.

The term 'primary natural things' is totally missing from the doxography of Diogenes Laertius and occurs only twice in Arius Didymus. In one passage (*Ecl.* 2.82) the meaning is clearly unrelated to the other texts which we have been examining and is certainly not temporal.[29] The other text (*Ecl.* 2.80) is corrupt and needs some emendation. Hirzel's solution (p. 830 n. 1) would remove the term from the text, as would Schaefer's (p. 294). Of these two suggestions, Hirzel's seems preferable.[30] Wachsmuth's simple supplement would leave the term *prôta kata phusin*. But since Arius reports a quite different use of the term at 2.82, where no corruption is suspected, it may seem wiser to get rid of the term here; otherwise we would be attributing two unconnected senses of a technical term to the same Stoic doxography.

If we do accept Wachsmuth's correction, though, the text in question supports a predominantly non-temporal reading of the force of *prôton*. The text would read thus: 'They say that the doctrine concerning these things [i.e. natural and unnatural things] is made from [i.e. on the basis of] primary natural and unnatural things. For the significant (*diapheron*) and the indifferent are relative concepts.' This is a clear case of the early Stoic use of the term 'primary' for which I have argued. On this reading of the text a primary natural thing would not be something which is natural to someone right at the beginning of his life and characteristic of that stage of his life; it would be a natural thing with reference to which other natural things are said to be natural. There is, then, no reason to believe that the old Stoics used the term 'primary' in a predominantly temporal sense to designate the first stages of a newborn animal's life and traits which are characteristic of those stages.

Appendix 2

The Kinds of Impulse

For the detailed classification of the kinds[1] of impulse in early Stoicism we are dependent on a short section of Arius Didymus' doxography of Stoic ethics preserved by Stobaeus (ch. 9–9a, pp. 86–7 Wachsmuth). Other evidence is relevant and will be adduced in the appropriate places; we begin, however, with a close look at the Stobaeus text.

9 They say that what stimulates impulse is nothing but a hormetic presentation of what is obviously [or immediately; the sense of *authothen* is uncertain] appropriate. And impulse is in general a movement of the soul towards something. The impulse occurring in rational animals and that in irrational animals are understood to be its species. But they have not been given names. For *orexis* is not rational impulse but a species of rational impulse. And one would properly define rational impulse, saying that it is a movement of mind towards something involved in action. Opposed to this is *aphormê*, a movement ⟨of mind away from something involved in action⟩. They say in a special sense too that *orousis* is impulse, being a species of practical impulse. And *orousis* is a movement of the mind to something in the future (*epi ti mellon*). So this far impulse is used in four senses, and *aphormê* in two. When you add the hormetic disposition too, which indeed they also call impulse in a special sense, and from which the active impulse occurs, impulse is used in five senses.

9a There are several species of practical impulse, among which are these: *prothesis, epibolê, paraskeuê, encheirêsis, ⟨hairesis⟩, prohairesis, boulêsis, thelêsis.* So they say that *prothesis* is an indication of accomplishment; *epibolê* is an impulse before an impulse; *paraskeuê* is an action before an action; *encheirêsis* is an impulse in the case of something already in hand; *hairesis* is a *boulêsis* based on analogy; *prohairesis* is a choice (*hairesis*) before a choice; *boulêsis* is a rational [i.e correct] *orexis*; *thelêsis* is a voluntary *boulêsis*.

It is apparent at first glance that this does not pretend to be a complete list of the material it deals with. The first section discusses only those kinds of impulse to which the Stoics were willing to apply the name 'impulse' without restriction. These are no doubt the most common and useful kinds. The second section is incomplete by its own admission. The indications we have about the nature and relationship of the various kinds are only the paltry remains of text-book definitions. When Arius Didymus compiled his synopsis of Stoic ethics, he no doubt excerpted his source; this earlier hand-book may itself have been incomplete. Moreover, we have no idea of how much of Arius' version was omitted by Stobaeus. In the text of section 9 there is at least one lacuna. We have no hope of recovering a complete Stoic discussion of the kinds of impulse. We shall have to do our best with the information we do have, hypothesizing that it is not a treacherously unrepresentative selection.

Section 9a discusses the kinds of practical impulse, a term which is synonymous with rational impulse.[2] The text we are considering supports this when it explains that rational impulse is 'towards something involved in action' (*epi ti tôn en tôi prattein*). Moreover, *orexis*, which is a form of rational impulse, also appears in the list of the kinds of practical impulse in section 9a.

Let us consider first the general outline of Arius' discussion. Section 9 outlines five kinds of *hormê* and two kinds of *aphormê* as the *eidê* of impulse. What are these seven kinds and how are they related to each other? The first distinction made is between impulse in rational animals (1) and in non-rational animals (2). Arius observes that the Stoics did not distinguish these with separate names, such as *orexis* or *boulêsis*. In a similar way rational and non-rational *phantasia* were given the same name, despite important differences between them.[3] Nevertheless, because of the importance of distinguishing rational and irrational forms of impulse, the former are designated *logikê*,[4] just as rational presentations are designated *logikê*. The irrational forms of these two psychological capacities or activities are not even dignified with labels of this type, but are simply referred to 'homonymously with the genus' (see n. 3). If there were to be a special designation for them, it would have to be *alogos*; but for this usage we have no evidence.

Orexis is the third of the five senses of impulse mentioned in section 9; the hormetic disposition is the fifth. It follows that the fourth kind was called *orousis* (4). Thus it cannot be correct to emend the word to *orexis*,[5] for this would leave the list of five kinds short by one.

Since type (5), the disposition, is special and type (2) does not apply to humans, we are left with three kinds of impulse to consider in more detail: rational impulse (1), *orexis* (3), and *orousis* (4). How are these related? As far as can be determined from the definitions, it is not the case that (1) is the genus of which (3) and (4) are species. For although *orousis* (4) is, like *orexis* (3), a form of rational or practical impulse (1), it is contrasted to (1) in a way that *orexis* is not. *Orousis* is defined as being to something future, and *orexis*, we shall see, is defined as a form of impulse to the good. These two differentiae are not mutually exclusive and it is quite possible that the same impulse could count as an *orexis* and as an *orousis*.

Nevertheless these are the two main subtypes of rational impulse and it seems likely that the distinction between them forms the organizational principle for the more detailed list of kinds of impulse in section 9a. Thus we will be returning to them shortly. But another problem arising out of section 9 demands our attention first. In section 9 Arius says that he has given two senses of *aphormê* as being kinds of impulse. Yet only one is indicated in our text, and the description of it is lost in the lacuna which has been partially filled by Wachsmuth.[6] The same lacuna is probably the cause of the complete omission of the second sense of *aphormê*. We are told that the first sense of *aphormê* is opposed to rational impulse (1). What, we may ask, is the missing sense of *aphormê* meant to be opposed to?[7]

Is it opposed to irrational impulse (2), to *orexis* (3), or to *orousis* (4)? Certainty is impossible, but all likelihood supports the suggestion that it is opposed to irrational impulse. For when the lacuna occurs, *orousis* has not yet been mentioned. If the second *aphormê* is opposed to *orousis* a second lacuna will be needed. This is Dyroff's solution (p. 22). But it is preferable to keep the lacunae to the necessary minimum, and it is already necessary to posit the earlier one which Wachsmuth indicates. Moreover, it would be odd if *aphormê* were opposed to either *orousis* or to *orexis* and not the other. For they are both subtypes of rational impulse. Last, the distinction of rational and irrational impulse is the more important, and the kinds of *aphormê* are more likely for this reason to correspond to it.

Probably, then, the two senses of *aphormê* mentioned in the conclusion of section 9 are rational and irrational and correspond to rational and irrational impulse. At this point we may ask what is meant by the opposition of *aphormê* to *hormê*. *Aphormê* designates the impulse to avoidance behaviour rather than to pursuit behaviour. Thus the two are opposed as contraries rather than contradictories. When *aphormê* occurs in this sense in our sources it is always analogous to *hormê*.[8] It differs only by being directed at the avoidance of something rather than the pursuit of it, or at the abstention from action which is possible in the circumstances rather than at the performance of it.

Abstention from action must clearly be counted as a kind of action when it is the result of an *aphormê*. In many circumstances abstention and omission are properly considered actions.[9] This important feature of the analysis of action is reflected in chapter 11 of Plutarch's *Stoic Self-Contradictions*, where *hormê* is explained as a command to do something of moral significance and *aphormê* as a command not to do something. (*Hormê* is a *logos prostaktikos* and *aphormê* is a *logos apagoreutikos*.) Avoiding theft, to use the example Plutarch gives, in relevant circumstances is action just as much as burglary is.

When the avoidance behaviour is of the more obvious type, however, the case is even more clear that *aphormê* causes an action. It follows from these considerations that Dyroff's conception of *aphormê* as something which essentially involves inaction must be wrong. He is not very clear about the sense he wants to give to inaction,[10] but he commits himself to the view that it does not lead to something which counts as a *praxis*, a responsible human action.[11] This must be wrong if it is a kind of impulse at all. It seems that his notion that the missing sense of *aphormê* involves inaction comes from a phrase in Wachsmuth's supplement to the lacuna in section 9. He supplied *tôn en tôi mê prattein* in a critical spot; it is not supported by the text of Galen which he cites to support his supplement,[12] and von Arnim and Grilli[13] have already seen that the *mê* must be deleted from the supplement to the lacuna. With it disappears all reason for regarding *aphormê* as a cause of any kind of non-action.[14] It is simply the kind of impulse which causes avoidance or abstention.

We may now return to the question of the relationships among rational impulse (1), *orexis* (3), and *orousis* (4). For by considering this we may be able to clarify the general outline of sections 9 and 9a and thus shed light on the way the Stoics organized the classification of impulses.

First the term *orexis* demands a short explanation. Bonhoeffer[15] showed that we must recognize that Stoic usage included two distinct senses of *orexis*. It was used as a general term to designate a certain type of impulse (that directed at the apparent good) with no presumption that the impulse was correct (according to Right Reason) or incorrect (contrary to Right Reason). But it was also used specifically to designate a kind of correct impulse. Like impulse generally, every *orexis* which occurs will in fact be either correct or incorrect;[16] this is in line with Stoic tendencies to nominalism and their beliefs that right and wrong are contradictories, not contraries, in their proper range, which is human behaviour. There is no room in the set of things which exist or occur for a 'general' impulse which is not either right or wrong. Every one that occurs is the product of a virtuous or vicious mind and takes its moral character from that of the mind which produces it. It follows that the use of *orexis* as a general term is a convenient fiction, an abstraction as Bonhoeffer says,[17] which is being used when *boulêsis* is defined as *eulogos orexis*[18] and *epithumia* as *alogos orexis*.[19] When *orexis* is used in this sense, each instance of it is either a *boulêsis* or an *epithumia*. The term in this sense could be dispensed with except for its usefulness in drawing attention to similarities between *boulêsis* and *epithumia*. As we shall see, the most important similarity it indicates is with respect to the object of such an *orexis*, the apparent good.

The second sense of *orexis* is, as Bonhoeffer says,[20] the normative or standard-setting sense. This is the *orexis* which Stoic writers can say is directed only at the 'good'. They can say this because in Stoic doctrine man is by nature (i.e. normatively, not normally) an animal who is attracted to the good. In a prescriptive sense, therefore, man's *orexis* is for the good. But as a matter of regrettable fact, most instances of *orexis* will be *epithumiai* or wrong *orexeis*, since so few men ever achieve virtue.

In sections 9 and 9a the abstract sense of *orexis* is being used. *Orousis* and *orexis* are both kinds of rational impulse and *orousis* is characterized as being 'to something in the future'. Note, now, that in section 9a *hairesis* (choice), *prohairesis*, *boulêsis*, and *thelêsis* are all types of *orexis*. The diagrams will make their relations clear.

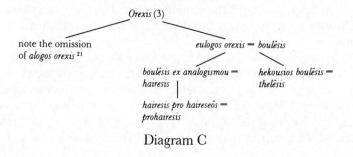

Diagram C

The abstract sense of *orexis* is being used, but the counter-rational forms are omitted.

Since *orousis* is the other major subtype of rational impulse in section 9, the suggestion may be made that *orousis* is the general term under which the other forms of impulse in section 9a are to be placed. This suggestion will be supported if, as I shall argue, these impulses can be plausibly interpreted as being directed 'at something in the future'. While I think that this is the likeliest hypothesis, I am aware that it must remain tentative in view of the dismal state of our evidence on the kinds of impulse.

Orousis and *orexis* are not necessarily mutually exclusive as we have seen. That means that any diagram showing their relations will be somewhat misleading; nevertheless, it is worth while to sketch the relations between the terms in sections 9 and 9a as organized by the doxographer. We must not suppose that this represents a regular genus/species classification.

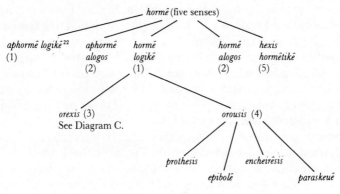

Diagram D

Before discussing the individual kinds of impulse, two remarks may be made about the range of the classification. It is quite extensive, even though it is not the full Stoic classification. At least one purpose of such a wide-ranging set of types of impulse must have been to provide a sufficiently comprehensive framework of types and subtypes to include all ethically significant actions and intentions. For the classification differentiates impulses in a variety of ways: as correct and incorrect; as aimed at pursuit and avoidance behaviour; and according to the sort of hormetic proposition involved, that is according to the features of the predicate. The paucity of subdivisions for irrational impulse is consistent with the greater complication of human behaviour and with the predominantly ethical interests of the Stoics. Second, it is worth pointing out that as far as our sources indicate, the subdivisions of *aphormê* are less numerous and complicated than for *hormê*, although where we do have information about *aphormê* it is exactly analogous to that for *hormê*. This may be explained in three ways: by the neglect of our tradition, which found avoidance behaviour less interesting and so omitted it from the reports we have; by the hypothesis that the Stoa had less to say about avoidance behaviour, from sheer disinterest; or more probably, because the Stoa explicitly believed that avoidance behaviour is not as complex as pursuit behaviour and so analysed it into fewer subtypes.

Orousis

Despite the limitations of our evidence, two questions may profitably be asked about the kind of impulse designated as *orousis*. What does it mean for an impulse to be 'a movement of the mind to something in the future (*epi ti mellon*)'? And is it probable that *prothesis, epibolê, paraskeuê*, and *encheirêsis* are subtypes of *orousis*? In answering these questions we shall get at least a rough idea of how the Stoics extended their psychology of action to include a wider range of plans, endeavours, and intentions.[23]

Since it is an impulse, *orousis* will be directed at a predicate, i.e. an action expressed in a verbal formula. Predicates have tense as well as grammatical voice; twice we are told of 'past-tense predicates'.[24] We do not have specific reference to 'future-tense' predicates in our sources, but it would make sense for the Stoics to have noticed them. Let us suppose then that an *orousis* is 'directed at something future' in virtue of being directed at a predicate in the future tense. This is easily expressed in Greek, although it is awkward in English. Instead of a *hormê epi to pheugein* one would have a *hormê epi to pheuxesthai* (in English, an impulse to being going to flee). An *orousis* must be, on this hypothesis, an impulse to an action which is more remote in the future, not to be performed in the immediate situation in which the agent finds himself. It would, then, be an appropriate form of impulse to use when one wanted to speak of planning and long-range intentions. For these are states which determine future actions as a result of a decision made in the present.

One might, for example, have an *orousis* in a situation like this. One has a presentation of a buried treasure in a neighbour's garden; one forms the proposition that it is right to steal it when possible, assents to this, and thereby one has an impulse to dig it up as soon as the neighbour leaves town for the weekend.[25] This impulse would be a movement of the mind to something future; the predicate in the proposition to which assent was given was in the future tense. This is the sort of mental act (and it is an act for which one may be praised or blamed, even if no overt action occurs until Saturday morning) which I think is meant by the technical term *orousis*. By means of the various kinds of *orousis* the Stoics would be in a position both to account for planning and long-range intentions and also to hold people responsible for the moral quality of the plans they make even if, by some chance, they should not carry them out.

In addition to the passage in Stobaeus which we are considering, the four terms which I suggest are kinds of *orousis* are common in Epictetus; reference to some is made by Plutarch[26] and by Origen.[27] The range of their occurrence assures us that we are dealing with genuine old Stoic terminology, probably Chrysippean in origin. The meaning of these terms is discussed briefly by Voelke and Dyroff;[28] but only Bonhoeffer[29] makes a serious attempt to analyse their meaning. His account is helpful, but not correct (see below). Let us look at the four types one by one and see whether they may be interpreted as forms of *orousis*.

Prothesis

This term is defined as a *sēmeiōsis epiteleseōs*,[30] i.e. an 'indication of accomplishment'.[31] In ordinary Greek the word *prothesis* means purpose or end, and occurs in the phrase *kata prothesin*, which means 'purposely' (LSJ s.v. *prothesis* II 1).[32] But in its Stoic use as a kind of impulse it is much harder to understand. It is true that there is an Aristotelian precedent; the corresponding verb *protithesthai* means something like 'intend'.[33] But this is not a reliable guide, since the Stoics often altered the sense of terms borrowed from Aristotle.

Thus we are forced to rely on the definition in Stobaeus and on the ordinary sense of the word which must have imposed some constraints on the technical Stoic usage. What, then, can be made of *sêmeiôsis epiteleseôs*? *Sêmeiôsis* appears nowhere else as a Stoic term. *Sêmeion*, of course, is common enough. But its use for a special sort of inferential proposition is unlikely to help us here.

The word *sêmeiôsis* can mean an object or event functioning as a sign, an inference drawn from such a sign or, according to LSJ, the noting of a symptom in medical practice. Since an impulse is a mental event not itself observable by someone else, it is unlikely that *sêmeiôsis* here means sign or inference. A more promising guess is that it is the verbal noun formed from the verb *sêmeiousthai* in the sense to 'note for oneself'. Thus the term would indicate a self-conscious registering of one's own intentions to act.

This guess about the technical sense of *sêmeiôsis* is consistent with the ordinary sense of 'purpose' or 'intention' for *prothesis*. I suggest that *prothesis* is a self-conscious impulse to a future action, with emphasis on determination to accomplish the action mentioned in the proposition to which assent is given. This would rule out the possibility that the assent given is implicit assent. If, as seems reasonable to suppose, the proposition contains a future-tense predicate, *prothesis* would be a form of *orousis*. *Prothesis*, a future-directed intention, involves deliberate and self-conscious planning; by making it a form of impulse the Stoics brought such planning within the psychology of action.

Epibolê

The frequent use of this term by Epictetus in the sense of 'project' or 'basic plan of life'[34] is a considerable help in elucidating its sense for the old Stoa. For Epictetus' use is certainly consistent with the claim that it is a form of *orousis*, a future-directed plan or intention. But I doubt whether Epictetus is using the term exactly as the old Stoics did; Epictetus' freedom with other technical terms from the old Stoa should make us cautious. Let us see what may be learned from its old Stoic usage.

In Stobaeus the term is defined as 'an impulse before an impulse'.[35] We also know that it was the key term in the Stoic definition of *erôs*, passionate love.[36] What can be deduced from the definition of *epibolê* in Stobaeus which is consistent with its use in the definition of *erôs*?

An impulse in itself is not an action. If the *epibolê* is an impulse before an impulse, we may conclude that two actions are involved, since each impulse should lead to an action. One could say that an *epibolê* is an impulse to an action A preceding an impulse to another action B. The two actions, A and B, must be closely connected, so that the *epibolê* causes A but is logically connected to B which is further in the future and will have its own impulse. This connection to the future action B is what makes it plausible to describe an *epibolê* as future-directed and so as an *orousis*. There is no indication that this link to a future action needs to be a conscious intention, as was the case with *prothesis*. Assent leading to an *epibolê* can be implicit. Accordingly, it is not surprising that the phrase *kat'epibolên* does not occur with the meaning 'purposely'.

If the suggestion that one's present impulse may be connected to a future action, although the agent is unaware of it, seems odd, consider the following. We hold a man responsible for getting himself into a situation where an action of his which he intended to do (A) leads to another (B), even if he did not consciously acknowledge where his initial action would lead. We do so as long as B could be seen to follow upon A by a reflective, alert, and observant man. We say that he should have realized what he was getting himself into. For the Stoics, one is held responsible because the perhaps conscious assent to the doing of A involved the implicit assent to the doing of B.

What about *erôs*? It is the *epibolê* for 'making friends' (*philopoiia*) because of the appearance of beauty. The perception of a beautiful person elicits an impulse towards friendly behaviour (A); but this impulse is, in the circumstances, closely connected to future behaviour which is more appropriate to the sexual connotations of the word *erôs* (B). One may not be aware of what one is leading up to when smiling at a sexually attractive person; or perhaps one is. No matter. The friendly behaviour elicited by the sight of a beautiful person can have this further erotic aspect, and when it does, *erôs* is in the offing.

Paraskeuê

This term is oddly defined in Stobaeus: an action (A) before an action (B).[37] Since *paraskeuê* is a form of impulse, not of action, this wording must be designed to emphasize that the action corresponding to the impulse must in fact occur if the impulse is to count as a case of preparation. This emphasis is not pointless. For our impulses are not hindered by external interferences, but our actions are. If our action stopped in this way, we might say that an intention to act had occurred; but it is doubtful whether we would say that a preparation occurred at all if either the preliminary action (A) or the principal action (B) were hindered. The agent, no doubt, is thought of as being aware that A was a necessary condition to B, as seems to be suggested by the grouping of *paraskeuê* with *prothesis* and memory by Plutarch.[38]

Encheirêsis

This form of practical impulse is somewhat problematic.[39] Its definition is not repeated in Plutarch, as are those of the previous three kinds of impulse. Nor is it used by Epictetus or alluded to by Origen. There is no reason to doubt the term's authenticity, although its importance may be questioned in view of the silence of our authorities besides Arius Didymus.

Its definition (*hormê epi tinos en chersin êdê ontos*) does not immediately suggest that it is oriented to future action. But despite the difficulties imposed by our lack of other evidence, it is possible to speculate about its sense. I think it is at least possible that *encheirêsis* is a type of *orousis* in the sense which I have given to that term.

Note first that it is not an impulse *epi ti en chersin êdê on*. The object of impulse is not an action right at hand. It is rather an impulse 'in the case of' or 'dealing with' something already in hand. If it were a form of *orousis*, this would mean that *encheirêsis* is an impulse to a future action which could begin with or be introduced by some sort of action on something present. The impulse to an action in the future (B) occurs together with some immediate endeavour (A) leading to it. On this interpretation, *encheirêsis* would differ from *epibolê* and *paraskeuê* only in the fact that what is done here and now (A) is viewed as a part of the ultimate action (B), not a distinct action connected with it.[40] Like *epibolê* and *paraskeuê*, this kind of impulse would differ from *prothesis* in that it would involve starting immediately on some action connected with the future, as *prothesis* does not. Whether or not this is the correct account of *encheirêsis*, I think it is at least possible to take it as a form of *orousis*, an impulse to an action in the future.

Epictetus' use of the first three four forms of *orousis* is quite striking. But he does not seem to be following the details of the old Stoic usage of these terms. Bonhoeffer discusses the use of these terms,[41] and correctly emphasizes that Epictetus does not bother to distinguish among them. There is no need to repeat his discussion of Epictetus' usage. The special forms of impulse are treated by Epictetus as basically identical with *hormê* in general.

Bonhoeffer also discusses the old Stoic use of these technical terms. Here he is less reliable, for he has adopted a theory of the distinction between them which is calculated to de-emphasize the significance of the fact that Epictetus did not distinguish the meanings of these technical terms as the older Stoics seem to have done. For it is part of Bonhoeffer's plan in *Epictet und die Stoa* to represent Epictetus as being as orthodox as possible. In this case, as in several others, this simply will not work.[42] Although Epictetus is orthodox enough in the main outlines of his psychology of action, he is not scrupulously conservative on matters of terminology.

Bonhoeffer's view is that *epibolê, prothesis, paraskeuê,* and *encheirêsis* are not different kinds of impulse (which is what Arius Didymus tells us) but that they are stages of the impulse to action.[43] In this way Epictetus' treatment of them as basically the same as *hormê* becomes close enough to orthodoxy for Bonhoeffer's purposes. But no attempt is made to explain what is meant by calling them *eidê* of impulse, rather than aspects or parts; and no attempt is made to relate the classification of the *eidê* of impulse to the scheme of Arius' account or to *orousis*.

Orexis

The term *orexis* is used by the Stoics quite differently than by Aristotle; yet for both it is a key concept. For Aristotle it was a central concept of wide scope, covering all particular kinds of desire, motivation, and action in animals of all types. In this respect it is like the Stoic term *hormê.* For the Stoa, though, *orexis* is a definite kind of impulse found only in humans. The relation between the terms *orexis* and *hormê* in Stoic usage will be discussed here; for their relation in Aristotle's psychological and ethical works, see Appendix 3.

No definition is given of *orexis* in the text of Arius Didymus which we are considering. This is one of the reasons why we cannot be sure how it was thought to relate to *orousis*, the other major type of practical impulse mentioned there. The incompleteness of that account becomes more evident when we recall that an important type of impulse which contrasts with *orexis* in a fundamental respect is not even mentioned here. Selection (*eklogê*) is in many respects the natural complement to *orexis*, yet it is totally absent from the formal discussion of the kinds of impulse.[44]

I shall simplify the discussion by omitting the avoidance-behaviour counterparts of *hormê* and *orexis* (*aphormê* and *ekklisis*); they are analogous to the positive forms and a consideration of them would add nothing to the discussion. In our sources *orexis* is usually used in its abstract sense. Each individual occurrence of *orexis* is either according to or contrary to reason; but using *orexis* in the abstract sense enables the Stoics to differentiate the correct and incorrect forms of *orexis* (*boulêsis* and *epithumia* respectively) without losing sight of what they have in common.[45] The further classification of *orexis* in Arius Didymus is based on *boulêsis*, and so only concerns the correct forms of *orexis*.

But what do *boulêsis* and *epithumia* have in common which justifies the use of an abstract term to apply to both?[46] It appears from evidence elsewhere (for Arius Didymus does not give an account of *orexis* in this text) that both kinds of *orexis* are impulses to the apparent good. The difference is that *boulêsis* is to a correctly conceived good in the correct way and *epithumia* is to a mistakenly conceived good in an incorrect way. This is clear in many texts. At *TD* 3.24 *cupiditas* (= *epithumia*) is an *appetitus magni boni*; at *Peri Pathôn* 1 (= SVF 3.391) *alogos orexis* is glossed as 'the pursuit of an expected good'. Similar wording is used by Aspasius (SVF 3.386): *orexis* is of the apparent good. Again in the *Tusculans* (4.12), *boulêsis* is said to be an impulse to acquire something good which is according to Reason, i.e. correct.

The same close connection of *orexis* to the pursuit of apparent good is also seen at *Ecl.* 2.97–8, where the normative sense of *orexis* seems to be foremost in the compiler's mind. Good things are said to be the object of *orexis, boulêsis, hairesis,* and *apodexis*,[47] while the action in pursuit of such objects is indicated by the corresponding gerundives. Thus the close connection to what is good confirms the generalization that *orexis* in its abstract sense is an impulse to the apparent good. One may also note that at *Ecl.* 2.72 the good is said to be *haireton*, i.e. object of *hairesis*, and *areston*.[48]

The conclusion to be drawn is clear. In the old Stoa *orexis* and all of its forms and subtypes have for their object 'the good'. Let us turn to the subtypes of *orexis* which are included in Arius Didymus' list of the kinds of impulse. This can be done more quickly. For although two of them are of great importance in ethics (*boulêsis* or 'will' and *hairesis* or 'choice'), the others are of only passing interest. These two, moreover, seem to be very similar kinds of impulse. And although some consideration of Epictetus' usage is needed in the case of *prohairesis*, the others are not used by him in a technical sense,[49] while *thelêsis* does not even appear in his works.

Boulêsis

With *boulêsis* we have another type of impulse designated by the same term as a key Aristotelian concept.[50] *Boulêsis* is defined as a *eulogos orexis*, i.e. a correct desire. Thus it seems to have been inspired by Aristotle's use of the word to designate the correct form of *orexis*: *De Anima* 3.9, 432b5; 3.10, 433a23 ff.; *Rhetoric* 1.10, 1368b37 ff.; *Nicomachean Ethics* 3.2, 1111b19 ff.; 3.4, 1113a15–b2; *Politics* 7.15, 1334b22. The psychology behind Aristotle's usage is of course quite different from the Stoic psychology of 'desire'. The Stoics and Aristotle were no doubt influenced by earlier uses of *boulêsis* in this sense; Plato, for example, restricted the use of *boulesthai* to desires for things which the agent believes to be good.[51]

The most obvious fact about the use of the term *boulêsis* is that it is restricted almost completely to discussions of the *pathê* and *eupatheiai*.[52] *Boulêsis* is one of the *eupatheiai*; the other use of the word which merits attention is in the phrase 'the will of Zeus' or 'the will of nature'. This is a curious fact, but one which supports the attempt made in Chapter 5 to connect the doctrine of the passions more closely to the issue of man's place in a providentially determined world. Because *boulêsis* is so similar in meaning to *hairesis*, the fact that the context of *boulêsis* is so restricted explains why they kept two distinct terms.[53]

Thelêsis

This is defined as *hekousios boulêsis*, voluntary willing. This is a peculiar juxtaposition of traditional philosophical terms. Its significance can best be divined by reflecting on Aristotle's discussion of the voluntary in the *Nicomachean Ethics* (3.1). Aristotle considered cases which were on the borderline between being voluntary and involuntary. These 'mixed actions' are involuntary in the sense that they are not the sorts of things one would do if given a completely free choice (e.g. throwing cargo overboard), but voluntary in the sense that they are chosen as the best course to take in difficult circumstances (in a storm it may be a matter of jettisoning cargo or losing the ship). Such actions are not voluntary in an unqualified sense.

I want to suggest that for the Stoics a voluntary willing is an impulse to do something which is good and which is also the sort of thing one would choose *not* as a result of difficult circumstances or constrained alternatives. For a *boulêsis* could be an impulse to what is morally good, in a situation where the right action is not what one would want to choose in ideal circumstances. It may even be something *apoproêgmenon*, such as sickness. In contrast to this, a case of *thelêsis* would be a choice of the good in cases where there is no constraint of circumstances on one's choice; it would be a fully voluntary action. If one discovered that the right thing to do was to jettison the cargo in order to save lives, that might, if done by a sage, be a *boulêsis* or *hairesis* but not a *thelêsis*. If the right thing to do involves smooth sailing and the health of the crew and safety of the cargo, then one's voyage would be carried out by a *thelêsis*.

If this suggestion is right, the terminology is a sort of fossil of a larger Stoic discussion of some of the same issues in ethics which Aristotle raised. If this suggestion is correct, we see the Stoics aiming to cover the same ground as Aristotle did within the framework of their own theory of action.[54]

Hairesis

'Choice' is a much more important form of impulse, as a glance through the Index to SVF will confirm. Like *boulêsis*, the term has a history of use as a technical term in ethics; from its beginnings in Plato, it became an important ethical term for both Aristotle and Epicurus. In concentrating once again, as Plato sometimes had, on a normative use of the term (correct choice of the good), the Stoa elevated *hairesis* into a technical term for the highest and best expression of a human's practical intelligence.[55]

Like *boulêsis*, *hairesis* is an impulse to the good;[56] a question therefore arises about the difference between the meanings of the two terms, if indeed they are not synonyms. Because of the difference in application of the two terms, however, it is possible to make a suggestion about the difference in usage of the terms. *Boulêsis*, as we have seen, is found almost exclusively in discussions of passions and *eupatheiai*; *hairesis*, on the other hand, is found usually in a wider context; it is normally contrasted with selection (*eklogê*) in this respect. Selection is directed at the indifferents, while choice is directed at the good.[57] The significance of this has been discussed in Chapter 6 at some length, and there it appeared that choice was a special way of pursuing indifferents which converted mere selection into a morally correct pursuit of the good. With *boulêsis* matters are much simpler. As a correct form of *orexis* it appears to be a pursuit of the good and nothing more. Thus if one's impulse is directed at the good and at nothing else, if there is not a complicated interdependence of one's pursuit of something indifferent and of the good as there is in the case of choice, then that impulse is a case of *boulêsis*. Such a term is most useful in contrast with passions, for passions are caused by a misconception of the good. Choice has a wider use, because it describes the impulse to the good in the concrete setting in which it will usually occur, where a man is pursuing something not morally good in a morally proper way which converts that pursuit into a good act. *Hairesis* is free of the restrictions imposed on *boulêsis* by its use in the theory of *pathê* and *eupatheiai*.

Let us note a few particulars about the use of *hairesis*. It is defined as *boulêsis ex analogismou* by Arius Didymus. The usually accepted[58] interpretation of this is that the *analogismos* or reckoning up referred to here is not consideration or deliberation about what one is to do. For any choice of the good will be automatic and unreflecting, once the good is seen. And a sage will not have to deliberate about that. The consideration and reflection (if there is any) will be concerned with the selection of indifferents which provides the particular content of an act of choice. Choice is an impulse to the good, which is unconditionally desirable. On the usually accepted interpretation, the reference to *analogismos* is to be explained on the basis of the fact that the concept of the good is formed by analogy.[59] The mention of *analogismos* in the definition of choice, then, is simply a reflection of the way in which choice becomes possible. For without the analogical reflection which gives us a concept of the good, no choice will be possible.

This may be right;[60] I certainly have no concrete alternative to put in its place. But one objection to this is worth making. *Boulēsis* is also an impulse to the good. *Hairesis* is defined as a *boulēsis ex analogismou*. How can the analogical reasoning which is necessary in order to have a conception of the good serve to differentiate two forms of impulse which share the feature of being directed at the good? This seems impossible. It is at least worth considering the possibility that *analogismos* refers to the special feature of *hairesis*, its involvement with selection among indifferent things.

The standard Latin translation for *hairesis* and its verb forms is *expetere*.[61] Seneca is usually careful about this restriction on the use of *expetere* (see *Ep.* 117.17 *quod expetendum est, bonum est,*[62]) and Cicero is scrupulous about it in book 3 of the *De Finibus*.

In Stoic sources *hairesis* is clearly a form of impulse. We are told that it is directed at *katēgorēmata* (*Ecl.* 2.97) or *ōphelēmata* (*Ecl.* 2.78) which are actions. But it is stimulated by an object, the *haireton*.[63] Like all rational impulses, it involves assent to certain propositions and is also directed at action.

Aristotle and Epicurus[64] use *hairesis* and *phugē* as general terms for pursuit and avoidance behaviour. This pairing of the terms is also found in Stoic sources, and this may be a reflection of this more general philosophical usage.[65]

Prohairesis

The old Stoic use of this term diverges from its Aristotelian counterpart more than any other. It is defined obscurely in *Ecl.* 2.87 as *hairesis pro haireseōs*, a choice which is (temporally) before a choice. This is clearly a fairly unimportant term for the old Stoa,[66] yet it is an important, indeed a central, ethical concept for Epictetus.[67] Its use by Epictetus is so unrelated to that of the old Stoa that comparison of the two is not at all helpful for determining its earlier sense. Still, a brief look at Epictetus' usage is in order.

Like all forms of impulse it depends on opinions and is unhinderable and under the agent's control. For Epictetus it is the locus of good and bad for man and is set in sharp contrast to the body and the external objects which *prohairesis* uses as its raw material. In marked contrast to its trivial role in the old Stoa, *prohairesis* in Epictetus seems to be in control of the other impulses and faculties, and so is almost equivalent to the *hēgemonikon*.[68] The *prohairesis* is to be improved by moral training, for it must be made *kata phusin*, it must be put into its normatively natural condition. *Prohairesis* plays, for Epictetus, a central role in the accommodation to fate; he has elevated the term to stand for a man's entire free power of choice, which constitutes his moral programme for life, his *Lebensvorsatz* or *Beruf.*[69]

While in Epictetus *prohairesis* is such a central concept, indicating the essential moral personality of the agent, it is for the old Stoa one of the least important types of impulse. Some sources use the common philosophical phrase *kata prohairesin* to indicate free voluntary acts which a person intends to do, but this is not a technical Stoic use of the word *prohairesis.*[70] The only information we have on the technical use of the term, as opposed to its general use as a piece of philosophical jargon in later writers is *Ecl.* 2.87; and this suggests an absurdly restricted use of the term, in view of Aristotle's use of it. Aristotle defined *prohairesis* as *orexis bouleutikê*;[71] for him it was a central ethical concept, the intersection point of reason and desire which made possible rational and responsible behaviour. The concepts of rational *hormê* and assent played this role for the old Stoa, and they dismissed *prohairesis* to a lowly status indeed.

It seems likely, then, that Epictetus' use of the word reflects a tradition of Aristotelian usage more than it does earlier Stoic terminology. This reliance on a more general philosophical use of the term would explain why his use of the term is so different from that of the old Stoa, which rejected the Aristotelian use.[72] The older Stoics must have intended to 'correct' and so to displace Aristotelian *prohairesis*; by trivializing the central concept of Aristotle's analysis of rational action they made room for their own analysis which was based on the concepts of impulse and assent.

Bonhoeffer makes an attempt to salvage the orthodoxy of Epictetus' terminology even here. He tried to find in the old Stoa a comparably important use of *prohairesis*. What he found were a few texts, a worthless passage from the Suda and texts which merely reflect the generalized jargon of later philosophical writers.[73] It is not surprising that such texts are reminiscent of Epictetus' use, for they are also part of the general tradition dominated by Aristotelian, not Stoic, usage in this instance.

The old Stoic *prohairesis* was an insignificant 'choice before a choice'.[74] Pohlenz[75] tries to inject some importance into this by interpreting it as 'eine erstmalige, vorläufige Entscheidung'. But if this is right, we would have expected *prohairesis* to be a form of *orousis*, not of *orexis* as it is. Very little importance can be attached to the term at *Ecl.* 2.87, and the reason for this is most probably that it is only mentioned at all because Aristotle used the word. One may recall, of course, the Stoic adaptation of his term *boulêsis* and of the use made of his discussion of mixed actions. The old Stoics seem to have been attempting to subsume and displace Aristotle's framework for the analysis of ethically significant action. The downgrading of *prohairesis* was another part of this general programme; in view of the popularity of the term in later philosophical jargon and even in the works of a Stoic like Epictetus, it can only be said that in this case the attempt was a dismal failure.[76]

Appendix 3

Hormê in Plato, Aristotle, and the *Magna Moralia*

Hormê and *horman* are fully developed technical terms in the writings of the early Stoics.[1] They have a broad range of senses in Greek generally, and these are represented in the dialogues of Plato. The non-technical nature of his usage makes detailed exploration of it unnecessary, but it is worth while to point out that in several places Plato uses *hormê* in a way which shows why the Stoics should have chosen it as their key term in the theory of action. For one of the term's uses, which is frequently found in Plato, is to designate a desire, effort, or inclination to act, or more specifically to pick out that aspect of an action which is captured by the technical Stoic use of *hormê*. This is the moment of activated desire which causes action, that last stage of the activity of the soul before bodily movement is produced. It is interesting, too, to note that Plato often uses idioms similar to the one which became standard in the Stoa. A full survey of the relevant texts of Plato would be tedious here, and an illustrative selection of passages must suffice.

In the *Philebus* (35c12, d2) *hormê* is the thrust or desire of the soul; it is contrasted with the mere *pathêmata* of the body which may be at odds with the soul's desires and efforts. (The *hormê* is in this case a striving to drink, i.e. to replenish liquids, while the condition of the body is the opposite, the absence of liquids or thirst; we would say that the intentional object of desire is the opposite of the bodily condition[2].)

In the *Sophist* (228c2) *hormê* is used of an effort by the soul to acquire or to achieve something; it is an effort which can fail of its mark; but there is no explicit connection with desire in the context. The case is different in the *Laws* (866e2); here the *hormê* is the striving or activated desire of an agent acting under the influence of *thumos*.

If the Seventh Letter is genuine, it contains an interesting Platonic foreshadowing of Stoic phrasing (325e1); for the narrator says that at a certain time he was full of a great desire or drive or motivation to enter politics, and uses the idiom familiar from Stoic texts (*hormê epi to prattein ta koina*).[3]

The verb *horman* or *hormasthai* is more common in the dialogues, but has roughly the same range of meaning as the corresponding noun. It even turns up with the sense and construction seen in the Seventh Letter. At *Republic* 354b5 *hormêsai epi to* + infinitive means to try or undertake to do something. Similar sense is given to the verb, though with slightly different constructions, at a number of other places.[4] In these texts there is only a weak connection, if any, with the idea of a faculty of desire which is thought of as being activated to cause the action or effort or undertaking in question.

In some texts, however, this idea is present, and then we see how the Platonic use of the term blends easily into the Aristotelian use of *hormê* as a rough equivalent for *orexis* or its activation. A text in book 4 of the *Republic* (436b2) is the most important in this connection. Here Plato is introducing his theory of three 'parts' of the soul, each with its characteristic form of desire. He asks whether when a person acts in each of the three characteristic ways he is acting with the entire soul or with the appropriate one of the three parts. The phrasing is interesting: *ê holêi têi psuchêi kath' hekaston autôn prattomen hotan hormêsômen*, 'or is it with the entire soul that we act in each case, when we have an impulse'. The last phrase may be more naturally translated as 'when we set ourselves to it' or 'when we begin' or 'when we try', etc. The important point terminologically is the connection of *hormê* to the idea of activation of desire. That this is not accidental is indicated by the use of the verb for the activity of the spirited part of the soul in book 9 (581a10).[5]

A passage in the *Laws* (886b1) uses *hormasthai* to stand for the general tendency of a soul to live in a certain way (*hormasthai epi ton asebê bion*); the idiom with *epi* is interesting, but the cause of the tendency or undertaking is what should be pointed out. It is the result of a failure to control (*akrateia*) one's pleasures and desires. In a rather less pointed way, this text shows how the action of *hormê* was thought to be the result of the activation of desires.

As I said at the outset, Plato's use of *hormê* and the corresponding verbs is not technical. It shows the full range of idiomatic flexibility of which *hormê* is capable in Greek. Because of this he occasionally employs the words in ways which reveal which facets of its wide range made it suitable for the technical purposes to which it was put by the Stoics. When we turn to Aristotle's psychological and ethical works we can see the faint beginnings of a technical specialization of the term as a designation for *orexis* or a certain aspect of the activation of *orexis*. The Aristotelian use of the word no doubt further inspired the Stoics to adopt it as a strict technical term.

A review of Aristotle's use of the term *hormê* and its relation to *orexis* will show how easy and natural it was for later Greek philosophers, in the period when an eclectic philosophical jargon was being coined and became dominant, to conflate *hormê* and *orexis*. For although the one was the central theoretical term for the Stoa and the other for Aristotle, they could be blended together by those who were not interested in or did not understand the differences between the two psychological theories. This process continued to the point where, as noted in Chapter 5, the desiderative part of the soul could be called *to hormêtikon* rather than *to orektikon*.

Aristotle's use of *hormê* is well summed up by A. K. Griffin:[6] Impulse, he says,

is a word of general signification which was used a great deal in common speech and also in Plato's works. It occurs quite generally in Aristotle's writings, but not frequently except in *Magna Moralia*. It is used as synonymous with most of the other terms for desire. It appears to mean the same as 'desire' (*orexis*), as 'emotion' (*pathos*), as appetite (*epithumia*), as 'choice' (*prohairesis*). It may be said to have no precise meaning of its own which can be assigned to it over and above that of its synonyms.

This general characterization will need to be qualified somewhat, but Griffin's recognition that *hormê* is a synonym for the various forms of desire is correct. Let us look now a little more closely at the use of *hormê* in Aristotle and in the *Magna Moralia*.[7]

In the one sense *hormê* designates the tendency of a natural body to carry out its motion. This use is found at *EE* 2.8.4. Although at 2.8.5 Aristotle will go on to apply *hormê* in its more usual sense to animal motion, his analysis of the voluntary and the constrained begins from the fact that when, e.g., a stone or fire moves *kata tên phusei kai tên kath' hauta hormên*, it is not a constrained movement. When *hormê* is used at *Physics* 2.1 (192b18) and *Metaphysics* Δ 23 (1023a17 ff.; cf. 1015a26–7, *Post. An.* 94b37 ff.) this is the sense of the word. *Qua* bed or cloak these objects have no *emphutos hormê* to change, but *qua* stone or earth or some compound of natural bodies, they do have an inbuilt impulse to move to their natural places.

In this sense the term is rare. In fact, its only occurrence in the ethical works is the one now being considered. Here the ambiguity of *hormê* is used to make a plausible argument for a definition of the voluntary as that which is done according to an *archê* internal to man.

The common ethical sense of *hormê* (omitting *EN* 1116b35 where *horman* simply means 'rush') is as an equivalent for *orexis*, sometimes with a special emphasis on the active exercise of *orexis* in the determination of an action.

Thus at *EE* 2.8.5 ff., constrained or forced action is described as happening *hotan para tên en autôi hormên exôthen ti kinêi* (cf. *Met.* 1015a26–31). Aristotle goes on to point out that men have two *archai* of action, *orexis* and *logos*, which may sometimes be opposed, and that as long as action is according to one of these two, it may be considered voluntary.

At first sight, this suggests that *hormê* is not *orexis* but something common to the function of *orexis* and *logos*. However, as we shall see below and as is especially clear from *DA* 3.9–10 (432b3–7; 433a21–30), the actions which stem from reason are also driven by a kind of *orexis*, i.e. the *boulêsis* which obeys right reason (cf. Ross, *Aristotle*, p. 145). (But contrast *Met.* Δ 5 where *hormê* is used of irrational *orexis* and *prohairesis* is used for the deliberate *orexis* leading to action).

Thus *hormê* and *horman* are often used to designate the function of the *orexis* of either the rational or irrational part of the soul. This use is particularly clear in the discussion of *akrasia* at *EN* 1.13. The *hormai* are the desires which conflict in the acratic act: *epi tánantia gar hai hormai tôn akratôn* (1102b21). These are conflicting desires, not actions. For the acratic agent only carries out one act (the wrong one). The *hormai* are thus invisible events in the agent's soul, a point which Aristotle emphasizes by his comparison of them to bodily movements.

The same use of *hormê* is found elsewhere in the *EN*. At 10.9 (1180a23) Aristotle notes that people become angry if others oppose their *hormai*, which are clearly to be understood as desires or urges to act. And in 7.6 (1149a31–b1) the verb *horman* is used to designate the activities of *thumos* and *epithumia*—both of which are irrational *orexis*. The verb is similarly used at *DM* 7 (701a33–4) to refer to the desire which is actually functioning, not desire as a state or condition; *houtôs men oun epi to kineisthai kai prattein ta zôia hormôsi*.

Aristotle held that *orexis* was needed even for actions according to reason, but he usually preferred to use the term *orexis* to refer to the irrational sort. This accounts for his tendency to use the roughly synonymous *hormê* in just those cases where he wanted to emphasize that desire is common to the rational and irrational parts of the soul. Since Aristotle thought that irrational desire was exercised in an automatic way whenever an *orekton* appeared—providing there is not *logos* to oppose it[8]—*hormê* was also used for automatically occurring tendencies to motion, such as the movement of stones to their natural place.[9] Thus at *EE* 8.2.12 in the discussion of *eutuchia* after the rhetorical question, 'Are there not *hormai* in the soul, some from reasoning and others from irrational desire?' (another case of *hormê* being common to both parts of the soul—Kenny, *Aristotelian Ethics*, p. 168), Aristotle goes on to single out the 'prior' irrational *hormai*. Good luck is said to occur when our *hormai* are good and right even without reason. The ensuing discussion of good luck and its cause is marked by a recognition of the equivalence of *hormê* to *orexis* (8.2.12; also 1247b34–6). *Hormê* and *horman* are used of specific desires in action (e.g. 1248a30), but *hormê* has an overtone of 'inbred condition' or 'general tendency'. This is not surprising. *Orexis* itself is often used as a term for a persistent desire, a state or condition of a soul, as well as for the activation of this capacity. And in the present discussion of good luck it is only such irrational and undeliberated *hormai* which are being considered.

In this passage too, as in the discussion of *akrasia* and the voluntary, it seems to be the neutral connotations of *hormê* which lead to its use in place of *orexis* with its strong suggestion of the irrational part of the soul. For in *akrasia* Aristotle wished to focus on the conflicting desires which come from the two parts of the soul and the discussion of the voluntary demands a term which can be applied to either *archê* of motion. In the discussion of *eutuchia* in the *EE*, *hormê* is applied to desires or desiderative tendencies which are in fact irrational but give the appearance of being rational. The noncommittal *hormê* is thus more apt than *orexis*.

The tendency to use *hormê* as an equivalent for the Aristotelian *orexis* remained strong in the Peripatos (see e.g. Aristoxenus frr. 33, 37, 38 Wehrli); and this tendency is no doubt part of the reason for the *Magna Moralia*'s relatively high concentration of this use. As can be seen by going through the texts from the *MM* in detail, there are no clearly Stoic uses of *hormê* in it. Indeed, the tendency in later centuries was just the opposite; more and more the term came to be used with an 'Aristotelian' sense even by philosophers whose allegiance to Aristotle and familiarity with his ethical treatises were weak.

Space limitations preclude a full discussion of the date and authorship of the *MM*, which are quite controversial issues. I believe that it is a Hellenistic compilation based on Aristotle's ethical works. There are, some have argued, reasons to suspect that the *MM* must be at least late enough for its author to be familiar with Stoic doctrine. For example, D. J. Allan ('*Magna Moralia* and *Nicomachean Ethics*', p. 7) accepts a dating by Dirlmeier (late second or early first century BC), based on the contention that 1204a23 ff. refers to one Diodorus who studied under Critolaus. Allan sees an attempt to select Peripatetic ethical doctrine for use against Stoic views in the tendency of the *MM*'s author to treat moral virtue as the only virtue (a Stoic doctrine) and to take '*aretê* rather than *eudaimonia* as his fundamental conception' (see p. 7 and n. 6).

This dating of the *MM* is supported by Long ('Aristotle's Legacy', p. 73 and nn. 9–11), who is following Allan's analysis of the purpose of the treatise. In particular, he is ready to accept that the greater frequency of the term *hormê* in the *MM* is a sign of Stoic influence. But the use of *hormê* in the *MM* is an easy development from Aristotle's use, as we shall see, and any Stoic influence on the terminology must be very indirect. Discussion and criticism of the Stoic psychology of action may have led to a conflation of *hormê* and *orexis* and a more frequent use of *hormê* in place of *orexis*. Critics assimilated the Stoic *hormê* to Aristotle's *orexis*, but did not use *hormê* in the Stoic sense. This can be seen if we examine the use of *hormê* and *horman* in the *MM*.

In some cases the *MM* simply carries over the term *hormê* from the corresponding text of the *EE* or *EN*. Thus: *MM* 2.4.2 and 1.13.3 (cf. *EE* 2.8.5–6 and esp. *EN* 1.13); and *MM* 2.8.8–11 (cf. *EE* 8.2.12–24); cf. also *MM* 1.34.26 and 2.6.24–26 with *EN* 7.6.

Elsewhere *hormê* replaces *orexis*, marking the trend to use the former term more frequently than Aristotle himself. See *MM* 1.16.1. One or two texts speak of a general *hormê* to *ta agatha* or to *to kalon* (1.34.23 ff.; 2.7.30–1). But this is not a Stoicizing use. Aristotle too uses *orexis* for this sort of tendency to act (e.g. *EE* 8.2.12 *kai hê orexis ge epi to agathon badizoi an pantote*, Rackham's text in the Loeb edition).

The *MM* very often uses *hormê* to indicate *orexis* in the generation of an action. This use is found in the *EN* and *EE*. But those works will often refer to actions *tout court*, whereas the *MM* inserts the term *hormê* to refer to the same action. This is correct doctrine, for actions all require an *orexis*. Note: *MM* 1.4.9 (cf. *EN* 1.13); 1.20.10 (*EN* 3.7; *EE* 3.1); 2.6.35 (*EN* 7.7–8). At *MM* 1.17.5 the force of *hormê tis tou prattein* is clear, confirming the use of *hormê* to refer to *orexis* in the moment of causing an action. In this passage, *hormê* is replacing *orexis* in a discussion of *prohairesis*.

The last noteworthy use of *hormê* is at *MM* 2.16.3, which recommends that we have a number of friends suited to *tôi kairôi kai têi autou hormêi pros to philein*. The point seems to be different from that at *EN* 9.10 and *EE* 7.12.17–18. Cf. also *EE* 7.2.48. The *hormê* here might be either a desire for friends (but that would be circular, since the question at issue is how many friends we should want), a capacity for befriending people or a natural tendency to do so. The last is more probable, being a plausible blurring of the natural-tendency sense with the sense indicating desire. The author, in fact, seems to have it in mind that our desire or need for friends is in some sense a built-in part of our ethical make-up. While this notion does not appear in the *EE* or *EN*, the use of *hormê* is still based on uses there, and shows no sign of Stoic influence. It is perhaps closest to the *EE*'s discussion of *eutuchia*, which also shows a tendency to conflate *hormê* with natural virtue.

One may conclude, then, that the use of the term *hormê* in the *MM* is not evidence of direct Stoic influence. But while the sense of the term is an easy extension of Aristotle's use of it in the ethical treatises, its frequency is striking. It may be that *MM* is reflecting, by its choice of terminology, the dominance of Stoic ideas in ethical debate. This is plausible if the *MM* is dated to the Hellenistic period. It follows from this that the usage of the *MM* is not a guide to the doctrine of the old Stoa, although it is interesting to note that it displays eclectic tendencies in its terminology which are carried further by later philosophical writers.

Appendix 4

The Term *Kath' Hormên*[1]

The Stoic term *hormê* is a part of a distinct psychology of action; although it is similar to the Aristotelian term *orexis* in being a central theoretical term, it takes its meaning from the theory of which it is a part and cannot, therefore, be assumed to be equivalent to Aristotle's *orexis*. Later writers with eclectic tendencies and little interest in the differences between Aristotelian and Stoic theories did tend to conflate the terms *hormê* and *orexis*, and this tendency is nowhere more apparent than in the case of the phrase *kath' hormên*.

Let us begin with a bit of background and some distinctions. In Aristotle a distinction may be drawn between actions of an animal (rational or irrational) which are performed through the animal's own power of desire (*orexis*) and which are therefore its own actions in contrast to things done to it or automatic processes over which it has no control. Let us call the former actions 'voluntary' and emphasize that to label them as such is not to say that they are the sorts of actions for which the agent can be held morally responsible. Only adult humans can be held morally responsible for their actions; and I think it is likely that Aristotle regarded morally responsible actions as a subset of an adult's voluntary actions. Further conditions had to be satisfied before a voluntary action became responsible.

We have seen how things stand for the Stoa on these questions. Corresponding to voluntary actions are actions carried out through an animal's power of impulse (*hormê*); the Stoics would agree that only adult humans are bearers of moral responsibility, since the voluntary actions of children and irrational animals have no moral value as such. But unlike Aristotle, the Stoics did not mark off morally responsible actions as a subset of the voluntary actions of adults. Any voluntary action by an adult, any action carried out through the power of rational impulse, is a responsible action. They took this very hard line because they faced the challenge of reconciling human moral responsibility with a form of determinism, as Aristotle did not. And the theory of action reflects their desire to hold adults responsible for everything that they do.

All actions in the proper sense of the word are the result of assent as well as of impulse, and assent is just the sort of thing for which a man may be held to account.

Another distinction is needed. A term which has its origin in a Stoic theory may be used outside the framework of that theory. It may be adopted by other philosophers, eclectics or those with little interest in the precise details of the Stoic theory which originally spawned the terminology in question. When a term is used in this way it seems reasonable to call this a non-Stoic use of the term, despite its ultimate origin. When, however, a Stoic or someone professedly reporting Stoic views uses the term with an awareness of the theory of which it is a part, it is fair to say that such a use of the term is a Stoic usage. The question whether the term itself is Stoic is of less importance than the issue of how it is being used.

The term *kath' hormên* is an interesting case of interaction between Stoic and non-Stoic traditions in later Greek philosophy. For although it seems to have its origins in a Stoic use of the term *hormê*, the phrase later became a part of the general philosophical jargon and was used with no awareness of its specifically Stoic sense by a wide range of writers. Its sense in the later writers seems to be 'voluntary' in the 'Aristotelian' sense which has been outlined. The fact that Aristotle himself used the term *hormê* as a synonym for *orexis* (see Appendix 3) was a powerful encouragement for eclectic writers and philosophers unsympathetic to the Stoa to adopt the term *kath' hormên* in this sense.[2]

An action according to impulse should mean, in old Stoic theory, an action for which the agent (if it is a human being) can be held morally accountable. In attested Stoic uses of the term that is exactly what it does mean. At Diogenes Laertius 7.108–9 'activities according to impulse' are actions which can be subdivided exhaustively into three classes: appropriate actions, inappropriate actions, and those which are neither. Even the actions which are neither are subject to moral evaluation; they are not the general type of action to be appropriate or the opposite, but any individual occurrence of such an action would be right or wrong depending on the disposition of the agent. The actions described as being 'activities according to impulse' are responsible human actions; they are caused by assent and impulse. The phrase as it is used here is fully in accord with the old Stoic psychology of action.[3]

Chrysippus too uses the phrase *kath' hormên* in a narrowly limited sense. In his *Peri Pathôn*[4] he refers to the actions of running and walking as *kath' hormên*. By this he means just what one would expect from the general psychology of action: these activities are carried out by an agent as a result of impulse and assent, in accordance with the agent's practical decision. He also uses the term in this way in SVF 2.1000 = *NA* 7.2.12. Another case of a reliable Stoic use of the phrase is in Clement of Alexandria (SVF 2.714). Here the movements of animals are said to be *kath' hormên kai phantasian*; this too reflects an awareness of the psychology of action, according to which a presentation as well as an impulse are involved in each action by an animal.[5]

This very sparse use of the phrase in Stoic sources, suggests that it was not thought of as a technical term in its own right, but simply a phrase which could be used to indicate action which is according to impulse in the sense determined by the psychology of action. By contrast, later philosophical writers quite regularly employ the phrase (and the phrase *kath' hormên kinesis*) and do so with a fixity of meaning which indicates that for them the term has become technical, a part of the philosophical jargon of the day. It is used in the minimal sense of 'voluntary' sketched above, with no awareness that the term originally had its home in the Stoic theory of action. It is worth while to give a rough idea of the frequency with which this term is used in later writers, not just as a footnote to the history of the terminology of later Greek philosophy, but because some of these writers also use the term in reporting on Stoic theories.[6] An awareness of the non-Stoic use of this term by authors of this period ought to show that such reports are not a guide to Stoic usage and doctrine.

Alexander's use of the phrase *kath' hormên* in the *De Fato* may reflect some knowledge of Stoic use of *kath' hormên* (see n. 5). He refers to animal motion which is *kath' hormên* (at p. 182.5–6) and uses similar terminology later in the book.[7] But while it may be *based on* Stoic use of these terms, it cannot be taken for a reliable *report of* Stoic use. For Alexander is using the terms in an anti-Stoic argument characterized by a mixture of Stoic and Aristotelian premisses and by at least one significant distortion of Stoic doctrine.[8]

When he is not criticizing the Stoics Alexander persists in using the term *kath' hormên* to describe animal action. In the *De Anima*,[9] *kath' hormên energeia* seems to be a term meaning little more than 'voluntary activity', although the situation is complicated by the fact that Alexander has added a hormetic faculty to the orectic faculty he took over from Aristotle.[10] He probably did so under Stoic influence, but it is not the Stoic use of *hormê* which he has in mind (indeed it is hard to see just how he thinks *hormê* differs from *orexis*). In a somewhat similar way, Alexander added *hormê* to the faculties whose presence is needed to distinguish voice (*phônê*) from mere noise (*psophos*).[11] In doing so he was followed by later commentators.[12] Aristotle had distinguished voice from noise by the presence of *phantasia* alone.[13]

Both in his criticisms of the Stoa and in his own philosophical writing Alexander blends Aristotelian and Stoic ideas and terminology.[14] In this he may be taken as typical of the tendency in later writers to conflate *hormê* with non-Stoic concepts in such a way that the phrase *kath' hormên* could eventually be used to mean 'voluntary' with no reference to its original Stoic meaning. In particular, the term *kath' hormên kinêsis* or *energeia* came to be a regular term meaning nothing more than the 'voluntary motion' of animals *qua* animals[15] and having no particular Stoic sense. Let us look first at Nemesius.

He is important because he uses the phrase *kath' hormên kinêseôs* in reporting the psychological views of Panaetius.[16] One of the changes which Panaetius is supposed to have made in the traditional Stoic psychology is to have said that the power of voice was a part of the (faculty of) voluntary movement (*tês kath' hormên kinêseôs meros*); in earlier Stoic theory the power of voice was made a separate parcel of *pneuma* extending from the *hêgemonikon* to the organs of voice. The term *kath' hormên kinêsis* has sometimes been interpreted as a Stoic term,[17] but it is more likely that Nemesius is describing what he understands to be Panaetius' innovation in his own terms. We cannot be sure of this, since the term *kath' hormên* has some precedent in other sources for the Stoa. But nothing in this context suggests a characteristically Stoic use of the technical term, while the term *kath' hormên kinêsis* is common throughout Nemesius' book as a term for voluntary motion of the sort which characterizes animal life jointly with the power of perception. This is certainly the use made of the term in the dubious fragment 86a of Panaetius.[18] Here Nemesius is not reporting on Panaetius or any other named source, although some of the material in this account is similar to what he earlier reported for Panaetius. But the similarity has been overestimated, and it should be noticed that in fr. 86a Nemesius is giving in his own name a wide-ranging account of the powers of animals, powers of the soul (perception and voluntary motion), of *phusis*, and of life. In fr. 86 Nemesius attributes to Panaetius by name some changes from the general theory of the soul (and only the soul) of the earlier Stoics typified by Zeno, whose name is used in the report. Whether or not some of the changes in psychology which Panaetius introduced were the ultimate sources for the theory of animal powers given by Nemesius, fr. 86a is not direct evidence for Panaetius' theory.[19] The use by Nemesius there of the term *kath' hormên kinêsis* in a non-Stoic sense can provide no support for a claim that it is a Stoic term in fr. 86.

Nemesius' other uses of the term tend to support the conclusion that *kath' hormên kinêsis* is his own term being used with the minimal sense of voluntary motion. At the beginning of chapter 27 of *De Natura Hominis* (p. 250) *kath' hormên kinêsis* is a synonym of *kata prohairesin kinêsis*. This is virtually the same use of the phrase as is found in fr. 86a.[20] Here it clearly means 'voluntary motion'; the power of voice is said to be voluntary. It is likely enough that in fr. 86 Nemesius is reporting some change in traditional Stoic psychology by Panaetius which he interpreted in his own terms. For the use in ch. 27 is quite similar again to other uses of the term in Nemesius.

On pp. 38-9, for example, the *kath' hormên kinêsis* is given as one of the defining characteristics of animal soul. On p. 177 voice, perceptual powers, and the *kath' hormên kinêsis* are described as subordinate powers characterizing animal soul. On p. 243 the involuntary nature of the reproductive power is said to be balanced by the fact that the act of intercourse is itself voluntary: 'for it is accomplished through the *kath' hormên* organs (sc. of the body) and it is in our power to refrain from and master the *hormê*.' The simple meaning 'voluntary' for the term *kath' hormên* is even more clearly indicated at pp. 276-7. Nemesius is rephrasing Aristotle's point that the voluntary is what is done through an internal *archê* of action (desire) with knowledge of the particular circumstances in which one acts: 'No one says that what is according to calculation and *prohairesis* and *kat' oikeian hormên kai ephesin*, along with a knowledge of the particulars, is involuntary'. This use of *hormê* alongside *ephesis* is more reminiscent of Aristotelian terminology than of Stoic, as is the general point which is being made. Nemesius comes quite close to such a use of the term *hormê* again on p. 265 (cf. p. 60 and pp. 121-2).

In view of the general use made by Nemesius of the term *kath'
hormên* and the fact that when he does use it in reporting
Panaetius' ideas, he shows no sign of using it in a Stoic sense, it is
likely that for Nemesius *kath' hormên* is no more than the standard
philosophical jargon of his day. This jargon may have been deeply
influenced by Stoicism in its formative stages, but the influence of
Aristotelian terminology and of Peripatetics such as Alexander
was also important.

This very general use of the term *kath' hormên* is also found in
Numenius (quoted by Porphyry at Stobaeus *Eclogae* 1.349) in a
report of Stoic epistemology (SVF 2.74). Numenius says that for the
Stoics assent is *kath' hormên*. This would be odd if the phrase *kath'
hormên* were a Stoic term, since we know that *hormê* is a result of
assent in the psychology of action and does not play any role in the
theory of knowledge. All Numenius is trying to say is that assent is
voluntary, that it is in a man's power to give or refuse assent to a
presentation.[21] The Stoic way of saying this is to say that assent is *eph'
hêmin*, in our power.[22] Numenius is merely using the philosophical
terminology of his own day in reporting a genuine Stoic belief. In
this instance it is useful to have independent evidence for the claim
that *kath' hormên* was considered to be an equivalent for the Stoic *eph'
hêmin*. Pseudo-Plutarch (at *De Fato* 571c) uses *kath' hormên* as a
synonym for *eph' hêmin*. That is what Numenius is also doing.[23]

Nemesius also used this terminology, and we have seen that he
took voluntary motion and perception to be the two powers which
jointly characterize animal soul. This is, of course, similar to a
genuine Stoic doctrine; for they made *hormê* and *phantasia* the two
powers characteristic of animals. But the basic idea also has Aristotelian roots,[24] and in the form in which we frequently find it in later
authors (*kath' hormên kinêsis* and *aisthêsis* characterize animal soul)
the doctrine has become common property, with terminology and
content drawn from both sources.[25]

This is the nature of the doctrine as we find it in Clement of
Alexandria.[26] Clement does not associate the use of the term *kath'
hormên kinêsis* with any particular school; it is a quite generally
accepted criterion for the presence of animal soul. He uses the
phrase *kath' hormên* in different combinations,[27] but its sense is
always the same for Clement: it refers to voluntary movement in the
broad sense and never shows any signs of a characteristically Stoic
use (except for SVF 2.714, p. 252 above).

Galen also uses the phrase *kath' hormên* in this way, and this is one source where Nemesius would have found the term used in the way we see him using it. In the *De Usu Partium*[28] it is used adverbially to describe the control over excretion which animals have and which is absent in the foetus. As in Nemesius, *kath' hormên* seems to be used interchangeably with *kata prohairesin*; similarly, there is no reason to see a characteristically Stoic use of the term in Galen. The phrase *kath' hormên kinêsis* itself is not used, but *kath' hormên energeiai* are mentioned and these are clearly the same thing. Moreover, in another work[29] Galen does use *kath' hormên kinêsis* and it is linked there with *aisthêsis*.[30]

The Aristotelian commentators also use the term *kath' hormên* in its broad and non-Stoic sense. It is used to designate the sort of self-movement which is characteristic of animals *qua* animals, as for example by Simplicius:[31] a movement is described as being 'not physical in the narrow sense (*haplôs*), like that of fire, . . . but voluntary, which occurs in animals'. It is also used to indicate when human action is not constrained by external causes but comes from the agent's own desires, a use which is reminiscent of *Eudemian Ethics* 2.8.[32] It indicates the minimal condition for voluntary action, and does not by itself show that the action is also a fully responsible action in Aristotle's sense.

The wide currency of these ideas and the eclectic terminology in which they are cast is evident from their appearance in a Neoplatonic treatise falsely attributed to Galen which its editor, K. Kalbfleisch, suggests is actually the work of Porphyry.[33] As in Clement, the idea that voluntary action and perception are the generally accepted hallmarks of animal soul is used throughout; Plato's own rather different ideas are tortuously reconciled with it. His terminology for these two characteristic powers is interesting; for he uses not *kath' hormên* or *kath' hormên kinêsis*, but simply *hormê* and *aisthêsis* or *phantasia*. If there is Stoic influence on the choice of these terms, it is remote; for he attacks Stoic ideas[34] and conflates *orexis* and *hormê*[35] in a way which betrays the eclectic combination of Aristotelian and Stoic terms.

With this we may conclude our survey. The general sense of *kath' hormên* in later philosophical texts is clear. Even the simple term *hormê* came to be used in a non-Stoic sense by writers not interested in the psychology of action and under the influence of Aristotle's own somewhat fluid use of the term. These terminological developments need not be examined in any more detail. It suffices if this selective survey has shown that in one or two cases the term *kath'* *hormên* (which might otherwise be interpreted as a Stoic term in those contexts) is being used in this minimal and generally current non-Stoic sense.

Notes

Introduction

1. For this title cf. Strato's *Peri phuseôs anthrôpinês* (D.L. 5.59) and Aristotle's *Peri anthrôpou phuseôs*, no. 184 in the Hesychian life (see Düring, *Biographical Tradition*, p. 88 and P. Moraux, *Les Listes*, p. 263 and n. 70).
2. D.L. 7.4.
3. *Fin.* 2.40. It is highly probable that Antiochus is Cicero's source here.
4. For the views of Theophrastus see the recent discussion by W. W. Fortenbaugh, 'Arius, Theophrastus and the Eudemian Ethics', pp. 214–16.
5. Compare 2.140.
6. And certainly not the most valuable if taken on its own; see *Off.* 1.153.
7. This fragment was probably directed against Aristotle *EN* 10.7.
8. *Fin.* 3.17–18.
9. This concerns physics primarily; that the motivation for the study of dialectic was the same has recently been suggested by A. A. Long, 'Dialectic and the Stoic Sage', esp. p. 109. Rhetoric, the other half of logic, and ethics are obviously sciences with practical goals.
10. For example, Jonathan Bennett's in *Linguistic Behaviour.* His key theoretical terms are Goal, for the desiderative element, and Registration, for the informational component. Donald Davidson's study, 'Actions, Reasons and Causes', gives a scheme for explaining action in terms of pro-attitudes and beliefs about one's circumstances. He provides a defence of treating psychological factors like reasons or intentions as causes of action. Aristotle and the Stoics treated intentions or their analogues as causes. Unlike the Stoics, Davidson does not regard all 'intentions' as events in the mind.

Chapter 1

1. The most important work on Aristotle's theory since Furley is found in the interpretive essays of Martha Nussbaum's edition of the *De Motu Animalium.* Walter G. Englert has thoroughly re-examined the questions of Aristotle's influence on Epicurus and the nature of Epicurus' theory, differing from Furley in particular on the role of

the swerve in Epicureanism. His as yet unpublished dissertation was submitted to the Classics Department of Stanford University in 1981.

2. As Michael Bratman describes such theories, referring primarily to Donald Davidson's theory of action.

3. See 700b20 *kritika*.

4. See *DA* 3.9.

5. 701a25 ff. He notes that obvious premisses are often elided in dialectic too.

6. Pleasure and pain are the immediate results of perceiving something which matches or conflicts with one's apparent good. So *DA* 3.7, 431a8–14, is to be compared: pleasure and pain are states of activation with the perceptual apparatus with respect to the good or bad. The result of such pleasure or pain is pursuit or avoidance behaviour.

7. 701a34: *epi to kineisthai kai prattein ta zôia hormôsi*.

8. See ch. 3 n. 53.

9. See Appendix 3.

10. 3.10, 433b29; cf. 3.11, 434a5–7.

11. *DM* 701b34–5 and 701a36 indicate that Aristotle is more inclined to group *phantasia* with thought. But this is not his only position. At *NE* 7.3, 1147b5 animals are contrasted to men because they act according to *phantasia* and memory alone, without use of general concepts. (Cf. *DA* 3.10, 433b5 ff. on animals' lack of a sense of time.)

12. For further criticisms of Nussbaum on *phantasia* see H. B. Gottschalk's review in *AJP* 102 (1981), esp. pp. 92–4. Aristotle's theory of *phantasia* has also been discussed recently by Malcolm Schofield, 'Aristotle on the Imagination'. G. Watson's discussion '*Phantasia* in Aristotle, *De Anima* 3.3' is a sensible and comprehensive analysis of Aristotle's views.

13. pp. 256–8. It is by no means clear that Aristotle thought of *aisthêmata* as neutral and uninterpreted images, mechanical products of the interaction of the sense organs and external objects (despite the limited causal account given in *DA* 2). See Kahn, 'Sensation and Consciousness', pp. 72–3 and Cashdollar, 'Aristotle's Theory of Incidental Perception', pp. 164–7, 170.

14. *DA* 3.8, 432a8–9. Cf. *DA* 3.7, 431b2–10; NB b7, *hôsper horôn*.

15. As in *Post. An.* 2.19. Cf. also Nussbaum, p. 267 n. 68.

16. This approach might even work for the important text in the *NE* (3.5, 1114a32), 'but we are not responsible for our *phantasia*', i.e. for how things look to us. But Aristotle is not here using *phantasia* as a psychological faculty, nor is he giving his own opinion. So we need not insist that *phantasia* here be representational as it is in the psychological works.

17. p. 218. More recently, in 'Self-Movers', n. 14, p. 179, Furley is inclined to abandon his earlier stress on 'images' under the influence of Nussbaum's work. I do not think that this recantation is necessary in order to take account of Nussbaum's most important insights on *phantasia*.

18. For the Stoic way of combining these two elements, see below, pp. 56–59.

19. *Reason and Human Good*, Ch. 1.

20. e.g. *EN* 1142b21–6, discussed by Cooper, pp. 45–6. Also at *DM* 7, 701a17–22 a deliberation prior to the action is cast in syllogistic form; see Cooper, p. 25 n. 26.

21. pp. 174–5.

22. *DM* 7, 701a23–5.

23. Aristotle discusses this preparation in *DM* 8, esp. 702a15–21. In chs. 8 ff. he turns from the question of the psychology of action strictly speaking to the issue of how the activation of desire causes the bodily motions which constitute the action. This psycho-physical question is a distinct though closely related issue; for a discussion of it see Nussbaum's essay 3 and her commentary. The Stoics disagreed among themselves about this question (see below, p. 51). Epicurus (see Lucretius *DRN* 4.877–906) distinguished the question of what happened in the mind to cause action and the question of how the body was then set in motion (4.886 ff.).

24. See *DA* 3.10, 433b5 ff.

25. *EN* 7.3, 1147b3–5.

26. There is a Platonic precedent for the notion of assent in Aristotle and the Stoics. See *Rep.* 437bc on nodding 'yes' and 'no' in a discussion of desire and action. In the *Phaedo* 98–99 Plato strongly emphasizes the role of thought and decision in causing actions.

27. Ch. 7, 701a31 ff.

28. 3.11, 434a16–21.

29. 3.7, 431a8–14.

30. 7.3, 1147a25 ff.

31. This does not mean that the action too is not formulable as a conclusion which can be verbalized. See Cooper, op. cit., p. 48 n. 61 and pp. 56–7.

32. Cf. 1147a34 *legei pheugein touto*, where *legei* (says) has imperatival force. For *kôluein* in an imperatival sense see *Rep.* 439c6: to *keleuon*, to *kôluon*.

33. 3.9, 432b26–433a3.

34. Also: *legousês tês dianoias pheugein ti ê diôkein*.

35. *EN* 6.10, 1143a4–11, discussed below, p. 62; *EE* 2.2, 1220b5–6; 2.1, 219b27 ff. (cf. *EN* 1.13); 8.3, 1249b14.

36. He therefore avoided the problems mentioned in the preceding paragraph.
37. The closest he comes is at *DRN* 3.182–3 where *sibi mens fieri proponit* suggests an intention formulated in language.
38. The development of the *lekton* and its relation to the *phantasia* were essential.

Chapter 2

1. I regret that I received Long, 'Soul and Body in Stoicism', too late to make extensive use of it.
2. See Bonhoeffer, *Epictet*, pp. 67–76 for an early but still useful treatment of the topic of this section. More recently J. A. Akinpelu, 'The Stoic Scala Naturae', examines Cicero's treatment of the topic in *ND* 2.
3. Baldry, *The Unity of Mankind in Greek Thought*, pp. 11–12.
4. SVF 3.333 (= *Fin.* 3.64); 2.1127 (= *ND* 2.78–80).
5. *De Anima* 2.1 (413a5–10); 2.2 (413b24–7); 3.5; *NE* 10.7. Perhaps only the active intellect (*DA* 3.5) is separable. The details of Aristotle's views on this are problematic.
6. Seneca *Ep.* 95.36; 124.14; Cicero *ND* 2.34; at *Off.* 2.12 we are told that the gods do no harm. This recalls the natural goodness and generosity of Plato's demiurge in the *Timaeus* and of the gods in *Rep.* 2.
7. *DA* 2.3; see Hardie, *Aristotle's Ethical Theory*, pp. 24–7; Ross, *Aristotle*, pp. 129–31. Compare the rather different *scala naturae* Aristotle uses when he turns to scientific biology (Ross, pp. 114–17). No analogue to this is found in the Stoics.
8. *DA* 2.3 (414b29).
9. For Stoic indebtedness to Aristotle on this point see D. Hahm, *The Origins of Stoic Cosmology*, p. 164 and n. 69.
10. For a discussion see D. Furley, 'Self-Movers'.
11. Admittedly the discussions of rational and irrational *dunamis* do not contrast man and irrational animals, but rather man and inanimate objects; but *EE* 2.8 shows clearly Aristotle's position on the question.
12. D. Hahm, *The Origins of Stoic Cosmology*, p. 164; compare Bonhoeffer, *Epictet*, p. 69 and Long, 'The Logical Basis of Stoic Ethics', pp. 93–4. See too Seneca *Ep.* 76.9–11.
13. Aristotle used the term *psuchê* for the life force in plants as well; by using a different term for these two levels the Stoics sharpened up the distinctions between the levels, with no loss of continuity.
14. See Hahm, op. cit., Ch. 5, Rieth, *Grundbegriffe*, pp. 125–33, J. Gould, *The Philosophy of Chrysippus*, pp. 99–102, R. Todd, *Alexander of Aphrodisias on Stoic Physics*, pp. 34–49. Recently, Long, 'Soul and Body'.

15. These powers are also given as the characteristics of animal nature by Hierocles, *Ethikê Stoicheiôsis* 1.31-3, a treatise notable for its faithfulness to the doctrines of the old Stoa; they are also mentioned in several of the texts considered or referred to below. This doctrine is quite rigid by comparison with Aristotle's more nuanced (and unclear) position: perception is the one *sine qua non* of animal soul, and desire (*orexis*), *phantasia*, and the power of local motion are mentioned somewhat confusingly as powers possessed by either all animals or those above a certain minimal level of organization.

   By stipulating impulse and presentation as the marks of soul, the Stoics regularize Aristotle's remarks at the cost of ignoring the subtler gradations among the lower forms of animal life. Zeno was not a working biologist. Aristotle's *orexis* and local motion are combined in the Stoic *hormê*. *Phantasia*, whose relation to perception is problematic in Aristotle, is made a definite part of the perceptual process in Stoicism.

16. pp. 311-12 Koetschau, whose text I follow.

17. Stones cut off from a vein of metal, i.e. out of a mine, are removed from the 'living rock' which is thought of as growing like a plant; a stick cut from a tree is similarly made into a mere thing. The grammatical problems in the text I translate do not obscure the main point. The text may be corrupt here.

18. Here the text reads *autou* in place of *hautou* as we would expect. The sense is the same.

19. This word may be corrupt.

20. Reading *anaploi* with Kalbfleisch and Rieth (for his discussion of this text see op. cit., 127-31). Von Arnim's emendation *anaplêroi* does not greatly affect the sense.

21. An obvious correction by Kalbfleisch.

22. Corrected by Kalbfleisch in the addenda, p. 574. The word is *prattein*, the usual term for responsible human action.

23. We have several references to the natural virtue of gods (*ND* 2.34, *Ep.* 124.14 and 95.36). The parallel text at *De Aeternitate Mundi* (75) suggests that the reference may also be to the sage; and the sage is often said to be the equal of Zeus in virtue.

24. See A. Graeser, *Plotinus and the Stoics*, on Plotinus' use of Stoic ideas.

25. This is probably also true for the fifth level, gods. As well as being rational they also perceive, have *hormai*, have physical constitutions held together by *hexis*, and perhaps also grow and require some form of nutrition. This sounds strange, but a discussion of Stoic theology is not in order here.

26. Marcus Aurelius too (6.14) uses the familiar doctrine of the *scala*

naturae. It is behind Sextus' attacks on Stoic theology (*M* 9.78–91), for which see Akinpelu, op. cit.

27. *Stromates* 2.20.110–111 = SVF 2.714.

28. Simplicius, we recall, only mentions impulse. Presentation is also omitted by Galen (SVF 2.757) and Aëtius (SVF 2.708 = *Dox. Gr.,* p. 438). Presentation is mentioned by Philo in a text very generally inspired by the Stoic hierarchy (*Quis Rerum Divinarum Heres* 137–40).

29. *Off.* 2.11 and *ND* 2.34, 2.81, 2.122.

30. For Cicero's translations see also *Acad.* 2.24, *Fin.* 3.23, 4.39, 5.17, *ND* 2.58, *Off.* 1.101, 2.18. *Appetitus* and *appetitio* are usual, but *impetus* also occurs, as at *Off.* 2.11.

31. *Leg. Alleg.* 2.22–23; *Quod Deus* 35–45.

32. We must also suspect Plutarch's version of the inclusion doctrine at *Virt. Mor.* 451b–c. The level included in man's soul here is an irrational power which is to some degree independent of reason. As we shall see, this is just the opposite of the Stoic doctrine on the powers of the soul.

33. Bonhoeffer *Epictet,* pp. 69–70 and 106 ff. citing Diogenes Laertius 7.138, 86; cf. *M.* 7.234. Panaetius seems to have differed on this point; see van Straaten, pp. 96–7 and fr. 86. Van Straaten's argument that Panaetius had a Stoic predecessor on this point (pp. 98 ff.) seems implausible.

34. *Prep. Ev.* 6.6.24.

35. *Logismôi* and *prohairesei* are not Stoic terms here. And Eusebius errs in saying that sticks, stones, etc. are moved by *hexis.* Rather they are unified by *hexis* and moved by external force. No reliable Stoic source attributes the power of motion to natural place to the lowest entities on the scale. But see below on Alexander and Nemesius, pp. 88–91 and n. 220.

36. D.L. 7.88. Cf. *boulêsis tou theou* at *Ecl.* 2.105.25.

37. See Appendix 2, esp. p. 237.

38. *Diss.* 4.1.100.

39. *Meditations* 9.1.4; 9.28.

40. A.-J. Voelke, *L'Idée de volonté dans le stoïcisme,* pp. 28–9.

41. Philippson, 'Panaetiana', 'Zur Psychologie der Stoa'; Pohlenz principally in *Antikes Führertum,* 'Zenon und Chrysipp', and *Die Stoa.* The problem has a much longer history and stretches back into the 19th century.

42. Pohlenz thought it was Chrysippus' innovation.

43. For background, the reader might consult A. Bonhoeffer's discussion of the structure and function of the soul in *Epictet und die Stoa,* pp. 86–112.

44. One example of this is the report of Cicero at *Academica* 1.39 that

Zeno's psychology was monistic in the same sense as the Chrysippean psychology was: there is no separate power in the soul
able to oppose reason in the determining of human actions or
emotions.

45. Aëtius 4.4.4 (*Dox. Gr.* p. 390 = SVF 2.827); D.L. 7.110 = SVF 2.828,
where mind is called *dianoia*; Galen *PHP* 5.3.7, p. 306 DeLacy. Galen
insists correctly that these parts are distinct from powers; see too
Pohlenz, *Gnomon* 21 (1949), p. 117.

46. Porphyry in *Ecl.* 1.350 = SVF 2.830; Iamblichus in *Ecl.* 1.369 = SVF
2.831.

47. *Nat. Hom.* p. 212 = SVF 1.143. There is no reason to suspect that Zeno
held a different view; but Nemesius does not generally provide
accurate information about Zeno and he here attributes this doctrine
to him in terms strikingly similar to those of the other doxographic
versions which refer only to 'the followers of Zeno' or the Stoics
generally. Hence the need for caution in using his testimony.

48. *M* 7.234. On *sunektikon aition*, see Frede, pp. 243 ff. in *Doubt and
Dogmatism*.

49. Van Straaten, *Panétius*, pp. 97–101 argues that some old Stoics at least
anticipated Panaetius in distinguishing *phusis* from *psychê* in animals.
His arguments on that point are indirect and unconvincing.

50. Cf. Bonhoeffer, *Epictet*, p. 105.

51. *Ecl.* 1.369.

52. *Ecl.* 1.367–8.

53. Pohlenz, *Gnomon* 21 (1949), p. 117 properly emphasizes this, in
contrast to van Straaten who follows Schindler in refusing to
distinguish parts and powers of the soul (pp. 119–25).

54. *De Anima* 2.2, 413a22–5.

55. Moreover, the example of the apple which has various characteristics
in one body is traditional among the Aristotelian commentators. The
earliest use of it which I have found is in Alexander, *De Anima*, p. 31.4–
5, whence no doubt it entered the tradition. It appears not to be used
by Aristotle. Did Alexander who so frequently relies on Stoic sources
as well as Aristotle take this illustration from a Stoic source? Or is
Iamblichus drawing his example from ultimately non-Stoic sources?
Voelke, *L'Idée*, p. 21 and van Straaten, pp. 122–3 are both suspicious of
the attribution of *dunamis* to the Stoa by Iamblichus. This is sensible.
But unfortunately both repeat the error of Schindler (pp. 25, 28–9) in
that they do not distinguish sharply between parts and powers.

56. p. 224 = SVF 3.203.

57. Voelke, *L'Idée*, p. 28; Schindler and van Straaten ignore this text.

58. *Sumptôma* = event or occurrence; cf. Chrysippus' use at SVF 2.1181 =
St. Rep. 1050 f.

59. *Leg. Alleg.* 1.30 = SVF 2.844.

60. *Ecl.* 2.74 = SVF 3.112.

61. Philo's terminology is never very reliable, but in this case Arius confirms the genuineness of *tonikê dunamis*. *Nous* is Philo's usual word for *hêgemonikon* (see Rist, *Center for Hermeneutical Studies*, Colloquy 23 (1976), p. 3).

62. Voelke, *L'Idée*, pp. 41–9; 'Les Origines', pp. 11 ff.

63. These would perhaps be *katalêpseis*; cf. *M* 7.151 = SVF 2.90, SVF 1.68, 2.93, 2.95.

64. *Ecl.* 2.86; *Strom.* 2.13.59 = SVF 3.377.

65. Diogenes Laertius 7.110.

66. *M* 7.237. *Heteroiôsis* also refers to a stable state of the soul, a modification.

67. *Adv. Col.* ch. 26, 1122b. The reference to Zeno is secured by the fact that this text reports Arcesilaus (see Pohlenz, *Die Stoa*, vol. i, p. 90).

68. Cf. Bonhoeffer, *Epictet*, p. 112 and n. 99 below. Much more evidence about *hormê* can be found if we recall that a *pathos* is a kind of *hormê*, and specifically a *hormê* of the active variety. This goes back to Zeno. The 'movement' terminology is used by Zeno (D.L. 7.110), by Chrysippus (*PHP* 4.4.16, p. 254 = SVF 3.476; *PHP* 4.2.8 ff., pp. 240–2 = SVF 3.462), in *Ecl.* 2.88 and in the *Peri Pathôn* of pseudo-Andronicus (SVF 3.391 = ch. 1, p. 223). Zeno called *pathôs* a *ptoia* (*Ecl.* 2.39) and Arius correctly interprets this as a reference to the active sense in contrast to the potential sense. Arius uses his own terminology here, and also misrepresents Zeno on a point not relevant here (see below, p. 142). Note that I refer to the pages of DeLacy's edition of *PHP*.

69. *Prep. Ev.* 15.20.5 = *Dox. Gr.*, p. 471 = SVF 2.821. Cf. Philo *De Animalibus*, ch. 29.

70. *ND* 2.29. On this analogue of mind see Bonhoeffer, *Epictet*, pp. 74–6, 108, 111. Note too that impulses like those of *pathê* do occur in animals (*TD* 4.31; *De Ira* 1.3.4–8) but these cannot be *pathê* because animals lack reason. Compare Diogenes Laertius 7.55 on *phônê*: in animals it is air struck by *hormê* alone, while in men it comes from *dianoia* (presumably the mind strikes the air with a rational *hormê*). At *Ecl.* 2.86–7 impulse in general is defined as a 'movement of the soul', but impulse in men is a 'movement of the mind'.

71. Aristotle too held that animals and men alike had a controlling and dominant part of the soul which was 'located' in the heart. So did Epicurus: D.L. 10.66 schol., *DRN* 3.138–42.

72. van Straaten, pp. 121–2, 125, also seems to espouse a form of this interpretation, when he insists on reading *dunamis* as function and denies that the Stoa was sufficiently sophisticated to

distinguish between the faculty of doing something and the action itself.

73. Like the Stoics, I occasionally use 'soul' where the mind alone is meant. See *M* 7.234, Rist, *Stoic Philosophy*, p. 257 and Bonhoeffer, *Epictet*, p. 105.

74. The philosophical climate which made this distortion possible is well represented by such works as *Virt. Mor., St. Rep., Comm. Not.*, and *PHP.*

75. *Acad.* 1.39; cf. *TD* 3.74–5. In the latter text Zeno is said to identify passions with judgements, which some scholars think is a move made only by Chrysippus. At *Die Stoa*, vol. i. p. 143 Pohlenz tries to explain this away.

76. *Virt. Mor.* 441c–d. Pohlenz, 'Zenon und Chrysipp', p. 196 rejects this text, but his position is weak and *ad hoc.*

77. *L'Idée*, p. 24. Plutarch shows no awareness of a difference between the two on this point. Only Galen and possibly Posidonius thought that Zeno and Chrysippus disagreed. On the value (or lack of it) of this tradition see A. C. Lloyd, 'Emotion and Decision', pp. 234–5, 243 and Rist, *Stoic Philosophy*, pp. 29–30.

78. SVF. 2.824 = *Paraphrasis in DA* 1.1.

79. *De Anima Mantissa*, pp. 118–19 = SVF 2.823. I assume for convenience that Alexander wrote the entire *Mantissa* (and the *Problemata* and *Quaestiones*). The question of the authenticity of these texts affects nothing I have to say.

80. *Theôrêtikos nous* e.g. Similarly, Stoics would reject the equation of *to orektikon* with *to hormêtikon*. A Stoic might also disagree with what Alexander says about *to aisthêtikon*, that it has a theoretical *telos* in contrast to the practical goal of *to hormêtikon* and that it includes the powers of presentation, assent, and memory.

81. Pohlenz, 'Zenon und Chrysipp', pp. 185 and 210. Similarly at p. 190 n. 1 he uses a Galenic statement about 'one power in the soul' which has been shown to be useless (Philippson, 'Zur Psychologie', pp. 175–6).

82. 4.21 = *Dox Gr.*, p. 410 = SVF 2.836.

83. Voelke, *L'Idée*, p. 29, Pohlenz, 'Zenon und Chrysipp', p. 191 n. 1; and cf. Stein, vol. ii, p. 125.

84. *PHP* 3.5.31, p. 206 = SVF 2.896.

85. D.L. 7.159; Stobaeus SVF 2.840.

86. *M* 7.237.

87. 'Zenon und Chrysipp', pp. 190–1 citing *Virt. Mor.* 441c.

88. *Strom.* 2.16.72 = SVF 3.433 *tropas psuchês; Virt. Mor.* 446 f *henos logou tropên ep' amphotera; De Ira* 1.8.2–3 *mutatio animi.*

89. *Die Stoa*, i, p. 144.

90. Virtue is a *pôs echon*, which Pohlenz takes to be a fleeting transformation of the soul, at *Ep.* 113.2; yet at *Virt. Mor.* 3,441b, *Ecl.* 2.70--1, and elsewhere it is a *dunamis* and *diathesis*. *Epistêmê* is a *hexis* (D.L. 7.47) and a *sustêma* (Ecl. 2.73-4) as well as a *katalêpsis* (*M* 7.151). *Aisthêsis* is a *hexis* and a *dunamis* as well as an *energeia* (Aëtius 4.8.1 = *Dox. Gr.*, p. 394 = SVF 2.850; also D.L. 7.52).

91. 'Zenon und Chrysipp', pp. 182-3, citing SVF 2.400.

92. 'Zuständlich' by which Pohlenz seems to mean 'transient'.

93. Op. cit., p. 184, referring to *tropai* and *conversiones* to support his view.

94. At *Die Stoa*, i, pp. 90-1 he argues weakly that the Iamblichus text applies only to Zeno and not to Chrysippus. There is no evidence for this. His treatment of *Virt. Mor.* ch. 2-3 at 'Zenon und Chrysipp', p. 196 is similarly weak.

95. Rieth, *Grundbegriffe*, p. 61 and Exkurs 3. Rist, *Stoic Philosophy*, pp. 167-9; Long, *Hellenistic Philosophy*, pp. 162-3. On *psuchê pôs echousa* see Hahm, *The Origins of Stoic Cosmology*, Ch. 1, esp. pp. 4, 17-21.

96. *L'Idée*, p. 22.

97. Porphyry in *Prep. Ev.* 15.11.4 = SVF 2.806. Pohlenz refers to this definition at 'Zenon und Chrysipp', p. 183 but does not consider its implications for his interpretation of *pôs echon*.

98. Cf. *poiotês* as a *pôs echon* at SVF 2.379.

99. It seems at least possible that Zeno used this category, since the category *pros ti pôs echein* can be traced to Ariston (D.L. 7.161). If Hahm's claim (Ch. 1 of his book, op. cit.) that the Stoics developed their use of *pôs echein* from Aristotle's theory of categories, then the attribution to Zeno is strengthened.

100. As he does at 'Zenon und Chrysipp', p. 185.

101. *M* 7.230-1; 372-3. See Bonhoeffer, *Epictet*, p. 150. On *M* 7.236-241, an important text in this connection, see ibid., p. 112. It is apparent that the Stoics applied *heteroiôsis* somewhat indiscriminately to explain all sorts of mental phenomena, states, and events and that it came close to being trivialized as a result. But given the Stoic commitment to a thorough materialism it is hard to see how they could have dealt in detail with psychological problems without some such universal solvent. See also Graeser, *Zenon*, pp. 30-9, esp. 37.

102. pp. 27-9.

103. Except for the four clearly stated exceptions: the incorporeals void, time, place, and *lekta*. On Stoic materialism see the recent discussion in Hahm, op. cit., Ch. 1.

104. In addition to Iamblichus see Diogenes Laertius 7.159 and Alexander of Aphrodisias *De Anima*, p. 97. 11-16 = SVF 2.839. The latter text is inspired by Stoic doctrine but not a proper report of it.

105. *Comm. Not.* 1084a–b = SVF 2.848.
106. This is the implication of describing virtues, vices, actions, etc. as 'rational animals', *pôs echonta* of the rational soul. Cf. *Ep.* 113 and SVF 3.306. Voelke refers to this doctrine but fails to appreciate the implication of it for his Pohlenzian thesis (pp. 23–4; 26–7). For some *pôs echonta* are stable states while others are fleeting events.
107. *Ecl.* 2.87.
108. *Aph' hês sumbainei horman.*
109. On *hexis* and *dunamis* see Rist, op. cit., pp. 3–4: 'in fact the word *dunamis* is used to describe the use or operation of the *hexis*'. Cf. Seneca *Ep.* 113.7 where disposition (*habitus*) and power (*vis*) are identified.
110. Compare *DRN* 3.262–8 for the Epicurean version of this same doctrine.
111. pp. 237–8 = SVF 2.393. See Rieth, *Grundbegriffe*, pp. 22–9, Rist, *Stoic Philosophy*, Ch. 9.
112. Thus virtue is a *diathesis* and invariable (*Ecl.* 2 .70–1) while the *hexis hormêtikê* can be strong or weak, good or bad and so is properly called a *hexis*.
113. SVF 2.403 = Simplicius Comm. on *Categories*, pp. 165–6.
114. i.e. *logos*.
115. *Adv. Col.* 1122b.
116. See n. 99.
117. We know that Zeno thought the soul was pneumatic (SVF 1.134–141, 146).
118. In addition to the *hexis hormêtikê*, we hear explicitly about a *hexis logikê* (SVF 3.238, 512).

Chapter 3

1. Although since it is a material alteration of the mind according to the Stoics it would in principle be possible to observe it and thus to identify it independently of its relation to stimuli and actions.
2. Not everyone would agree today. See Robert Kirk, 'Rationality without Language', *Mind* 76 (1967), pp. 369–86 and Jonathan Bennett, *Linguistic Behaviour.*
3. *prophorikos logos*, i.e. uttered *logos*. See e.g. *Soll. An.* 972f–973a.
4. Cf. The distinction between *lexis* and *logos*, SVF 3 Diogenes 20 (= D.L. 7.57), 29.
5. *endiathetos logos*, see SVF 2.135, Sextus *M* 8.275 ff. Philo uses the contrast at *De Animalibus* 12 ff.
6. On *lekta* see e.g. A. A. Long, 'Language and Thought in Stoicism', esp. pp. 82–4 and 104–6; A. C. Lloyd, 'Emotion and

Decision' and 'Grammar and Metaphysics in the Stoa'; A. Graeser, 'The Stoic Theory of Meaning'.

7. *Theaetetus* 189e–190a; *Sophist* 263e. Compare the idea of writing in the soul at *Philebus* 39. Bruce Rosenstock pointed out to me the relevance of some of these texts.

8. Sextus *M* 8.409 = SVF 2.85.

9. D.L. 7.63, *M* 8.70. Below, pp. 56–59.

10. For example we are told (*M* 8.276) that rational animals differ from beasts not just by internal reason but by *metabatikē kai sunthetikē phantasia*; and that *lekta*, like 'place', are understood by a form of *metabasis* (D.L. 7.53). *Lekta* depend in some sense on rational *phantasia*, but the sense of *metabasis* and *metabatikē phantasia* and their relation in these texts is not completely clear.

11. See Pamela Huby, 'The First Discovery of the Freewill Problem'.

12. D.L. 10.133–4. See recently D. Sedley, 'Epicurus' Refutation of Determinism'.

13. See R. Sorabji, *Necessity, Cause and Blame*, Ch. 4, of which *Doubt and Dogmatism*, Ch. 10, 'Causation, Laws and Necessity' is a version.

14. *De Fato*, p. 184.20–22.

15. As is Gould, 'The Stoic Conception of Fate', pp. 23 ff., esp. p. 26.

16. A combination of Aristotelian deliberation and Stoic assent is, however, found in Alexander's own blend of Aristotelian and Stoic psychology of action.

17. See A. C. Lloyd 'Emotion and Decision', p. 245; A. A. Long, 'Stoic Determinism and Alexander of Aphrodisias', pp. 258–9; 'Early Stoic Concept', p. 92; 'Aristotle's Legacy to Stoic Ethics', p. 81; P. Grimal, *Sénèque ou la conscience de l'empire*, pp. 378–9. Epictetus is at one with the old Stoa on this point.

18. I should acknowledge here a great debt to the work of A. A. Long, especially in 'Early Stoic Concept' and 'The Stoic Concept of Evil'.

19. Pembroke 'Oikeiôsis', p. 117 distinguishes the Stoic concept of impulse from the later interpretation of it as 'instinct'. A. A. Long has done more than any other scholar to clarify the concept; see 'Early Stoic Concept', p. 78 n. 2.

20. A. Preus, 'Intention and Impulse in Aristotle and the Stoics', p. 48 interprets *hormai* as 'underlying drives, instincts, impulses, or passions', without argument or explanation.

21. J. Gould, *The Philosophy of Chrysippus*, p. 183, properly criticized by Preus, op. cit., p. 53.

22. *L'Idée*, pt. 1 Ch. 4. Because he does not distinguish the *hexis* and *kinêsis* senses of *hormê* he drifts into regarding it as an innate drive as well as a factor in the analysis of action.

23. The use of the word 'impulse' in question is now a bit old-fashioned,

but well exemplified by e.g. Havelock Ellis in *The Psychology of Sex*. Misunderstanding of Zeno's book title *On Impulse* or *On Human Nature* may also encourage this interpretation of *hormê*. No doubt the influence of earlier uses of the term is also important here. See Appendix 3 on this, but clearly the Stoic sense of the technical term must be worked out independently. The earliest verbatim quotation from a Stoic using the term is in the *Hymn to Zeus*, where the verbal form *horman* is used (SVF 1, p. 122 line 22) in a non-technical sense (meaning 'rush'). Pohlenz compares Solon *Elegy* 1.43: *speudei d' allothen allos* (*Hermes* 75 (1940), p. 121).

24. This sense of *aphormê* (found e.g. at D.L. 7.89) must be clearly distinguished from the *aphormê* which is a simple contrary of *hormê*. See Appendix 2, n. 7.

25. *Ecl.* 2.87, *hexis hormêtikê*. pp. 38–39 above.

26. Cicero *Acad.* 2.24–5. Cf. 2.108. Alexander *DA*, pp. 72–3 adapts this for his own purposes, but the main elements and the idea of a sequence are borrowed from the Stoic theory. See R. B. Todd, *Alexander of Aphrodisias on Stoic Physics*, p. 28.

27. On Cicero's sources for the *Academica* see the recent work of J. Glucker, *Antiochus and the Late Academy*, Ch. 1 and Excursus 2C, with the modifications to this picture proposed by D. Sedley *Phronesis* 26, (1981), 67–75.

28. Cicero *De Fato* 41–2.

29. For the different sequence which Seneca gives in *Ep.* 113 see below n. 193 and pp. 175 ff.

30. We shall see that the absence of *logos* from most accounts of the sequence of mental events generating an action is readily understandable. Below, p. 58–59.

31. *Ecl.* 2.88; Galen *PHP* 4.3.7, p. 248.

32. *St. Rep.* 1037f = SVF 3.175. I disagree strongly with Graeser's translation of *logos prostaktikos* as 'prescriptive sentence' ('The Stoic Theory of Meaning', p. 93). Reason is imperatival or commands by means of *prostaktika lekta*, and *these* are prescriptive sentences. Below, pp. 61–63.

33. The analysis of action reconstructed here is similar to the imperatival analysis of will set out by Kenny, *Action, Emotion and Will*, Chs. 10–11 and *Will, Freedom and Power*, Ch. 3. There are of course many differences, most noticeably in logical complexity and analytical sophistication. More important is the difference of status of the theories. Kenny gives an analysis of action and will, a philosophical re-description. The Stoics gave a causal analysis of action and 'will' (I use 'will' in Kenny's sense). The components of their analysis were believed to be mental events in a material soul which

caused the actions and emotions which the analysis is meant to explain.

34. Voelke's chapters on 'Connaissance et volonté', 'Connaissance et tendance', and 'Tendance et volonté', are often suggestive. But I propose a deeper and more comprehensive treatment of the question.

35. *Ecl.* 2.88 (cf. 2.97–8): 'Impulses are directed at predicates'.

36. The reconstruction should also make sense of the several weaker and partial statements of the connection between impulse and assent. See Sorabji, *Necessity, Cause and Blame*, p. 80 n. 47 = *Doubt and Dogmatism*, p. 273 n.62.

37. Preus is wrong, then, to contrast the causal role of Stoic *hormê* to Aristotle's theory (p. 52). But he conceives 'cause' here as the mechanical blind causation of underlying passions and contrasts it to Aristotle's intentional or teleological theory. Properly understood, the Stoic theory of action is causal in the same sense as is Aristotle's.

38. The intentional element is stateable, at least in principle, by the agent. Even where it is not consciously recognized by the agent, it is present as part of the cause of each action. Given that this is a causal analysis of action, it is natural to require that the intention be stateable by the agent to himself.

39. If it is, Aristotle cannot meet a requirement that intentions be stateable by the agent; an animal's purposes could be formulated in language, but only by a rational observer.

40. *DRN* 3.182–3 *nil adeo fieri celeri ratione videtur/quam sibi mens fieri proponit et incohat ipsa* is as close to a recognition of stateable intentions as we find in Epicurean theory. But the analysis of action seems not to leave room for anything of a verbal, logical, or linguistic nature. Probably the *proponit* here refers to a stimulative image rather than a proposition; see *DRN* 4.884–5 *providit.*

41. *Thought and Action*, pp. 98–9.

42. In his early work *Rationality* Jonathan Bennett argues for reasons different from Hampshire's or the Stoics' that linguistic ability is the *sine qua non* of rational purpose. In *Linguistic Behaviour* he retracts that claim for reasons too complex and sophisticated to be of relevance to the Stoics. Compare also Kenny, *Will, Freedom and Power*, Ch. 2 esp. pp. 19 ff. on Aquinas.

43. SVF 2.1000 = *NA* 7.2.

44. *De Fato* 41 ff. (above, p. 46).

45. See Long, 'Freedom and Determinism', pp. 182, 187.

46. Seneca *Ep.* 113.23.

47. *Stoic Philosophy*, p. 34.

48. See Bonhoeffer, *Epictet*, pp. 104–5.

49. Already a feature of Zeno's psychology: see Ch. 2, n. 117.
50. See Hahm, op. cit., Ch. 5. Compare the notions of Epicurus about the
    soul's constitution. The mixture of particles similar to warm *pneuma*
    suggests that he was giving an atomistic version of Aristotle's *pneuma.*
51. Epicurus too seems to have considered the problem of how the soul
    sets the body in motion as distinct from and subordinate to the
    question what events in the soul cause an action. See *DRN* 4.886 ff.
    and compare 3.152–60.
52. The Greek idiom is usually *hormê epi* or *horman epi* plus the accusative.
53. At *Ecl.* 2.87 impulse is defined as a 'movement of the mind toward [or
    directed at] something involved in action'; this replaces the vaguer
    expression 'directed at something' at *Ecl.* 2.86. At *Ecl.* 2.88, 97–8 we
    are told that predicates are the object of impulse. But predicates are
    the verbal representations of events or states of affairs (and actions are
    the examples most frequently given). So this is simply an alternative
    expression of the same view. Such predicates are incorporeal: 'exer-
    cising prudence and exercising temperance, which are incorporeal
    and predicates' (*Ecl.* 2.98). Further on incorporeal predicates:
    Voelke, *L'Idée*, pp. 54–5; Rieth, 'Über das Telos der Stoiker', p. 25;
    Long, 'Early Stoic Concept', pp. 86–90.
    The idiom *hormê/horman epi* + infinitive is anticipated by Plato and
    Aristotle (see *Republic* 354b5, Seventh Letter 325e1; *De Motu* 701a34).
    Stoic examples of the idiom: Galen *PHP* 3.7.25, p. 216.26 = SVF
    2.903; Origen *De Principiis* 3.1.2 & 4 = SVF 2.988; D.L. 7.85 (*hormê
    pros hêdonên* is also used, but only for the rejected Epicurean doctrine;
    note *hormê pros* + infinitive used by some unidentified but Stoically
    inspired philosophers reported at pseudo- Plutarch *De Libidine et
    Aegritudine* 7). As noted, the *epi ti* at *Ecl.* 2.86 is vague, but the *ti* no
    doubt stands for a verbal idea. This is probably also true for the diffi-
    cult phrase in the definition of *orexis, hormê logikê epi ti hoson chrê hêdon* at
    PHP 4.2.4 (p. 238.36–7). De Lacy's decision to print *epi tinos hoson chrê
    hêdontos* in this passage and at p. 250.9–12 and p. 342.30 is certainly
    wrong, as it breaks the pattern of *epi* + accusative found elsewhere.
    Epi ti hoson chrê hêdon designates an action which is satisfying to the
    proper degree. On this definition of *orexis* see Bonhoeffer, *Epictet*,
    pp. 236–7, Lloyd, 'Emotion and Decision', p. 241, and below.
    Some texts replace the verbal idea after *epi* with the object pursued:
    epi to phainomenon (*St. Rep.* 1057b); *epi to phanen* (Alexander *On Fate*, p.
    183.25). Similarly, *hupokeimenon* indicates the object pursued at Philo
    Leg. Alleg. 1.30. But when the *phantasia* presents as stimulus some-
    thing which is to be acquired or pursued, it is natural enough to refer
    to the thing pursued rather than the pursuit of the thing as the object
    of impulse. Kenny, *Action, Emotion and Will*, pp. 112 ff. notes 'wanting'

(which is a narrower concept than *hormê*) has a similar structure. Wanting some tangible object must always be filled out by a statement of what one wants to do with it: 'I want x' must be expandable to 'I want to ϕ x'. The Stoics made the form using the full specification of the predicate the basic idiom.

54. *De Fato*, p. 183 = SVF 2.980.

55. *Ep.* 113.2. See too 113.18, but this portrayal of the sequence is not wholly reliable. See below, p. 176.

56. The argument from *apraxia.* Cf. *Adv. Col.* 1122a ff. The argument goes back to Zeno or Chrysippus.

57. Technically the *quos*, 'these' could refer to the senses. But it would be perverse to take it so, given the parallel texts which give assent the key role in action. The intrusion of *sensus* here is one instance of the amalgamation of epistemology and action theory encouraged by the use of the argument from *apraxia.* It is common in the *Academica*.

58. *Acad.* 2.108; cf. 2.62: 'For by removing assent they have taken away every motion of the mind and every physical action.' Impulse is to be understood as one of the motions of the mind.

59. Simplicius *Comm.* on *Categories*, p. 306.

60. *Whether the Affections* 501c.

61. These 'activities according to impulse' are extensionally equivalent to 'things attributable to us'. On this term see C. Stough, 'Stoic Determinism and Moral Responsibility', p. 214.

62. *St. Rep.* 1057a. For *prattein* instead of *horman* being said to depend on assent see Galen *PHP* 5.4.12, p. 314.

63. Only Alexander's adaptation of Stoicism at *DA*, pp. 72-3 even suggests the possibility that a human impulse is not regularly followed by a *praxis.* But this text is untrustworthy evidence for the Stoic theory. At p. 72.16-18 his remarks on *phantasia* run counter to Stoic theory as reported elsewhere. Alexander says (p. 73.1-2) that 'there are some cases in which after an impulse we did not act' because our *boulêsis* no longer co-operated. This is Alexander's adaptation, for in Stoic doctrine *boulêsis* is a kind of *hormê* and one which cannot ever be altered (it is the correct impulse of the sage).

64. On *praxis* as action in the strict sense see Rieth, *Grundbegriffe*, pp. 130-1 and p. 131 n. 1. See too G. Nebel, 'Der Begriff des Kathekon', p. 444 and n. 2: a *kathêkon* is not a *praxis* when an animal does it, but only when a human does. He quotes Alexander *De Fato*, p. 205 (SVF 2.1002): 'And some animals will only be active (*energêsei*), but rational animals will act (*praxei*).' This special sense of *praxis* is no doubt taken over from Aristotle. 'And man is the starting point of *praxeis*, alone among animals. We would not say

that any other animal *acts*' (*EE* 1222b19-20). Also 1224a28 ff.; *EN* 1139a17-b5; 1111b2; 1094a1; 1097a21; *DM* 701a7-25.

65. SVF 2.991.

66. See Bonhoeffer, *Epictet*, p. 250.

67. Long, 'Early Stoic Concept', p. 80 disagrees. But this disagreement is based on a erroneous notion to be refuted below, p. 101 with n. 271.

68. Bonhoeffer, *Epictet*, p. 125.

69. Lloyd, 'Emotion and Decision', suggests that the stages of the sequence are not rigidly separate but telescoped into one another. He may be right, but the elements and ordering of the analysis are nevertheless distinct.

70. *Acad.* 2.24-5; 2.30. In the latter text we must read *ut* with the MSS and Reid in *deinde appetitio ab his pulsa sequeretur, tum ut sensus . . .* This makes it clear that the cognitive activity here described is not a part of the process involving presentation and impulse, but a distinct item in Cicero's list.

71. Origen *De Principiis* 3.1.2: *phantasiai . . . hormên prokaloumenai.*

72. *kinein, Ecl.* 2.75; 2.86. Cf. *Mantissa*, p. 161.12.

73. *M* 8.397 = SVF 2.91. On assent being *kath' hormên* see Appendix 4.

74. *M* 7.373 = SVF 1.64, 2.56.

75. See Sandbach, pp. 11-12 in *Problems in Stoicism*.

76. I shall not deal with the vexed question whether a man's assent to presentations which do not stimulate action but merely provide information can be 'free'. This question must be addressed by those concerned with Stoic epistemology and especially the *kataléptikê phantasia.* There is no reason to believe that any stimulative presentations are cataleptic. See below, p. 76 and n. 106.

77. *EN* 3.5, 1114a32. Cf. *EN* 3.1.

78. This seems to be the force of *phantasia* here.

79. *Helen* 15 ff.

80. Cf. too Gorgias' used of the word *prothumia* in 19. It recurs in Stoic discussions of the emotions.

81. *Philebus* 39-40 *(Cf. Sophist* 263-4). This is not the whole story about this difficult passage, but I wish only to emphasize that pictures in the soul have a role here. For the Stoic view on the relation between images and the statements which spell out their meaning see below, pp. 56-59. On Aristotle's somewhat uncertain view see Ch. 1.

82. Martha Nussbaum (Essay 5 of her edition of *De Motu Animalium*) disagrees. But see Ch. 1.

83. The *hexis hormêtikê* will, if it is corrupt, produce bad *hormai* and actions. For *eukataphoriai*, inclinations to bad actions, are *hexeis (Ecl.*

2.70–1). *Euemptôsia* is defined as an *eukataphoria eis pathos* (*Ecl.* 2.93) and a *pathos* is an incorrect *hormê.* Thus an *eukataphoria* is a form of *hexis hormêtikê.*

84. Seneca *Ep.* 95.57 = SVF 3.517. Cf. Plato *Laws* 862b.

85. See Long, 'Freedom and Determinism', esp. pp. 187, 193; *Hellenistic Philosophy*, p. 183; I. Hadot, *Seneca*, pp. 105–7. Like Aristotle, the Stoics held that bad characters were formed or strengthened by repeated bad actions: *TD* 4.23; Epictetus 2.18.1 ff.; Seneca *Ep.* 85.10 and 15; 75.10–11. And presumably they also believed the converse for good characters.

86. See R. Sorabji, *Doubt and Dogmatism*, p. 275; Long, 'Freedom and Determinism', pp. 181–2.

87. For *peri hormês* as a standard topic see D.L. 7.84. NB Long, 'Early Stoic Concept', p. 78: 'I would conjecture that there is no feature of early Stoic ethics concerning which we have lost more crucial evidence than the *topos* they called *peri hormês.*'

88. See C. Wachsmuth, Praefatio, esp. pp. xiii–xiv and *Studia* p. 67: *denique in hoc archetypo nullum mendum frequentius omissione.* He notes that such lacunae are particularly apt to occur in the ethical doxography of Arius. At p. xxxi of the Praefatio Wachsmuth invites scholars to continue the work of emending the text of Stobaeus, esp. his quotations from philosophical authors.

89. *Gorgias* 468 a–c.

90. *EN* 3.1, 1110b11. Cf. *DM* 701b33–702a1.

91. *DRN* 2.258 *quo ducit quemque voluptas.*

92. C. Imbert, 'Théorie de la représentation . . .', esp. p. 224 speculates on how this resemblance may occur. See too her essay, 'Stoic Logic and Alexandrian Poetics', in *Doubt and Dogmatism*.

93. On presentations as referring, see Kerferd, 'The Problem of Synkatathesis and Katalepsis', p. 252 (in *Les Stoïciens et leur logique*). Some important ancient texts are Aëtius 4.21.1–2 (*Dox. Gr.*, pp. 401–2); *M* 7.162, reporting Antiochus; *M* 8.70; Nemesius *Nat. Hom.*, p. 172.

94. Strictly speaking, of the *hêgemonikon*. See *M* 7.227–31. Sextus continues this discussion to *M* 7.241.

95. *M* 7.154. Arcesilaus is, characteristically, exploiting Stoic doctrine to criticize the Stoics themselves. For the doctrine that assent is properly speaking given to propositions is itself a Stoic doctrine. Yet for the sake of brevity they would speak of assent to a presentation rather than to the accompanying proposition, as this criticism shows. Neither Arcesilaus nor Sextus was above taking advantage of such trivial verbal inconsistencies. Michael Frede has suggested to me that there may be significance in the claim that assent is to presentations rather than to propositions. But this text is the only

one I am aware of which presents these two formulations as alternatives and its *bona fides* is suspect.

96. *M* 7.242; SVF 2.74 (von Arnim's emendation of *Ecl.* 1.349); Alexander *DA*, p. 71; Aëtius at *Dox. Gr.*, p. 396.

97. What I shall present is more or less the orthodox view, as Kerferd describes it ('The Problem of Synkatathesis and Katalepsis', pp. 255–6). He mentions other possible interpretations on p. 256 which would supplement the orthodox view. Kerferd's alternative to the orthodox view seems unnecessary and unconvincing. See too the discussions of Graeser, *Zenon*, pp. 42–5 and C. Stough, *Greek Skepticism*, pp. 39–40. More recently Julia Annas has supported the traditional view ('Truth and Knowledge', pp. 88–98); for her view of Kerferd see her n. 18 on p. 104.

98. This seems to be the implication of the description of rational presentations at D.L. 7.51 as 'those of rational animals'. Irrational presentations are 'those of irrational animals'. Kerferd (op. cit., p. 253) and Imbert ('Théorie de la représentation', pp. 226 ff.) support this reading. *Phantasmata* are treated in a parallel fashion at SVF 2.83 = *Dox. Gr.*, pp. 400–1. For a different view see Long, 'Thought and Language', p. 83.

99. Sextus *M* 8.70 and D.L. 7.63 report it in identical words. The doctrine is confirmed at D.L. 7.49.

100. Opinions have varied on how strictly the Stoics maintained this technical distinction. See, e.g., Lloyd, 'Emotion and Decision', p. 237: 'Stoics were willing to treat images themselves as objects of assent, so that the distinctions of image (representation) and judgement tended to dissolve.' Others take a stronger position; see Rieth, 'Über das Telos', p. 25, Bonhoeffer, *Epictet*, pp. 140, 176–8, and Philippson, 'Zur Psychologie der Stoa', pp. 158–9. See also Sandbach, *The Stoics*, p. 88, 'Phantasia Kataleptikê', pp. 12–13, and Long, 'Thought and Language', pp. 82–4 and *Hellenistic Philosophy*, pp. 126–31. *M* 7.154 (n. 95) shows that some Stoics did refer, for the sake of brevity, to assent given to presentations.

101. Sextus says that a rational presentation 'presents the object of presentation to reason', presumably for assent or rejection (*M* 8.70).

102. As is said at *M* 7.244. Again I follow the older and, I think, the correct interpretation of this text against Kerferd's innovative views (op. cit., pp. 262 ff.). See Imbert, 'La théorie de la représentation', p. 239, Long, 'Language and Thought', p. 92, Rist, *Stoic Philosophy*, p. 149, Frede, *Die stoische Logik*, p. 41.

103. *Ecl.* 2.76–7 and Long, 'Early Stoic Concept', pp. 86–90.

104. *Ecl.* 1.138–9.

105. *Philebus* 39–40. Cf. *Sophist* 264ab: *phantasia* is an internal discourse

occurring through perception. It is not clear how the representational and the discursive elements are thought to be related by Plato (or by Aristotle, who criticizes Plato and gives his own account in *DA* 3.3). But both elements are present in the theory. My thanks to Bruce Rosenstock for pointing out the significance of these texts.

106. One should be noted here. As Striker has seen ('Sceptical Strategies', pp. 71-2), no hormetic presentation can be cataleptic. Thus there are no hormetic presentations which force man's assent, no matter what his character. If it were otherwise, Chrysippus' attempt to retain responsibility by means of the special role of assent would be a conspicuous failure.

107. Cicero *De Fato* 42.

108. Sextus *M* 7.385 suggests that there is no other way, if we may trust his statement that 'the intellect can receive nothing except by experiencing a presentation.'

109. 'Thought and Language', p. 82.

110. 431b2-19; 432a3-13. The similarity of these passages to the Stoic view would be illusory if Nussbaum's view of *phantasia* were correct.

111. 'Emotion and Decision', p. 236. Lloyd is using the word 'predicate' in a sense more appropriate to Aristotelian logic than to Stoic.

112. SVF 3.172.

113. 'Early Stoic Concept', p. 80; cf. Bonhoeffer, 'Zur stoischen Psychologie', p. 427.

114. Below, p. 101 with n. 271.

115. *M* 8.70 ff.; D.L. 7.63.

116. If we were told that 'a rational presentation is accompanied by *a lekton*' I would be reluctant to make the hypothesis I am making here.

117. 6.10, 1143a4-11.

118. Not of course by overt bodily motion, which may be hindered by external obstacles; by obedience I mean the psychic *kinêsis* (which might be described as 'setting oneself to do something') which normally causes such overt movement if not hindered. For a reason given in the next paragraph (1) I think it preferable to identify the *hormê* strictly speaking with the invariable response to the command and not to the command itself. But our sources state that a *hormê* is a command. This identification, which my interpretation subtly modifies, is comprehensible and reasonable if such commands are by definition obeyed in this unhinderable fashion.

119. See for example *Virt. Mor.* 446e-447a.

120. Again, allowing for the possibility of external hindrance. I assume this qualification throughout.

121. SVF 3.466. Below, pp. 148-153.

122. As at *Ecl.* 2.98: *to phronein kai sôphronein.*

123. Or a *pragma suntakton peri tinos ê tinon*. This difficult phrase probably means the same as the simpler version quoted in the text.

124. As David Sedley noted after a brief examination of the roll in Naples. Von Arnim worked from Cronert's edition in *Hermes* 36 (1901).

125. *to prostattomenon*, the content of the speech act commanding.

126. This translation is indicated by the *de* in *ei de mê* and by the parallel sentence at p. 108. 28-30. Cronert's punctuation (*Hermes* 36 (1901), p. 564 indicates that he interpreted it thus.

127. The translation would change slightly if we restored *prostattetai* instead of *prostattesthai*.

128. i.e. a predicate like this.

129. *St. Rep.* ch. 11, 1037 d-e.

130. Passages are collected at SVF 2.974-1007. Eight distinct attempts at reconciliation are detected by R. Sorabji, 'Causation, Laws and Necessity', in *Doubt and Dogmatism* (= *Necessity, Cause and Blame*, Ch. 4).

131. 'Stoic Determinism and Moral Responsibility'. I shall try to avoid unnecessary repetition of her presentation where I agree with it.

132. G. Verbeke, 'Aristotélisme et Stoïcisme dans le *De Fato* d'Alexandre d'Aphrodisias'; A. A. Long, 'Stoic Determinism and Alexander of Aphrodisias' *De Fato* (i-xiv)', 'Freedom and Determinism', 'The Stoic Concept of Evil'; M. Reesor, 'Fate and Possibility in Early Stoic Philosophy'; J. B. Gould, 'The Stoic Conception of Fate'; P. L. Donini, 'Fato e volontà umana in Crisippo'. Several chapters of *Doubt and Dogmatism* are also relevant: see in particular G. Striker, pp. 67 ff., M. Frede, esp. p. 236 and Sorabji's essay.

133. p. 222 and n. 38. I do not follow her remark that 'the idea of an action seems to be logically independent of the notion of cause and effect' in this context.

134. Cicero *De Fato* 7-11 attributes such a position to Chrysippus and then criticizes it. See Burnyeat, 'Can the Sceptic Live his Scepticism?', p. 42 n. 38 on the determination of assent by character.

135. See Long, 'Freedom and Determinism', p. 193. Compare Furley, *Two Studies*, pp. 235-6 on Epicurus and Aristotle.

136. Stough, op. cit., p. 226 makes this point.

137. D.L. 7.89, and below, Ch. 6.

138. SVF 1.518.

139. Cicero *De Fato* 7-8.

140. Lucretius *DRN* 3.319-322. Cf. Furley, *Two Studies*, pp. 198-200 and 227 ff. and Long, 'Freedom and Determinism', n. 46, p. 197.

141. Sorabji is not sure that this is correct as a description of the Stoic position. But a version of his third interpretation (*Doubt and Dogmatism*, pp. 274-6) seems to me to be the best reading of Chrysippus.

142. p. 275.
143. On the special character of the 'internal' causes of human action, see Davidson, 'Actions, Reasons and Causes', p. 694. He thinks that an agentless cause of a human action does not make him a 'helpless victim' of the cause (p. 700).
144. In one text assent is said to be *kath' hormên* (SVF 2.74). This might suggest that assent is thought of as an action like observable external actions and so that the Stoics were indeed exposed to the regress argument. But this text does not reflect Stoic views about the nature of assent; see Appendix 4 on the term *kath' hormên*.
145. SVF 1.537, p. 122 lines 11–13.
146. Cleanthes' views on determinism, necessity, and possibility did differ from Chrysippus'. But I think that their disagreement was limited to the question of how best to respond to the 'sophistic' Master Argument of Diodorus.
147. It must be understood that 'rational' means 'produced by reason', not 'corresponding to Right Reason' i.e. correct.
148. Pohlenz *Hermes* 75 (1940), p. 120.
149. D.L. 7.88. Long, 'Freedom and Determinism', p. 179 interprets it as 'not planned by god'. Reesor, 'Necessity and Fate', takes Cleanthes to be saying that the acts of bad men do not happen 'according to the common nature and its *logos*'.
150. See below, p. 156.
151. See A. A. Long, 'The Stoic Concept of Evil'.
152. See above, Ch. 2, pp. 32–33.
153. Long, 'Soul and Body', p. 50 and n. 41 disagrees. But the 'assent' he grants to animals is different from what he attributes to human adults. Below I argue that such animal 'assent' was called *eixis*. I suspect our disagreement on this point is merely verbal.
154. See *TD* 4.31; Seneca *De Ira* 1.3.4–8.
155. SVF 3.477. Compare Galen at *PHP* 5.5.
156. *hosa ton logon mêdepô sumpeplêrôken*.
157. Aëtius *Dox. Gr.*, p. 400. See too SVF 3 Diogenes 17, 2.764 and Pohlenz, *Die Stoa*, vol. ii, p. 33.
158. SVF 2.841.
159. Rist, *Stoic Philosophy*, pp. 40–1 disagrees and speaks of a 'weak assent' in children. There is no textual evidence for this use of the phrase. Seneca, *Ep.* 124, emphasizes that children and animals are in the same position from a moral perspective, despite the potential of a child for developing reason (esp. 124.9). On the 'seeds of reason' see also Philo *De Animalibus* 96. See Pohlenz, *Die Stoa*, vol. i, p. 89.
160. *EN* 1111a25–6 (cf. 1100a1–4). Pembroke, 'Oikeiôsis', p. 120 and n. 35 lists more texts. See too *EN* 1111b8–9, 12–13; *EE* 2.8.6, 7.2.7 and

Fortenbaugh, *Aristotle on Emotion*, Ch. 4. Also Irwin, 'Reason and Responsibility'.

161. Compare Philo's description of the non-rational *hêgemonikon* at *De Animalibus* 29.

162. D.L. 7.55 = SVF 3 Diogenes 17.

163. *Ep.* 124.1. Cf. *Fin.* 3.21.

164. *Ep.* 124.16 ff.

165. Cf. Bennett, *Rationality*, pp. 79-93 on the interdependence of language, sense of time, and the ability to form universal concepts.

166. *De Lingua Latina* 6.56 = SVF 2.143.

167. This does not fit too well with Diogenes' selection of fourteen as the transitional point. But Varro may be softening the paradoxical appearance of the Stoic view that reason is not present in all its glory until the age of fourteen, which is particularly implausible when applied to the case of language use. That Varro has adapted Chrysippus to some degree is shown by his pun on *locus* and *loqui*, which cannot be drawn directly from a Greek source.

168. M. Frede, 'The Principles of Stoic Grammar', pp. 54-8.

169. Philo *De Animalibus* 85 says that real thought requires immaterial entities which animals do not have.

170. *De Ira* 1.3.7. Cf. *amudra* used of the quasi-passions by Origen, SVF 3.477. Compare Philo *De Animalibus* 29 for the 'unclearness' of the non-rational mind.

171. Hampshire, *Thought and Action*, pp. 99-100, agrees that children start out like animals and correctly emphasizes that there is a long period of hazy transition to the status of responsible, intending agents.

172. And their memory is quasi-memory, their anger quasi-anger, etc. See *Soll. An.* 961ef.

173. 7.51. The phrase *apo huparchontôn* does not prove that only cataleptic presentations are meant. There is a problem with the text here as well.

174. See Sandbach, 'Phantasia Katalêptikê'; Rist, *Stoic Philosophy*, Ch. 8; A. Graeser, *Zenon von Kition*, pp. 30-68; J. Annas, 'Truth and Knowledge'.

175. The 'voluntariness' of assent is mentioned by Cicero *Acad.* 1.40; the use of *kath' hormên* to express this idea at *Ecl.* 1.349 = SVF 2.74 is not a reflection of Stoic usage. See Appendix 4.

176. Op. cit., pp. 14-15.

177. *PH* 1.193, 1.230; *M* 7.225.

178. Alexander *De Fato*, pp. 183.21-184.5; Plutarch *St. Rep.* 1056f-1057a. Below, pp. 86-91.

179. Plutarch *Virt. Mor.* 447a, on passions. Note too *rhopas* here, which is used in polemical treatments of the *apraxia* argument (*Adv. Col.* 1122b).

180. Cicero's use at *Acad.* 2.66 would,,I suggest, be typical. It is used of an adult human, and that is not Stoic (but Cicero speaks here as an Academic). But he uses it it disclaim personal responsibility for his opinions: *itaque visis cedo nec possum resistere.* Cf. n. 177.

181. *Acad.* 2.38–9.

182. 'Phantasia Katalêptikê', p. 15. But cf. Epictetus 3.3.1–4.

183. Further on this question see Cherniss, Loeb *Moralia* 13.2, pp. 600–1 n.; Bonhoeffer, *Epictet,* pp. 164–5, 177–8; Voelke, *L'Idée,* part 1, Ch. 3.

184. *The Stoics,* p. 60.

185. Plutarch (*Adv. Col.* 1119f–1120a) uses the Stoic belief that assent requires *lekta* to attack the Epicureans.

186. 3.1.2 ff. Stough, 'Stoic Determinism and Moral Responsibility', p. 220 treats Alexander as the more reliable source. It seems preferable to use Origen's non-polemical account, which all agree is based on Stoic sources, rather than the polemical Aristotelianism of Alexander. Stough's particular concern is with the application of *phusis.* By using it to refer to one level of the *scala naturae* Origen is adhering to a legitimate Stoic usage; Alexander's use of the term for all the levels is also found in other Stoic sources. My reasons for preferring Origen's usage are substantive rather than terminological. It is certain that Origen had and used reliable Stoic sources: see von Arnim, preface to SVF 1, p. xlvi; Todd, *Alexander of Aphrodisias on Stoic Physics,* p. 24 and n. 14. Long, 'Stoic Determinism . . .', esp. pp. 266–8 shows a healthier suspicion of Alexander than he does in 'Freedom and Determinism'. Chadwick, 'Origen, Celsus and the Stoa', p. 34 concludes that Origen was 'on terms of easy familiarity' with the works of Chrysippus himself. Recent papers by L. Roberts, 'Origen and Stoic Logic', and J. M. Rist, 'The Importance of Stoic Logic in the *Contra Celsum*', confirm that in the field of logic as well Origen had access to technical works of the orthodox Stoa. Another case of Origen's use of orthodox Stoic views has been brought to light by Jonathan Barnes (p. 9 of 'La doctrine du retour éternel'); he notes that Origen's version of this doctrine is orthodox at a point where other sources report post-Chrysippean innovation.

187. See Stough, op. cit., pp. 206–7, 220–2 on this text.

188. The Stoics did not think such skills to be true arts because they defined a *technê* as made up of propositional entities. See *M* 7.373; SVF 2.94; 3.214. See Pohlenz, *Grundfragen,* p. 5; Hahm, *The Origins,* p. 204 and n. 12. Compare the position of Bennett, *Rationality,* pp. 98 ff.

189. Bennett, op. cit., uses the example of the non-rational skill of the

bee throughout his book. Compare *ND* 2.123 *machinatio quaedam atque sollertia.*

190. For the ancient debate see Philo *De Animalibus*, Plutarch *De Amore Prolis, De Sollertia Animalium*; on the examples see S. O. Dickerman, 'Some Stock Examples of Animal Intelligence in Greek Psychology'. Further discussion in Pohlenz, *Die Stoa*, vol. i, pp. 84-5, 'Tierische und menschliche Intelligenz bei Poseidonios'; A. Dyroff, 'Zur stoischen Tierpsychologie'; Chadwick, op. cit., pp. 36-7; Brink, 'Theophrastus and Zeno on Nature in Moral Theory', pp. 130-1. Some ancient texts: SVF 2.714-737, esp. 2.729, 729a, 729b; 1.515; Seneca *Ep.* 121.22-4. A. Terian brings the discussion up to date in his edition of Philo *De Animalibus*. Philo's essay gives a reasonably clear version of the Stoic position as well as that of their opponents.

191. *PH* 1.69; cf. *Soll. An.* 969a-c; Philo *De Animalibus* 45-6, 84. A different canine inference is mentioned at *M* 8.271.

192. Compare Sandbach, 'Phantasia Kataleptikê', p. 12.

193. In one discussion of the psychology of action, which otherwise appears to be orthodox, Seneca (*Ep.* 113.18) refers to an impulse occurring in a preliminary way before as well as after assent is given: 'every rational animal does nothing unless it is first stimulated by a presentation of something, *then has an impulse*, and then assent confirms this impulse.' On this theory it would be the preliminary impulse which is blocked by a refusal of assent or confirmed by assent, rather than the presentation. But this new stage is unique and occurs nowhere else in our sources for the old Stoa. Moreover, it is likely that Seneca's source, which is post-Chrysippean, may be adapting Chrysippean doctrine (Seneca does not attribute this version of the theory to Chrysippus and it conflicts with the rest of our evidence for the early Stoa). See Ch. 5 on *propatheiai*, esp. p. 179 for a suggestion as to the reason for the adaptation of Chrysippus.

194. *On Tranquillity* 12.5.

195. This is to be understood with appropriate restrictions on the term 'action'. Actions must be the result of assent and impulse and so occurrences like sweating, trembling, and digestion may be excluded. See below, pp. 175 ff. on *propatheiai*. The Stoic approach to voluntariness and responsibility is clearly different from Aristotle's. For one thing, the Stoic approach tends to make the voluntary and the responsible converge, where Aristotle arguably does not. Although Aristotle's position on responsibility and voluntariness is not completely clear, I take it that responsible action is prohairetic action and this sort of action is a distinct subset of voluntary action characterized by the occurrence of deliberation before action (*EN* 5.8, 1135b8-11). For a fuller discussion see T. Irwin, 'Reasons and Responsibility in

Aristotle'. For another view of Aristotle's opinions on the relation of voluntary and prohairetic action, see Kenny, *Will, Freedom and Power*, Ch. 2.

196. Cooper, *Reason and Human Good*, pp. 9–10 attributes this sort of move to Aristotle; see also T. Irwin, op. cit., p. 131.

197. D. Glidden, 'The *Lysis* on Loving One's Own', p. 52.

198. On implicit assent see G. Striker, 'Skeptical Strategies', p. 67 n. 39.

199. Given their doctrines of psychological materialism, however, these theories are at least verifiable in principle.

200. *De Principiis* 3.1.5.

201. Cf. *M* 8.397, which shows that epistemology and action are similar in this respect.

202. See Voelke, *L'Idée*, p. 145. Epictetus also contrasts the rational use of presentations to the *mere* use of them by irrational animals: Bonhoeffer, *Epictet*, p. 74, Goldschmidt, *Le Système*, pp. 116–17; *Diss.* 1.6.12–22; 2.8.1–8; 2.14.15.

203. The ethical importance of getting one's assent right is stressed at D.L. 7.48. Note the reference to untrained or unexercised presentations.

204. *Diss.* 2.18.24–6. Cf. 1.28.28–33, *Ench.* 20.

205. *Strom.* 2.20.111.

206. With Clement's *sunapopheresthai* compare *sunharpazein* at *Ench.* 10, 20, 34; *Diss.* 2.18.24 and *helkuein* at 2.18.23.

207. *Ecl.* 2.85.

208. *Officium* at *Acad.* 2.25 reflects *kathēkon*. But *oikeion* and its opposite lie behind *accommodatum naturae, alienum naturae* (2.24–5, 38) and are found at D.L. 7.85 ff and in Philo *Quod Deus* 44 (here *hôs heterôs* is a stylistic variant for *allotriôs*).

209. *St. Rep.* ch. 47, esp. 1056ef; cf. *M* 7.405.

210. This entails the belief that every time Plutarch says 'Chrysippus says' he need not be accurately quoting anything ever said by Chrysippus, but may only be attributing to him a line of reasoning to which Plutarch thought he should be committed.

211. *M* 7.242, D.L. 7.75; cf. *St. Rep.* 1056a.

212. This is a feature of all reported versions of the argument: *St. Rep.* 1057ab, *Adv. Col.* 1122cd, and in Cicero's *Academica*. See the excellent discussion of Striker in 'Sceptical Strategies', esp. pp. 66–9, 74–9; also Pohlenz, *Die Stoa*, vol. i, pp. 174–5.

213. The cross-over is further encouraged by the parallel treatment of assent in hormetic and non-hormetic applications; the Academics denied that assent was needed for perception (*Ecl.* 1.350) just as they denied it was needed for action (e.g. *St. Rep.* 1057ab, *Adv. Col.* 1122cd).

214. *Adv. Col.* 1122a–d.

215. Similarly, Stoic definitions of *aisthêsis* are usually definitions of

human perception only: SVF 2.72 = *Dox. Gr.*, p. 396, SVF 2.74 = *Ecl.* 1.349, *Acad.* 2.145.

216. *Adv. Col.* 1122cd.

217. *phusikôs*, cf. Origen's *tetagmenôs*.

218. Voelke, *L'Idée*, pp. 32 ff. uncritically assimilates Antiochus to the Stoa with no argument. Sandbach, 'Phantasia Katalêptikê', p. 15 had already cast doubt on *Acad.* 2.38.

219. He attributes assent to animals at *Acad.* 2.38. A less distinct form of this assimilation seems to lie behind the loose wording of 2.30 too.

220. On these texts see W. Theiler, 'Tacitus und die antike Schicksalslehre', pp. 65–7. Even their exposition of the Stoic hierarchy of nature arouses suspicion. For Alexander attributes to the lowest level, exemplified by stones and fire (the latter an example not found in more reliable sources), the power of movement to natural place and intrinsic powers. This is not the point mentioned by the Stoics. Nemesius gives the power to cool as the natural power of water and repeats the examples of the natural motion of fire and water. He also refers to the power of each plant to produce its characteristic fruit, another example absent from better Stoic sources.

221. Nemesius is writing in a well-worn polemical tradition; the same example is found at pseudo-Plutarch *De Fato* 571cd. Walking was a standard Stoic example (D.L. 7.98, 109; *Ecl.* 2.69, 72, 96–7; Seneca *Ep.* 113.18–19, 23). But they in turn borrowed it from Aristotle (*DM* 701a10–16, 702a15–21), who was perhaps writing with *Gorgias* 468b in mind. Cf. *DRN* 4.877 ff.

222. Reesor, 'Fate and Possibility', pp. 286–7 vaguely senses that Nemesius is distorting the Stoic position, but does not see how. She is apparently satisfied with Alexander's account, who makes what I shall argue is the same move as Nemesius.

223. Alexander's own psychology of action is an interesting blend of Stoic and Aristotelian elements (see e.g. *De Anima* 72–3). Todd, op. cit., mentions this blend briefly, but does not discuss it. Preus, op. cit., does deal with the question but starts from a misunderstanding of the Stoic position.

224. 180.9–181.7. Alexander, unlike Aristotle, is probably committed to the view that an act of deliberation occurs before each rational action, if only unconsciously.

225. 196.24–197.3 = SVF 2.984.

226. One might also point out that Alexander employs a definitely un-Stoic notion of *hormê*, using it to define an Aristotelian concept of *prohairesis* not shared by the Stoa (180.8–9). On terminology see Appendices 2, 3, 4.

227. 181.15–182.20.

228. 182.3–4; 182.12.
229. 182.11–13.
230. 182.16 ff.
231. 183.22–3.
232. 182.16 ff; 183.5–10.
233. 205.27–9.
234. 205.15–16.
235. *logikē sunkatathesis*, 184.11–12.
236. *phantasiais monais*, a difficult phrase, tr. after Sharples.
237. 184.1–4.
238. 184.20–2.
239. 183.27–185.7.
240. 184.11–12. On the difference between assent and rational assent compare *DA* 67.17–18 and 73.11–13.
241. 205.16–18. Cf. the definition of *prohairesis* involving *boulē*. Also 178.17–24.
242. I refer only to the explicit theory. No doubt Aristotle presupposes our ability to entertain propositions from time to time.
243. I should direct the reader's attention to two essays by Claude Imbert, which deal in part with this question: 'Théorie de la représentation et doctrine logique' and 'Stoic Logic and Alexandrian Poetics'.
244. At *Speech Acts*, p. 30 Searle calls it the propositional content in contrast to the illocutionary force. In 'The Intentionality of Intention and Action' Searle develops his earlier analysis in detail, applying it to the problem of intention.
245. In 'Imperative Sentences' Hare calls it the descriptor in contrast to the dictor; in *The Language of Morals* he replaces these terms with the now familiar phrastic and neustic, the latter term reappearing in 'Practical Inferences' as tropic. For similar distinctions see Rescher, *The Logic of Commands*, pp. 8–9 and Kenny, *Action, Emotion and Will*, pp. 222 ff. and 'Practical Inference', pp. 67 ff.
246. I am supposing that the Stoa recognized that 'it is fitting ...' sentences differ from 'it is the case that ...' sentences in a way analogous to the way they thought that 'You, do...' sentences differ.
247. *Linguistic Behaviour*, p. 238.
248. *Speech Acts*, p. 122. His later work 'The Intentionality of Intention and Action' should be compared to this.
249. Hare, p. 70 of 'Practical Inferences', notes that the formal consequences of an approach like that taken by Bennett and his own are 'very similar'.
250. Although the Stoics did use 'not' as a negation operator governing whole sentences.
251. See the lists of complete *lekta* at D.L. 7.66 ff. and *M* 8.70 ff.; SVF

2.188-92. These are all definite modes of asserting a sentence content, phrastics plus neustics in Hare's terms.

252. This may be because of the ambiguous position of the referring component of a complete *lekton*. It seems (see Long, 'Language and Thought', pp. 104-6) that this is not an incomplete *lekton* as the predicate is. These are semantic questions which cannot be discussed here.

253. See Hare, 'Practical Inferences', p. 70, Kenny, 'Practical Inference' and Ch. 5 of *Will, Freedom and Power.*

254. Cf. Davidson, 'Actions, Reasons and Causes', pp. 686-7. The agent's reason for acting helps to determine the correct description of his action. I do want to suggest that any element in the Stoic analysis is identifiable with a Davidsonian reason. When comparing the Stoic analysis of intention to Davidson's I have in view Davidson's earlier and more general discussion of intentional *action*, rather than his later remarks on the problem of 'pure intending' in the essay 'Intending'.

255. On assent and intention see J. M. Rist, *Stoic Philosophy*, Ch. 12, esp. p. 220.

256. 'Early Stoic Concept', p. 91.

257. This is the approach taken by Gilbert, 'The concept of Will in Early Latin Philosophy', and by Voelke in *L'Idée* and in his two related articles.

258. *Aristotle's Theory of the Will*, pp. vii-viii.

259. Although it seems not to upset Searle, 'The Intentionality', which I think is to his credit. Davidson, 'Actions, Reasons and Causes', pp. 687-8, defends treating reasons as causes by arguing that the stateable reason and the described action are logically independent (although grammatically connected, p. 695). It may be that the predicate corresponding to the action is more general than and so distinct from the action performed in a particular time, place, and fashion. But apart from the question whether the predicate in a hormetic proposition can be regarded as a Davidsonian reason, I doubt that the Stoics saw this clearly enough to use it in their own defence. (For one thing, the Stoics are accounting for intentional actions by positing mental events of the sort which many modern philosophers, including Davidson, would prefer to avoid. In this respect the Stoic position is perhaps more like that of Searle in 'The Intentionality of Intention and Action'.) It is more in keeping with their psychological materialism to get them off the hook by exploiting the fact that the mental events which cause actions, according to their theory, are 'distinct existences' and so capable of playing the role of Humean causes (see Kenny, *Will, Freedom and Power*, pp. 117-18). This is the defence I attribute to the Stoics in the following lines.

260. *Ecl.* 1.138-9 = SVF 1.89, 2.336.
261. See the comments of Frede, 'The Original Notion of Cause', pp. 245-6.
262. See N. Rescher, 'On the Characterization of Action', Davidson, 'Actions, Reasons and Causes'.
263. Epictetus *Diss.* 1.6.10 gives a sketchy account of the manipulation of presentations in thought. He does not address the problem, assuming as he usually does that all internal mental events are free or seem so to the agent. For other references by Stoics to the mental manipulation of presentations see D.L. 7.51, SVF 2.83 (Aëtius), *M* 8.276, and others listed recently by Sharples (*Alexander of Aphrodisias: On Fate*, pp. 140-1, 149-50); I doubt that *De Ira* 2.3 f. belongs in this list. But what is striking is the failure of the Stoics to apply this very general theory of the manipulation of presentations to specific problems of action and determinism. Yet we have fragments (SVF 2.1000 e.g.) where references to this rather than vague allusions to one's character would be relevant. I suspect, therefore, that there is a real gap in the theory and that Alexander's criticisms of the Stoics on this point are not quite as unfair as Sharples thinks (pp. 149-50): Alexander is exploiting a genuine gap in the theory, although his distinction between *phantasia* and *phainomenon* is not Stoic.
264. See Stough, op. cit., pp. 214, 222.
265. See n. 221.
266. See *Ecl.* 2.66: 'Similarly, the sensible man does everything well, the things he *does* and, by Zeus, yes! the things he doesn't do.' See Appendix 2.
267. The distinction between internal and external actions is mentioned by Cicero at *Fin.* 3.32: offences *in effectu* are overt actions; offences *sine effectu* are internal actions, exemplified by the passions.
268. *PHP* 4.7.14, p. 284 = SVF 3.466. For discussion see pp. 147-151.
269. Alexander also restricts *hormê* in this way (*DA* 72.20-73.1).
270. Voelke, *L'Idée*, p. 52 and n. 1. In general, pp. 51 ff.
271. The only indication that there was such a thing as a theoretical impulse is at *Ecl.* 2.88: 'All impulses are acts of assent and the practical also contain the power to move [sc. the agent].' At first sight this suggests the existence of non-practical impulses, and Long, 'Early Stoic Concept', p. 80, Tsekourakis, *Studies*, pp. 77-8, and Bonhoeffer, *Epictet*, p. 255 take it in this way. Only Bonhoeffer realizes how untenable the notion of a non-practical impulse is, and his puzzlement was the motivation for some unpromising speculation about non-practical impulse by Dyroff (*Die Ethik*, pp. 22-3; see Appendix 2). But as Striker saw ('Sceptical Strategies', p. 78 n. 55) it is possible to take *praktikas* as an explication of *hormas*, not as a

designation for a distinct sub-group of impulses. She further suggests that if we are to keep *praktikas* as such a designation, which is after all the most natural reading of the text, it may refer to passions, some of which are impulses to internal reactions and do not necessarily produce overt action. But there are reasons for doubting this solution. For *boulēsis*, one of the *eupatheiai* which are analogues to the passions, is said to be a practical impulse. At best only some of the passions could be non-practical. This is a difficult text, and I prefer to suspect a lacuna between *einai* and *tas de* and to fill it with *sunkatatheseis de kai allas einai*. This would distinguish practical *assents* which cause impulses from theoretical assents, a distinction which we know from the rest of the theory of action. It is true that there is no overt sign of a lacuna in F or P (which I have examined on microfilm); but Wachsmuth himself noted the frequency of such lacunae in the archetype of F and P, our best witnesses to the text (*Studia*, p. 67), and invited historians of philosophy to continue the job of emending a badly corrupt text on philosophical grounds (intro. to his edition, p. xxxi). The suggested supplement is needed on philosophical grounds, is explicable by haplography, and is no longer than many other postulated gaps whose supplements are generally accepted (see e.g. 87.6–7, 75.3, 90.16–17).

Chapter 4

1. *Ecl.* 2.75–6.
2. Compare the more detailed discussion of Rist, 'Zeno and Stoic Consistency', pp. 167 ff.
3. D.L. 7.87.
4. *Ecl.* 2.102.22–103.4; 2.106.12–20.
5. e.g. *Ep.* 34.4; 35.4; 120.9 ff. Compare Marcus 11.21.
6. *Ep.* 95.58.
7. *Ep.* 20.5.
8. D.L. 7.88.
9. D.L. 7.88.
10. *Ben.* 6.23.
11. *M* 11.200–1; *Ecl.* 2.66–7.
12. *M* 7.373; SVF 3.214; 2.93–5; 2.731; 1.73.
13. *Ecl.* 2.63.6 ff.; 2.66–7.
14. *Ecl.* 2.60.7–8. Cf. 2.74.4–5.
15. *Ecl.* 2.75. Cf. Clement's definition of a *hairesis* at SVF 2.121, p. 37 (= *Strom.* 8.5.16.2): 'an inclination to many judgements possessing consistency (*akolouthia*) with each other and the *phainomena*, which contributes to living well'. See also *Ecl.* 2.62.23–4; 63.3–5.

16. D.L. 7.87–8.
17. *Phronêsis* is also defined as the knowledge, presumably complete, of what to do and not to do. Passages are listed in the Index to SVF, vol. 4, p. 157. And this is what the Law of Nature and Right Reason are said to command: see SVF 3.314, 323; 2.1003 (= Alexander *De Fato*, p. 207); and compare *Ecl.* 2.59 and Alexander *De Fato* 210.19–21.
18. Epictetus *Ench.* 26; cf. SVF 3.180.
19. D.L. 7.88.
20. See Appendix 2.
21. *ND.* 2.58.
22. *St. Rep.*, ch. 11.
23. This similarity is also mentioned by Cicero, *ND* 2.58.
24. *Ecl.* 2.96.10–17.
25. *ND* 2.37.
26. In addition to the freedom from passions which will be discussed below.
27. Aristotle's discussion of deliberation in *EN* 3 does not commit him to a belief in indeterminacy in human action, but it does seem to be strongly suggested. Alexander seems to have thought he was taking Aristotle's position when he connected deliberation with indeterminacy. For an attempt to sort out Aristotle's complex views on this sort of question see R. Sorabji, *Necessity, Cause and Blame.*
28. This must be what is meant by making Right Reason a criterion (D.L. 7.54).
29. Epictetus *Diss.* 1.2.12 ff.
30. 'Early Stoic Concept', p. 84.
31. As Origen points out (SVF 2.1185) it is harder to predict the actions of men than of animals because so much would have to be known about their bodily and psychic states.
32. D.L. 7.127; SVF 3.238–9. Cf. Seneca *Ep.* 113.8. Chrysippus seems to be filling in something Cleanthes failed to consider rather than attempting to introduce an important new doctrine about virtue.
33. Rist, *Stoic Philosophy*, pp. 131–2 suggests that Chrysippus' opinion that virtue may be lost opens a way to free action which is not merely a 'reflex of character'. But I cannot reconcile this suggestion with his fuller discussion of the loss of virtue, pp. 16–17.
34. *Ben.* 6.21.2–3.
35. See Long, 'Freedom and Determinism', pp. 188–9; SVF 2.965–967.
36. See Stough, op. cit., p. 224.
37. How the sage acts in view of his inevitable uncertainty about the details of fate and god's will is a question still to be answered. See below, pp. 119 ff. on reservation and Goldschmidt, *Le Système*, p. 215.
38. *De Vita Beata* 15.7.

39. *Ecl.* 2.115.5-9. Cf. Cicero *Paradoxa* 34. Cicero also points to freedom from passions and errors.

40. As has been noted above, Aristotle's position is complex and cannot be discussed here. He often speaks of it being in a man's power to do or not to do something as the result of a deliberation. But Sorabji suggests (pp. 250-1) that he might have been content with a position very like the Stoa's.

41. 'Language and Thought', esp. pp. 95-6, 102-4; and 'Dialectic and the Stoic Sage', esp. pp. 108-10, 113-18.

42. On the Stoic commitment to astrology see A. A. Long, 'Astrology: arguments pro and contra'.

43. Chs. 9 and 9a of *Ecl.* 2, pp. 86-7 Wachsmuth.

44. This is also true of *hormê* itself. See Appendix 3.

45. *Eklogê.* See Ch. 6 p. 198 and n. 73 for evidence on *eklogê*. We almost always read of *eklogê* being directed to things which are 'according to nature' in contrast to true goods. The opposite of selection is *apeklogê*, rejection, directed at 'things contrary to nature'.

46. *Diss.* 3.2.1-4. I am not concerned with his third *topos* here. There is no reason to make Epictetus' topics match up with the traditional Stoic tripartite division of philosophy as a whole.

47. *Epictet*, pp. 256-7.

48. *Diss.* 3.3.2; 1.4.1-2.

49. *Diss.* 3.2.1-2.

50. *Ench.* 2.1; *Diss.* 2.8.29; 3.23.9.

51. *Diss.* 3.2.1-2.

52. D.L. 7.108; *Ecl.* 2.86.

53. *Ecl.* 2.93.

54. *Diss.* 1.18.1-2 is the closest he comes to adopting the old Stoic usage. See Bonhoeffer, *Epictet*, p. 256.

55. There are, for example, no distinctive labels for non-rational presentation or impulse, so that they must go by the general name. But rational presentation and rational impulse do have distinct labels (*noêsis* and *praktikê hormê*).

56. *Diss.* 3.25.3; *Ench.* 2; *Diss.* 1.4.2-3.

57. *Diss.* 1.22.1.

58. See e.g. *Diss.* 3.3.1-5.

59. See Hijmans, *Askêsis*, p. 68; on this aspect of passions, see below, pp. 146 ff.

60. *Ench.* 48.3.

61. *Diss.* 3.13.21.

62. Bonhoeffer, *Epictet*, pp. 240-2 is very good on this point.

63. See e.g. Goldschmidt, *Le Système*, pp. 87, 145-6, 157; Sandbach, *The Stoics*, pp. 44; Forschner, *Die stoische Ethik*, pp. 203 ff., 208-11.

64. SVF 2.975.
65. Seneca *Ep.* 109.5; *De Divinatione* 1.127–8. See Kerferd, 'What Does the Wise Man Know?' and Rist, *Stoic Philosophy*, p. 146.
66. *Diss.* 2.6.9–10 = SVF 3.191. I agree with Oldfather ad loc., Long, *Hellenistic Philosophy*, p. 194, and Rist, op. cit., p. 6, n. 3 (who is less certain) that this is a verbatim quotation.
67. *Ben.* 4.34.4. The doctrine is applied to a different sort of case, but the general point is the same.
68. *Ecl.* 2.115.5–9.
69. *TD* 3.58.
70. *Tranq.* 13.2–14.1.
71. Marcus 4.1; 5.20;6.50; 11.37 (= fr. 27 of Epictetus).
72. Seneca's term *levius* at *Tranq.* 13.3 is clearly a rendering of the Greek *kouphôs*. The term therefore goes back to earlier Stoics.
73. He speaks here of a reservation in one's love for or attachment to certain things. But this implies a desire that they should continue to exist. This desire and the corresponding efforts are forms of impulse, as indeed is love itself (sexual love, *erôs*, is a form of *epibolê*).
74. *Ben.* 4.34.4.
75. *Diss.* 3.24.23–4 and 85 ff.
76. *Ecl.* 2.75. Long, 'Early Stoic concept', pp. 82–4 does not entertain this interpretation of the unique phrase *hormê autotelês*. Thus he wishes to emend the text. His argument is ingenious, but I think that this interpretation of *autotelês* is plausible enough to make emendation unnecessary.
77. *Ecl.* 2.115.
78. 6.50.

Chapter 5

1. Aristotle wrote a book on *pathê*, if the dubious text at D.L. 5.23 is to be believed. Theophrastus definitely wrote a *peri pathôn* (D.L. 5.45, cf. 5.44 *On Grief*).
2. *Fin.* 3.35; *TD* 3.7. The latter is the fuller account.
3. Since it can mean 'state' or 'condition' it may be used as a substitute for *nosos* in a medical context, e.g. *Airs, Waters, Places* 22. See also *M* 7.247. But in its literal sense *pathos* is much wider in meaning. Democritus B 31 treats the soul's *pathê* as analogous to bodily diseases, but that is not evidence for the literal meaning of *pathos*.
4. In *PHP* 5.2–4 Galen discusses Posidonius' disagreement with Chrysippus over the body–soul analogy. In this connection *nosêma* and *nosos* seem to have been used interchangeably. See also *TD* 4.23 ff., SVF 3, pp. 102–4.
5. Galen also discusses the interesting passage at *Sophist* 227–8.

6. It is the particular merit of R. Rabel, *Theories of the Emotions in the Old Stoa*, Ch. 1 to do this.

7. When using a different source at *TD* 4.23–33 Cicero gets the distinction between diseases in the soul and actual *pathê* correct.

8. *PHP* 5.5.

9. SVF 3.476 ad fin. = *PHP* 5.1.10, p. 294; SVF 3.477; *De Ira* 1.3.6; *TD* 4.31.

10. On the general temper of Posidonius' thought see I. G. Kidd, 'Posidonius on Emotions'.

11. *Doxai* are by definition incorrect judgements.

12. Naturally enough, if Fortenbaugh (*Aristotle on Emotion*) is correct that Aristotle had popularized this insight in the late 4th century.

13. *TD* 4.14.

14. Pohlenz ('Zenon und Chrysipp' and in *Die Stoa*) is the most important champion of the view that Chrysippus made a radical change. For a criticism of it see Voelke, *L'Idée*, pp. 81–3. For other views see Anne Glibert-Thirry, 'La théorie stoïcienne de la passion . . .', pp. 401–3. Galen frequently alludes to the question which Posidonius seems to have raised (e.g. *PHP* 4.2–4.3, 5.1.4 ff.). It seems that Galen did not have a clear view on the problem (5.6.42). See also Graeser, *Zenon*, pp. 168–72.

15. e.g. Rist, *Stoic Philosophy*, pp. 30–1; Lloyd, 'Emotion and Decision', pp. 240–1; see also Bonhoeffer, *Epictet*, p. 95.

16. *Ecl.* 2.88 illustrates how the judgement and the passion could be identified or distinguished without changing the underlying theory. For in discussing impulse and assent Arius begins with an identification of the two and then distinguishes them according to their objects. There is no suggestion that the theory is being modified, just explicated.

17. *TD* 3.74–5 = SVF 1.212.

18. Chrysippus' monism is attacked throughout *PHP* 4–5, but see the expression *mia dunamis* at 5.1.8 (p. 294) and 5.5.38–9 (p. 326).

19. For an account of the shift from Chrysippus' monism to the more complex theory of Posidonius see most recently Glibert-Thirry, op. cit. Kidd, op. cit., gives a lucid account of Posidonius' theory of the passions and sets it in the context of his broader philosophical approach. I would put Panaetius too among the innovators, and argue that he adopted a form of psychological dualism which allows non-rational powers in the soul to oppose reason. M. van Straaten argues against this claim (*Panétius, sa vie*, pp. 104–15). But see the discussions by Rist (*Stoic Philosophy*, pp. 182–4), Grilli ('Studi Paneziani', pp. 73–4), Pohlenz (*Die Stoa*, vol. i, pp. 198–9), Schindler (*Die stoische Lehre*, pp. 76–7), and Holler (*Seneca*, pp. 48–50). Voelke,

L'Idée, pp. 115–17 cautiously accepts dualism for Panaetius. Van Straaten replies to his critics in a recent essay (in *Images of Man*, pp. 104–9). But he offers no new arguments to defuse the obvious implications of *Off.* 1.101, 132 which are the main support for the dualistic interpretation. Van Straaten has focused narrowly on the fact that Chrysippus and Panaetius agree in regarding *logos* and *hormê* as powers and not parts of the mind. But the important point is the relationship between these powers. Chrysippus would not admit that *hormê* was an independent force able to disobey *logos*. On this point, which is the nub of the dualism problem, van Straaten offers us nothing.

20. *PHP* 4.7.12–44.
21. For a discussion of this attempt see below.
22. For just one example, note Galen's report of Posidonius (*PHP* 5.5.21): 'for sometimes impulse occurs in the animal as a result of the decision of the calculative [sc. part of the soul] but many times it occurs as a result of a movement in the passionate part.'
23. 'How is Weakness of the Will Possible?', p. 93 in *Moral Concepts*, ed. J. Feinberg = *Essays on Actions and Events*, p. 21.
24. Because weak will has such a broad scope, Aristotle discusses it in *De Anima* 3.11 as well as in his ethical works. Some ethically oriented discussions have, of course, shed useful light on general psychological questions.
25. Either Euripides' version (in the great speech, *Medea* 1019–80) or Ovid's, at the beginning of *Metamorphoses* 7.
26. In what follows I owe a great deal to C. C. W. Taylor's valuable discussion of the shortcomings of 'Plato, Hare and Davidson on Akrasia'.
27. A somewhat similar position is taken by Gary Watson in 'Skepticism about Weakness of Will', esp. pp. 338–9.
28. Taylor, op. cit., p. 518.
29. Taylor's account of Hare does not do full justice to the complexities of his discussion in Ch. 5 of *Freedom and Reason*, 'Backsliding'. But I am not sure whether Hare's discussion there is fully compatible with the important texts which Taylor does discuss.
30. 'Socrates on Akrasia', pp. 83–4. It is of course no accident that Vlastos acknowledges inspiration from the work of Davidson in this article. But his is nevertheless a highly convincing account of Socrates' approach in this dialogue (and in many other early or transitional dialogues, including the *Gorgias*).
31. See Taylor, pp. 203–4 in *Plato: Protagoras* for a summary discussion of the evolution of Plato's views on weak will.
32. e.g. *EN* 1.13, 1102b16–25.

33. *EN* 7.3, 1147a31–4.
34. *EE* 2.8.12–3.
35. He is careful to say (2.8.14) that the man is not compelled as a whole, as long as one of these 'parts', reason and appetite, determines the action.
36. As Aristotle himself does apropos of weak will, *EN* 9.8, 1168b34–5.
37. Cf. Adkins, *Merit and Responsibility*, p. 320: 'Any psychology which divides, or seems by its language to divide, the personality into independent and conflicting functions—intellect, passion, and appetite, or any others—will be faced with Aristotle's difficulties, as soon as its users grow analytical. If one function interferes with or inhibits another, surely the man acts under constraint: how then can he be held responsible for any action performed while in this condition?'
38. Op. cit., pp. 432, 434.
39. *Antiteinousi*; cf. *EN* 1102b17–18.
40. 'Sceptical Strategies', p. 79.
41. *PHP* 4.4.24, p. 256 $\doteq$ SVF 3.476.
42. D.L. 7.93.
43. See Bonhoeffer, *Epictet*, p. 254. *Enkrateia* is 'unconquerable knowledge of what appears according to Right Reason' (*Ecl.* 2.61.11–2; cf. D.L. 7.93). *Sôphrosunê* is 'knowledge of what should be chosen, what should be avoided and what is neither of these' (SVF 3.266; *Ecl.* 2.59.8–9). At *PHP* 4.2.39–44 Galen gives a dualistic interpretation of *akrasia, enkrateia, sôphrosunê*, and *akolasia* which is modelled on Aristotle. He argues that Chrysippus does not disagree with this, but this distorts the text Galen is discussing. See p. 171 ff. below.
44. The meaning of *akrasia* in Epictetus seems compatible with Chrysippus' usage: *Diss.* 2.16.45; 2.18.6; 3.1.8.
45. *De Anima*, p. 27.4–8. Or Epicurus may be meant. Cf. *Mantissa*, p. 118.6–9.
46. *Virt. Mor.* 7, 446e–447a, cf. 3, 441c–d.
47. See Long, *Hellenistic Philosophy*, p. 177.
48. For Hare, many cases of weak will are cases where the assent was insincere (see *Language of Morals*, p. 20). This is one of the ways he uses to eliminate full-blooded cases of weak will.
49. *Virt. Mor.* 447b–c.
50. For a different non-dualistic account of what Aristotle called *akrasia*, cf. Melden, *Free Action*, p. 157.
51. I hesitate to attribute serious misunderstandings of the orthodox position to Posidionius, Galen's source for much of the discussion.

But Posidonius did disagree with the early Stoics about these fundamental issues.

52. *PHP* 4.2.12, p. 240.
53. At *PHP* 4.3.7, p. 248 Galen himself suggests how this phrase could
be reconciled with Chrysippus' views; but he does not let this hinder
his polemical attack.
54. Cf. SVF 1.205.
55. For this connection of Pythagoras and Plato, cf. *Dox. Gr.* pp. 389–90.
PHP 4.7.39, p. 290 suggests that Posidonius may have originated the
connection. He certainly exploited it.
56. *Ecl.* 2.38–9.
57. *EN* 1105b21–3.
58. See J. Dillon, *The Middle Platonists*, pp. 77–8.
59. *Virt. Mor.* 444b–445a; cf. 449d 'the greater and the lesser'.
60. See Albinus *Epitome*, ch. 24; *Virt. Mor.* 444a–b; Posidonius fr. 31. It is
sometimes called *to hormêtikon* too: *Ecl.* 2.117; *Leg. Alleg.* 2.99; 3.131.
61. This time in the main account of Stoic ethics, rather than in prefatory
material: *Ecl.* 2.89.4–90.6.
62. See Bonhoeffer, *Epictet*, p. 284 on the Platonic influence. I. G. Kidd
has recently shown its Posidonian affinities in some detail
('*Euemptôsia*').
63. See e.g. Posidonius frr. 31, 166 and *Virt. Mor.* 446e. Note too Galen's
metaphor *aphêniazein* at *PHP* 4.2.27, p. 244; 4.5.18, p. 262. Philo
retains both the one-horse (*Leg. Alleg.* 2.99) and the two-horse (*Leg.
Alleg.* 3.118) versions. The difference between bipartition and
tripartition was not considered to be of critical importance by many
eclectic philosophers. The precedent for this occasional indifference
is to be found both in Plato and in Aristotle (see D. A. Rees,
'Bipartition of the Soul in the Early Academy', for example). Galen
seems to be more rigid in his preference for tripartition than either
Posidonius or Plato. Aristotle's view on the matter is notoriously
flexible.
64. *PHP* 4.2.8–18, pp. 240–2.
65. Arius does not seem to be referring to Chrysippus' reluctant
recognition that sometimes passions continue after the judgement
which originally produced them has stopped. But this aspect of
Chrysippus' discussion of the passions is sufficiently puzzling in
itself that comparisons with this passage of Arius cannot be certain.
66. It is possible too that Arius was misled by Chrysippus' occasionally
casual language in discussions of the passions.
67. I do not mean to deny that Chrysippus refined some of the
terminology used to describe the theory and elaborated the
definitions of various subtypes of passions.

68. See *Diss.* 1.4.27–29 for Chrysippean remarks which justify this approach (esp. 1.4.28): 'In order to find out that the doctrines which produce a smooth flow [sc. of life] and generate freedom from passions are not false, take up my books and you will learn that the views which make me free of passions are in agreement and harmonious with nature.' It is interesting to recall that D.L.'s account of vicious actions (7.97) gives particular emphasis to the reaction of men to the events of the external world which are beyond their control: *kataplêxis, tapeinotês, douleia, aterpia, dusthumia, perilupia.*

69. *Ecl.* 2.92–3, *TD* 4.22 ff. and Epictetus *Diss.* 2.18.8 ff. suggest that the *kinêsis* and the *hexis* which govern it are related much as Aristotle said that bad actions and bad habits are related. Repeated bad actions produce the bad *hexis* which causes further bad actions.

70. Cicero seems to misunderstand his source when he discusses *spanis* at *TD* 4.21. Other accounts make it a proper subtype of *epithumia* (D.L. 7.113; SVF 3.397).

71. The propositional element is mentioned explicitly in the definitions of some passions, as shown by the word *dokounta* in the definition of *orgê* (*Ecl.* 2.91). Cf. *philarguria* at D.L. 7.111. Most definitions, though, leave this propositional element to be understood by inference. It is in the general description of passions that it comes into prominence.

72. Regularly termed *doxa*, a weak or incorrect assent. Chrysippus' view is reported at D.L. 7.111 and reflected at *Ecl.* 2.88–9.

73. *TD* 4.14; 4.65; Clement *Strom.* 2.13.59 = SVF 3.377; *Strom.* 1.17.83–4; Epictetus *Diss.* 3.24.23. This analysis of responsibility has a corollary in the Stoic theories about the 'cure' of the passions. Chrysippus held that the real and proper cure lay in changing the erroneous opinions which lead regularly to such acts of improper assent. Origen (SVF 3.474) makes it clear that the 'first-aid' for *pathê* which is compatible with any set of ethical principles was not regarded as the true cure. Cicero makes the same point in his discussion of cures, based ultimately on Chrysippus' *Therapeutikon*, i.e. book 4 of the *Peri Pathôn* (see *TD* 4.58 ff., esp. 60, 62–3). *TD* 3.77 suggests that Chrysippus was deliberately adding this 'first-aid' as an adaptation of the strict position of Cleanthes, who said that passions could only be cured by means of a total reform of a man's opinions.

74. 'Fear' is a slight exception to this. See below, n. 85.

75. Abbreviated accounts sometimes identify these impulses with their results, as at *Ecl.* 2.90. But the fuller accounts make the distinction clear.

76. See *Ecl.* 2.89, e.g. This is clinched by Chrysippus' reference to 'the impulse to contraction' of the soul at SVF 3.466, p. 117.28 = *PHP* 4.7.14, p. 284. DeLacy mistranslates the phrase ad loc.

77. On passions as affective responses in the soul, compare Lloyd, 'Emotion and Decision', pp. 238-9.

78. Except in so far as we respond to these physical feelings in a certain way.

79. Cf. Kenny, *Action, Emotion and Will*, p. 55.

80. On this topic, which is not often discussed with the attention it deserves, I follow in large measure the views of Bonhoeffer, *Epictet*, pp. 266 ff.

81. Compare Epictetus *Diss.* 4.1.84. A distinction roughly comparable to this was made by Epicurus, who made present pleasure and pain basic (D.L. 10.34) and fear based on the expectation of evil subordinate to it. In the letter to Menoeceus (D.L. 10.125) he says that 'that which does not cause trouble when present gives vain grief when it is expected'.

82. *Ench.* 2; *Diss.* 2.1.11 ff.; 3.2.3 ff.; 3.22.61; 4.1.84.

83. At *Ecl.* 2.90 we are told that the opinion that something good or bad is coming is the cause of the erroneous *orexis* or *ekklisis*. This is compatible with their being impulses to pursuit or avoidance, since such opinions are regularly supposed to stimulate such behaviour.

84. *TD* 3.24-5; 4.11 ff.; pseudo-Andronicus at SVF 3.391, D.L. 7.110-14. But the definitions in the *Excerpta Menonis* cols. 2.39-3.7 include the important distinctions.

85. It is apparent from one or two texts that some allowance was made for the affective aspect of fear, though there is no evidence at all that this was done for desire. At *Ecl.* 2.90.3 *lupeisthai* and *phobeisthai* are grouped together, and this might lead us to suspect that they have more in common than the texts so far considered suggest. Similarly, at *TD* 4.15 Cicero gives definitions of pleasure and pain which highlight their affective nature; the definition of desire as *effrenata adpetentia* does not indicate affectivity, since it refers only to excess in the pursuit of something. But his description of fear picks out, in addition to its character as the cause of avoidance behaviour (*fuga*), an affective aspect too (*recessus quidam animi*). But the principal evidence for the recognition of an affective element in fear is at *Ecl.* 2.90. For here we read: 'Fear is an avoidance disobedient to reason, and the cause of it is the judgement that something bad is coming, the judgement that it is to be avoided in this way having in it the stimulative and fresh.' This last phrase, *to kinêtikon kai prosphaton*, represents an extension to fear of the sort of affective element which other texts lead us to expect only for pleasure and pain. The text of this entire section is disputed, and Bonhoeffer discusses the problems it presents at some length (*Epictet*, pp. 271-3). I agree that Wachsmuth is wrong to delete the *kai* from this phrase, which he

seems to do because he takes *prosphaton* to mean 'temporally recent'.
Bonhoeffer convincingly argues that this is wrong. But Bonhoeffer
also accepts the usual supplement to the account of *epithumia: prosphaton tou ontôs auto orekton einai.* The effect of this is to extend the
unusual application of *prosphaton* to desire as well as to fear. It is
tempting to do so, since there is a lacuna in this section (lines 16–18).
But the supplement to the account of desire is unnecessary. Even
with the supplement its definition will not be parallel to that of fear,
since the adverb *ataktôs* is not present in the account of fear as it is in
that of desire. But the other two texts considered in this note (*TD* 4.15
and *Ecl.* 2.90.3) suggest strongly that fear, unlike desire, was given a
subordinate affective aspect and there is no reason to suppose that
the same was done for desire which is always treated *solely* in terms of
pursuit behaviour. I would also retain the *houtôs* of the MSS in line
13, in place of Heeren's intrusive emendation to *ontôs.* We should,
then, acknowledge that some Stoic did concede that fear too had an
affective aspect subordinate to its principal significance as a certain
kind (NB *houtôs*) of avoidance behaviour. But it is doubtful whether
we should follow Pohlenz (*Die Stoa,* vol. ii, p. 80) in supposing that
Chrysippus made this concession to the more usual notion of what
fear involves. We should recall that *Ecl.* 2.89–90 shows other signs of
post-Chrysippean developments, probably Posidonian, and that the
addition of *prosphaton* to the account of fear conflicts with the explication of its meaning at *Ecl.* 2.89.2–3. But certainty is impossible.

86. One point may be dealt with briefly. Sometimes the adjective 'fresh'
is applied not to the opinion but to the object about which the
opinion is held; see, e.g., *Ecl.* 2.90 and *PHP* 4.7.5, p. 280. Bonhoeffer
(*Epictet,* pp. 266–8) explains this variation in usage and makes it clear
that it is not significant. The application of the adjective to the
opinion is primary.

87. *PHP* 4.7.1–5 = SVF 3.481. Bonhoeffer, *Epictet,* pp. 269–70.

88. Pohlenz (*Die Stoa,* vol. i, p. 148 and vol. ii, p. 80) ignores Bonhoeffer's
arguments and claims that Zeno interpreted 'fresh' in terms of time
while Chrysippus innovated by interpeting it in terms of force. But
TD 3.74–5 attributes a 'force' interpretation to Zeno, and
Posidonius had grounds for giving Chrysippus a temporal interpretation, even if he did exaggerate it.

89. *Ecl.* 2.90, confirmed by pseudo-Andronicus' definitions of pleasure
and pain at SVF 3.391 and by other texts.

90. On this clause see the Stoically inspired ch. 7 of pseudo-Plutarch
On Desire and Pain (*De Libidine et Aegritudine*) and *Excerpta Menonis*
2.44–5.

91. *TD* 3.74–5.

92. I interpret this sentence as an explanation of the previous, not as the addition of a new point. Heine, in his commentary, correctly refers to *Ecl.* 2.89.2–3 as a parallel explanation of 'fresh'.

93. *PHP* 4.7.12–17, p. 284 = SVF 3.466.

94. There is some doubt about what *tautês* refers to here. Galen takes it as referring to the opinion at 4.7.18, immediately following this text. This is the most natural reading in the context. But the *kai* may introduce a new point. Moreover, *hormê* is the nearest antecedent, and Posidonius (at 4.7.36, p. 288) seems to have taken it to refer to *hormê*. In this text Chrysippus says that the contraction of the soul, i.e. the affective reaction, and the impulse to it relax together, and Posidonius (loc. cit.) also supposes that the impulse and the contraction are closely connected. Therefore, I suspect that the correct reference is to *doxa* here, as the context suggests, and that Posidonius is interpeting this difficult and ambiguous passage according to his own polemical intent. This problem is closely connected to the textual problem discussed in n. 95.

95. The *mê* is transmitted by the MSS here, but omitted at the parallel text 4.7.37, p. 288. Editors have either deleted it here or supplied it there. Müller and von Arnim take the first course and DeLacy the second. I follow DeLacy with some reservations in view of the uncertainties mentioned in n. 94. The suspicion remains that Galen did not fully understand what he read, hampered by his dependence on Posidonius and his own hostility to Chrysippus. Note too that all the quotations from Chrysippus marked as such by DeLacy are not accurate; 4.7.36 is supposed to be a re-quotation of the text here, but *tês hormês diamenousês* is substituted for *tautês diamenousês*.

96. Op. cit., p. 418.

97. See n. 85 on fear, if the modification there is in fact Chrysippus'. Also below, pp. 175 ff. on preliminary passions.

98. n. 94.

99. *Epictet*, pp. 281–2. My only qualification to his solution is that he extends the importance of the 'fresh opinion' to all the passions. But since the problem only arises for *lupê*, he need not have done so.

100. Cf. *TD* 3.61: *oportere, rectum esse, ad officium* [cf. *kathêkon*] *pertinere ferre illud aegre quod acciderit.*

101. *TD* 4.14. In this and other passages the definition of pleasure is analogous.

102. Thus Posidonius' substitution of *hormê* for *doxa* is not justified. Although the judgement and its own impulse are always found together, the judgement which Chrysippus said continued is not that which directly governs the impulse to contraction.

103. At *TD* 3.52 which reports Chrysippus' views, we have another

instance of his use of several opinions to explain pain. For here it is said that the contraction of pain may be made worse by the additional opinion that we are at fault for the presence of the bad thing. This text confirms that Chrysippus did give temporal factors a role in his analysis of passions such as pain, but not the only (*non sunt in hoc omnia*) role nor even the most important. Chrysippus seems to be analysing the force of sudden events to stimulate passions more strongly than other events in terms of the opinions we form.

104. *TD* 3.52.

105. It is a shame that Galen has not given us the means to interpret Chrysippus' reference to the causes of laughing. It may have helped with the interpretation of this point.

106. *Pathêtikê phlegmonê*. The text is *PHP* 4.7.25–7, p. 286 = SVF 3.467. Note here Chrysippus' phrase 'as though they were sated' with the passion. This and the reference to inflammation are good examples of the sort of vivid language which Posidonius pounced on as indications of Chrysippus' recognition of phenomena which were inconsistent with his psychology.

107. Is this the 'interference' referred to in the text of Chrysippus quoted on p. 149?

108. On the basis of the text of *On Passions* 2 considered above (SVF 3.467).

109. See also SVF 3.474 = Origin *Contra Celsum* 1.64 and 8.51.

110. At *Fin.* 4.23 Cicero praises Panaetius for not undertaking in his consolation for Tubero to argue that pain is not a bad thing. This may only mean that he limited his attention to 'first aid', not that he denied that pain was indifferent.

111. See e.g. *Fin.* 3.21, 33–4, 43–8. Also *ND* 1.16. Seneca gives us (in *Ep.* 74) a fairly orthodox discussion of how the error about whether something is good or bad in this orthodox sense opens men up to passions by making them think that their happiness depends on things ultimately beyond their control. Cf. *Ep.* 75.11.

112. *PHP* 4.5.24 ff., pp. 264 ff., 4.7.6 ff., pp. 280 ff.

113. Which Cicero provides at *TD* 3.68; 4.61. The *Tusculans* do, however, show signs of the unorthodox interpretation (3.24–5; cf. *Fin.* 2.13), which suggests perhaps that Cicero did not himself appreciate the importance of the distinction made by his source. The unorthodox view appears in the Cyrenaic or eclectic discussion of *TD* 3.52–61 which is corrected by the orthodox account in 3.74–8. This passage and book 4 (see esp. 4.11–5, 24–6, 59–61) treat the error about good in the orthodox way.

114. Voelke, *L'Idée*, p. 88 and Philippson, 'Zur Psychologie . . .', p. 163 have interpreted the *pleonasmos* of impulse in this way.

115. *PHP* 4.5.21 = SVF 3.480.

116. *alla kai kata to epi pleon ekpeptōkenai pros tauta tou kata phusin.*
117. The standard definition of passion: D.L. 7.110; *Ecl.* 2.88.
118. *PHP* 4.2.8–18, pp. 240–2 = SVF 3.462.
119. Closest to my eventual solution are Bonhoeffer, *Epictet*, pp. 262–3 and Sandbach, *The Stoics*, p. 61. Von Fritz, *RE* Band 10A, p. 120 also adumbrates it. The connection of the excess to the poor tone (*tonos*) of the soul, which is emphasized by E. Bréhier (*Chrysippe*, pp. 246–9), Philippson ('Zur Psychologie', pp. 162 ff.), and Voelke (*L'Idée*, pp. 87 ff.), is correct as far as it goes. But it must be stressed that Chrysippus' own account of excess, which we have, does not bring it in. The tone of the soul is the *hexis* which if correct produces correct assents and impulses and if not correct produces improper assents and an excessive impulse. *Tonos* is a characteristic of the *hexis hormētikē*, but 'excessiveness' is a characteristic of the *kinēsis.*
120. The phrasing in the Greek makes it clear that these movements are movements in the soul, i.e. impulses. Cf. *Ecl.* 2.87.4–7. Cf. 'in his soul' below.
121. *apestrammenon ton logon.* Cf. *TD.* 3.24 *aspernans rationem.*
122. A reference to Zeno, whose definition Chrysippus is explaining? Or should we read 'we outline' with Müller?
123. DeLacy, whose translation I sometimes follow, takes *metaballein* as 'change his pace'.
124. e.g. *Ecl.* 2.90, *Strom.* 2.13.59 = SVF 3.377, *TD* 3.7, 3.24, 4.47.
125. It is characteristic of Galen's polemical approach that he explicitly considers how 'irrational' should be interpreted (*PHP* 4.4.9 ff., pp. 252 ff.) and does not even raise the possibility that Right Reason may be the reason disobedience to which is intended.
126. SVF 3.386; *Ecl.* 2.89.15–6; *TD* 4.11; 4.61. This normative Right Reason is also called 'the conclusive' or 'proving reason' (*ho hairōn logos*) and is mentioned in the definitions of passion at *Ecl.* 2.88.9 and in the *Excerpta Menonis* col. 2.29–30. On 'the conclusive' or 'proving reason' see *Virt. Mor.* 449c, D.L. 7.108, *Comm. Not.* 1070b. A possible Platonic model for the phrase is at *Crito* 48c. *Hairesis* is defined as a form of correct impulse at *Ecl.* 2.87 (see Appendix 2).
127. D.L. 7.88.
128. Or (see below) to one's own reason just in so far as one has assimilated it to the Right Reason.
129. *Strom.* 2.13.59 = SVF 3.377; *Ecl.* 2.88–9; SVF 3.446, 391; *TD* 4.11; 4.47.
130. SVF 3.390 = *Virt. Mor.* 450c–d.
131. *Strom.* 2.13.59 = SVF 3.377.
132. *Diss.* 4.1.84.
133. D.L. 7.87–8; cf. *Ep.* 124.14.

134. Cf. Marcus 2.16 where disobedience to this is linked to some of the passions.
135. On the *daimôn* cf. the similar view of Posidonius fr. 187 = *PHP* 5.6.3 ff., pp. 326 ff. In this text the goal of living according to reason is contrasted to living according to passion.
136. *PHP* 5.5.4–5, p. 326.
137. SVF 3.175 = *St. Rep.* 1037f–1038a. Cf. *Ep.* 95.40.
138. D.L. 7.88. and Epictetus *Ench.* 26. *Boulêsis* is an impulse and thus the *hormêta* of Zeus mentioned by Marcus in a discussion of passions (9.1.4) are the events willed by Zeus. On the topic of god's impulses see *Diss.* 4.1.100; 4.1.89. According to *ND.* 2.58 god's impulses are his providential will and they are impulses like those of men. On Nature's will see Voelke, *L'Idée*, pp. 106–9.
139. See ch. 4(*a*) above on the assimilation of human to divine will and cf. Marcus 9.28 and in general Zeller, *Die Philosophie der Griechen*, ed. 5, vol. iii 1, pp. 226 ff. If it is true that the will of Zeus is what causes the events of the providentially determined world order (the disposition or *dioikêsis* of things), then the assimilation of human to the divine will guarantees that our human actions will be in complete consistency with the fated events of our own lives. Also Voelke, *L'Idée*, pp. 99 ff.
140. *Dox. Gr.*, p. 323 col. a.
141. SVF 2.975.
142. See for example the fragment at SVF 2.1003, and also SVF 3.308 = D.L. 7.128, SVF 3.314, 332, 613, 614.
143. Note the coupling of *tên kath' hautous* with *phusikên* in the text translated on p. 156.
144. *PHP* 4.6.35, p. 276 = SVF 3.478.
145. It is interesting that Marcus (7.20) speaks of doing what 'the constitution of man' wills much as he and other Stoics speak of doing the will of Zeus.
146. M. Kubara, 'Acrasia, Human Agency and Normative Psychology', comes to a somewhat similar position in his attempt to eliminate the paradox of *akrasia* by viewing the acratic agent as a 'diminished' (p. 230) or downgraded version of one's normal self.
147. *PHP* 4.6.35, p. 278.
148. SVF 3.390 = *Virt. Mor.* 450c–d. They do not displace our reason as such.
149. D.L. 7.89.
150. Galen (*PHP* 4.3.7, p. 248) in fact suggests that the difficult phrase 'without reason and judgement' (see above, p. 156) may have been intended by Chrysippus in exactly this sense, 'without circumspection' (*aneu periskepseôs*). He may be right, though the phrase is used

only in reference to customary ways of speaking. Characteristically, Galen does not let this insight affect his polemic. Cf. too *PHP*4.6.29, p. 276 *aperiskeptoteron kai aneu epistrophês logikês*.

151. SVF 2.83, 841.
152. *PHP* 4.6.11, p. 272 = SVF 3.473.
153. *PHP* 4.6.41 ff., p. 278 = SVF 3.478. Von Arnim thinks the words in question are a quotation; DeLacy is right to take them as a paraphrase by Galen.
154. Recall too the orthodox definition of *enkrateia* as *epistêmên anhuperbaton tôn kata ton orthon logon phanentôn* (*Ecl.* 2.61); cf. SVF 3.275.
155. *Ecl.* 2.93 and D.L. 7.115.
156. *Hairesis* is an impulse to the good.
157. *Arrostêma* is also defined here as a *nosêma* coupled with weakness. I shall not go into the various refinements of Chrysippus on the doctrine of disease in the soul.
158. In this account of disease in the soul I follow the sound remarks of Bonhoeffer, *Epictet*, pp. 275-7.
159. p. 314.
160. Galen goes on to give a tendentious criticism of this position.
161. The difference between assent as a *kinêsis* and the disposition of the soul which constitutes a persistent opinion is important here.
162. Cf. Seneca *De Vita Beata* 8.6.
163. *Ecl.* 2.66.14-67.4 = SVF 3.560.
164. SVF 3.392; Marcus 8.1; *TD* 4.23-4 uses this to explain diseases in the soul. See also *Ecl.* 2.62.23-4, 63.3-5 and Clement SVF 2.121.
165. SVF 3.471-471a = *PHP* 5.2.20-5.3.11, pp. 298-308. It is hard not to sympathize with Galen's criticisms of Chrysippus for calling this sort of thing a 'part' of the soul.
166. Thus Arius describes the opinion which causes an emotion as *asthenês hupolêpsis* (*Ecl.* 2.89).
167. On inconsistency and vacillation see also *Tranq.* 2.7-8.
168. SVF 3.490. For inconsistency as a sign of moral failings, cf. *Diss.* 2.22.6 ff. and 25 and *TD* 4.24, 29-31.
169. *PHP* 4.6.1-11, pp. 270-2.
170. *Orexis*, in its normative form (i.e. correct *orexis*), is defined as *logikê hormê epi ti hoson chrê hêdon*. On the text of this definition see Ch. 3 n. 53. A correct *orexis* is an impulse to something which is satisfying to the degree to which it should be. This notion of the proper degree, if it were better understood, would help elucidate the notion of 'excess'. As a *pathos*, incorrect *orexis* (i.e. *epithumia*) is excessive. The two terms *hoson chrê* and *pleonazousa* are correlative.
171. *Ecl.* 2.88.
172. *PHP* 4.5.6, p. 260 = SVF 3.476.

173. The statement in Arius (*Ecl.* 2.92.18–20) that some passions are distinguished not by their objects (*to eph' hôi gignetai*) but by the peculiarities of their movements may be a reference to the movement of the *hormê* itself. But more likely it is a reference to the differences among the movements in the soul which the movement of *hormê* brings about, i.e. various distinctions among the contractions and expansions etc. These affective reactions are occasionally identified with the impulse itself, but this is a result of the search for brevity and punch in the account of passions, not technical accuracy.

174. *PHP* 4.4.24, p. 256 = SVF 3.476.

175. See also *Ep.* 96 on this and Voelke, *L'Idée*, pp. 196–7.

176. Fictive, but not completely artificial. See *Tranq.* 13.2.

177. *Tranq.* 1.10.

178. See below, Ch. 6(*d*).

179. Cf. Marcus 6.50.

180. See *Ecl.* 2.99.14–15; 102.20–103.4.

181. *kouphôs . . . kai aneimenôs, Ench.* 2.2. See also *Diss.* 4.7.12.; *Tranq.* 13.3; *Ben.* 4.34.4 and 4.39.4; Marcus 4.1; 5.20; 6.50; 8.41.

182. Marcus 11.37.

183. *Ep.* 75.11.

184. *TD* 4.26.

185. 'Choose' here represents the Latin *expetere* which is the standard translation for *haireisthai.*

186. *Ecl.* 2.93.

187. SVF 3.386.

188. For example *Virt. Mor.* 449f, 441d in paraphrases of Stoic texts. Also ch. 7 of *De Libidine et Aegritudine.*

189. *TD* 4.14 and elsewhere.

190. It is also noteworthy that even a genuine bad thing, such as folly, is not enough to justify a contraction in the soul (*TD* 3.68); for Posidonius' criticisms see *PHP* 4.7.6–7, p. 282 = SVF 3.481. At *TD* 4.61 Cicero emphasizes that even in the case of a genuine good, one can respond with elation in a way that goes beyond Right Reason. What, if anything, he has in mind here is not clear, but see below, pp. 174–5 on the need for one's entire life to be in order if a genuine *eupatheia* is to be possible.

191. The key evidence was in *Diss.* 2.6.6–10.

192. SVF 3.377; *Diss.* 4.1.84.

193. *Virt. Mor.* 450e–451b; 444c.

194. Note his misinterpretation of Chrysippus' runner analogy in *PHP* 4.2.28 ff. This also turns up at *De Ira* 1.7.2–4; 2.35.1–2. Note especially the reference (similar to Galen's) to the inertia of body weight at 1.7.4 and Plutarch's *proekthein* at *Virt. Mor.* 446de. Seneca,

Galen, and Plutarch are using a common source, which must be
Posidonius, for this criticism.

195. Recall the contrast between the Chrysippean notion of excess and
the eclectic version, which shows up at *Ecl.* 2.88–9. On one page
'excessive' is glossed by 'disobedient to Right Reason (*tôi hairounti
logôi*)' and on the next there is the strange reference to a man in a
passion being swept away by the *sphodrotês* of the passion 'as though
by some disobedient horse'. No doubt Posidonius is behind this too.

196. Or change his pace, on DeLacy's interpretation of *metaballein*.

197. This analogy brings out the imperatival character of Right Reason
quite clearly.

198. *heôs tosoutou heôs autos axioi.* I agree with DeLacy in excising *kai* before
the second *heôs*, although nothing vital turns on it. On the connection of this symmetry and a proper estimate of *axia*, cf. Marcus 4.32.

199. Cf. *Ench.* 8; 31.1; 32.

200. *PHP* 4.4.16–18, p. 254 = SVF 3.476. Fear and desire are cited.

201. *PHP* 4.4.24–26, p. 256 = SVF 3.476. I think Müller was right to
excise *êtoi apatheis eisi* at p. 256 line 11 as a gloss. DeLacy restores it.

202. The word *tonôi* used here (*hoi tonôi trechontes*) is not a reference to the
soul's *tonos*, but simply means 'vigorously'.

203. *Diss.* 2.6.6–10.

204. *PHP* 4.4.31, p. 256, still SVF 3.476.

205. *PHP* 4.4.32, pp. 256–8, also SVF 3.476. Galen dully asks, 'What does
he mean by "in this sense"?'

206. *PHP* 4.4.13–4, p. 262 = SVF 3.479.

207. Dyroff, *Die Ethik der alten Stoa*, p. 174 is sceptical about Chrysippus'
role in systematizing the doctrine (although he misunderstands *Virt.
Mor.* 449c; there is no suggestion that the rest of the chapter is not
Chrysippean). On p. 98 and p. 173 n. 1 he cites evidence suggesting
that other *eupatheiai*, such as *euphrosunê* and *tharros*, were as important
for Chrysippus as the canonical trio. See Epictetus *Diss.* 2.1 on the
importance of *tharros* beside *eulabeia*. A. C. Lloyd also expresses
doubt about the origin and date of the formal doctrine of *eupatheiai*
('Emotion and Decision', pp. 233–4). Pohlenz (*Die Stoa*, vol. i, p. 152
and vol. ii, p. 83) thinks the term is post-Chrysippean. Rist (*Stoic
Philosophy*, pp. 31, 73) thinks that the doctrine if not the term goes
back to Zeno; soo too Grimal, *Sénèque*, pp. 331–2. It is clear that
Chrysippus distinguished *chara* (SVF 3.439, 440; 2.900; *St. Rep.*
1046b) and *eulabeia* (SVF 3.175) in the canonical sense.

If, as Pohlenz says (vol. ii, p. 83) the term *eupatheia* is a *contradictio in
adiecto* and therefore unlikely to have been Chrysippus' coinage,
then perhaps we can follow Sandbach (*The Stoics*, p. 67) when he
suggests that Cicero's term *constantia* (*TD* 4.12–14, cf. Voelke, *L'Idée*,

p. 91 n. 2) derives from *eustatheia*. Sandbach thought this would have been a simple error on Cicero's part, but this is unlikely. Could it not be that *eustatheia* was an earlier Stoic term for *eupatheia*? *Eustatheis hormai* do constitute a smoothly flowing life and reflect the consistency of opinions and actions. On *eustatheia* see Epictetus *Diss.* 1.29. Also note that Epictetus *Diss.* 1.4.27 ff. shows the relationship of *apatheia* to *euroia* and *têi phusei sumphônia* for Chrysippus. See *TD* 3.18 on the relation of *apatheia* to *constantia*. On the other hand, for this suggestion to be appealing, one would have to agree with Pohlenz's rather scrupulous objections to the term *eupatheia*.

208. Is this the *phronimê hormê* of *Ecl.*2.68-9?
209. Cf. Epictetus *Diss.* 1.4.27-9.
210. For *apatheia* and virtue see SVF 3.201.
211. *Ecl.* 2.72, cf. 2.73 and *Ep.* 66.5.
212. *Ecl.* 2.58.
213. *Ecl.* 2.69; D.L. 7.98.
214. D.L. 7.94.
215. SVF 3.432; D.L. 7.116.
216. *aspasmos* and *agapêsis*. Bonhoeffer, *Epictet*, p. 287; Voelke, *L'Idée*, pp. 59-60.
217. *Epictet*, pp. 285-98; cf. pp. 233-48. He does, however, make a regrettable distinction of *pathê* and *eupatheiai* into his categories of *Gefühle* and *Willensakten*. These categories correspond to the real distinction between future-oriented and reactive passions; but these foreign categories obscure the important point which Bonhoeffer almost admits despite himself, that the reactive passions (*Gefühle*) are properly kinds of 'action' (i.e. *Willensregungen*, see *Epictet*, p. 285). At SVF 3.85 Chrysippus calls the *eupatheia* joy a *katorthôsis*.
218. See Dillon, op. cit., pp. 77-8 and 151. For Philo see SVF 3.436.
219. *Ecl.* 2.97.
220. *Ecl.* 2.58.
221. *The Stoics*, p. 67.
222. *Virt. Mor.* 449a.
223. SVF 3.437. Cf. SVF 3.434.
224. Cf. *Ep.* 95.57; *Diss.* 4.8.3.
225. There is no correct counterpart to irrational contraction (*TD* 4.14) for that would be a correct response to the presence of something bad. But nothing bad ever happens to the sage.
226. If, that is, anyone noticed: see SVF 3.539, p. 144.
227. I wish to thank Prof. J. M. Rist for his persistent criticism of my earlier views on this topic. He cannot be held responsible for their present form. I am also grateful to Michael Frede for discussions of his view of *pathê*, which differs from my own.

228. This is not a Stoic theory, as Yon, the Budé editor, *seems* to think, pp. 39–41 and n. 3 to pp. xxviii. His discussion, however, is quite unclear.

229. I am not convinced, as Bonhoeffer, *Epictet*, p. 252 n. 1 is, that *Academica* 2.30 contains a hint of this doctrine too: *quem ad modum primo visa nos pellerent, deinde adpetitio ab his pulsa sequeretur, tum ut sensus ad res percipiendas intenderemus* (reading *ut* with the MSS and Reid).

230. *Ep.* 113.18. See above, Ch. 3 n. 193.

231. Bonhoeffer, loc. cit., argues that the unorthodoxy here is only apparent. But he is overreaching the evidence in his effort to keep Seneca orthodox—which he demonstrably is not on other important points. There are *no* orthodox references to preliminary impulse.

232. *Propatheiai*, although they are no more passions than *eupatheiai* are. It is not clear when the term itself originated.

233. *Noctes Atticae* 19.1.14–20 = fr. 9. Holler (*Seneca*, pp. 70–1) thinks that Gellius is wrong about its orthodoxy. But he is convinced (incorrectly in my view) that the doctrine of *propatheiai originated* with Posidonius. I simplify by omitting some phrases which Gellius gives in both Greek and Latin.

234. Gellius' statement is puzzling. The word is not found elsewhere in Epictetus or in Stoic fragments.

235. *De Ira* 1.16.7 = SVF 1.215. This text is connected to *propatheia* by Hadot, *Seneca*, p. 132 n. 38 and p. 183.

236. Prof. Rist (in correspondence) compares these responses to *eixis* or irrational yielding to presentations. The sage, then, is reverting to a pre-rational stage when he has a *propatheia*. But I am reluctant to accept that a sage has such a pre-rational disposition.

237. Cf. also *TD* 3.13 *necessarium*. Seneca also refers to such reactions in similar terms.

238. *Virt Mor.* 449ab, which certainly refer to Chrysippus (contra Holler, op. cit., p. 71). On the odd word *suneorseis* see Bonhoeffer, *Epictet*, p. 310.

239. He also deals with *eupatheiai* here.

240. *MA* 703b5–8; *DA* 432b30–2. Cf. Rist, *Stoic Philosophy*, pp. 42–3.

241. Galen *PHP*4.2.2, p. 248 lets *dêxeis* slip into his list of genuine passions. This is probably an error, but see n. 242 on Epictetus' use of *daknein*.

242. Epictetus is firm on this in the fragment quoted above and in *Diss.* 3.24.108: 'when the presentation bites you—for this is not in your power'. Epictetus also uses 'bite' of one's voluntary reaction based on an opinion: *Ench.* 46.2; *Diss.* 3.2.8; 3.24.117; 4.6.10; 4.8.23; 4.10.23. This only emphasizes the similarity of the two phenomena and so the difficulty of the Stoic position.

243. 2.1–4.

244. Shivering when cold water is splashed on you; a revulsion from certain tactile sensations—2.2.1.
245. 2.2.5 *omnia ista motus sunt animorum moveri nolentium, nec adfectus sed principia proludentia adfectibus.*
246. 2.2.2; cf. 2.4.1–2. NB 2.3.4 *numquam autem impetus sine adsensu mentis est* and cf. 2.1.4. *Const. Sap.* 10.4 should be compared too.
247. 2.3.1–2; cf. 2.1.2. Some of these seem to me to depend on psychic reactions: pallor, tears, deep sighs, etc.
248. But note that he includes in this the sudden *announcement* of a peril.
249. Hadot, *Seneca*, p. 132 n. 41 juxtaposes *Ep.* 113.18 with passages of *De Ira* which deal with *propatheia.*
250. The standard example 'walking' is used there.
251. So Bonhoeffer in his full discussion of *propatheiai, Epictet,* pp. 307–11; also Hadot, op. cit., pp. 131–3; 182–4. Further bibliography on *propatheiai* includes Holler, *Seneca* esp. pp. 21–4, 68–72; Pohlenz, *Die Stoa,* vol. ii, p. 154; Grimal, *Sénèque,* pp. 331–42, also p. 400 (criticized by Reesor, *Phoenix* 33 (1979), pp. 284–5); Griffin, *Seneca,* pp. 180–1.
252. Pohlenz, loc. cit., thinks he succeeds. But the wording Seneca uses in 1.7 makes this claim implausible. Seneca was trying to avoid committing himself to dualism, but the result is a muddle. On Seneca's tendency to self-contradiction on the details of psychology see Hadot, pp. 90 ff.
253. *Ep.* 71.27 is clear on this. For his dualism see Grimal, op. cit., pp. 398 ff.
254. *Ep.* 57.3–6; 74.30–4; 99.14 ff.; *Cons. Marc.* 7.
255. *Ep.* 11.1–7; 71.29; 74.31–2. Note the Platonic precedent for attributing such *pathê* to the body in *Philebus* 33de and in the *Phaedo.*
256. The term may be his coinage.
257. As at *PHP* 5.5.21, p. 320. *Philebus* 33e would suggest to Posidonius how the Stoic ideal of *apatheia* might be reconciled with such dualism. Cf. *Ep.* 71.27.
258. 'Posidonius on Emotions' p. 207.
259. *Over the Teacups* (Houghton, Mifflin, 1890–1), p. 296.
260. *The Right Stuff* (Bantam, 1980), p. 265.
261. *Freddy's Book* quoted in the *New York Times Book Review,* 23 March 1980, p. 26.

Chapter 6

1. D.L. 7.89.
2. Posidonius criticized Chrysippus on this very point (*PHP* 5.5.9–21, pp. 318–20).
3. For the debate over the *telos* see A. A. Long, 'Carneades and the

Stoic *Telos*', O. Rieth, 'Über das Telos der Stoiker', W. Wiersma, '*Telos* und *Kathêkon*', R. Alpers-Gölz, *Der Begriff Skopos*, pp. 62–106, and I. G. Kidd, 'Stoic Intermediates and the End for Man'.

4. In the case of the development of central doctrines in physics, I think there is enough evidence; see e.g. M. Lapidge, '*Archai* and *Stoicheia*'. But even on the *telos*, for the various formulations of which we are relatively well informed, I think that a case can be made for the essential agreement of Zeno and Chrysippus.

5. The Stoics tended to put the ideal state of full wisdom at the end of the moral development from birth. Despite the fact that people do not in fact normally become sages, it is still the final stage of their moral development and fullest realization of man's rational nature. So in the normative account of human development it has a right to be considered the final goal of human development and moral maturation.

6. *Ecl.* 2.83.13–14.

7. *Oikeios* is a much commoner term in philosophy and is not exclusively Stoic.

8. For discussions of the meaning and history of the word see Kerferd, 'The Search for Personal Identity', and Pembroke, 'Oikeiôsis'.

9. Fundamental works on the problem are Kerferd, op. cit.; Pohlenz, *Grundfragen*; Pembroke, 'Oikeiôsis', which includes references to most of the significant earlier literature. Also helpful are Rist, 'Zeno and Stoic Consistency'; Long, 'Logical Basis' and *Hellenistic Philosophy*, pp. 172–5, 184–99; Sandbach, *The Stoics*, pp. 31–6, 121. White, 'The Basis of Stoic Ethics' is misleading on several points and must be used with caution.

10. That there are significant precedents for or analogues to the Stoic theory in the work of Epicurus (depending on one's view of the relative chronology) is apparent from *Basic Doctrine* 7, D.L. 10.53, 10.34, and possibly 10.127–8. See also H. Steckel, *Epikurs Prinzip*, Ch. 1.

11. Aristotle's discussion of self-love was probably influential. Cf. Plato's *Lysis* on the *prôton philon* (esp. 219cd) and Glidden, 'The *Lysis* on Loving One's Own'. Rist, 'Zeno and Stoic Consistency', argues persuasively for the role of Polemo in stimulating Zeno's thoughts on the foundations of ethics.

12. Post-Chrysippean developments would be easier to document, but this is beyond the scope of my discussion. For Philo see Pembroke, n. 130, p. 149. On Posidonius see Kidd, 'Posidonius on Emotions', p. 205. For another development see Pembroke n. 89, p. 146. Philippson, 'Das erste Naturgemässe', p. 456 discusses Panaetius (as represented at Gellius *NA* 12.5.7 ff.). See also Pohlenz, *Grundfragen*, pp. 3 ff. esp. p. 7 n. 2.

13. SVF 1.197.
14. See Pembroke, op. cit., p. 121 and Kerferd, op. cit., p. 179.
15. See my 'The Two Forms of *Oikeiôsis* in Arius and the Stoa'.
16. For the supplements to the text see n. 30.
17. See n. 42.
18. The precise meaning of the Greek word is uncertain.
19. Perhaps, as A. A. Long suggested to me, one should read *hote* (when) for *hoti* (because), following the early MSS and Sandbach (*The Stoics*, p. 33).
20. See Pembroke, op. cit., pp. 120–1 for a more sympathetic description of the Stoics as observers of child development. This is based largely on the account of children's love of learning in *Fin.* 3.17. But this section, like those immediately following it (18–19), interrupts the main flow of the text; they may be elaborations added by Cicero from another source. Pembroke also gives a good account of the Stoic penchant for these unrealistically sharp evaluative transitions (cf. Long, *Hellenistic Philosophy*, p. 173).
21. *PHP* 5.5.1–21, pp. 316–20 = fr. 169.
22. See Appendix 1.
23. See Bonhoeffer, *Epictet*, pp. 252–3 for an account of *protê hormê*.
24. See, e.g., Kidd, 'The Stoic Intermediates', p. 155; Long, 'Carneades and the Stoic *Telos*', p. 67. For further discussion see Appendix 1.
25. This view was taken already by Dyroff, *Die Ethik der alten Stoa*, pp. 30–1, who also thought that the doctrine of D.L. 7.85–6 was Zenonian in substance. We may see a precedent for Chrysippus reporting and refining his predecessors' opinions in his own works in his treatment of presentation (SVF 2.56). White, op. cit., p. 172 insists that D.L. 7.85–6 cannot be taken as evidence for Zeno's views. It is true that it is only an inference that the Stoics whose views are reported in those sections include Zeno; but since Zeno's views on the *telos* are reported from his *On Human Nature* or *On Impulse* (cited in the next section), the inference is sounder than is indicated by White's dogmatic claim (p. 173) that Zeno did not base his *telos* on the specific nature of man and primary impulse. Cleanthes is said to have held that the *telos* was *no longer* based also on human nature (7.89), which surely suggests that Zeno said that it was. See too Rist, op. cit., pp. 167 ff. of which White seems unaware.
26. On the significance of this see Long, 'Arius Didymus and the Exposition of Stoic Ethics'.
27. There is one precious and usually ignored text which proves that Cleanthes dealt with this theme. At Hierocles col. 8.9 ff., admittedly a very fragmentary text, we have the beginning of a

comparison of the views of Cleanthes and Chrysippus on a point concerning the perception and *phantasia* of newborn animals. As the context is a discussion of the role of these in the *oikeiôsis* to itself of a newborn animal, it must be the case that Cleanthes discussed *oikeiôsis* and the primary impulse, even if not in those words. Since it is unlikely that Cleanthes first introduced the theme to Stoicism, this suggests that Zeno too had something to say on the topic.

28. I would not claim that the basic text is verbatim Chrysippus. But there is no reason to believe that the relations between the key theoretical terms have been altered by the excerptor.

29. A point properly emphasized by Pembroke, op. cit., p. 116 and n. 7. The verb *oikeioô*, to orient, here no doubt has the technical sense 'give an orientation to'. There is an earlier use of the active voice of *oikeioô* (Thucydides 3.65.3). Cf. Kerferd, p. 182, Pembroke, n.1. While the sense here is non-technical, the force of the active is very like what I propose for the Stoic passage. In Thucydides the leaders of the city are said to give over the city to a kinship-based alliance. That is, an agent gives something a new relationship to a third thing; the agent brings about a state of belonging for something else. In Chrysippus the third thing in question is the animal itself and so the relationship created by the action of *oikeioô* is a reflexive one. (I do not think that Sextus *M* 7.12 = SVF 1.356 suffices to show that Ariston used the word. The sense of *oikeioô* in Sextus' paraphrase is not paralleled by other old Stoic uses. It may be no more than Sextus' gloss for *protrepein*. Certainty is impossible.)

30. Reading *oukeiousês auto hautôi*. Two MSS have *auto* here, one has *autôi*. Kerferd, op. cit., p. 185 follows H. S. Long's conservative text (OCT) and reads only *auto*. Von Arnim (SVF 3.178) recommends but will not print the conjecture by Koraes which I adopt. Long's reluctance to supply *hautôi* is peculiar in view of his willingness to do the same in line 9 on von Arnim's suggestion. The second supplement is not even supported by the MSS variation which points to the cause of the omission by haplography. The *hautôi* is needed in both places to justify the conclusion of the argument (*oikeiôsai pros heauto*). Without the supplements the sense must be the same, but the form of expression much more difficult.

31. It is taken in this sense by Kerferd, Sandbach, Pembroke, and A. A. Long.

32. Respectively SVF 3.180 = *Mantissa*, p. 163; SVF 3.181 = *NA* 12.5.7; SVF 3.146 = *Comm. Not.* 1060c; col. 6.40–3.

33. *Fin.* 3.16, 21; 3.22 refers to the *initia naturae*.

34. We may interpret the middle-passive forms of *St. Rep.* 1038b and Alexander (SVF 3.183, 185) as passive in force. Similarly the passive

verb in the adaptation of the eclectic Eudorus (*Ecl.* 2.47) also suggests external agency. Eudorus' discussion is cast in orthodox Stoic terminology (see Long, 'Arius Didymus and the Exposition of Stoic Ethics', p. 55). The so-called Peripatetic version in Arius (*Ecl.* 2.118) took *phusis* in Aristotelian fashion as an impersonal force.

35. In speaking of *oikeiôsis* in the basic text I am taking some liberties with the wording. For only the verbal and adjectival forms occur here. In fact there is no fragment which preserves a verbatim use of the noun by Chrysippus. But Plutarch does use the word (*St. Rep.* 1038bc) to describe his theory, and I shall do the same. Caution about the terminology is not pointless. For some uses of the term are not reliable evidence for Chrysippus and indicate later developments. *Fin.* 3.21 refers to the *prima conciliatio* but makes it refer to the 'natural things', not the self or one's constitution. These are arguably to be identified with the *oikeia* an animal pursues on the basis of the *oikeiôsis* in D.L. 7.85. But in D.L. they are distinguished from the *prôton oikeion.* Similarly the use of *oikeiôsis* at SVF 1.197 and Posidonius' use in fr. 169 are not reliable evidence for Chrysippus. The latter is adapting and arguing against Chrysippus' theory.

36. It is probably best to describe the orientation as a disposition, since it is an ongoing state. In calling the orientation a process Kerferd (op. cit., p. 186) probably wants to emphasize the development of this relational disposition as the animal matures. But as the constitution matures and changes (*Ep.* 121) the orientation is still directed at it; the proper description of the relational disposition does not change; it is always true to say that the orientation is to the constitution. Plutarch's definition of *oikeiôsis* (*St. Rep.* 1038c) as *aisthêsis . . . tou oikeiou kai antilêpsis* is unreliable. It conflicts with the basic text and is offered as an explanatory addendum to a polemical criticism. Orientation *depends on* perception but is not itself a form of perception.

37. It might be objected to my insistence on the difference between the orientation and primary impulse that 'being directed at oneself' is a shorthand expression for 'being directed at self-preservation', just as *pros hêdonên* is shorthand for *epi to tuchein tês hêdonês*. I do not think that D.L. 7.85 can be interpreted in this way. For the *prôton oikeion*, the primary object of the orientation, is one's own constitution *and* an awareness of it. The predicates to which this might be thought to correspond would be 'to preserve oneself' and 'to be aware of oneself'. But the primary impulse is only to self-preservation, and impulse is nowhere else directed at cognitive states, but only at actions such as the pursuit and avoidance behaviour given as the result of the orientation at the end of D.L. 7.85.

38. 'Constitution' is my translation of *sustasis*. I borrow it from Seneca's *constitutio* (*Ep.* 121). Cicero's *status* (*Fin.* 3.16) is less literal.

39. I agree with Pohlenz (*Grundfragen*, p. 9) and Philippson ('Das erste Naturgemässe', p. 455) that the specification of the constitution rather than oneself as the object of orientation is Chrysippus' improvement on earlier terminology, probably Zeno's. Pembroke (op. cit., p. 145 n. 77) disagrees. Alexander's testimony (SVF 3.183 = *DA*, p. 150) supports my view. So, I think, does the interchange of the terms in the basic text. However, Pohlenz and Philippson, unlike Pembroke, do not see the importance of distinguishing the orientation from the primary impulse.

40. *Ep.* 121.10: *principale animi quodam modo se habens erga corpus*. In Greek: *hêgemonikon pôs echon pros to sôma*. Another description of the constitution is *kata phusin kataskeuai* (D.L. 7.108), where its role in determining what is *kathêkon* in Zeno's theory is emphasized.

41. These *oikeia*, in contrast to the *prôton oikeion*, are also called 'natural things', *ta kata phusin*. See *Comm. Not.* 1069f–1070a; 1060c; SVF 3.145 = Alexander *Mantissa*, p. 167. An extended use is also found: *St. Rep.* 1038b = SVF 3.674. Cf. *Ecl.* 2.105.26–106.1; 2.69.13.

42. *Sunaisthêsis*. I accept this emendation for the transmitted *suneidêsis*, following Pembroke, op. cit., n. 25. It is supported by Hierocles' use of *sunaisthêsis* and *aisthêsis heautou*, and by Cicero's and Seneca's *sensus sui*. *Suneidêsis* (self-knowledge) seems inappropriate for rudimentary animals and the newborn, who are included at this point. It is also supported by reference to *sunaisthêsis* by the eclectic Eudorus at *Ecl.* 2.47, a passage modelled closely on Stoic sources.

43. The references to *aisthêsis* at *St. Rep.* 12 and SVF 1.197 are no help. The object of perception here is not oneself but other things.

44. This includes Seneca *Ep.* 121 and Hierocles, which are our longest discussions of *sunaisthêsis*.

45. Despite *phantasia hautou* at Hierocles 6.24–8.

46. Col. 3.19 ff.

47. Note again the assumption of the equivalence of the self and the constitution.

48. Note the use Chrysippus makes of one of Aristotle's analyses of pleasure as an *epigennêma* (*EN* 10, 1174b33) in dismissing the role which pleasure plays in motivating animals.

49. Col. 6.24–30.

50. Note *eikos*. Hierocles (6.40–4) is explicit about this presumption and his word *matên* recalls Aristotle's formulation of the teleological assumption. *Ep.* 121.24 seems to be based on the same teleological argument. Compare too Marcus 10.7.1.

51. Hierocles 5.56–60.
52. Cf. Harman, 'Practical Reasoning', p. 458.
53. Col. 6.59–7.27; *Ep.* 121.7–9.
54. Its description will be just as specific, although the disposition will have to be said to be directed at the act type; the occurrent impulse causes a token of that type.
55. This emphasis on *houtô* is also indicated in the translations of Long ('Logical Basis', p.103), Pembroke (p. 116), Sandbach (*The Stoics*, p. 33) and Kerferd (p. 185). Sandbach in particular catches the nuance which I emphasize: the orientation to self is the reason for the behaviour in question.
56. This broad generality in the description of self-preservatory acts is found also in the accounts of Gellius (SVF 3.181), Cicero (*Fin.* 3.16), and Hierocles (6.54–9).
57. At least not in Chrysippus' theory. It may refer to something like neo-natal desires in the Antiochean version (see *Fin.* 5.55, 61, 17–18, and Appendix 1). The Stoics (see Alexander SVF 3.183, Plutarch *St. Rep.* 1038b, and Hierocles 6.42) do emphasize that this orientation and the resultant primary impulse exist from birth onwards; but there is no *exclusive* interest in the activities of the newly born animal.
58. Cicero or his source has blurred together the object of orientation and that of the primary impulse. Still, he makes clear how orientation to oneself is the cause of the impulse to self-preservation. A similar inaccuracy is seen in the fact that Cicero interprets *epigennêma* as indicating that pleasure is temporarily posterior to the action and not that it is dependent on it, as Chrysippus and Aristotle said.
59. For the material in the rest of this chapter see Voelke, *L'Idée*, pp. 65–81, whose account is very good. Much as been written on *ta kata phusin* and I propose to deal with one small aspect of this and related topics.
60. The converse is also true: something contrary to an animal's nature (*para phusin*, an unnatural thing) stimulates *aphormê*, an impulse to avoidance behaviour. Because this symmetry between contraries is so complete, I will usually omit the unnatural things and *aphormê* from my discussion. What is said of the positive side applies to these *mutatis mutandis*.
61. White, op. cit., pp. 150, 153 puts great emphasis on the distinction between self-preservation and self-enhancement and uses it to argue the implausible thesis that early Stoic ethics did not see the full realization of one's own nature as part of the *telos*. But I doubt that the line between self-preserving and self-enhancing things can be drawn with any clarity (as Aristotle might say, having good vision, a *kata phusin*, is both for the sake of living and of living well), and I am con-

vinced it cannot have the significance White gives it solely on the basis of Cicero's silence in *Fin.* 3. There are other important sources for early Stoic ethics, and if White had considered, say, Arius' discussion of *kata phusin, proêgmena* etc. (*Ecl.* 2.79 ff.) his picture of Stoic ethics would have been different.

62. Seneca takes pleasure and pain to be *kata phusin* and *para phusin* respectively. This view was not shared by Chrysippus but there was room for genuine debate within the school (see Rist, *Stoic Philosophy*, pp. 46–9, 103 ff.). The disagreement whether pleasure was natural may well have turned on different views as to whether pleasure was a useful guide to self-preservatory things and actions. All Stoics presumably agreed that it was a mere *epigennêma* of actions (D.L. 7.85), but may have disputed its heuristic value.

63. *Ep.* 121.17.

64. *tôn pros ti legomenôn einai. Ecl.* 2.80.9.

65. They are best represented at *Ecl.* 2.79–86. D.L. 7.102–10 provides some additional information, but in general is less helpful for my purposes. *Fin.* 3 will not be used in my discussion here. Sextus is useful in a number of places, esp. *PH* 3.177 and *M* 11.59–63. See also *M* 11.125, 135; *PH* 3.191. Long, 'Arius Didymus and the Exposition of Stoic Ethics' provides the best recent discussion of the structure and organization of the doxographical material and references to earlier discussions. My interest in what follows is not in the organizational principles of the doxographers but in the conceptual relationships underlying their handbooks.

66. See *Ecl.* 2.84; D.L. 7.84; *M* 11.73. Chrysippus too made his contribution to the theory of indifferents (D.L. 7.102; *St. Rep.* 1047e–1048c), no doubt partly because of the need to refute Ariston (*M* 11.64 ff). Chrysippus insisted on the definition of the indifferent as that which can be used well or ill—part of the Stoa's Socratic heritage. But he seems to have added a new sense of the word too (*M* 11.60; *PH* 3.177; *St. Rep.* 1045d–f).

67. On *to kata phusin, ho kata phusin bios* see SVF 3.145; *Fin.* 3.20, 50. Similarly for the relation of natural things to impulse, *Ep.* 121.2–3; *ND* 3.33.

68. *Ecl.* 2.79. Cf. D.L. 7.102–3. Also *Fin.* 3.20 which I will not be using here.

69. They are called *kathapax adiaphora. Ecl.* 2.79; D.L. 7.104–5. For a third sense of indifferent see n. 66.

70. D.L. 7.102–3.

71. *Ecl.* 2.79; 2.82; D.L. 7.104–5; *M* 11.59 and 61; cf. 125, 135; *PH* 3.177.

72. *Ecl.* 2.79; D.L. 7.104–5.

73. Although it is not listed at *Ecl.* 2.86–7. See Appendix 2. Also Voelke,

L'Idée, pp. 65 ff. Note the use of *eklogê* as a kind of impulse by Chrysippus at *Diss.* 2.6.9. Compare impulse and selection at *Ecl.* 2.79 with *Ecl.* 2.82.5-10 noting the contrast of *eklogê* to the impulses *hairesis* and *phugê* at 2.79. Further on *eklogê* in section (*c*). *Lêpsis* seems to be a synonym of *eklogê* (see the uses of it at *Comm. Not.* 1071a, 1070a; *Ecl.* 2.75, 82-3, 86.15; *Fin.* 3.59, 4.30, 39; *Acad.* 1.36-7.

74. The terminology used here (*axia eklektikê*) is of later origin, but the doctrines are demonstrably Chrysippean. See Rist, *Stoic Philosophy*, pp. 219 ff.; Rieth, 'Über das telos', pp. 14-19, 44.

75. The variation of this to *pollê axia* at *Ecl.* 2.80 is a refinement which does not affect the main point that value determines preferred status.

76. *Ecl.* 2.82. D.L. 7 does not connect impulse to *kata phusin* in this way. This seems to be an unimportant omission.

77. See Long, 'Logical Basis'.

78. Cf. p. 75 above. But our sources do not tell us what *this* factor is.

79. For a discussion of the complicated relations between the approriate and the natural see Kidd, 'Moral Actions and Rules in Stoic Ethics', pp. 250 ff. In general on *kathêkon* see Rist, *Stoic Philosophy*, Ch. 6 and Bonhoeffer, *Die Ethik*, Exkurs 3.

80. See *M* 11.66 and Chrysippus at *Diss.* 2.6.9.

81. D.L. 7.108 *energêma de auto einai tais kata phusin kataskeuais oikeion*. *Ecl.* 2.85 *energei gar ti kakeina akolouthôs têi heautôn phusei.* Cf. Chrysippus SVF 3.491 = *Comm. Not.* 1069e.

82. D.L. 7.86.

83. D.L. 7.107. It follows that 'appropriate action' is not an applicable translation in this case.

84. Although David Winston reminds me that Philo toys with the idea of an *oikeiôsis* in the case of plants. See *De Animalibus*, chs. 79-80, 94-5.

85. D.L. 7.107; *Ecl.* 2.85 for irrational animals.

86. *ta kath' hormên energoumena*, D.L. 7.108.

87. *Ecl.* 2.86.12-6.

88. SVF 3.491 = *Comm. Not.* 1069e.

89. D.L. 7.107; *Ecl.* 2.85.

90. On the meaning of reasonable see Rist, *Stoic Philosophy*, pp. 107-11.

91. See Goldschmidt, *Le Système*, pp. 134-40; Voelke, *L'Idée*, pp. 65-8.

92. *Ecl.* 2.84.24-85.1. I owe the translation of *kata prohêgoumenon logon* to A. A. Long.

93. *Ecl.* 2.83.13-84.3. Again the formulations are Antipater's but the ideas are easily traceable to Chrysippus.

94. *Comm. Not.* 1069e.

95. *Diss.* 2.6.9.
96. *Ep.* 92.11-2. His closeness to a Greek source is indicated by the Grecism *in electione quali* (12) for *en eklogēi poiāi* (cf. *qualia* at *Acad.* 1.28).
97. If the relation of this to primary impulse seems too tenuous to make this point, recall that in 13 Seneca goes on to say that this same relation exists between man's selection and his body, health, strength, etc.
98. *Fin.* 2.34; 3.31. His name is not mentioned. Cf. *Ecl.* 2.76 attributed to Chrysippus without the clause on selection. There is no reason to doubt that Chrysippus' intent is conveyed by the fuller formulation and I am confident that it is in fact an alternate formulation by Chrysippus himself. (For another slight variation in his formulation see *PHP* 4.6.12, p. 328. The addition of *holēn* to *phusin* does not affect the meaning.) For discussion see Rieth, 'Über das Telos', pp. 17-19, Long, 'Carneades and the Stoic Telos', p. 69, and Rist, *Stoic Philosophy*, p. 219.
99. See Striker, 'Sceptical Strategies', p. 65 and n. 32.
100. See Kidd, 'Moral Actions and Rules in Stoic Ethics'; Bonhoeffer, *Die Ethik*, pp. 230-1 (cf. 193-8). For the probabilistic nature of ethical rules, cf. Ross, *The Foundations of Ethics*, pp. 148 ff. For the notion of act-types in contrast to individual actions see Rescher, 'On the Characterization of Actions', p. 249.
101. For more on Ariston see J. Moreau, 'Ariston et le Stoïcisme', and N. P. White, 'Two Notes on Stoic Terminology', pp. 111-15. Chrysippus' nominalism was less extreme and he had no compunction about being guided by and talking about what occurs for the most part.
102. White's translation for *peristasis* ('Two Notes').
103. Cf. *Ecl.* 2.81.4-5.
104. *M* 11.66. The example is Ariston's.
105. The distinction between *per se* values and those things which are valuable with reference to them (see D.L. 7.107; *Ecl.* 2.75, 82-3; *Fin.* 3.56), because they help to produce things which are valuable *per se* is important here. One general rule for selection would be not to choose a derived value (such as wealth) over a *per se* value (such as health), except in unusual circumstances. Similarly, the interests of the soul should be put ahead of those of the body (*Ecl.* 2.82).
106. In the following discussion I am especially indebted to the discussion by Goldschmidt (op. cit., 145 ff. esp. p. 158) on the relation of the goal to action. He alone among earlier commentators has put proper emphasis on the importance of impulse with reservation.
107. *Ep.* 92.12; *Fin.* 3.20.

108. *Comm. Not.* 1069e. Cf. *Fin.* 3.31.

109. Above, p. 125 and Appendix 2; cf. *Ep.* 118.9 *perfecte petendum.* In *Fin.* 3 Cicero does a good job of keeping selection and choice distinct.

110. D.L. 7.94, confirmed by *Ep.* 124, *Fin.* 3.33. Good is also defined as what is truly advantageous (SVF 3.74–7), in Socratic fashion; also as what contributes to happiness, which is a smooth flow of life (*M* 11.30).

111. Cicero's discussion should be read in conjunction with *Ep.* 120.4–5.

112. See *Ep.* 124.13–5.

113. See Voelke, *L'Idée*, p. 64; *Ep.* 118.13–4.

114. *Ep.* 124.14.

115. *Fin.* 3.20–1. White, op. cit., pp. 154 ff. discusses this text. Unfortunately, he focuses on it in isolation from other relevant evidence.

116. *St. Rep.* 1035cd = SVF 3.68.

117. *Ecl.* 2.75. See Long, 'Early Stoic Concept', pp. 81–5. My interpretation of the text differs from his in the interpretation of the *autotelês hormê.* See above, p. 125.

118. *Ecl.* 2.86; Rist, *Stoic Philosophy,* pp. 98–9.

119. SVF 3.510, tr. after Long, *Hellenistic Philosophy,* p. 204. See also Bonhoeffer, *Die Ethik,* pp. 215–16, and Rieth, op. cit., pp. 17–18 whose interpretation of the passage differs from mine.

120. *Meson* is used to bring out the contrast to the *teleion kathêkon* which is a virtuous act (*katorthôma*); see *Ecl.* 2.85–6 and D.L. 7.109 (virtuous actions are always appropriate).

121. D.L. 7.98 and SVF 2.393. Sextus (SVF 3.516) emphasizes that a *katorthôma* is a *kathêkon* performed from the proper disposition (*M* 11.200–01) and with consistency (*M* 11.207).

122. Here we must recall the Stoic habit of shifting between descriptive and prescriptive modes. What is a description of a perfectly rational sage is a prescription for the rational adult.

123. *Acad.* 2.131 says explicitly that the virtuous life is derived from this orientation (*honeste autem vivere quod ducatur a conciliatione naturae*).

124. *Ecl.* 2.69.13; cf. 105.26–7.

125. The analogy is made clear in the contrast of the two kinds of value at D.L. 7.105.

126. Seneca *Ep.* 118.14 ff. argues that difference in degree can amount to difference in kind. Difference in degree is also suggested by *pluris quam* at *Fin.* 3.21 and by *megistê* at *Comm. Not.* 1070b and *Ecl.* 2.85. 3–4. But the contexts in these places show that moral value is meant to be incommensurable with the indifferents (as at D.L. 7.105) and this is the key point in saying that the difference is one of kind. Also *Fin.* 3.34; *ND* 1.16.

127. *Fin.* 4.28. The entire critique of *Fin.* 4 turns on this point.

128. Frr. 160, 169. The point was controversial in Carneades' day (SVF 3, Antipater 56), but *oikeiôsis* was not used. On Ariston SVF 1.356 see n. 29.

129. *St. Rep.* 12.

130. Recall that on my interpretation of *Ecl.* 2.75 the *haireton* is described as that which stimulates an unreserved impulse.

131. See *Fin.* 3.34.

132. *Fin.* 3.23. At *Diss.* 3.3 Epictetus deals with the overriding of lower values by the good.

133. *Ep.* 76.18, *ad haec faciendi et non faciendi ratio derigitur.*

134. SVF 3.181.

135. D.L. 7.109.

136. Rist, *Stoic Philosophy*, pp. 98–9.

137. e.g. *Comm. Not.* 1070b.

138. Cf. Rieth, op. cit., pp. 22–3.

139. The example of the archer illustrates Antipater's formulation of the *telos* which adapted earlier Stoic formulations in order to meet Academic criticism; see Long, 'Carneades and the Stoic Telos', esp. sections 4 and 5. The focus of the definition has changed in that explicit reference to the ultimate standard of goodness, rational Nature and harmony with it, has been suppressed in favour of emphasis on selections. Cf. Rist, *Stoic Philosophy*, pp. 221–2.

140. The need for an awareness of the good as one's reason is the element suppressed in Antipater's formulation.

141. *EN* 1115b12–13; 22–4; 1119b16–18; 1122b6–7; 1120a23–9; *EE* 1229a1–2; 1230a27–9.

Conclusion

1. D.L. 7.40.

2. Ibid.

Appendix 1

1. Kerferd, 'The Search for Personal Identity', pp. 190–1; Pembroke, op. cit., n. 8; Philippson, 'Das erste Naturgemässe', esp. p. 445; Pohlenz, *Grundfragen*, pp. 13–14.

2. See Long, *Hellenistic Philosophy*, pp. 186–7; Voelke, *L'Idée*, p. 66.

3. 'Über das Telos', p. 33.

4. Op. cit., p. 191.

5. e.g. Brink, 'Theophrastus and Zeno on Nature', pp. 143–4; Pohlenz, loc. cit.; Long, *Hellenistic Philosophy*, pp. 189–90.

6. Obviously the social *oikeiôsis* develops later, since it is based on love for one's children. But it does not evolve out of the orientation to

oneself in any obvious way. See my 'The Two Forms of *Oikeiôsis* in Arius and the Stoa'. The social *oikeiôsis* is never called secondary, either temporally or logically.

7. Ch. 6 n. 41.

8. At col. 1.1–5 Hierocles seems to say that a newborn animal's first experiences tell us something about its *prôton oikeion*. But this is merely the use of the newborn as an especially clear case illustrating the facts of pre-rational and irrational life. This is discussed in Ch. 6.

9. The *prôton oikeion* as interpreted here has clear similarities to Plato's *prôton philon* as interpreted by David Glidden ('The *Lysis* on Loving One's own', p. 56): 'The *prôton philon* on the contrary explains why the objects men cherish are cherished at all.'

10. Pohlenz (*Grundfragen*, p. 14 n. 1) saw that Eudorus' use of the phrase *prôton oikeion* was unorthodox (*Ecl.* 2.47).

11. Of course, it also explains actions which are obviously aimed at self-preservation (*Ep.* 121.9; Hierocles 3.19–30).

12. Cf. *Fin.* 3.16: *ex quo intellegi debet principium ductum esse a se dilegendo.*

13. I shall be arguing against the assumption made in various forms by: A. A. Long, 'Carneades and the Stoic Telos', p. 67 n. 24, p. 70 n. 32; Kerferd, op. cit., p. 191, followed by Rist, 'Zeno and Stoic Consistency', pp. 165–6; Philippson, 'Das erste Naturgemässe', p. 445; Voelke, *L'Idée*, p. 66; Pohlenz, *Grundfragen*, pp. 13–14, 17–21; *Die Stoa*, vol. i, pp. 114, 119, vol. ii, p. 66; Kidd, 'The Stoic Intermediates', pp. 155, 166 ff.

14. I have traced this view and the careful support of it as far back as Hirzel (*Untersuchungen*, vol. ii, Excurs 6, pp. 829–40). He discusses Madvig's thorough but mistaken exposition and the views of Zeller. Hirzel was followed by Bonhoeffer, *Die Ethik*, pp. 175–7. Schaefer (*Ein frühmittelstoisches*, Excurs 2, esp. pp. 304–5) is also correct on this point. See Cherniss, Loeb *Moralia*, vol. xiii.2, p. 749 note g.

15. On the *Carneadea divisio* see the most recent and authoritative account in John Glucker's *Antiochus and the Late Academy*, pp. 52 ff., 391, 394–5. Note esp. (pp. 52–3 and n. 135) the limited degree of certainty we may claim for our knowledge of this doctrine and its origin. Also, M. Giusta, *I Dossografi di etica*, vol. i, pp. 223 ff., 240 ff.

16. See Long, 'Carneades and the Stoic Telos'.

17. See Hirzel, op. cit., pp. 834 ff.

18. See Glucker, pp. 55 ff., 391 ff. on the Ciceronian texts and p. 54 for a suggestion that the Greek accounts are derived from a later Stoic version.

19. SVF 3.12 = *PHP* 5.6.9–12, p. 328.

20. Rieth, 'Über das Telos', p. 35 n. 2 thinks that Posidonius uses the

term here in its 'Academic' sense. But one version of Antipater's *telos* formula (*Ecl.* 2.76.13–5) refers to the *prohêgoumena kata phusin* where other versions and reports mention only the *kata phusin*. Long identifies Posidonius' formulation of the view he rejected (SVF 3.12) with Antipater's formula (op. cit., p. 84), and this must be correct, *prohêgoumena* being a synonym of *prôta*.

21. See Glucker, p. 54 n. 143.
22. That Chrysippus used some sort of classification of the *telê* is not inherently improbable (see *Fin.* 2.44). It would account for the book title *Peri Telôn* rather than *Peri Telous* (D.L. 7.85, cf. Cleanthes D.L. 7.175). But if he did have some sort of division of *telê* it was not influential, for all later classifications seem to be inspired by Carneades' version (Glucker, p. 54).
23. Lucian is not reliable. See Hirzel, op. cit., p. 833 and n. 1 for this text and *Acad.* 2.138.
24. Glucker, p. 54; cf. Giusta, op. cit., vol. i, p. 224.
25. *Grundfragen*, p. 14.
26. See Hirzel, op. cit., p. 832; Schaefer, p. 298, pp. 303–8 suggests a slight, basically non-temporal distinction in meaning for the middle Stoic period.
27. Of course there were disagreements about whether pleasure and wealth should be counted; but that is also the case for the *kata phusin*.
28. See *NA* 12.5.10 and Philippson, 'Das erste Naturgemässe', p. 456; Hirzel, op. cit., p. 833. Rist thinks the inspiration is Posidonian, *Stoic Philosophy*, pp. 38–9, 41.
29. Hirzel, op. cit., pp. 831–2. I doubt that Schaefer, pp. 295–6 is right to identify the doctrine here with that of Eudorus at *Ecl.* 2.47–8.
30. He would read: *prohêgeisthai de legousi ton peri toutôn logon ton peri tôn kata phusin kai para phusin.* Wachsmuth did not know this suggestion when he established his text (vol. i, introduction, pp. xxxii–xxxiii).

Appendix 2

1. The kinds are *eidê*; at the beginning of the passage the contrast is between impulse in general (*kata to genos*) and impulse in species (*en eidei*). For the emendation to *en eidei*, see Hirzel, op. cit., vol. ii, p. 384 n. In section 9 the doxographer discusses ways in which the term *hormê* is used, the point being that some of the kinds of impulse are also referred to by the label 'impulse' by the Stoics. Throughout it is important to note that despite the *genos/eidos* jargon the Stoics are not arranging their classification in the familiar genus/species pattern. This principle of division was not favoured by the Stoics (see Rieth, *Grundbegriffe*, Chs. 1 and 2 and p. 30).
2. For the sense of *logikê* here see Bonhoeffer, *Epictet*, pp. 233–4; Rieth,

Grundbegriffe, pp. 130–1 and n. 1. Compare the definition of *phantasia* at D.L. 7.51. A rational impulse is simply the impulse of a rational animal; so too is a practical impulse, since a *praxis* is behaviour by a rational animal. Only one text has been taken as evidence against the equation of practical and rational impulse, *Ecl.* 2.88. 1–2. For a discussion of this text see Ch. 3, n. 271.

3. For the Stoic habit of not giving separate names to subtypes in a classification scheme see D.L. 7.78: some conclusive syllogisms do not have a separate term to designate them, but are referred to 'homonymously with the genus'.

4. That *logikê hormê* is the term for the first sense of impulse (1) is implied by the sentence, 'For *orexis* is not rational impulse but a kind of rational impulse.'

5. The suggestion is Zeller's. It is entertained by Bonhoeffer, (*Epictet*, p. 255) and Dyroff (*Die Ethik*, pp. 22 n. 3). Hirzel (op. cit., vol. ii, p. 383 n. 1–385) and Wachsmuth, ad loc., reject it. The term is not so peculiar that it should be expunged. The one other Stoic use, if it counts, is at Philo *De Mutatione Nominum* 160 (an emendation by Mangey). If the emendation is right, the definition assigned to the term by Philo is unorthodox or muddled.

6. I have translated Wachsmuth's supplement, less the word 'not' (*mê*). I shall discuss this presently.

7. I am supposing that another sense of *aphormê*, which has little to do with the psychology of action, is not a likely candidate for this lacuna. *Aphormê* also refers to a general tendency, part of the innate constitution of an animal (D.L. 7.89, Origen *De Principiis* 3.1.3; *Ecl.* 2.62; 2.65) and has an extended sense as well in the definition of the probable (D.L. 7.76). Bonhoeffer (see his index in *Die Ethik*, p. 252) clearly separates the two senses of *aphormê*; so too Adler in his index to SVF (vol. 4, p. 31). The term is also discussed by Grilli, 'Studi Paneziani', part 1.

8. e.g. SVF 3.118, 119, 121, 122.

9. See N. Rescher, 'On the Characterization of Actions', p. 248. Keeping oneself from doing something (Rescher suggests the example of refraining from scratching a mosquito bite) 'is importantly different from a second type of inaction' which is made up of all those things which someone happens not to be doing. 'But these *nonactions* are not doings of any sort, I am not somehow active in keeping myself from doing them.' An *aphormê* leads to 'doing not-X' rather than to 'not doing X', in Rescher's terms.

10. He describes *aphormê* as (p. 21) as 'eine Art Getragenwerden des Geistes von etwas weg, was auf dem Lassen beruhe'.

11. Op. cit., 23 he calls *aphormê* a *hormê logikê apraktos*, in an attempt to

answer Bonhoeffer's puzzlement about the reference to *praktikai hormai* at *Ecl.* 2.88.1–2. The term *apraktos* occurs nowhere in our sources.

12. *PHP* 4.2.11, p. 240.

13. SVF 3.169 n.; 'Studi Paneziani', p. 32.

14. This also means that the extra lacuna after *orousis* which Dyroff wants is unnecessary. In addition he errs by taking *praktikê hormê* as one of the senses of impulse in section 9; the wording of *Ecl.* 2.87.1–3 shows that *orexis* is the term in question.

15. *Epictet*, pp. 223–9.

16. Op. cit., p. 235.

17. Op. cit., p. 235.

18. *Ecl.* 2.87.21–2.

19. D.L. 7.113; cf. *Ecl.* 2.90.7–8.

20. *Epictet*, p. 235.

21. The *alogoi orexeis* belong here. *Epithumia* is the counterpart of *boulêsis*. See SVF 3.391; *Ecl.* 2.90; D.L. 7.113.

22. The *aphormai logikai* or *praktikai* belong here. The general term for the *aphormê* corresponding to *orexis* is *ekklisis* (also used in the abstract sense). The two forms of *logikê aphormê* = *ekklisis* are *eulabeia* (*eulogos ekklisis*) and *phobos* (*alogos ekklisis*). See SVF 3.391; *Ecl.* 2.88.14–8; *St. Rep.* 1037f = SVF 3.175.

23. By this extension they were able to take account of future-directed intentions and plans as well as the more limited sort of intention which accompanied intentional or voluntary action. For the contrast see e.g. Davidson, 'Intending', and J. Searle, 'The Intentionality of Intention and Action'.

24. SVF 2, p. 99 lines 28–31; *De Sollertia Animalium* 961c. See also M. Frede, 'The Principles of Stoic Grammar', p. 35.

25. Compare the remarks of Cooper, *Reason and Human Good*, pp. 26–32 and Nussbaum, pp. 191–4 on Aristotelian practical syllogisms whose conclusions may be reached now but executed later.

26. *De Sollertia Animalium* 966b; the definitions of three of the four kinds of impulse are repeated in the Stobaean form at 961c (see W. C. Helmbold, 'Stoica'.

27. *De Principiis* 3.1.14.

28. *L'Idée*, pp. 60 ff.; *Die Ethik*, pp. 23–4.

29. *Epictet*, pp. 257–61.

30. *epiteleiôseôs* in Plutarch.

31. Helmbold, 'indication of intent to complete'. Dyroff, 'Vorsatz'. Bonhoeffer, 'Andeutung der Ausführung'. Voelke, 'l'annonce de l'accomplissement'.

32. The phrase *kata prothesin* occurs in Nemesius *Nat. Hom.* p. 229 =

SVF 3.416 in a report of Stoic doctrines. But this does not seem to be a specifically Stoic technical usage, being used to explicate the Stoic term *prohêgoumenôs*. Elsewhere Nemesius shows no sign of familiarity with the technical classification of the kinds of practical impulse. Alexander uses *kata prothesin* in this same way to explain an Aristotelian distinction (*De Fato*, p. 167.22); there is no reason to take it as a Stoic term.

33. See G. E. M. Anscombe, 'Thought and Action in Aristotle', p. 63.
34. See Voelke, *L'Idée*, pp. 140–1.
35. Cicero renders it *conatus*. Dyroff 'Drang'. Voelke, 'projet préalable'. To Bonhoeffer it is an 'Absicht' or 'Anschlag', 'der erste Ansatz des Willens ... im Gegensatz zum fertigen Entschluss'. Helmbold renders it 'design'.
36. *Ecl.* 2.91; 2.115; *M* 7.239; D.L. 7.113, 129; pseudo-Andronicus SVF 3.397; *TD* 4.72. See Pembroke, 'Oikeiôsis', p. 130 and n. 78 and Hirzel, op. cit., vol. ii, pp. 387 ff.
37. Dyroff, 'Vorbereitung'. Voelke, 'préparation'. Helmbold, 'preparation'. Bonhoeffer, 'das die Ausführung des Entschlusses vorbereitende Handeln'.
38. *De Sollertia Animalium* 966b.
39. Dyroff translates 'Angriff'. Voelke calls it 'entreprise' and 'effort touchant déjà au but'. Bonhoeffer describes it as 'den auf das bereits begonnene Werk gerichteten Willen'.
40. It is not too much to suppose that the Stoics recognized the possibility of describing actions in different ways, so that what is a part of one act may also be viewed as another, simpler act. A may be part of the complex act AB or a simple act leading up to B. This would be a version of the accordion effect described by J. Feinberg in 'Action and Responsibility'.
41. *Epictet*, pp. 257–9.
42. Bonhoeffer also argues that the old Stoics shared Epictetus' belief in innate moral concepts, insists that Epictetus' three *topoi* must correspond to the three parts of philosophy in the old Stoic system, and underrates Panaetius' influence on Epictetus' version of the doctrine of *personae*.
43. pp. 255, 258.
44. On *eklogê* see Voelke, *L'Idée*, pp. 65 ff.; above, pp. 115, 198 and Ch. 6, n. 73. It is rational impulse directed not at the good or apparent good, but at the *adiaphora*.
45. On *boulêsis* and *epithumia* (an *eupatheia* and a *pathos* respectively), see D.L. 7.116; *TD* 4.12 and 14–15; pseudo-Andronicus *Peri Pathôn* 1 and 6 = SVF 3.391 and 432.
46. After all, the use of the abstract sense of *orexis* as well as the

normative sense did have disadvantages. It gave captious critics such as Galen a splendid opportunity to tie the Stoic distinctions in knots by confounding the two senses. Galen took a similar tack with the two senses of *alogos* as the opposite of rational (*logikos*) i.e. occurring with a *lekton* in a rational animal and as the opposite of rational (*eulogos*) i.e. correct, according to Reason. See SVF 3.441-2, 463-4.

47. On *apodexis* see n. 48.

48. I omit *epaineton* and *dokimaston* which are mentioned here as designations of *agathon*, since they seem not to be forms of impulse. But *apodexis* and (*eu*)*arestēsis*, although not listed as kinds of *orexis* at *Ecl.* 2.87, are almost certainly subtypes of *boulēsis* (and so of *orexis*). They seem to be synonyms of *agapēsis* and/or *aspasmos* which are listed among the forms of *boulēsis* at *Peri Pathon* 6 = SVF 3.432. See Bonhoeffer, *Epictet*, p. 287, *Die Ethik*, p. 48; also Voelke, *L'Idée*, pp. 59-60. SVF 2.912 (note *euarestēsis pros ta sumbainonta*) suggests that these forms of *boulēsis* are important with respect to the doctrine of harmonizing one's will with that of Zeus or nature.

49. As Bonhoeffer notes, *Epictet*, p. 261. There is an exception, for the phrase *boulēma tēs phuseōs* occurs frequently and seems to reflect the *boulēsis tou tōn holōn dioiketou* mentioned by Chrysippus (D.L. 7.88). Cf. too the *boulēma tēs phuseōs* in Alexander (SVF 3.180). Nature's will is an impulse.

50. See Voelke, *L'Idée*, pp. 58-9.

51. *Gorgias* 468c ff.

52. D.L. 7.116; *Peri Pathōn* 6 = SVF 3.432; Lactantius SVF 3.437; *TD* 4.12.

53. Other uses of *boulēsis* are at *Ecl.* 2.97 (in the list illustrating the point that impulses are directed at predicates rather than objects), 2.58 (it is not a virtue, since virtues are states and *boulēsis* is a *kinēsis*); *boulēsis* may be the term behind Seneca's *voluntas* at *Ep.* 95.57, but that is by no means certain.

54. Bonhoeffer's dismissive remarks are not a very promising line of interpretation (*Epictet* p. 261). A better effort (not incompatible with my own suggestion) is made by Voelke (*L'Idée*, p. 60n. 4).

55. The term has been studied thoroughly by earlier scholars. See esp. Voelke, *L'Idée*, pp. 61 ff. to which my discussion owes much. He documents the Platonic background on p. 61, singling out *Phaedo* 99ab. See also the studies by Long, 'Early Stoic Concept', esp. 79-90; Tsekourakis, *Terminology*, pp. 102-14; Hirzel, *Untersuchungen*, vol. ii, pp. 383, 330 n.

56. *M* 11.99; *Ecl.* 2.64, 72, 78, 97; D.L. 7.98, 101, 127, etc.

57. See *Ecl.* 2.79, SVF 3.190–6; *Ecl.* 2.75; 2.82–3. Also, Voelke, *L'Idée*, pp. 65 ff. and Long, 'Early Stoic Concept', pp. 81–3.
58. Long and Voelke take it in this way (see n. 55).
59. *Fin.* 3.20–2, 33; D.L. 7.52; *Ep.* 120.4.
60. See Galen's description of *analogismos* at SVF 2.269; cf. Sextus *PH* 1.147.
61. Compare *Ecl.* 2.64 with *Fin.* 3.27, 36; 4.50.
62. At *Ep.* 95.57 Seneca uses *voluntas* where one might expect a form derived from *expetere*. No doubt he was avoiding the use of *expetitio*.
63. Long, 'Early Stoic Concept', pp. 86 ff. and n. 14.
64. For Aristotle see Bonitz, *Index Aristotelicus* for *haireisthai* and *hairesis*. For Epicurus D.L. 10.27, 128.
65. SVF 3.256; *Ecl.* 2.79.1–2 and 7–8; D.L. 7.105; *St. Rep.* 1040 f. At *St. Rep.* 1034e Cleanthes opposes *hairesis* and *ekklisis* in the definition of temperance. At *Ecl.* 2.72 *eulogos hairesis* is used somewhat surprisingly in place of *eulogos orexis* (cf. *eulogôs haireisthai* at D.L. 7.99).
66. It is used very infrequently, and one doubts whether its sense is the technical one given here or the general philosophical sense largely shaped by Aristotelian use of the word: e.g. *Ecl.* 2.99.14–15. See below.
67. On Epictetus and later use of the word, as well as on the historical background, see Bonhoeffer, *Epictet*, pp. 259–60, Hijmans, *Askêsis*, pp. 23 ff., Pohlenz, *Die Stoa*, vol. i, pp. 332 ff., Rist, *Stoic Philosophy*, pp. 228–32 and 'Prohairesis: Proclus, Plotinus et alii', Voelke, *L'Idée*, pp. 142 ff.
68. Voelke, *L'Idée*, p. 154 and n. 4.
69. Bonhoeffer, *Epictet*, p. 260 on *Diss.* 2.23.43; 3.23.5. Also: '. . . die *prohairesis* bedeutet . . . nichts anderes als die Fähigkeit freier, vernünftiger Selbstbestimmung'.
70. e.g. *Ecl.* 2.99.14–15 = SVF 1.216 and Aëtius 1.29.7 = *Dox. Gr.*, p. 326 = SVF 2.966. But cf. *Ecl.* 1.87 = Aëtius 1.29.2 = *Dox. Gr.*, p. 325. I disagree with Rist, *Stoic Philosophy*, p. 232 n. 2 who would attribute the phrase to Zeno.
71. *EN* 1113a11; cf. 1139b4–5.
72. Rist, *Stoic Philosophy*, p. 5.
73. *Epictet*, p. 260.
74. At *Epictet*, p. 260 Bonhoeffer criticizes the temporal *pro-* of the definition at *Ecl.* 2.87. But the *pro-* must be temporal (see above on *hormê pro hormês*). On the sense of *pro-* in Aristotle's *prohairesis* see Hardie, *Aristotle's Ethical Theory*, pp. 165–8.
75. *Die Stoa*, vol. i, p. 332.
76. See Appendix 4 below for a case where the Stoic influence on the later tradition of philosohical terminology was much stronger.

Appendix 3

1. There is an exception. Cleanthes uses *horman* in a non-technical sense in the *Hymn to Zeus* SVF 1, p. 122 line 22.
2. In the *Republic* too (439b1) *horman* is used of the activated desire thirst, with a turn of phrase which anticipates the Stoa: *toutou* [i.e. *tou piein*] *oregetai kai epi touto hormâi*.
3. Note the early Academic uses of *hormê* in the *Definitions* ascribed to Plato. At 415e6 it is used in a definition of *thumos* (cf. the *Laws* text above) and in 416a3 it means activity or drive to action (it is what *oknos*, hesitation, counteracts).
4. *Rep.* 439b1, *Alcibiades* I 111cl, *Rep.* 336b2, *Sophist* 242c5, *Rep.* 352c6, 391d1, *Symposium* 190a5, *Rep.* 510d3, 582c5, *Laws* 694c4, *Theages* 129c1.
5. It may suggest, though, that Plato felt that *hormê* was particularly suited to the desires of *thumos*, although not restricted to them. See the Academic definition of *thumos* (see n. 3).
6. *Aristotle's Psychology of Conduct*, pp. 24–5.
7. On Aristotle's use see Preus, 'Intention and Impulse'. But his discussion of Aristotle often seems questionable and must be used with caution. His account of *hormê* in the Stoa is unreliable. He seems to have missed the important difference between Aristotle's wide-ranging use of *orexis* and the much narrower use of it in the Stoics, when he says that the term is used by the Stoa 'roughly in the Aristotelian way' (p. 49).
8. Cf. *EE* 2.8.5–6; *EN* 7.3 1147a25–31 with its contrast to the case involving conflict at 31 ff.; *DM* 7.
9. On this transfer of *hormê* from the inanimate to the animate see Gauthier-Jolif on 1102b21 (pp. 95–6).

Appendix 4

1. I wish to thank A. A. Long for his comments on an earlier version of this discussion.
2. In the *Eudemian Ethics* 2.8 Aristotle maintained that action which was caused by either of the two basic kinds of desiderative principle (*archai* of action) was responsible; he ought perhaps to have restricted himself to a claim that such action was voluntary, but the context makes it clear that the other conditions necessary for action to be responsible are thought of as having been fulfilled.
3. The phrase *apo idias hormês* at SVF 2.499 (= Simplicius Comm. on *Categories*, p. 306.25) has the same sense as *kath' hormên* in Diogenes.
4. SVF 3.462 = *PHP* 4.2.15–16, pp. 240–2, quoted above, p. 155–6.
5. Von Arnim marks the phrase *kath' hormên kinêsin* in a passage of

Alexander (*De Fato*, p. 182.7 = SVF 2.979, p. 285.28) as a quotation from a Stoic source. This is not certain, as the polemical context ought to indicate. But it is quite possible that Alexander's use here is based on a knowledge of the Stoic use of the phrase *kath' hormên* as a description of voluntary action in the weak sense of the word. See n. 8.

6. Nemesius in reporting on Panaetius (p. 212 Matthaei = fr. 86) and Porphyry in reporting on Stoic epistemology (*Ecl.* 1.349 = SVF 2.74). See below on these passages.

7. On p. 205.15 ff. he refers to *kath' hormên energeia* and *kath' hormên energoumenon, kath hormên ginomenon*, etc. These seem to have the same meaning as *kath hormen kinêsis*. So too does the phrase *di' hormês* at p. 182.16.

8. *Pace* Striker (p. 78 n. 55 of *Doubt and Dogmatism*), Alexander's use here is not a case of the minimal sense of 'voluntary action' found in later writers who are not at all concerned with Stoic doctrine. It is, rather, a distortion for polemical purposes of genuine Stoic ideas. In his arguments Alexander specifies various senses of *kata phusin kinêsis* which correspond to the various levels of the Stoic *scala naturae*. *Kath' hormên* is attached to *kinêsis* to distinguish animal movement from the necessity of the invariable natural movements of fire (upwards) and stones, etc. (downwards). In contrast to these Alexander says, the *kata phusin* movement of animals is *kath' hormên*. But, Alexander argues, such movement is just as rigidly determined by fate as is that of fire and stones. The notion that animal movement is characterized by *hormê* is Stoic, although Alexander omits any reference to *phantasia* which is jointly characteristic (in SVF 2.714 Clement mentions both). Alexander's polemical use of the Aristotelian doctrine of natural motion is not based on the Stoic arrangement and definition of the *scala naturae*; in fact, it reminds us of Aristotle's transference of the automatic *hormê* of inanimate objects to their natural place to the *hormê* which is identified with animal *orexis*. The concept of rational action and assent which Alexander uses here and elsewhere in the *De Fato* is also non-Stoic. He assimilates human to animal action by attributing assent to both alike, whereas for the Stoics assent is what distinguishes man from the irrational animals. Alexander then claims that action is only free or responsible if it is a result of deliberate choice between alternatives, an Aristotelian concept of responsibility not shared by the Stoics. See Ch. 3, pp. 89 ff.

9. pp. 76.17, 77.7.

10. *De Anima*, pp. 73 ff. Similarly he adds a Stoically inspired faculty of assent to an Aristotelian account of perception and action.

11. *De Anima* 49.3–5; 50.7–8; Comm. on *Topics* (*CAG* 2.2, p. 109.25–31). For the Stoic definition of voice see D.L. 7.55.

12. e.g. Philoponus Comm. on *De Anima* (*CAG* 15, p. 379.9–10.

13. *De Anima* 420b29–33.

14. Michael of Ephesus followed Alexander's eclecticism quite closely and used it in his own work. See his Comm. on *De Motu CAG* 22.2, p. 115.7, 14–15, 24–5 where the Stoicizing interpretation of Aristotle is quite clear. Donini ('Il De Anima di Alessandro di Afrodisia e Michele Efesio' and Preus 'Intention and Impulse' pp. 56–7) show that Michael was dependent on Alexander. He did not draw on the Stoics himself.

15. Alexander used *kata phantasian tina kai kath' hormên ginomena* as a gloss for 'what is done by an animal *qua* by an animal'. This excludes what is done *to* an animal and its lower plant-like functions.

16. Fr. 86 van Straaten = *De Natura Hominis*, Ch. 15, p. 212.

17. It is accepted as a Stoic term by Bonhoeffer, *Epictet*, pp. 86–9; Schindler, *Die stoische Lehre*, pp. 35 ff.; Holler, *Seneca*, pp. 48 ff.; van Straaten (1946 edition), pp. 126–9;, Grilli, 'Studi Paneziani', pp. 73, 76 ff.; Voelke, *L'Idée*, pp. 118–20. Schmekel, *Die Philosophie der mittleren Stoa*, pp. 200–1 and n. 4, Pohlenz, *Die Stoa*, vol. ii, p. 100, and Verbeke, *L'Évolution*, p. 94 have seen that the term is Nemesius' rather than Panaetius' own.

18. Ch. 26, pp. 249–50.

19. The most likely account of the change made by Panaetius in the status of voice in the soul is the one given by Pohlenz (*RE* 18.3, 433) who is followed (approximately) by Rist, *Stoic Philosophy*, pp. 180–1. Voice, Panaetius will have said, does not need to be allotted a separate stream of *pneuma* from the *hêgemonikon* to the vocal organs (in the way that the senses are given distinct streams of *pneuma* from the *hêgemonikon* to the sense organs—SVF 2.885). Panaetius will have noted that Chrysippus held that the voice originated right in the area of the heart (SVF 2.840, 894), which made the separate stream of *pneuma* or part of the soul unnecessary. Thus speech was considered by Panaetius to be one of the activities of the *hêgemonikon*, like all other actions. If Panaetius said simply that voice was a voluntary activity of the soul, and if he believed with Diogenes of Babylon (D.L. 7.55) that *hormê* was required for the production of speech, then he could easily have expressed his position in a way which encouraged Nemesius to use his own term *kath' hormên kinêsis* in reporting it. The possibility that Panaetius actually wrote *kath' hormên kinêsis* cannot be ruled out, but given the frequency of the term in the non-Stoic use in Nemesius and the paucity of evidence for Stoic uses of the term, it is more economical to take it as Nemesius' term here.

20. There is a slight difference. In fr. 86a the psychic powers are *kata pro-hairesin* and these are divided into voluntary motion and perception, so that voluntary motion is a subdivision of *ta kata prohairesin*. But this is a minor difference from Ch. 27, merely an indication of Nemesius' terminological hesitation or his confusion (what does it mean to say that perception too is *kata prohairesin*?). Again, later in Ch. 27 (p. 252) voice and perception are said to be *kata prohairesin* and so presumably both voluntary (*kath' hormên*). Cf. pseudo-Plutarch *De Fato* 571c–e where *kath' hormên* (= *to eph' hêmin*) is given a wider sense than *kata prohairesin*. There is other evidence (below, p. 256) that *kath' hormên* was sometimes seen as an equivalent for Aristotle's term *kata prohairesin*.

21. This has been seen by Gisela Striker at p. 78 n. 55 of *Doubt and Dogmatism*. She also makes the point for Nemesius, p. 250. See W. Theiler, 'Tacitus', p. 62 and n. 1. Bonhoeffer, *Epictet*, p. 125 seems to accept the phrase as Stoic.

22. Cf. too Cicero's description of assent as *in nobis positam et voluntariam* at *Academica* 1.40.

23. Numenius reveals on p. 350 that he takes *kath' hormên* and *eph' hêmin* as equivalent.

24. Aristotle held that voluntary action, i.e. movements generated by the animal's own desire, and perception were powers that marked off animals from plants, although he did not say so in the blunt terms of the doxographer Aëtius, who reports that Aristotle believed that all animals were *hormêtika and aisthêtika* (*Placita* 5.26 = *Dox. Gr.* p. 438). Aëtius' terminology, of course, reflects the Stoically influenced use of *hormê* as well as the Aristotelian preference for *aisthêsis* over *phantasia*. Strictly speaking Aristotle makes *aisthêsis* alone the characteristic of animal life (cf. too *EE* 7.12.6). But *aisthêsis* is always found together with *orexis* (*DA* 414a32–b2). Locomotion is characteristic of all animals which have more than the sense of touch (*DA* 1.5, 410b16–21; 3.12; 3.9, 432b19 ff.); but animals with only the sense of touch are not typical; animal soul is said to be characterized by the powers of discrimination and locomotion (3.9, 432a15–17; cf. 1.5, 411a26 ff). Even those very low forms of animal life have *orexis* and, Aristotle concedes, an indefinite sort of motion (3.10–11, esp. 433b31–434a5). Thus Aristotle's position is somewhat fluid on this point, but the doxographer was clearly justified in reporting Aristotle's position as he did. (Cf. Alexander's view at *DA*, p. 29.11–22.) Aristotle himself reports that motion and perception are the traditional and commonly accepted criteria of animal soul (*DA* 1.2, esp. 403b26–7).

25. Cf. Plotinus *Enn.* 4.3.20.44–5 and 4.3.23.12–15 and 21 ff. His use of terminology is flexible.

26. *Stromates* 8.4.
27. p. 86.12, 86.22.
28. 15.5, p. 357, vol. ii of Helmreich's Teubner edition (Leipzig, 1909).
29. *PHP* 7.1.7, p. 430.
30. Galen is criticizing the Stoics, but gives it as a generally held view that 'the source of sensation and voluntary motion is the governing part (of the soul)' (tr. DeLacy). See too the use of *kath' hormên kinein* at *PHP* 5.7.1, p. 336.
31. Comm. on *De Anima* (*CAG* 11), p. 291.14–15, 38–41. Other uses are pseudo-Alexander *Quaestiones* 1.1, p. 3.15–16; Simplicius Comm. on *Physics* (*CAG* 10), p. 1037.13–17; Philoponus Comm. on *De Anima* (*CAG* 15), pp. 110.9–17, 576.25–8; 185.1–6.
32. Pseudo-Alexander *Quaestiones* 4.9, p. 129.20–3; Simplicius Comm. on *Categories* (*CAG* 8), p. 318.25–6. For the combination in Simplicius of *kata prohairesin kai zôtikên hormên*, cf. *EE* 8.2.14: *ta men gar prattetai apo tês hormês kai proelomenôn praxai.*
33. Pseudo-Galen, *To Gauros on How Embryos Receive Soul. Abhandlungen der königlichen Akademie der Wissenschaften zu Berlin* (Phil.-hist. Kl.), 1895. On Porphyry as the author, p. 25. Kalbfleisch, ibid., cites Hermippus *De Astrologia* 2.17 for similar doctrine: 'what is characteristic of animals is the voluntary, and perception and presentation'.
34. At 14.3.
35. See 4, 5, 15.3, 18.

Bibliography

A. Ancient Works

The basic collection of fragments is *Stoicorum Veterum Fragmenta*, ed. H. von Arnim. Three vols. Leipzig: Teubner, 1903–5. Vol. 4 Indices (M. Adler), 1924. Repr. four vols., Stuttgart: Teubner, 1979.

Stobaeus, *Anthology* Books 1–2, i.e. *Eclogae Physicae et Ethicae* is cited by book, page, and line from the edition of C. Wachsmuth (vol. i). Berlin: Weidmann, 1884.

Posidonius is cited by fragment and line from *Posidonius, vol. 1: The Fragments*, edd. L. Edelstein and I. G. Kidd. Cambridge: Cambridge University Press, 1972.

Panaetius is cited according to the numbering of M. van Straaten in *Panaetii Rhodii Fragmenta* (ed. 3). Leiden: Brill, 1962.

Nemesius' *De Natura Hominis* is cited by page and line from the edition of C. F. Matthaei. Madgeburg: Gebauer, 1802.

The ecclesiastical writers, Clement of Alexandria, Origen, and Eusebius, are cited from the most recent editions in the series *Die griechischen christlichen Schriftsteller*. Berlin: Akademie-Verlag. The only exception is Origen, *Vier Bücher von den Prinzipien*, edd. H. Görgemanns and H. Karpp. Darmstadt: Wissenschaftliche Buchgesellschaft, 1976.

Galen's *De Placitis Hippocratis et Platonis* is cited according to the pagination of the new text and translation by P. DeLacy in the series *Corpus Medicorum Graecorum* (first part, books 1–5: *CMG* V 4.1.2. Berlin: Akademie-Verlag, 1978; books 6–9, 1980).

Themistius' paraphrases, Alexander of Aphrodisias, and other Aristotelian commentators have been cited from the standard Berlin Academy editions. Unfortunately, R. W. Sharples's edition, *Alexander of Aphrodisias on Fate*, appeared too late to be used (London: Duckworth, 1983).

The various doxographical writers have been quoted from H. Diels, *Doxographi Graeci*. Berlin: Reimer, 1879.

Pseudo-Andronicus of Rhodes *Peri Pathôn* is cited from the edition of A. Glibert-Thirry (Leiden: Brill, 1977).

Hierocles is cited by column and line from the edition *Ethische Elementarlehre* (Papyrus 9780), ed. H. von Arnim with W. Schubart. Berlin: Weidmann, 1906 (= Heft 4 of *Berliner Klassikertexte*).

Other ancient authors are available in standard editions.

B. Modern Works

1. Adkins, A. W. H., *Merit and Responsibility: A Study in Greek Values*. Oxford: Clarendon Press, 1960.
2. Akinpelu, J. A., 'The Stoic *Scala Naturae*', *Phrontisterion* 5 (1967), 7–16.
3. Allan, D. J., '*Magna Moralia* and *Nicomachean Ethics*', *Journal of Hellenic Studies*, 77 pt. 1 (1957), 7–11.
4. Alpers-Gölz, R., *Der Begriff Skopos in der Stoa und seine Vorgeschichte*. Hildesheim and New York: Olms, 1976.
5. Annas, J., 'Truth and Knowledge', pp. 84–104 in 180.
6. Anscombe, G. E. M., 'Thought and Action in Aristotle', pp. 61–71 in *Articles on Aristotle*, vol. ii, edd. J. Barnes, M. Schofield, and R. Sorabji. London: Duckworth, 1977. This is reprinted from *New Essays in Plato and Aristotle*, ed. R. Bambrough. London: Routledge and Kegan Paul, 1965.
7. Baldry, H. C., *The Unity of Mankind in Greek Thought*. Cambridge: Cambridge University Press, 1965.
8. Barnes, J., 'La doctrine du retour éternel', pp. 3–20 in 17.
9. Bennett, J., *Linguistic Behaviour*. Cambridge: Cambridge University Press, 1976.
10. —— *Rationality*. London: Routledge and Kegan Paul, 1964.
11. Bonhoeffer, A., *Epictet und die Stoa: Untersuchungen zur stoischen Philosophie*. Stuttgart: Enke, 1890.
12. —— *Die Ethik des Stoikers Epictet*. Stuttgart: Enke, 1894.
13. —— 'Zur stoischen Psychologie', *Philologus* 54 (1895), 403–29.
14. Bonitz, H., *Index Aristotelicus*. Berlin, 1870. Reprinted Darmstadt: Wissenschaftliche Buchgesellschaft, 1960.
15. Bréhier, E., *Chrysippe et l'ancien stoïcisme*, ed. 2. Paris: Presses Universitaires de France, 1951.
16. Brink, C. O., '*Oikeiôsis* and *Oikeiotês*: Theophrastus and Zeno on Nature in Moral Theory', *Phronesis* 1 (1956), 123–45.
17. Brunschwig, J., ed., *Les Stoïciens et leur logique*. Paris: Vrin, 1978.
18. Burnyeat, M., 'Can the Sceptic Live his Scepticism?', pp. 20–53 in 180.
19. Cancrini, A., *Syneidesis: Il tema semantico della 'conscientia' nella Grecia antica*. Rome: Ateneo, 1970.
20. Carnois, B., 'Le désir selon les stoïciens et selon Spinoza', *Dialogue* 19 (1980), 255–77.
21. Cashdollar, S., 'Aristotle's Theory of Incidental Perception', *Phronesis* 18 (1973), 156–75.
22. Chadwick, H., 'Origen, Celsus and the Stoa', *Journal of Theological Studies* 48 (1947), 34–49.

23. Cherniss, H., ed., *Plutarch's Moralia*. vol. xiii.2 Cambridge, Mass.: Harvard University Press; London: Heinemann, 1976.

24. Colardeau, T., *Étude sur Épictète*. Paris, Thorin, 1903.

25. Cooper, J., 'The *Magna Moralia* and Aristotle's Moral Philosophy', *American Journal of Philology* 94 (1973), 327–49.

26. —— *Reason and Human Good in Aristotle*. Cambridge, Mass.: Harvard University Press, 1975.

27. Daraki-Mallet, M., 'Les fonctions psychologiques du Logos', pp. 87–119 in 17.

28. Davidson, D., 'Actions, Reasons and Causes', *Journal of Philosophy* 60 (1963), 685–700. Also pp. 3–19 in *Essays on Actions and Events*.

29. —— 'How is Weakness of the Will Possible?', pp. 93–113 in *Moral Concepts*, ed. J. Feinberg. Oxford: Clarendon Press, 1969. Also pp. 21–42 in *Essays on Actions and Events*.

30. —— 'Intending', pp. 83–102 in *Essays on Actions and Events*. Repr. from *Philosophy of History and Action*, ed. Y. Yovel. D. Reidel, and the Magnes Press, The Hebrew University, 1978.

31. —— *Essays on Actions and Events*. Oxford: Clarendon Press, 1980.

32. Dickerman, S. O., 'Some Stock Examples of Animal Intelligence in Greek Psychology', *Transactions of the American Philological Association*, 42 (1911), 123–30.

33. Dillon, J., *The Middle Platonists*. London: Duckworth, 1977.

34. Dirlmeier, F., *Die Oikeiosis-Lehre Theophrasts, Philologus* Supp. 30, 1 (1937).

35. —— 'Die Zeit der "grossen Ethik"', *Rheinisches Museum* 88 (1939), 214–43.

36. —— tr. and comm. *Aristoteles: Magna Moralia*. Berlin: Akademie-Verlag, 1958.

37. Donini, P. L., *L'etica dei Magna Moralia*. Turin: Giappichelli, 1965.

38. —— 'Il *De Anima* di Alessandro di Afrodisia e Michele Efesio', *Rivista di filologia e di istruzione classica* 96 (1968), 316–23.

39. —— *Tre studi sull' aristotelismo nel II secolo d. C.* Turin: Paravia, 1974.

40. —— 'Fato e volontà umana in Crisippo', *Atti della Accademia delle scienze di Torino* (Classe di Scienze Morali, Storiche e Filologiche) 109 (1975), 187–230.

41. Düring, I., *Aristotle in the Ancient Biographical Tradition*. Göteborg: Studia Graeca et Latina Gothoburgensia V, 1957.

42. Dyroff, A., *Die Ethik der alten Stoa*. Berlin: Calvary, 1897.

43. —— 'Zur stoischen Tierpsychologie', *Blätter für das bayerische Gymnasialschulwesen* 33 (1897), 399–404; 34 (1898), 416–30.

44. Evans, J. D. G., 'The Old Stoa on the Truth Value of Oaths', *Proceedings of the Cambridge Philological Society* 200 (N.S. 20) (1974), 44–7.

45. Fahnenschmidt, G., *Das Echtheitsproblem der Magna Moralia des Corpus Arisotelicum*. Diss: Tübingen, 1968.
46. Feinberg, J., 'Action and Responsibility', pp. 95–119 in *The Philosophy of Action* ed. A. R. White. Oxford: Oxford University Press, 1968. Reprinted from *Philosophy in America*, ed. M. Black (Allen and Unwin, 1965), pp. 134–60.
47. Forschner, M., *Die stoische Ethik.* Stuttgart, Klett–Cotta, 1981.
48. Fortenbaugh, W. W., *Aristotle on Emotion*. London: Duckworth, 1975.
49. —— ed., *On Stoic and Peripatetic Ethics: The Work of Arius Didymus.* New Brunswick, N. J.: Transaction Books, 1983.
50. —— 'Arius, Theophrastus and the *Eudemian Ethics*', pp. 203–23 in 49.
51. Frede, M., *Die stoische Logik.* Abhandlungen der Akademie der Wissenschaften zu Göttingen, phil.-hist. Kl. 3° Folge, 88 (1974).
52. —— 'The Principles of Stoic Grammar', pp. 27–75 in 167.
53. —— 'The Original Notion of Cause', pp. 217–49 in 180.
54. Furley, D., *Two Studies in the Greek Atomists.* Princeton: Princeton University Press, 1967.
55. —— 'Self Movers', pp. 165–79 in *Aristotle on Mind and the Senses*, edd. G. E. R. Lloyd and G. E. L. Owen. Cambridge: Cambridge University Press, 1978.
56. Gauthier, R. A. and J. Y. Jolif, *L'Éthique à Nicomache: Introduction, Traduction et Commentaire*, vol. ii (ed. 2). Paris: Béatrice-Nauwelaerts; Louvain: Publications Universitaires, 1970.
57. Gilbert, N. W., 'The Concept of Will in Early Latin Philosophy', *Journal of the History of Philosophy* 1 (1963), 17–35.
58. Guista, M., *I dossografi di etica.* Two vols. Turin: Giappichelli, 1964–7.
59. Glibert-Thirry, A., ed., *Pseudo-Andronicus de Rhodes Peri Pathôn.* Leiden: Brill, 1977.
60. —— 'La théorie stoïcienne de la passion chez Chrysippe et son évolution chez Posidonius', *Revue philosophique de Louvain* 75 (1977), 393–435.
61. Glidden, D., 'The *Lysis* on Loving One's Own', *Classical Quarterly* N.S. 31 (1981), 39–59.
62. Glucker, J., *Antiochus and the Late Academy.* Göttingen: Vandenhoek and Ruprecht, 1978.
63. Goldschmidt, V., *Le Système stoïcien et l'idée du temps.* Paris: Vrin, ed. 3, 1977.
64. Gottschalk, H. B., Review of Nussbaum, ed., *De Motu Animalium, American Journal of Philology* 102 (1981), 84–94.
65. Gould, J. B., 'Chrysippus: on the Criteria for Truth of a Conditional Proposition', *Phronesis* 12 (1967), 152–61.

66. —— *The Philosophy of Chrysippus*. Leiden: Brill, 1970.

67. —— 'The Stoic Conception of Fate.' *Journal of the History of Ideas* 35 (1974), 17–32.

68. Graeser, A., *Plotinus and the Stoics*. Leiden: Brill, 1972.

69. —— 'Zirkel oder Deduktion: zur Begründung der stoischen Ethik', *Kant-Studien* 63 (1972), 213–24.

70. —— *Zenon von Kition: Positionen und Probleme*. Berlin and New York: De Gruyter, 1975.

71. —— 'The Stoic Theory of Meaning', pp. 77–100 in 167.

72. Griffin, A. K., *Aristotle's Psychology of Conduct*. London: Williams and Norgate, 1931.

73. Grilli, A., 'Studi Paneziani', *Studi italiani di filologia classica* n.s. 29 (1957), 31–97.

74. Grimal, P., *Sénèque, ou la conscience de l'empire*. Paris: Les Belles Lettres, 1979.

75. Hadot, I., *Seneca und die griechisch-römische Tradition der Seelenleitung*. Berlin: De Gruyter, 1969.

76. Hadot, P., 'Un Clé des pensées de Marc Aurèle: les trois *topoi* philosophiques selon Épictète', *Les Études philosophiques* 1978, 65–83.

77. Hahm, D., *The Origins of Stoic Cosmology*. Columbus: Ohio State University Press, 1977.

78. Hamlyn, D. W., *The Psychology of Perception*. London: Routledge and Kegan Paul, 1957.

79. Hampshire, S., *Thought and Action*. London: Chatto and Windus, 1965.

80. Hardie, W., *Aristotle's Ethical Theory*. Oxford: Clarendon Press, 1968. Second edition 1980.

81. Hare, R. M., 'Imperative Sentences', pp. 1–21 in *Practical Inferences*. Reprinted from *Mind* 58 (1949), 21–39.

82. —— *The Language of Morals*. Oxford: Clarendon Press, 1952.

83. —— 'Practical Inferences', pp. 59–73 in *Practical Inferences*. Reprinted from *Festskrift til Alf Ross*, 1969.

84. —— *Practical Inferences*. London: Macmillan, 1971.

85. Harman, G., 'Practical Reasoning', *Review of Metaphysics* 29 (1976), 431–63.

86. Haynes, R. P., 'The Theory of Pleasure in the Old Stoa'. *American Journal of Philology* 83 (1962), 412–19.

87. Helmbold, W. C., 'Stoica', *Classical Review* n.s. 2 (1951), 146–7.

88. Hijmans, B. L., *Askêsis: Notes on Epictetus' Educational System*. Assen: Van Gorcum, 1959.

89. Hirzel, R., *Untersuchungen zu Ciceros philosophischen Schriften*, vol. ii. Leipzig: Hirzel, 1882.

90. Holler, E., *Seneca und die Seelenteilungslehre und Affektenpsychologie der Mittelstoa*. Diss. Munich, 1933. Kallmünz: Lassleben, 1934.

91. Huby, P., 'The First Discovery of the Freewill Problem', *Philosophy* 42 (1967), 353–62.

92. Imbert, C., 'Théorie de la Représentation et doctrine logique dans le stoïcisme ancien', pp. 223–49 in 17.

93. —— 'Stoic Logic and Alexandrian Poetics', pp. 182–216 in 180.

94. Inwood, B., 'The Two Forms of *Oikeiōsis* in Arius and the Stoa', pp. 190–201 in 49.

95. Irwin, T., 'Reason and Responsibility in Aristotle', pp. 117–55 in *Essays on Aristotle's Ethics*, ed. A. O. Rorty. Berkeley and Los Angeles: University of California Press, 1980.

96. Kahn, C., 'Sensation and Consciousness in Aristotle's Psychology', *Archiv für Geschichte der Philosophie* 48 (1966), 43–81.

97. Kenny, A., *Action, Emotion and Will*. London: Routledge and Kegan Paul, 1963.

98. —— 'Practical Inference', *Analysis* 26 (1965–6), 65–75.

99. —— *Will, Freedom and Power*. Oxford: Blackwell, 1975.

100. —— *The Aristotelian Ethics*. Oxford: Clarendon Press, 1978.

101. —— *Aristotle's Theory of the Will*. New Haven: Yale University Press, 1979.

102. Kerferd, G., 'The Search for Personal Identity in Stoic Thought', *Bulletin of the John Rylands University Library of Manchester* 55 (1972), 177–96.

103. —— 'The Origin of Evil in Stoic Thought', *Bulletin of the John Rylands University Library of Manchester* 60 (1978), 482–94.

104. —— 'What Does the Wise Man Know?', pp. 125–36 in 167.

105. —— 'The Problem of Synkatathesis and Katalêpsis in Stoic Doctrine', pp. 251–72 in 17.

106. Kidd, I. G., 'Stoic Intermediates and the End for Man', pp. 150–72 in 122.

107. —— 'Posidonius on Emotions', pp. 200–15 in 122.

108. —— 'Moral Actions and Rules in Stoic Ethics', pp. 247–258 in 167.

109. —— '*Euemptôsia*—Proneness to Disease', pp. 107–13 in 49.

110. Kirk, R., 'Rationality without Language', *Mind* 76 (1967), 369–86.

111. Kovesi, J., *Moral Notions*. London: Routledge and Kegan Paul, 1967.

112. Kubara, M., 'Acrasia, Human Agency and Normative Psychology', *Canadian Journal of Philosophy* 5 (1975), 215–32.

113. Lapidge, M., '*Archai* and *Stoicheia*: A Problem in Stoic Physics', *Phronesis* 18 (1973), 240–78.

114. Lloyd, A. C., 'Activity and Description in Aristotle and the Stoa', *Proceedings of the British Academy* 56 (1970), 227–40.

115. —— 'Grammar and Metaphysics in the Stoa', pp. 58–74 in 122.
116. —— 'Emotion and Decision in Stoic Psychology', pp. 233–46 in 167.
117. Long, A. A., 'Carneades and the Stoic *Telos*', *Phronesis* 12 (1967), 59–90.
118. —— 'The Stoic Concept of Evil', *Philosophical Quarterly* 18 (1968), 329–43.
119. —— 'Aristotle's Legacy to Stoic Ethics', *Bulletin of the Institute of Classical Studies* (London) 15 (1968), 72–85.
120. —— 'Stoic Determinism and Alexander of Aphrodisias' *De Fato* (i–xiv)', *Archiv für Geschichte der Philosophie* 52 (1970), 247–68.
121. —— 'The Logical Basis of Stoic Ethics', *Proceedings of the Aristotelian Society* n.s. 71 (1970–1), 85–104.
122. —— ed., *Problems in Stoicism*. London: The Athlone Press, 1971.
123. —— 'Language and Thought in Stoicism', pp. 75–113 in 122.
124. —— 'Freedom and Determinism in the Stoic Theory of Human Action', pp. 173–99 in 122.
125. —— *Hellenistic Philosophy*. London: Duckworth, 1974.
126. —— 'The Early Stoic Concept of Moral Choice', pp. 77–92 in *Images of Man in Ancient and Medieval Thought: Studia Gerardo Verbeke*. Louvain: Leuven University Press, 1976.
127. —— 'Dialectic and the Stoic Sage', pp. 101–24 in 167.
128. —— 'Arius Didymus and the Exposition of Stoic Ethics', pp. 41–65 in 49.
129. —— 'Astrology: Arguments pro and contra', pp. 165–92 in *Science and Speculation*, edd. J. Barnes, J. Brunschwig, M. Burnyeat, M. Schofield. Cambridge and Paris: Cambridge University Press and Éditions de la maison des Sciences de l'Homme, 1982.
130. —— 'Soul and Body in Stoicism', *Phronesis* 27 (1982), 34–57.
131. Mates, B., *Stoic Logic*. Berkeley: University of California Press, 1961.
132. Melden, A. I., *Free Action*. London: Routledge and Kegan Paul, 1961.
133. Moraux, P., *Les Listes anciennes des ouvrages d'Aristote*. Louvain: Éditions universitaires de Louvain, 1951.
134. More, P. E., *Hellenistic Philosophies*. Princeton: Princeton University Press, 1923.
135. Moreau, J., 'Ariston et le stoïcisme', *Revue des Études Anciennes* 50 (1948), 27–48.
136. Nebel, G., 'Der Begriff des *Kathêkon* in der alten Stoa', *Hermes* 70 (1935), 439–60.
137. North, H., *Sophrosyne: Self-Knowledge and Self-Restraint in Greek Literature*. Ithaca, N.Y.: Cornell University Press, 1966.
138. Nussbaum, M. C., *Aristotle's De Motu Animalium: Text with*

Translation, Commentary and Interpretive Essays. Princeton: Princeton University Press, 1978.

139. Pachet, P. 'L'impératif stoïcien', pp. 361–74 in 17.

140. Pembroke, S. G., 'Oikeiôsis', pp. 114–49 in 122.

141. Philippson, R., 'Panaetiana', *Rheinisches Museum* 78 (1929), 337–360.

142. —— 'Das "erste Naturgemässe"', *Philologus* 87 (1931-2), 445–66.

143. —— 'Zur Psychologie der Stoa', *Rheinisches Museum* 86 (1937), 140–79.

144. Pohlenz, M., *Antikes Führertum: Cicero de Officiis und das Lebensideal des Panaitios.* Leipzig and Berlin: Teubner, 1934.

145. —— 'Zenon und Chrysipp', *Nachrichten der Gesellschaft der Wissenschaften zu Göttingen,* phil.-hist. Kl. Fachgr. 1, 2 (1938), 173–210.

146. —— *Grundfragen der stoischen Philosophie.* Abhandlungen der Gesellschaft der Wissenschaften zu Göttingen, phil.-hist. Kl. 3° Folge, 26 (1940).

147. —— 'Kleanthes' Zeushymnus', *Hermes* 75 (1940), 117–23.

148. —— 'Tierische und menschliche Intelligenz bei Posidonios', *Hermes* 76 (1941), 1–13.

149. —— Review of van Straaten, *Panétius, Gnomon* 21 (1949), 113–20.

150. —— *Die Stoa: Geschichte einer geistigen Bewegung.* 2 vols. Ed. 4. Göttingen: Vandenhoek and Ruprecht, 1970.

151. Preus, A., 'Intention and Impulse in Aristotle and the Stoics', *Apeiron* 15 (1981), 48–58.

152. Rabel, R. J., *Theories of the Emotions in the Old Stoa.* Diss. Michigan, 1975.

153. Rees, D. A., 'Bipartition of the Soul in the Early Academy', *Journal of Hellenic Studies* 77 pt. 1 (1957), 112–18.

154. —— 'Aristotle's Treatment of *Phantasia*', pp. 491–504 in *Essays in Ancient Greek Philosophy,* edd. J. P. Anton and G. L. Kustas. Albany: State University of New York Press, 1971.

155. Reesor, M., 'The "Indifferents" in the Old and Middle Stoa', *Transactions of the American Philological Assocation* 82 (1951), 102–10.

156. —— 'Fate and Possibility in Early Stoic Philosophy', *Phoenix* 19 (1965), 285–97.

157. —— Review of Grimal, *Sénèque, Phoenix* 33 (1979), 284–85.

158. Regenbogen, O., 'Theophrastos'. Cols. 1354–1562 in Paulys *Realencyclopädie der classischen Alterumswissenschaft,* Supp. 7, 1940.

159. Rescher, N., *The Logic of Commands.* London: Routledge and Kegan Paul, 1966.

160. —— 'On the Characterization of Actions', pp. 247–54 in *The Nature of Human Action,* ed. M. Brand. Glenview, Ill.: Scott, Foresman and Co., 1970.

161. Rieth, O., *Grundbegriffe der stoischen Ethik: eine traditionsgeschichtliche Untersuchung*. Berlin: Weidmann, 1933.

162. —— 'Über das Telos der Stoiker', *Hermes* 69 (1934), 13–45.

163. Rist, J. M., *Stoic Philosophy*. Cambridge: Cambridge University Press, 1969.

164. —— 'Prohairesis: Proclus, Plotinus et alii', pp. 103–22 in *De Jamblique à Proclus*. Geneva: Fondation Hardt, 1975.

165. —— 'The Use of Stoic Terminology in Philo's *Quod Deus Immutabilis Sit* 33–50', *The Center for Hermeneutical Studies, Colloquy* 23 (1976).

166. —— 'Zeno and Stoic Consistency', *Phronesis* 22 (1977), 161–74.

167. —— ed., *The Stoics*. Berkeley, Los Angeles, and London: University of California Press, 1978.

168. —— 'The Importance of Stoic Logic in the *Contra Celsum*', pp. 64–78 in *Neoplatonism and Early Christian Thought*, ed. H. Blumenthal and R. A. Markus. London: Variorum, 1981.

169. Roberts, L., 'Origen and Stoic Logic', *Transactions of the American Philological Assocation* 101 (1970), 433–44.

170. Robinson, T. M., *Plato's Psychology*. Toronto: University of Toronto Press, 1970.

171. Ross, W. D., *Aristotle*. London: Methuen, 1923. Ed. 5, revised, London: Methuen; New York: Barnes and Noble, 1949.

172. —— *Foundations of Ethics*. Oxford: Clarendon Press, 1939.

173. Sandbach, F. H., 'Ennoia and Prolêpsis', pp. 22–37 in 122.

174. —— 'Phantasia Katalêptikê', pp. 9–21 in 122.

175. —— *The Stoics*. London: Chatto and Windus, 1975.

176. Schaefer, M., *Ein frühmittelstoisches System der Ethik bei Cicero*. Diss. Munich, 1933. Munich: Salesianische Offizin, 1934.

177. Schindler, K., *Die stoische Lehre von den Seelenteilen und Seelenvermögen insbesondere bei Panaitios und Poseidonios und ihre Verwendung bei Cicero*. Diss. Munich, 1934. Munich: Salesianische Offizin, 1934.

178. Schmekel, A., *Die Philosophie der mittleren Stoa in ihrem geschichtlichen Zusammenhange*. Berlin: Weidmann, 1892.

179. Schofield, M., 'Aristotle on the Imagination', pp. 99–140 in *Aristotle on Mind and the Senses*, ed. G. E. R. Lloyd and G. E. L. Owen. Cambridge: Cambridge University Press, 1978.

180. ——, M. Burnyeat and J. Barnes edd., *Doubt and Dogmatism: Studies in Hellenistic Epistemology*. Oxford: Clarendon Press, 1980.

181. Schwyzer, H.-R., '"Bewusst" und "Unbewusst" bei Plotin', pp. 343–90 in *Les Sources de Plotin*. Geneva: Fondation Hardt, 1960.

182. Searle, J., *Speech Acts*. Cambridge: Cambridge University Press, 1969.

183. —— 'The Intentionality of Intention and Action', *Inquiry* 22 (1979), 253–80.
184. Sedley, D., 'The End of the Academy', *Phronesis* 26 (1981), 67–75.
185. —— 'Epicurus' Refutation of Determinism', pp. 11–51 in *Syzêtêsis*, Studi ... offerti a Marcello Gigante. Naples: Gaetano Macchiaroli, ed., 1983.
186. Sharples, R. W., 'Aristotelian and Stoic Conceptions of Necessity in the *De Fato* of Alexander of Aphrodisias', *Phronesis* 20 (1975), 247–74.
187. Sorabji, R., 'Causation, Laws and Necessity', pp. 250–82 in 180. This essay is adapted from Chapter 4 of his *Necessity, Cause and Blame*. Ithaca, N.Y.: Cornell University Press, 1980.
188. Steckel, H., *Epikurs Prinzip der Einheit von Schmerzlosigkeit und Lust*. Diss. Göttingen, 1960.
189. Stein, L., *Die Psychologie der Stoa*. 2 vols. Berlin: Calvary, 1886–8.
190. Stough, C., 'Stoic Determinism and Moral Responsibility', pp. 203–31 in 167.
191. Striker, G., 'Epicurus on the Truth of Sense Impressions', *Archiv für Geschichte der Philosophie* 59 (1977), 125–42.
192. —— 'Sceptical Strategies', pp. 54–83 in 180.
193. Tatakis, B. N., *Panétius de Rhodes*. Paris: Vrin, 1931.
194. Taylor, C. C. W., ed., *Plato: Protagoras*. Oxford: Clarendon Press, 1976.
195. —— 'Plato, Hare and Davidson on Akrasia', *Mind* 89 (1980), 499–518.
196. Terian, A., ed., *Philonis Alexandrini De Animalibus*. Chico, Calif.: Scholars Press, 1981.
197. Theiler, W., 'Tacitus und die antike Schicksalslehre', pp. 35–90 in *Phyllobolia* für Peter von der Muehll. Basel: Schwabe, 1946.
198. Todd, R. B., *Alexander of Aphrodisias on Stoic Physics*. Leiden: Brill, 1976.
199. Tsekourakis, D., *Studies in the Terminology of Early Stoic Ethics, Hermes* Einzelschrift 32 (1974).
200. van Straaten, M., *Panétius: sa vie, ses écrits et sa doctrine avec une édition des fragments*. Amsterdam: A. J. Paris, 1946.
201. —— 'Notes on Panaetius' Theory of the Constitution of Man', pp. 93–109 in *Images of Man in Ancient and Medieval Thought: Studia Gerardo Verbeke*. Louvain: Leuven University Press, 1976.
202. Verbeke, G., *L'Évolution de la doctrine du pneuma du stoïcisme à S. Augustine*. Paris and Louvain: de Brouwer and Éditions de l'institut supérieur de philosophie, 1945.
203. —— 'Aristotélisme et stoïcisme dans le *De Fato* d'Alexandre d'Aphrodisias', *Archiv für Geschichte der Philosophie* 50 (1968), 73–100.

204. Vlastos, G., 'Socrates on Acrasia', *Phoenix* 23 (1969), 71–88.
205. Voelke, A.-J., 'L'Unité de l'âme dans l'ancien stoïcisme', *Studia Philosophica* 25 (1965), 154–81.
206. —— 'Les origines stoïciennes de la notion de volonté', *Revue de théologie et de philosophie* 1969-I, 1–22.
207. —— *L'Idée de volonté dans le stoïcisme.* Paris: Presses Universitaires de France, 1973.
208. von Arnim, H., 'Die drei aristotelischen Ethiken', *Akademie der Wissenschaften in Wien*, phil.-hist. Kl., *Sitzungsberichte* 202 (1924).
209. —— 'Arius Didymus Abriss der peripatetischen Ethik', *Akademie der Wissenschaften in Wien*, phil.-hist. Kl., *Sitzungsberichte* 204 (1926).
210. von Fritz, K., 'Zenon von Kition'. Cols. 83–121 in *Paulys Realencyclopädie der classischen Altertumswissenschaft* Band 10 A (2° Reihe, 1972).
211. Wachsmuth, C., *Studien zu den griechischen Florilegien.* Berlin: Weidmann, 1882.
212. Warnock, M., *Imagination.* London: Faber and Faber, 1976.
213. Watson, Gary, 'Skepticism about Weakness of Will', *Philosophical Review* 86 (1977), 316–39.
214. Watson, Gerard, *The Stoic Theory of Knowledge.* Belfast: Queen's University, 1966.
215. —— '*Phantasia* in Aristotle *De Anima* 3.3', *Classical Quarterly* 32 (1982), 100–13.
216. White, N. P., 'Two Notes on Stoic Terminology', *American Journal of Philology* 99 (1978), 111–19.
217. —— 'The Basis of Stoic Ethics', *Harvard Studies in Classical Philology* 83 (1979), 143–78.
218. Wiersma, W., '*Telos* und *Kathêkon* in der alten Stoa', *Mnemosyne* Ser. 3, 5 (1937), 219–28.
219. Winston, D., 'Freedom and Determinism in Philo of Alexandria', *Studia Philonica* 3 (1974-5), 47–70.
220. Yon, A., ed., *Cicéron: Traité du Destin.* Paris: Les Belles Lettres, 1933.
221. Zeller, E., *Die Philosophie der Griechen in ihrer geschichtlichen Entwicklung.* Ed. 5, Leipzig: Reisland, 1923.

Selective Index of Subjects and Terms

Selective Index
of Philosophers